Hard Times

Studs Terkel

THE NEW PRESS

NEW YORK

An Illustrated Oral History
of the Great Depression

Hard Times

For my wife, my son, and my editor

Requests for permission to reproduce selections from this book should be mailed to:
Permissions Department, The New Press, 38 Greene Street, New York, NY 10013.

Published in the United States by The New Press, New York, 2012
Distributed by Perseus Distribution

This is an abridged edition of *Hard Times*. The original edition included an additional
sixty interviews.

CIP data is available
ISBN 978-1-59558-703-9 (pb)

Now in its twentieth year, The New Press publishes books that promote and
enrich public discussion and understanding of the issues vital to our democracy
and to a more equitable world. These books are made possible by the enthusiasm
of our readers; the support of a committed group of donors, large and small; the
collaboration of our many partners in the independent media and the not-for-profit
sector; booksellers, who often hand-sell New Press books; librarians; and above all by
our authors.

www.thenewpress.com

Book design by Lovedog Studio
Composition by Westchester Book Composition
This book was set in Fairfield Light

Printed in the United States of America

10 9 8 7 6 5 4 3 2 1

Contents

Book One

THE MARCH

THE SONG

HARD TRAVELIN'

THE BIG MONEY

GOD BLESS' THE CHILD

Book Four

Book Five

Acknowledgments

FRIENDS, ACQUAINTANCES AND, IN astonishing number, strangers were gracious in offering suggestions. Without their hunches and tips, this work may not have been possible. Among these casual scouts: Richard Lamparski, Robert Cromie, Herman Kogan, Mike Royko, Lew Frank, Jr., Lucy Fairbank, Robert Sherrill, Phyllis Jackson, James Patton, Clifford and Virginia Durr, John Dierkes, Lou Gilbert, Phil McMartin, Sanka Bristow, Harry Bouras, King Solomon, Brendan McMahon, Earl Doty, Lou Abraham, Elizabeth Cooper, Jesse Prosten and Leon Beverly.

As in a previous work, *Division Street: America*, it was Cathy Zmuda who did more than transcribe the hundreds of thousands of spoken words onto pages. She offered gratuitous editorial comments and thus provided me with a perspective that might otherwise have been missing.

My colleagues at radio station WFMT, notably Norm Pellegrini, Ray Nordstrand and Lois Baum, were remarkably understanding and ingenious during my leaves of absence. My daily programs, re-broadcasts, had an air of contemporaneity, thanks to them. My gratitude, too, to Jim Unrath for beyond-the-call-of-duty chores as my companion and chauffeur, during a memorable trip through Arkansas.

Especially am I grateful to my editor, André Schiffrin, whose idea this was. His insistence and quiet encouragement are evident in all these pages. And to his perceptive associates Verne Moberg and Linda Faulhaber, for their bright-eyed look at what was becoming a burdensome matter—a salute.

Foreword
(*January–February 1986*)

Hard times come again no more . . .

As these words are being written, the Stephen Foster lyric rolls around in my head like a loose cannonball.

It is early in 1986, yet the Dirty Thirties come to mind. The bleak decade was so defined by a long-gone congressman, whose remembrances you will find in these pages.

How come this foreboding reflection? The Six O'clock News and the financial sections of our most respected journals inform us, via administration handouts, that things have seldom looked better. Even the phrase BOOM YEAR is occasionally headlined in a spirit of cheery prophecy.

True, there is the casual caveat, solemnly offered: something to do with "deficits." But aside from the warnings of the usual Cassandras, it's nothing to cause sleepless nights. It's too arcane a word anyway, an accountant's term. It's nothing like "hunger" or "homeless." These shadow words appear back in the feature pages, as "human interest" stories, adjacent to the gossip columns and theatrical news.

Up front are IMPORTANT developments. Look at the market. "Stocks jump another 12 . . . boosting the Dow Jones industrial average to a record and proving that optimism over economic growth and corporate earnings remains high."* Look at Dow Jones. Look at the corporate ads, offered with an air of Responsibility. Look at the bright and morning faces of Business Administration School graduates, attaché cases responsibly in hand, as they commute to the bustling office and the even more bustling floor.

---

* *Chicago Sun-Times*, February 8, 1986.

Unavoidably, you look at the face of the farmer as he is caught by the TV camera. You know the one: the desperate Iowan, who killed his neighbor and himself. I believe a minor bank official got it, too. It wasn't his fault either. He was as distraught as the man who killed him. It was bigger than both of them.

> Last month, in Union County, which has the richest land in South Dakota, a young Farmers Home Administration supervisor killed his wife, daughter, son and dog while they slept, then went down to his office and shot himself dead. He left a note: "The job has got pressure on my mind, pain on left side." . . . Because he was an out-of-stater, the F.H.A. moved him about the state, apparently figuring he would be more willing to get tough with local farmers who were behind on their loan payments than would a native South Dakotan.*

Who do I shoot? cried out Muley Graves, Steinbeck's near-crazed Okie, as he was being bulldozed off the land. God, I don't know, replied the town's bank officer, who was going sort of crazy himself.

Muley was a small farmer of the thirties. The Iowan was a small farmer of the eighties. Though a half-century separates them, their tether's end was commonly caused: neither could meet the payments.

Never since the Great Depression has the family farmer experienced such hardship, such despair. Scores of thousands are, with a growing sullenness, sampling the grapes of wrath. If help is not forthcoming one way—say, from Big Guv'mint—they will seek another. It's a natural for the nearest con artist at hand.

> Kearney, Nebraska—Huddled under blankets last weekend in a cold, dark grain-storage shed, 200 men and women from around the Midwest listened intently to a tall man in a dark business suit pledge to take up arms in defense of dispossessed farmers. "Christ told us he didn't come to bring peace but to bring us a sword," said the boyishly handsome 32-year-old Larry Humphreys. "When the banking system collapses, the logical thing to do is to come out bearing arms. . . . It's pretty much common knowledge that most of the international banks are Jewish. . . ."†

---

* "Broken Heartland," by Bob McBride, *The Nation*, February 8, 1986.
† "Farm Country's New Right Knight," by James Ridgeway, *Village Voice*, February 4, 1986.

There was farm anger and militancy in the thirties too, but with a difference. The Posse Comitatus and the Aryan Nation would have been hooted off the wheatlands as clownish and diversionary. There was some awareness of root causes, an awareness that has diminished considerably during a half-century of amnesia. The farmers of the thirties drew a bead on Washington.

Emil Loriks of South Dakota remembers: "The situation was tense in ten or eleven states. You could almost smell the powder. When Governor Herring of Iowa called out the militia, Milo Reno* said, 'Hold off. I'll not have the blood of innocent people on my hands.' We had a heck of a time getting the farmers off Highway 75. There were probably a thousand of them out there. Reno called a meeting at Sioux City. About thirty thousand farmers showed up. We decided to go to Washington and settle for a farm program. If Roosevelt hadn't come in in '32, we'd a' been in real trouble."

Then and Now. In the thirties, an administration recognized a need and lent a hand. Today, an administration recognizes an image and lends a smile. Larry Humphreys recognizes a bitter fruit, ripe for the picking.

The latest communiqué from Chicago's Far South Side informs us that the Southworks of U.S. Steel is laying off six thousand. That leaves a thousand on the job—for the time being. It had not been unexpected. The community had known it was coming: merely a few more thousand swelling the roster of idle hands in heavy industry.

Recently, Ed Sadlowski, a union officer, whose grandfather, father, and himself were steelworkers, drove me around the plant area. Like Leslie Howard, the dreamy hero of the film *Berkeley Square*, I was transported into another time. The Englishman found himself a subject of George IV. I found myself reliving the last days of Herbert Hoover's presidency.

Smokeless chimneys. No orange flashes in the sky. Empty parking lots. Not a Chevy or a Ford to be seen, not even for those with 20–20 vision. An occasional abandoned jalopy, yes, evoking another image of the thirties. Ours was the only moving vehicle for miles around. A stray dog; no humans. And it wasn't that cold a day. In fact, the weather was unseasonably mild, accentuating the landscape's bleakness.

The business end of the neighborhood wasn't all that busy either. A boarded-up store or two or three. Ed pointed at a men's clothing store: Open For Business. "He's closing next month."

South Chicago has joined Youngstown, Johnstown, and Gary. Steel Town circa eighties has become Ghost Town circa thirties. Recently, at an

---

* Head of the Holiday Association, a militant farmers' group of the thirties.

art-film house, I saw Willard Van Dyke's 1940 documentary, *Valley Town*. It was Lancaster, Pennsylvania, a steel city of the Great Depression, stone cold dead. It was an experience of *déjà vu* in reverse. I saw Ed Sadlowski's South Chicago

Where to? What next? At the time Carl Sandburg raised those questions in his celebrated long poem, he was assuming a tribal remembrance, generations hence. He did not count on a generation's amnesia. Would he have today renamed his work *The People, Maybe*?

As newspapers gather in my living room, in the manner of an old bum's bundle, last week's and the week's before, I'm able to make out headlines about bullish markets. A stray item in the same week-old edition catches my eye. Dateline, Waterloo, Iowa: "Another 200 employees will be laid off at Deere and Co., bringing to more than 1,000 the number of workers idled at the plant since October." Don Page of UAW Local 838 is quoted: "You keep saying it can't get worse, but it does."

It appears that Don Page and the president are on different wave lengths; certainly not on the same planet. Today's Murdoch headline positively glows: THE GREAT COMEBACK. Subheadline: *U.S. Grows Stronger Every Day—Reagan*. Though the *Wall Street Journal* and the *New York Times* are less flamboyant, they are equally euphoric.

Back to the bundle. Dateline, Schenectady, N.Y.: "At least 1,500 jobs will be eliminated this year at General Electric's turbine division. . . ." In 1974, 29,000 were employed at the plant. By 1980, it was under 17,000.

As the comics page is turned—barely discernible, pentimento-esque, are the outlines of *Bloom County*—there's a serious message from Eastern Airlines: 1,700 attendants will be fired and the pay of the survivors will be cut 20 percent. The Transport Workers Union explains elsewhere that it's a 32 percent cut in real wages.

AT&T, as well, has an announcement. It does not appear in its TV messages. There is no need for actor Cliff Robertson here. Its Aurora plant roster will be cut from 4,000 to 1,500. As Kurt Vonnegut would say, So it goes.

Last week, near my building of work, a line of young people was snaking all around the block. At first I thought they were hopefuls awaiting Chicago Bears tickets. There was one such line a block away. This file was overwhelmingly black, about two hundred. One of these hopefuls, age nineteen, told me he and the others were job applicants. Later that day, an acquaintance in the personnel department let me know there were about five openings.

Ed Paulsen was nineteen in 1931. He was a job applicant, too. San Francisco. "I'd get up at five in the morning and head for the waterfront.

Outside the Spreckels Sugar Refinery, outside the gates, there would be a thousand men. You know dang well there's only three or four jobs. The guys would come out with two little Pinkerton cops: 'I need two guys for the bull gang. Two guys to go into the hole.' A thousand men would fight like a pack of Alaskan dogs to get through there. Only four of us would get through."

Young Paulsen took to the road, along with millions of others. He rode the freights. Half the time, the boxcar, standing room only, was his home. Somewhere out there, in Kansas or Nebraska or who knows where, there might be a job of some sort.

A black World War Two vet, Louis Banks, shares the memory. "Black and white, it didn't make any difference who you were, 'cause everybody was poor. All friendly, sleep in a jungle. Sometimes we sent one hobo to walk, to see if there were any jobs open. He'd come back and say: Detroit, no jobs. He'd say: they're hirin' in New York City. Sometimes, fifteen, twenty guys were in that one boxcar. More. Women even, quite a few tryin' to disguise themselves. Oh, everybody was ridin', hopin'."

Fifty years later, the *Sacramento Bee* sent a couple of young journalists, Dale Maharidge and Michael Williamson, out on the road. They rode the freights for several months. Their elders had told them of the thirties. They had studied the photographs of Dorothea Lange, Walker Evans, the others. They saw the same faces. "When people are down and out," said Williamson, "they always look the same."

They too found boxcars, with hardly room to move. The new nomads have come from the rust belt, the abandoned farm, small failed businesses; many of them had voted for Reagan because "he made us feel good." Now they don't feel so good, but few blame the president. They resent being called losers, though that *is* what they are called these days. In the thirties (at least in retrospect), they were called victims. If there is a core difference between Then and Now, it is in language. Then, the words of the winners reflected discomfort in the presence of losers. Now, they reflect a mild contempt.

"I didn't know it was illegal to be poor in America," says one of the travelers. Did you know it was illegal to sleep in a car in Louisiana? And that it's illegal to sleep under an overpass in Portland? And illegal to eat out of a dumpster in Fort Lauderdale? Maharidge and Williamson were told that rat poison is often added to these trash cans.

This is not quite as astonishing as it might seem. In the thirties, vagrancy was the most frequent charge in arrest and detention. Burglary ran a close second. Today, the FBI reports that burglaries and robberies have doubled in cities where plant closings have become the norm.

A Vietnam veteran, on the move with his wife, two small children, and a tent, is thinking the unthinkable. "I'm trying my damndest to be an upright citizen. I've never committed any crimes before, but I'm thinking of hitting that 7-Eleven. I'm not gonna shoot anyone, just food for the kids."

Ed Paulsen would understand. "Hell, in the thirties, everybody was a criminal. You were getting by, survival. Stole clothes off lines, stole milk off back porches, you stole bread. I remember going through Tucumcari, New Mexico, on a freight. We made a brief stop. There was a grocery store, a supermarket kind of thing for those days. I beat it off the train and came back with rolls and crackers. This guy is standing in the window shaking his fist at you. It wasn't a big thing, but it created a coyote mentality. You were a predator. You had to be."

Today's paper reports another record-breaking day in the stock market. The financial columnist is euphoric: "The economy will turn in a performance superior to anything that could be dismissed as 'mediocre.' The year will be much better than lots of economists, including a number who operate in Wall Street, are willing to concede."

Business Week is singularly less sanguine. A cover story is called "The Casino Society." In a stunning piece, at considerable variance with other established journals, it explodes: "No, it's not Las Vegas or Atlantic City. It's the U.S. financial system. The volume of transactions has boomed far beyond anything needed to support the economy. Borrowing—politely called leverage—is getting out of hand. And futures enable people to play the market without owning a share of stock. The result: the system is tilting from investment to speculation."[*]

It rings a distant bell. Were Arthur A. Robertson still around, he'd recognize the tolling sound—at least, the alarm. He was an industrialist, "a scavenger. I used to buy broken-down businesses that banks took over." He was a millionaire at twenty-four. He knew all the legendary figures of the market, who'd "run up a stock to ridiculous prices and unload it on the unsuspecting public."

"In 1929, it was strictly a gambling casino with loaded dice. The few sharks taking advantage of the multitude of suckers. It was exchanging expensive dogs for expensive cats. Frenzied finance that made Ponzi[†] look like an amateur. Everything was bought on hope."

---

[*] *Business Week*, September 16, 1985.
[†] A Boston financier of the twenties. His "empire" crashed, and many people were ruined. He went to prison.

Sidney J. Weinberg whistled in amazement as he remembered October 29, 1929. "It was like a thunder clap. Everybody was stunned. The Street had general confusion. They didn't understand it any more than anybody else. They thought something would be announced." I hadn't the heart to ask him by whom. Emile Coué? God? Roger Babson? Weinberg was senior partner of Goldman Sachs and an adviser to presidents.

"A Depression could not happen again, not to the extent of the one in '29. Unless inflation went out of hand and values went beyond true worth. A deep stock market reaction could bring a Depression, yes. There would be immediate government reaction, of course. A moratorium. But in panic, people will sell regardless of worth. Today, you've got twenty-odd million stockholders owning stock. At that time you probably had a million and a half. You could have a sharper decline now than you had in 1929."

There is a sort of government action today, but not what Weinberg had in mind. Regulations that came into being after the Crash of '29 have been loosened more than somewhat. Especially for our banks.

In Banks We Trust is Penny Lernoux's chilling account in chapter and verse. The 1982 collapse of the Penn Square Bank in Oklahoma, Marx Brothers and W. C. Fields in style, may be the metaphor. This small fish, in its wild pursuit of high-interest debtors, attracted schools of much bigger fish. How close the call was for Chase Manhattan, Continental Illinois, and Citibank, we'll never quite know. Much too close for comfort. Big Guv'mint saved their hides, just as in a wholly different way it bailed out the Depression-stunned banks.

With New Deal regulatory agencies gutted by the Reagan Revolution, aggressive banking—a phrase dear to free-marketeers—has become the order of the day. Free translation: speculation in money. In the go-go climate created, banks are Brewsters profligately handing out their (our) millions in the wild expectation of even wilder returns. Not a penny may come back.

Latin American countries, the biggest debtors, owe $350 billion to a few American banks. If one or two of them default—say, Brazil, Argentina, or Mexico—it could wipe out the capital of our nine largest banks. Talk about panic. Talk about a run on two or three. Or nine.

"In '29 and '30, bank closings got into thousands." David Kennedy, years before he was appointed by Richard Nixon as secretary of the treasury, had served in the early thirties on the Federal Reserve Board. "There was one bank in New York, the Bank of the United States—in the wake of that closing, two hundred smaller banks closed. Because of the deposits in that bank from the others."

Penny Lernoux concludes, "It could lead to a situation that would make 1929 look like a birthday party."

Yet other voices, mostly frequently heard, tell us the outlook is not at all that bleak, no matter what parallels may be drawn between Then and Now. James Nathenson, past president of the Chicago Homebuilders Association, sees as glowing a future as the present president of the United States. Mr. Nathenson is a devout Chicago Bears fan and a season ticket holder. "I see everything that's happening with the Bears as a positive thing for Chicago housing—if they win." His reference was to the upcoming Super Bowl game. (The Bears won, of course.)

Fortunate is the city—and the society—that is blessed with the legs of Walter Payton, the arm of Jim McMahan, and the .heft of William Perry. Never mind the smokeless chimneys and boarded-up stores of South Chicago. Never mind two hundred young lining up for five jobs. Never mind history. Mr. Nathenson's euphoria is undiminished: "In Chicago, once we become winners, we begin to think like winners in our pursuits in life. If we're losers, we have that loser syndrome permeating our attitude."* Ronald Reagan couldn't have said it any better.

In the following pages, testimony is offered by scores who thought "like winners" until they suddenly, astonishingly, wound up losers. "It was like a thunder clap," Sidney Weinberg recalled. Have our weathervanes been dismantled? No storm signals at all? Or have lessons been learned from an experienced trauma that to some seems only yesterday, to others centuries ago. A young woman, on being told of the Great Depression by her grandparents, says, "It seemed like a fairy tale to me, something of a bedtime story."

Lessons learned? As with the drunk before the judge, when asked whether his plea be guilty or not guilty, the reply is: I stands mute.

Ours, the richest country in the world, may be the poorest in memory. Perhaps the remembrances of survivors of a time past may serve as a reminder to others. Or to themselves.

* *Chicago Tribune*, January 25, 1986.

NOTE

This being a book about Time as well as *a* time;
for some the bell has tolled. Heroes and dragons of
a long-gone day were old men, some vigorous, some
weary, when I last saw them. Some have died.

Hard Times

A Personal Memoir
(and parenthetical comment)

THIS IS A MEMORY BOOK, *rather than one of hard fact and precise statistic. In recalling an epoch, some thirty, forty, years ago, my colleagues experienced pain, in some instances; exhilaration, in others. Often it was a fusing of both. A hesitancy, at first, was followed by a flow of memories: long-ago hurts and small triumphs. Honors and humiliations. There was laughter, too.*

Are they telling the truth? The question is as academic as the day Pilate asked it, his philosophy not quite washing out his guilt. It's the question Pa Joad asked of Preacher Casy, when the ragged man, in a transient camp, poured out his California agony.

"Pa said, 'S'pose he's tellin' the truth—that fella?' The preacher answered, 'He's tellin' the truth, awright. The truth for him. He wasn't makin' nothin' up.' 'How about us?' Tom demanded. 'Is that the truth for us?' 'I don' know,' said Casy."*

I suspect the preacher spoke for the people in this book, too. In their re-memberings are their truths. The precise fact or the precise date is of small consequence. This is not a lawyer's brief nor an annotated sociological trea-tise. It is simply an attempt to get the story of the holocaust known as The Great Depression from an improvised battalion of survivors.

That there are some who were untouched or, indeed, did rather well isn't exactly news. This has been true of all disasters. The great many were wounded, in one manner or another. It left upon them an "invisible scar," as Caroline Bird put it.† To those who have chosen to reveal it in this work, my gratitude. And to those hundred or so others, in scattered parts of this land, whose life fragments I did not include, my apologies as well as my profound appreciation: they have enriched my own sense of this neglected time.

* John Steinbeck, *The Grapes of Wrath* (New York, Viking Press, 1939), p. 261.
† Caroline Bird, *The Invisible Scar* (New York, David McKay Co., 1965).

There are young people in this book, too. They did not experience the Great Depression. In many instances, they are bewildered, wholly ignorant of it. It is no sign of their immaturity, but of ours. It's time they knew. And it's time we knew, too—what it did to us. And, thus, to them.

I myself don't remember the bleak October day, 1929. Nor do I recall with anything like a camera eye the events that shaped the thirties. Rather, a blur of images comes to mind. Faces, voices and, occasionally, a rueful remembrance or a delightful flash. Or the astonishing innocence of a time past. Yet a feeling persists. . . .

Even now, when on the highway, seeing in faint neon, VACANCY, outside a modest motel, I am reminded of my mother's enterprise, the Wells-Grand. I ask myself, with unreasonable anxiety, perhaps, "Will it survive? Will this place be here next year?"

Fear of losing things, of property, is one legacy of the thirties, as a young colleague pointed out. An elderly civil servant in Washington buys a piece of land as often as she can afford. "If it comes again, I'll have something to live off." She remembers the rotten bananas, near the wharves of New Orleans: her daily fare.

That, thanks to technology, things today can make things, in abundance, is a point psychically difficult for Depression survivors to understand. And thus, in severe cases, they will fight, even kill, to protect their things (read: property). Many of the young fail to diagnose this illness because of their innocence concerning the Great Depression. Its occasional invocation, for scolding purposes, tells them little of its truth.

In the mid-twenties, all fifty rooms of the Wells-Grand were occupied. There was often a waiting list. Our guests were men of varied skills and some sense of permanence. The only transients were the wayward couple who couldn't afford a more de luxe rendezvous. Mysteriously, there was always room at the inn, even for sinners. Ours were the winking Gospels.

On Saturdays, most of our guests paid their weekly rent. On those evenings, I walked at a certain pace to the deposit window of the neighborhood bank. All the guests, with the exception of a few retired boomers and an ancient coppersmith (made idle by the Volstead Act), had steady jobs. It was a euphoric time.

The weekly magazines, *Judge* and *Life* (pre-Luce), were exciting with George Jean Nathan and Pare Lorentz critiques and Jefferson Machamer girls. *Liberty* carried sports pieces by Westbrook Pegler—the most memorable, a tribute to Battling Siki, the childlike, noble savage destroyed by civilization. *Literary Digest* was still around and solvent, having not yet forecast Alf Landon's triumph some years later. On the high school debating team, we resolved that the United States should or should not grant independence to the Philippines, should or should not join the World Court, should or should not recognize the Soviet Union. We took either side. It was a casual time.

Perhaps it was the best of times. Or was it the worst? Scott Nearing inveighed against dollar diplomacy. Bob La Follette and George Norris took to the hustings as well as the Senate floor in Horatio-like stands against the Big Money. Yet two faces appear and reappear in my mind's eye: Vice Presidents Charles G. Dawes and Charles Curtis; the first, of the responsible banker's jaw, clamped determinedly to an underslung pipe; the other, a genial ex-jockey, of the Throttlebottom look. There was an innocence, perhaps. But it was not quite Eden's.

As for the Crash itself, there is nothing I personally remember, other than the gradual, at first, hardly noticeable, diminishing in the roster of our guests. It was as though they were carted away, unprotesting and unseen, unlike Edward Albee's grandma. At the entrance, we posted a placard: VACANCY.

The presence of our remaining guests was felt more and more, daily, in the lobby. Hitherto, we had seen them only evenings and on weekends. The decks of cards were wearing out more quickly. The black and red squares of the checkerboard were becoming indistinguishable. Cribbage pegs were being more frequently lost. . . . Tempers were getting shorter. Sudden fights broke out for seemingly unaccountable reasons.

The suddenly idle hands blamed themselves, rather than society. True, there were hunger marches and protestations to City Hall and Washington, but the millions experienced a private kind of shame when the pink slip came. No matter that others suffered the same fate, the inner voice whispered, "I'm a failure."

True, there was a sharing among many of the dispossessed, but, at close quarters, frustration became, at times, violence, and violence turned inward. Thus, sons and fathers fell away, one from the other. And the mother, seeking work, said nothing. Outside forces, except to the more articulate and political rebels, were in some vague way responsible, but not really. It was a personal guilt.

We were carrying the regulars on the books, but the fate of others was daily debated as my mother, my brother and I scanned the more and more indecipherable ledger. At times, the issue was joined, with a great deal of heat, as my brother and I sought to convince our mother that somehow we and our guests shall overcome. In reply, her finger pointed to the undeniable scrawl: the debts were mounting.

With more frequency, we visited our landlord. (We had signed a long-term lease in happier days.) He was a turn-of-the-century man, who had no telephone and signed all his documents longhand. His was a bold and flowing penmanship. There was no mistaking the terms. His adjustments, in view of this strange turn of events, were eminently fair. A man of absolute certainties, who had voted the straight ticket from McKinley to Hoover, he seemed more at sea than I had imagined possible. I was astonished by his sudden fumbling, his bewilderment.

A highly respected Wall Street financier recalled: "The Street had general confusion. They didn't understand it any more than anybody else. They thought something would be announced." (My emphasis.) In 1930, Andrew Mellon, secretary of Treasury, predicted, ". . . during the coming year the country will make steady progress." A speculator remembers, with awe, "Men like Pierpont Morgan and John Rockefeller lost immense amounts of money. Nobody was immune."

Carey McWilliams suggests a study of the Washington hearings dealing with the cause of the Depression: "They make the finest comic reading. The leading industrialists and bankers testified. They hadn't the foggiest notion. . . ."

As for our guests, who now half-occupied the hotel, many preferred relief checks as rent rather than the accustomed cash. It was no longer a high-spirited Saturday night moment.

There was less talk of the girls in the Orleans street cribs and a marked increase in daily drinking. There was, interestingly enough, an upswing in playing the horses: half dollar bets, six bits; a more desperate examination of *The Racing Form. Bert E. Collyer's Eye*, and a scratch sheet, passed from hand to hand. While lost blacks played the numbers, lost whites played the nags.

Of my three years at the University of Chicago Law School, little need be said. I remember hardly anything, other than the presence of one black in my class, an African prince, whose land was a British—or was it a French?—possession. Only one case do I remember: it concerned statutory rape. The fault lay not in the professors, who were good and learned men, but in my studied somnolence. Why, I don't know. Even to this day. Was it a feeling, without my being aware, at the time, of the irrelevance of standard procedure to the circumstances of the day? Or is this a rationalization, ex post facto, of a lazy student? It was a hard case all around.

Yet those years, '31 to '34, at the university, did lead to an education of sorts. On my way from the Wells-Grand to the campus, I traveled through the Black Belt. Was it to escape Torts and Real Property that I sought out the blues? I don't know.

I do know that in those gallimaufry shops I discovered treasures: "race records," they were called by men with dollar signs for eyes. The artists, Big Bill, Memphis Minnie, Tampa Red, Big Maceo, among those I remember, informed me there was more to the stuff of life—and Battling Siki and Senegal, for that matter—than even Westbrook Pegler imagined. Or my professors.

Survival. The marrow of the black man's blues, then and now, has been poverty. Though the articulated theme, the lyric, is often woman, fickle or constant, or the prowess of John the Conqueror, its felt truth is his "low-down" condition. "The Negro was born in depression," murmurs the elderly black. "If you can tell me the difference between the depression today and the Depression of 1932 for the black man, I'd like to know."

It accounts for the bite of his laughter, as he recalls those "hard times": "Why did these big wheels kill themselves? He couldn't stand bringing home beans to his woman, instead of steak and capon. It was a rarity to hear a Negro kill himself over money. There are so few who had any."

And yet, even during the Great Depression, when the white man was "low-down," the black was below whatever that was. This hard fact was constantly sung around, about, under, and over in his blues.

> *I'm just like Job's turkey,*
> *I can't do nothing but gobble,*
> *I'm so poor, baby,*
> *I have to lean against the fence to gabble.*
> *Yeah, now, baby, I believe I'll change town,*
> *Lord, I'm so low down, baby,*
> *I declare I'm looking up at down.*
>
> *The men in the mine, baby,*
> *They all looking down at me. . . .*

—BIG BILL BROONZY

Here the images blur and time turns somersaults. It is the year of Repeal. A classmate and I appear at suddenly-legal taverns. A ritual, in the spirit of the day, comes into play: the house "pops" for every third beer.* It was so in all the taverns we visited. Today, it is a custom more honored in the breach than in the observance.

None I know was more rewarded by the triumph of the Wets than the coppersmith old Heinicke. He had been the lobby elder, ill, hard of hearing, grown weary with life. Suddenly, his services were in desperate demand by any number of breweries. The shortage of skilled coppersmiths was in direct ratio to the unslaked thirst for beer.

As a result of the six-day week he was putting in, the unexpected harvest of money and, most significantly, the delight in his skills, he was transformed, Faustlike, into a younger man. His newly purchased, superheterodyne radio set, in a baroque cabinet that occupied half his room, was heard loud and clear in all fifty quarters. Ascribe it to his exhilaration as much as to his deafness.

As for the others, political argument, often bitter, often hilarious, replaced desuetude. Aside from F.D.R.'s fireside chats, on Sundays a new voice dominated the lobby. It was Father Charles E. Coughlin, coming through the box radio, high on a wooden pedestal. There were those who muttered, "Turn the Roman off." But it was Matthew McGraw, our gaunt, bespectacled, fiery-eyed night clerk (his resemblance to Father Coughlin was remarkable), who insisted the voice be heard.

Matt was something of an intellectual. Before the Crash, he had been a master carpenter. He was constantly quoting from books, weeklies and monthly radical journals. He inveighed against the moneyed interests, against the privileged, against monopoly. He quoted Debs, Darrow, Paine. . . . Somewhere between October, 1929, and November, 1934 (when the Union for Social Justice was formed), something had happened to Matthew McGraw. A forgotten man, his cup of wormwood had flowed over.

A printer remembers his father swinging from Bob La Follette, Wisconsin's progressive senator, to Father Coughlin. The hurt, frustrated man, hearing of the powerful, alien East, sought an answer. So did the gentle, soft-spoken salesman, who hardly questioned anything. "He has the right idea," his daughter remembers him saying of the priest from Royal Oak. The salesman had voted for Roosevelt.

As for my mother, most of her tight-fisted savings were lost with the collapse of Samuel Insull's empire. My errands to the bank were for nothing, it

---

* It was "on the house."

seemed. It was a particularly bitter blow for her. She had previously out-jousted a neighborhood banker. R. L. Chisholm insisted on the soundness of his institution—named, by some ironic God, the Reliance State Bank. Despite his oath on his mother's grave and his expressed admiration for *my* mother's thrift, she withdrew her several thousand. His bank closed the following day. Yet, the utilities magnate took her, a fact for which she forgave neither him nor herself.*

It was 1936. Having long abandoned any thoughts of following the law, I joined the Illinois Writers' Project. I was a member of the radio division. We wrote scripts inspired by paintings at the Art Institute. They were broadcast over WGN, the *Chicago Tribune*'s station. Colonel McCormick, the publisher, was quite proud of these contributions to the city's culture. Though the front page of his paper invariably featured a cartoon of a loony, subversive professor in cap and gown, or a WPA boondoggler leaning on his shovel, he saw no inconsistency in programming the Great Artists series, with credits: ". . . under the auspices of the Works Progress Administration, Harry Hopkins, Director." I am told he listened to them regularly, with a great deal of pleasure.

By chance, I became a gangster in radio soap operas, among them, "Ma Perkins," "Betty and Bob" and "First Nighter." The jobs were fairly frequent, but tenure was lacking. Cause of dismissal: electrocution, life imprisonment, or being shot to death.

As the fervor of unionism spread, with an assist by the Wagner Act, the American Federation of Radio Artists was formed. There was hardly any dissent among the performers. There were, of course, obstinate executives, who played Canute, but the waves rolled over them. The climate, in this instance, was salubrious.

Not so, with other professional unions. The Newspaper Guild, for example. Perhaps my most vivid single memory—certainly my most traumatic—of the thirties, with which I bring these impressions to a close, concerns this battle in Chicago. The Hearst morning newspaper the *Herald-Examiner* was suffering a long and critical strike. Outside the building, journalists picketed. The Hearst delivery trucks were manned by a hard lot; some I remembered as alumni of my high school; some with syndicate friendships. They were employed in a dual capacity: as delivery

---

* Subsequently, during Insull's trial in Chicago, *Little Orphan Annie,* the comic strip, was featuring the ordeal of Daddy Warbucks, the indomitable redhead's benefactor. He, too, was being crucified by alien forces.

men and as terrorists. Whenever the situation presented itself, they'd slug a journalist-picket.

I see a tableau: a pale, bloodied reporter lying on the pavement as colleagues and passersby stare in horror. In the middle of the street stands a squat heavyweight, an auto jack in his grasp. His arms and legs are spread-eagled. He appears to be challenging all comers. Yet, I see, quite unblurred, the terror in his eyes.

The rest is history, which I leave to those whose less-flawed memories and reflections comprise this book.

See, I never heard that word "depression" before.
They would all just say hard times to me. It still is.

Roger, a fourteen-year-old
Appalachian boy, living in Chicago

A Depression might be interesting today. It could *really* be something. To be on the bum, and have nobody say: "Look, I'll give you $10,000 if you'd just come back and go to school." We have a choice today. What would it be like if we had no choice?

Tom, twenty

This I remember. Some people put this out of their minds and forget it. I don't want to forget it. I don't want it to take the best of me, but I want to be there because it happened. This is the truth, you know. History.

Cesar Chavez

They loved us who had passed away.
They forgot all our errors. Our names were mixed.
    The story was long.
The young people danced. They brought down new boughs for the flame. They said, Go on with the story now. What happened next?
    For us there was silence. . . .

Genevieve Taggard, 1940

Book One

The March

Jim Sheridan

It is a large hotel: a halfway house for its hundreds of guests, who are convalescing from nervous breakdowns. The benches near the entrance—and the lobby—are overflowing with the elderly and the young, engaged in highly animated conversations. On this summer's evening, it was certainly the most alive area in the neighborhood.

He is sixty-three years old.

THE SOLDIERS WERE WALKING the streets, the fellas who had fought for democracy in Germany. They thought they should get the bonus right then and there because they needed the money. A fella by the name of Waters, I think, got up the idea of these ex-soldiers would go to Washington, make the kind of trip the hoboes made with Coxey in 1898,* they would be able to get the government to come through.

D. C. Webb organized a group from Bughouse Square to go on this bonus march. Not having been in the army—I was too young for World War I and too old for World War II (laughs)—I was wondering if I would be a legitimate marcher. But the ten or fifteen other fellas were all soldiers, and they thought it would be O.K. for me to go. Webb said, "Come along, you're a pretty good bum." (Laughs.)

We went down to the railyards and grabbed a freight train. Our first stop was in Peru, Indiana. We jungled up there for a little while, and then we bummed the town, so to speak. Go to different grocers and give them a tale of woe. They would give us sausage or bread or meat or canned goods. Then we'd go back to the railroad yards, the jungle, where we'd build a little fire and we'd cook it up in these cans. We'd sit around the fire and eat. . . .

---

* In 1894, Jacob S. Coxey led a march of unemployed into Washington. It failed in its purpose. The small size of the group led to the coinage of the derogatory phrase "Coxey's Army."

Peru was the first division point outside of Chicago on the C & O.* We'd stop off and rest and scrounge up something to eat. We'd generally be told by the conductors the train was made up and ready to go out. Some of these fellas had come with their families. Can you imagine women and children riding boxcars?

The conductor'd want to find out how many guys were in the yard, so he would know how many empty boxcars to put onto the train. Of course, the railroad companies didn't know this, but these conductors, out of their sympathy, would put two or three empty boxcars in the train, so these bonus marchers could crawl into them and ride comfortable into Washington. Even the railroad detectives were very generous.

Sometimes there'd be fifty, sixty people in a boxcar. We'd just be sprawled out on the floor. The toilet . . . you had to hold it till you got a division point. (Laughs.) That's generally a hundred miles. You didn't carry food with you. You had to bum the town. It was beggary on a grand scale.

In one town, D. C. Webb got up on the bandstand and made a speech. We passed the hat, even, among the local citizenry. The money was used to buy cigarettes for the boys. Townspeople, they were very sympathetic.

There was none of this hatred you see now when strange people come to town, or strangers come to a neighborhood. They resent it, I don't know why. That's one of the things about the Depression. There was more camaraderie than there is now. Even more comradeship than the Commies could even dream about. That was one of the feelings that America lost. People had different ideas, they disagreed with one another. But there was a fine feeling among them. You were in trouble . . . damn it, if they could help ya, they would help ya.

One incident stuck in my memory. We had reached a place in Virginia. It was a very hot day. In this jungle, there was a man, a very tall man. He had his wife with him and several small children. We invited them over to have something to eat with us, and they refused. Then I brought something over to them in an old pie plate. They still refused. It was the husband who told me that he didn't care for anything to eat. But see, the baby was crying from hunger.

Finally, me and some others went down to bum the center of the town. I remember going into a drugstore and bumming a baby bottle with a nipple. Now, can you imagine a guy bumming a baby bottle with a nipple? It took me a few guts to work it up. I explained the circumstances. Then I went and bummed the milk.

* Chesapeake and Ohio Railway.

Toward Los Angeles, California

Dorothea Lange, 1937

When I got back to the jungle camp, it was kinda dark. I first reported in to Captain Webb and then he kidded me about the baby bottle. "Christ," I said, "that baby there's gotta eat." And he said, "This afternoon you got pretty much of a rebuff." "Well," I said, "I'm gonna try again." So I went over and addressed myself to his wife. And I told her: here is the baby bottle. We had even warmed up the milk. But she looked at her husband, and her husband said he didn't want it.

What could I do about it, but just feel blue? I didn't look upon it as charity. It seemed to me that here was a fella's pride getting the best of him.

The tragedy came when the train was going through Virginia.

We had to go through these mountain countries. The smoke from the stacks of the engines, and the soot, would be flying back through the tunnels and would be coming into the boxcars. So in order to avoid getting choked, we'd close the boxcars and hold handkerchiefs over our noses. There was quite a discussion about this. What would happen to the little infant? We was afraid it would smother. The mother was holding the baby, but the baby seemed very still. The mother screamed. We didn't know what the scream was about. After we reached Washington, we found out that the baby had died going through the tunnels.

When the baby died, a feeling of sadness came over those in the boxcar. It seemed that they had lost one of their own.

When we got to Washington, there was quite a few ex-servicemen there before us. There was no arrangements for housing. Most of the men that had wives and children were living in Hooverville. This was across the Potomac River—what was known as Anacostia Flats. They had set up housing there, made of cardboard and of all kinds. I don't know how they managed to get their food. Most other contingents was along Pennsylvania Avenue.

They were tearing down a lot of buildings along that street, where they were going to do some renewal, build some federal buildings. A lot of ex-servicemen just sort of turned them into barracks. They just sorta bunked there. Garages that were vacant, they took over. Had no respect for private property. They didn't even ask permission of the owners. They didn't even know who the hell the owners was.

They had come to petition Hoover, to give them the bonus before it was due. And Hoover refused this. He told them they couldn't get it because it would make the country go broke. They would hold midnight vigils around the White House and march around the White House in shifts.

The question was now: How were they going to get them out of Washington? They were ordered out four or five times, and they refused. The police chief was called to send them out, but he* refused. I also heard that the marine commander, who was called to bring out the marines, also refused. Finally, the one they did get to shove these bedraggled ex-servicemen out of Washington was none other than the great MacArthur.

The picture I'll always remember . . . here is MacArthur coming down Pennsylvania Avenue. And, believe me, ladies and gentlemen, he came on a white horse. He was riding a white horse. Behind him were tanks, troops of the regular army.

This was really a riot that wasn't a riot, in a way. When these ex-soldiers wouldn't move, they'd poke them with their bayonets, and hit them on the head with the butt of a rifle. First, they had a hell of a time getting them out of the buildings they were in. Like a sit-in.

They managed to get them out. A big colored soldier, about six feet tall, had a big American flag he was carrying. He was one of the bonus marchers. He turned to one of the soldiers who was pushing him along, saying: "Get along there, you big black bastard." That was it. He turned and said, "Don't try to push me. I fought for this flag. I fought for this flag in France and I'm gonna fight for it here on Pennsylvania Avenue." The soldier hit him on the side of the legs with the bayonet. I think he was injured. But I don't know if he was sent to the hospital.

This was the beginnning of a riot, in a way. These soldiers were pushing these people. They didn't want to move, but they were pushing them anyway.

As night fell, they crossed the Potomac. They were given orders to get out of Anacostia Flats, and they refused. The soldiers set those shanties on fire. They were practically smoked out. I saw it from a distance. I could see the pandemonium. The fires were something like the fires you see nowadays that are started in these ghettoes. But they weren't started by the people that live there.

The soldiers threw tear gas at them and vomiting gas. It was one assignment they reluctantly took on. They were younger than the marchers. It was like sons attacking their fathers. The next day the newspapers deplored the fact and so forth, but they realized the necessity of getting these men off. Because they were causing a health hazard to the city. MacArthur was looked upon as a hero.†

* General Pelham D. Glassford.
† He was aided by General George Patton and Major Dwight Eisenhower. "Thank God," said President Hoover, "we still have a government that knows how to deal with a mob."

And so the bonus marchers straggled back to the various places they came from. And without their bonus.

POSTSCRIPT: *After the Bonus March, I bummed my way to New York. I couldn't get on relief there because I wasn't a resident. So I resorted to one of the oldest professions—that is, begging. I became a professional panhandler. I had quite a few steady clients. One of them was Heywood Broun. Every time I put the bite on him, he'd say, "For Chrissake, don't you know any other guy in the city beside me?" (Laughs.)*

■   ■   ■   ■

A. Everette McIntyre

Federal trade commissioner.

ON A PARTICULAR MORNING—I believe this was on the twenty-sixth or twenty-seventh of June, 1932—the police blocked the avenue and turned the marchers back. The bonus men had undertaken to march around the White House. The president didn't like that. A lot of other people didn't like it, either, because they were clogging up Pennsylvania Avenue, in the busy part of the day.

About five thousand of the bonus marchers and their families were camping in some of the demolished buildings. The police encircled them. There was some brick throwing. A couple of the police retaliated by firing. A bonus man was killed and another seriously wounded.

During lunchtime, the following day, I heard some army commands. To my right, down by the ellipse toward the monument, military units were being formed. It looked like trouble. We didn't have long to wait.

A squadron of cavalry was in front of this army column. Then, some staff cars, and four trucks with baby tanks on them, stopped near this camp. They let the ramps down and the baby tanks rolled out into the street. When the army appeared, the bonus people, who were in these old buildings, started beating on tin pans and shouted: "Here come our buddies." They expected the army to be in sympathy with them.

One of these staff cars unloaded—not very far from where I was standing—and out of it came MacArthur, Chief of Staff. He had a youngish major as an aide. His name was Dwight Eisenhower. With their hands on their hips, they surveyed the situation.

The 12th Infantry was in full battle dress. Each had a gas mask and his belt was full of tear gas bombs. They were given a "right face," which caused them to face the camp. They fixed their bayonets and also fixed the gas masks over their faces. At orders, they brought their bayonets at thrust and moved in. The bayonets were used to jab people, to make them move.

Soon, almost everybody disappeared from view, because tear gas bombs exploded. The entire block was covered by tear gas. Flames were coming up, where the soldiers had set fire to the buildings to drive these people out. The infantry was apparently under orders to drive this group toward the bridges, across the Potomac. Through the whole afternoon, they took one camp after another.

My colleagues and I decided that the army would assault the camp in Anacostia Flats, across the river. There were about twenty thousand to forty thousand bonus people there. We went on the roof of a building and watched what occurred there that evening. It happened after dark.

The 12th Infantry did march across the bridge, in full battle dress as before. This was quite a sight. We could see the fires. Soon, all the occupants of that camp were driven into the Maryland Woods, into the night.

The next day, I read accounts of some of the people who had been jabbed with bayonets. Some had been injured seriously. People who had raised their arms had their arms cut by some sabres. Others were hit by the flat of the sword. In some instances, ears were cut off. . . .

■   ■   ■   ■

Edward C. Schalk

A veteran of World War I.

WHEN THE ARMY CAME out, what else could they do? They just walked off, like good Spartans would do.

I remember when they come back from Washington. They landed over here on State Street. They had sort of a reunion. It was nice weather, summertime. And all kinds of people came to visit 'em. They had a flag spread out, and everyone was throwin' money in—quarter, half a dollar. Showin' that they were welcomin' 'em back and were all for 'em. They had quite a time. After that, where they went, nobody knows.

The Song

Once in khaki suits,
Gee, we looked swell,
Full of that Yankee Doodle-de-dum.
Half a million boots went sloggin' through Hell,
I was the kid with the drum.
Say, don't you remember, they called me Al—
It was Al all the time.
Say, don't you remember I'm your pal—
*Brother, can you spare a dime.**

E. Y. (Yip) Harburg

Song lyricist and writer of light verse. Among the works in which his lyrics were sung are: Finian's Rainbow, The Bloomer Girl, Jamaica, The Wizard of Oz *and* Earl Carroll's Vanities.

I NEVER LIKED THE idea of living on scallions in a left bank garret. I like writing in comfort. So I went into business, a classmate and I. I thought I'd retire in a year or two. And a thing called Collapse, bango! socked everything out. 1929. All I had left was a pencil.

Luckily, I had a friend named Ira Gershwin, and he said to me, "You've got your pencil. Get your rhyming dictionary and go to work." I did. There was nothing else to do. I was doing light verse at the time, writing a poem here and there for ten bucks a crack. It was an era when kids at college were interested in light verse and ballads and sonnets. This is the early thirties.

I was relieved when the Crash came. I was released. Being in business was something I detested. When I found that I could sell a song or a poem, I became me, I became alive. Other people didn't see it that way. They were throwing themselves out of windows.

Someone who lost money found that his life was gone. When I lost my possessions, I found my creativity. I felt I was being born for the first time. So for me the world became beautiful.

With the Crash, I realized that the greatest fantasy of all was business. The only realistic way of making a living was versifying. Living off your imagination.

We thought American business was the Rock of Gibraltar. We were the prosperous nation, and nothing could stop us now. A brownstone house was forever. You gave it to your kids and they put marble fronts on it. There was a feeling of continuity. If you made it, it was there forever. Suddenly the big dream exploded. The impact was unbelievable.

I was walking along the street at that time, and you'd see the bread lines. The biggest one in New York City was owned by William Randolph Hearst. He had a big truck with several people on it, and big cauldrons of hot soup, bread. Fellows with burlap on their shoes were lined up all around Columbus Circle, and went for blocks and blocks around the park, waiting.

There was a skit in one of the first shows I did, *Americana*. This was 1930. In the sketch, Mrs. Ogden Reid of the *Herald Tribune* was very jealous of Hearst's beautiful bread line. It was bigger than her bread line. It was a satiric, volatile show. We needed a song for it.

On stage, we had men in old soldiers' uniforms, dilapidated, waiting around. And then into the song. We had to have a title. And how do you do a song so it isn't maudlin? Not to say: my wife is sick, I've got six children, the Crash put me out of business, hand me a dime. I hate songs of that kind. I hate songs that are on the nose. I don't like songs that describe a historic moment pitifully.

The prevailing greeting at that time, on every block you passed, by some poor guy coming up, was: "Can you spare a dime?" Or: "Can you spare something for a cup of coffee?" . . . "Brother, Can You Spare a Dime?" finally hit on every block, on every street. I thought that could be a beautiful title. If I could only work it out by telling people, through the song, it isn't just a man asking for a dime.

This is the man who says: I built the railroads. I built that tower. I fought your wars. I was the kid with the drum. Why the hell should I be standing in line now? What happened to all this wealth I created?

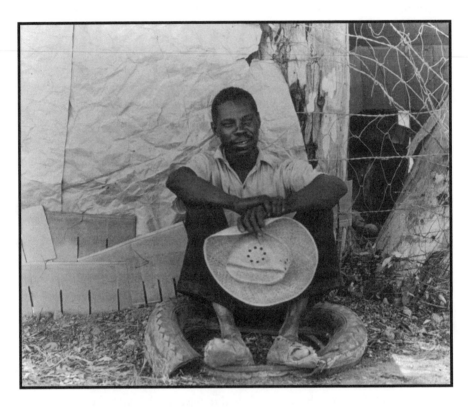

Negro field worker, Holtville, Imperial Valley, California.
"He has just made himself shoes out of that old tire."

DOROTHEA LANGE, 1935

I think that's what made the song. Of course, together with the idea and meaning, a song must have poetry. It must have the phrase that rings a bell. The art of song writing is a craft. Yet "Brother, Can You Spare a Dime?" opens up a political question. Why should this man be penniless at any time in his life, due to some fantastic thing called a Depression or sickness or whatever it is that makes him so insecure?

In the song the man is really saying: I made an investment in this country. Where the hell are my dividends? Is it a dividend to say: "Can you spare a dime?" What the hell is wrong? Let's examine this thing. It's more than just a bit of pathos. It doesn't reduce him to a beggar. It makes him a dignified human, asking questions—and a bit outraged, too, as he should be.

Everybody picked the song up in '30 and '31. Bands were playing it and records were made. When Roosevelt was a candidate for president, the Republicans got pretty worried about it. Some of the network radio people were told to lay low on the song. In some cases, they tried to ban it from the air. But it was too late. The song had already done its damage.

Hard Travelin'

I've been doin' some hard travelin',
I thought you knowd
I've been doin' some hard ramblin'
Away down the road. . . .

. . . I've been layin' in a hard rock jail,
I thought you knowd
I've been laid out ninety days
Way down the road.
The darned old judge, he said to me,
It's ninety days for vagrancy,
And I've been doin' some hard travelin', Lord.

—WOODY GUTHRIE[*]

Ed Paulsen

From 1926 on, when he was fourteen, he, himself, knocked around and about the states—"I rode the freights" across the land. "I always went back to my home in South Dakota. My sister and her husband had a little farm. It was a retreat. I played semipro baseball up there at one time. You know who I faced? Satchel Paige. He was pitching for Bismarck. I worked punching cattle, $10 a month. I was never satisfied to stay there. I was always taking a pop at L.A. or San Francisco.

"Everybody talks of the Crash of '29. In small towns out West, we didn't know there was a Crash. What did the stock market mean to us? Not a dang

[*] Words and Music by Woody Guthrie TRO-© Copyright 1959, 1963 by Ludlow Music, Inc. New York, N.Y. Used by permission.

thing. If you were in Cut Bank, Montana, who owned stock? The farmer was a ping-pong ball in a very tough game.

"I finished high school in 1930, and I walked out into this thing. . . ." He picked apples in Washington, "hustled sheets" in Los Angeles, and worked on road gangs all along the coast. "It got tougher. We didn't know how to make out in the city. It was terrifying. There were great queues of guys in soup lines. We didn't know how to join a soup line. We—my two brothers and I—didn't see ourselves that way. We had middle-class ideas without a middle-class income. (Laughs.)

"We ended up in San Francisco in 1931. I tried to get a job on the docks. I was a big husky athlete, but there just wasn't any work. Already by that time, if you were looking for a job at a Standard Oil Service Station, you had to have a college degree. It was that kind of market. . . ."

I'D GET UP AT five in the morning and head for the waterfront. Outside the Spreckles Sugar Refinery, outside the gates, there would be a thousand men. You know dang well there's only three or four jobs. The guy would come out with two little Pinkerton cops: "I need two guys for the bull gang. Two guys to go into the hole." A thousand men would fight like a pack of Alaskan dogs to get through there. Only four of us would get through. I was too young a punk.

So you'd drift up to Skid Row. There'd be thousands of men there. Guys on baskets, making weird speeches, phony theories on economics. About eleven-thirty, the real leaders would take over. They'd say: O.K., we're going to City Hall. The mayor was Angelo Rossi, a dapper little guy. He wore expensive boots and a tight vest. We'd shout around the steps. Finally, he'd come out and tell us nothing.

I remember the demands: We demand work, we demand shelter for our families, we demand groceries, this kind of thing. . . . Half the guys up there making the demands were Negroes. Now there wasn't a big black colony in San Francisco in those days. But they were pretty cagey, the leaders—they always kept a mixture of black and white.

I remember as a kid how courageous this seemed to me, the demands, because you knew that society wasn't going to give it to you. They'd demand that they open up unrented houses and give decent shelters for their families.* But you just knew society wasn't yielding. There was nothing coming.

---

* "Thirteen public aid families squatted in a vacant building . . . they defied the police to evict them. Most were victims of a recent fire. The others decided to abandon their substandard housing in favor of the three-story building. . . . 'Man, we're going to stake out

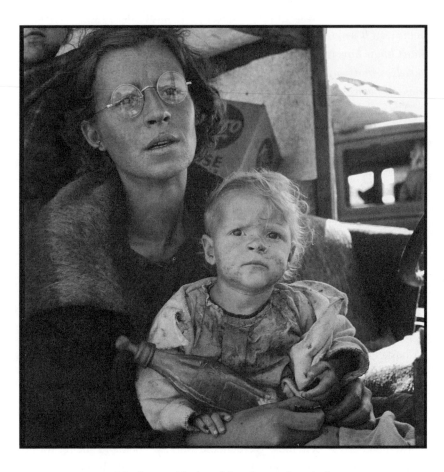

Mother and baby of family on the road,
Tulelake, Siskiyou County, California

DOROTHEA LANGE, 1939

This parade would be four blocks long, curb to curb. Nobody had a dime. There were guys on the corner trying to sell apples to this moneyless wonder. (Laughs.)

The guys'd start to yell and there come some horses. They used to have cops on horseback in those days. Then there'd be some fighting. Finally it got to killing. I think they killed three people there that day, besides the wounded. It really got rough because the guys had brought a bunch of marbles and threw them on the street, and the horses were slipping and sliding around. This made the cops mad and they got rough.

There'd be this kind of futile struggle, because somehow you never expected to win. We had a built-in losing complex. That's the way those crowds felt. A lot of them would drift back into the Sally.* By now it's one o'clock, and everybody's hungry. We were a gentle crowd. These were fathers, eighty percent of them. They had held jobs and didn't want to kick society to pieces. They just wanted to go to work and they just couldn't understand. There was a mysterious thing. You watched the papers, you listened to rumors, you'd get word somebody's gonna build a building.

So the next morning you get up at five o'clock and you dash over there. You got a big tip. There's three thousand men there, carpenters, cement men, guys who knew machinery and everything else. These fellas always had faith that the job was gonna mature, somehow. More and more men were after fewer and fewer jobs. So San Francisco just ground to a halt. Nothing was moving.

We were always trying to get to sea, but I didn't have any ticket. Oh, I made that waterfront a thousand times. There used to be those great old liners that sailed out to Hawaii. You could hear the band play "Aloha Away," and all the guys were standing there with tears in their eyes. As though you had somebody going some place. And you didn't know a damn soul. (Laughs.)

We weren't greatly agitated in terms of society. Ours was a bewilderment, not an anger. Not a sense of being particularly put upon. We weren't talking revolution; we were talking jobs.

We'd grown up in small-town high schools. There wasn't much expression, in the press, of the intelligentsia. It was just a tough world, and you had been born into it. I had no great sense of fervor until I went to L.A. and

---

those apartments just like the early settlers when they took it away from the Indians,' announced Mrs. Pearl Moore, a Tenants' Union representative." (Chicago *Daily News*, February 21, 1969).
* The Salvation Army.

ran into Upton Sinclair in 1934. If I were picking a time when I began to say, "What the hell's this all about?" it came when I wandered into a meeting one day where Upton Sinclair was talking.* This was the winter of '33, '34. There was this litttle pink-and-white guy up there speaking, the least likely guy ever to be a radical you ever saw. You automatically think of pince-nez glasses and a shock of white hair. His audience was made up mostly of working stiffs.

He pointed out the great piles of oranges, the piles of lumber laying there idle. . . . They'd put up a rick of oranges and apples, put gasoline over it and set fire to them. Vegetables were being destroyed and everything. Everybody who cried so much later about federal programs destroying little pigs . . . they should have seen what industry was doing at this time. To keep the price up.

Sinclair's idea was to relate the unemployed to the resources not being used. This appealed to me tremendously. It made sense to have this food eaten up by hungry people. I got a job singing with the quartet that was campaigning with him.

If I had to pick one constant enemy during this time, it was the American Legion. They were made up of home guard types. They were the most vicious enemies of this drifting, reckless, hungry crowd of people. Every place I went, Hoovervilles—they were raided. This bunch of Legionnaires with those damn caps on. Guys with baseball bats, driving them out of the jungles around the railroad grounds. Even in the little towns I lived in. I had a war with those guys by the time I was in high school. They were always the bane of my existence.

They were the Main Streeters. They were doing all right. Merchants, storekeepers, landowners. They had a fix that was just awful to live with. They were hard on the little candidate for governor. They'd come to his meetings with baseball bats and clubs and break it up. Once, when we sang in the Valley, they attacked us and beat the hell out of us. We barely got out of there.

During the Sinclair campaign, I was going to the library, picking up books I'd never read before, books that never crossed my track. You'd go down to look for work in the morning, and then you'd give up at eleven o'clock and drift into that library. I got my education there, really.

By this time, Roosevelt was president. There was the NRA . . . mystical things were going on we didn't understand at all. People were talking price fixing and what have you. Very, very weird world. It didn't mean a damn

---

* He was candidate for governor of California. EPIC was his symbol and credo: End Poverty In California.

to us. There were three brothers of us, we got a freight and went down to Portland. They'd started to work on the Bonneville Dam. Beautiful sight down that river. On a decent day, if you set on top of a boxcar, it was beautiful. . . .

We drifted down to the jungle. We go into a beanery, 'cause there was no train out till eleven that night. In comes a Mexican whore and a colored whore. They order a hamburger. The proprietor says, "I don't serve niggers. Get that dame out of here." The Mexican girl comes back and orders two hamburgers. The guy grumbles, fries up a couple. The colored girl walks in. This guy goes under the counter and comes up with a sap.* He lashes out at the girl's head, bong! Jeez, I think he's killed her. She groans and staggers back off this stool. He cuts around the corner in a wild rage. I put my foot out and trip him. He just went ass over Tecumseh. The girls get out in time. He'd a killed that girl, I believe. We lam out of there, too. We grab the midnight freight and get off at Phoenix. It's a hostile town, so we beat it.

We make an orange freight. We rode in the reefer.† Clear to Kansas City. It goes like a bat out of hell, a rough ride. We broke through the wire netting and ate the oranges. We got vitamins like mad. (Laughs.) But your mouth gets burnt by that acid juice and your teeth get so damn sore from that ride. By the time we got off at K.C., I could hardly close my mouth.

We catch a train into Kansas City, Kansas, that night. At the stops, colored people were gettin' on the trains and throwin' off coal. You could see people gatherin' the coal. You could see the railroad dicks were gettin' tough.

Hal and I are ridin' on the top of the boxcar, it's a fairly nice night. All of a sudden, there's a railroad dick with a flashlight that reaches a thousand miles. Bam! Bam! He starts shooting. We hear the bullets hitting the cars, bam! like that. I throw my hands up and start walking towards that light. Hal's behind me. The guy says, "Get off." I said, "Christ, I can't." This thing's rollin' fifty miles an hour or more. He says, "Jump." I says, "I can't." He says, "Turn around and march ahead." He marches us over the top. There's a gondola, about eight feet down. He says, "Jump." So I jumped and landed in wet sand, up to my knees.

We come to a little town in Nebraska, Beatrice. It's morning. I'm chilled to the bone. We crawl into a railroad sandbox, almost frozen to death. We dry out, get warmed up, and make the train again. We pull into Omaha. It's night. All of a sudden, the train is surrounded by deputies, with pistols. The guy says, "Get in those trucks." I said, "What for? We haven't done

* A blackjack.
† The refrigerator car.

anything." He said, "You're not going to jail. You're going to the Transient Camp."

They drive us up to an old army warehouse. They check you in, take off your clothes, run them through a de-louser, and you take a bath. It's midnight. We come out, and here's a spread with scrambled eggs, bacon, bread, coffee and toast. We ate a great meal. It was wonderful. We go upstairs to bed. Here's a double-decker, sheets, toothbrush, towels, everything. I sat down on this damn bed, I can't tell you, full of wonderment. We thought we'd gone to heaven. Hal's a young punk, he's seventeen. He said, "What the hell kind of a place is this?" I said, "I don't know, but it's sure somethin' different."

The next morning, they called us up to a social worker. By this time, there's a thousand guys in there. They're playing baseball, some guys are washing down walls—bums, bindlestiffs, cynical rough guys who've been on the road for years. It's kind of like a playhouse. It's unbelievable.

Through a social worker, he is assigned to a job with the National Youth Administration, at "a little cold-water college" in Aberdeen, South Dakota. "And then the good life began for me.

"Before Roosevelt, the federal government hardly touched your life. Outside of the postmaster, there was little local representation. Now people you knew were appointed to government jobs. Joe Blow or some guy from the corner.

"It came right down to Main Street. Half of them loved it, half of them hated it. There was the immediacy of its effect on you. In Aberdeen, Main Street was against it. But they were delighted to have those green relief checks cashed in their cash registers. They'd have been out of business had it not been for them. It was a split thing. They were cursing Roosevelt for the intrusion into their lives. At the same time, they were living off it. Main Street still has this fix."

The NYA was my salvation. I could just as easily have been in Sing Sing as with the UN.* Just every bit a chance. Hell, yes. Everybody was a criminal. You stole, you cheated through. You were getting by, survival. Stole clothes off lines, stole milk off back porches, you stole bread. I remember going through Tucumcari, New Mexico, on a freight. We made a brief stop. There was a grocery store, a supermarket kind of thing for those days. I beat it off the train and came back with rolls and crackers. This guy is standing in the window shaking his fist at you.

* He has an administrative job with UNICEF.

It wasn't a big thing, but it created a coyote mentality. You were a preda-tor. You had to be. The coyote is crafty. He can be fantastically courageous and a coward at the same time. He'll run, but when he's cornered, he'll fight. I grew up where they were hated, 'cause they'd kill sheep. They'll kill a calf, get in the chicken pen. They're mean. But how else does a coyote stay alive? He's not as powerful as a wolf. He has a small body. He's in such bad condition, a dog can run him down. He's not like a fox. A coyote is na-ture's victim as well as man's. We were coyotes in the thirties, the jobless.

No, I don't see the Depression as an ennobling experience. Survivors are still ridin' with the ghost—the ghost of those days when things came hard.

■   ■   ■   ■

Pauline Kael

Film critic, The New Yorker.

THE FIRST VIOLENCE I had ever seen was along the Embarcadero. The an-ger of the men. I never saw it again until recently in Philadelphia—between cops and little Negro kids.

Angry men were yelling. They had weapons and were angry at other men. I was in a car with my father. I had seen passive bread lines. But this was different. Girls don't usually see this, particularly if you're a bookish girl from a bookish family.

It may have been a prelude to the San Francisco General Strike. I'm not sure. That was almost like a blackout. It had a sense of paralysis.

The kids with lots of money had actually been moved to the peninsula out of harm's way. The rich people thought there was going to be a revolu-tion, and they moved out of town.

My neighbors were angry with my mother, because she fed hungry men at the back door. They said it would bring others, and then what would she do? She said, "I'll feed them till the food runs out." It wasn't until years later, I realized the fear people had of these men. We didn't have it in our house.

I understand why these neighbors were afraid. They had lived with do-mestic violence all their lives. They were beaten up by their husbands every Saturday night. You could hear them screaming. So their fear of men was generalized. I'm sure my father never hit my mother. Ours was a nonviolent family, so we weren't particularly scared of these strange men.

■   ■   ■   ■

Frank Czerwonka

"I'm a garbage man. Work for the city. I have a steady income, twice a month. My wife has an independent income—me.

"I mean, there's a conditioning here by the Depression. I'm what I call a security cat. I don't like the job I have, but I don't dare switch. 'Cause I got too much whiskers on it, seniority.

"I won't hang around with failures. When you hang around with successful people, it rubs off on ya. When you hang around with failures, it may rub off on ya, too. So I'm a snob, so do me somethin'."

WHEN MY FATHER DIED, my mother involved herself in speakeasies, blinds and beer flats. Married a couple of times.

In 1928, I started working. And I got laid off a week before the Depression. I had everything I wanted. I didn't want much. My life's ambition was to be a bum, and I failed at that. (Laughs.)

In 1930, my stepfather had this flat, where we had a speakeasy going. People from a small syndicate moved in the next flat. In our neighborhood, we wouldn't drink moonshine, just refined alcohol. My stepfather would peddle the moonshine on the South Side.

These moonshiners, they got the gas company men to tap the main with a three-inch pipe. Using company tools to steal their own gas. The gas company men, I mean, they take money, too. They tapped the gas main pipe and ran it up to the second floor and put a burner on it. Put a hundred-gallon still on it, going twenty-four hours a day. Just time off to put a new batch in.

There was cooperation in the neighborhood. Like this friend of mine, his father ran a joint. He got a job with the utility company to repair meters. Things got rough in the neighborhood. So everybody was cheatin' on gas, electricity, everything they could. A lot of people had their meters taken out. So he'd rig up jumpers on the meters in the whole neighborhood. He warned 'em: if they see anybody climbin' up a pole to put a meter on, let him know. The electric company came around, put a meter on it. So he climbed the pole and put a jumper* on the meter.

---

* "A jumper is a way of puttin' a wire on it so the current goes around the meter instead of through it and doesn't rotate the wheels. The current is goin' all the time, but not registerin'."

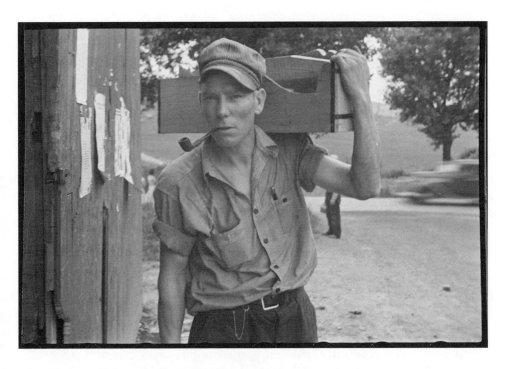

Carpenter, Westmoreland County, Pennsylvania

WALKER EVANS, 1935

The whole neighborhood would cooperate . . . ?

Yeah, to beat the utility. And there's the bit about the case workers, too. The case worker was the enemy. They'd see case workers snoopin' around— they'd know 'em by sight—they'd pass the word around. If they were havin' parties or they were eatin' or the old man was moonlighting somewhere to pick up a few bucks, they'd cover up for each other.

The syndicate boys had barrels of mash all over the place. One day my stepfather gets drunk—he was goofy that way. He liked to get arguments goin' and get pounded up. So they asked my mother if it's all right to kill him. She said: "No, I haven't got insurance on him."

Our speakeasy had a candy-store front. That was the come-on. The fuzz wasn't botherin' us. They were just shakin' down the syndicate. They were tryin' to get money from them because it was a big operation. They'd take out two truckloads of this moonshine. In five-gallon cans that were always a quart short. Even the one-gallon cans were about four ounces short. They never gave you a full measure. That was the standard practice in them days. They were gyppers.

Did you pay off the syndicate?

No, we bought through their channels. We bought alcohol. This moonshine was obviously for the South Side trade, the colored. The syndicate got a big place cheap to cook, about eight rooms. They used to get knocked off every so often, but not too often. Because the police captain was taken care of. They didn't believe in payin' off the men on the beat. They'd give him a drink and that was it. Because it would run into many expenses otherwise. 'Cause if one got something, he'd tell everybody else, and they'd all be in on it. This way, they'd pay the captain off and he wouldn't come around.

We'd been raided a couple of times, but they never could find the booze. My mother had a clever gimmick. She'd drive a nail in the wall, take a jug of booze and put a hat and coat on top on it. They never found it.

There was another candy-store front used by a woman. A cop started comin' around and gettin' friendly. She knew he was workin' up to a pinch. So she prepared a bottle for him. He talked her into sellin' it to him. He pinches her, takes her to court. He said: "I bought this half a dog of booze. Half a pint." The woman said, "How do you know it's booze?" The cop takes a swig of it and spits it out. It was urine. Case dismissed.

When we had this place, the downtown Cadillac squad came in there— the open cars with sawed-off shotguns. They didn't want to drag us in. They wanted money. They wanted $40. My mother wasn't holding that day.

So she had to wait for the customers to come in and borrow it from 'em. It took about three hours to pay these guys off.

Later on, in 1933, when Prohibition was lifted, alcohol dropped from $40 a gallon to $5. For a while $8 was the standard price, but $5 was the low point.

I wanted to get out of this. Get a job, more or less. I was goin' to work one day with seven cents and my lunch in my pocket. Believe it or not, I was waitin' for a streetcar. A truck was goin' out of town. Its tail gate was down. I jumped on it and was gone for six months. This was maybe '31. Still in Hoover's time. I went as far as the truck went. A freight train comes by.

I had my seven cents, but I ate my lunch. I bought a pack of Bull Durham, but I needed food. I found a jungle, ate somethin', and learned a few tricks from these 'boes.

Freight trains were amazing in them days. When a train would stop in a small town and the bums got off, the population tripled. So many ridin' the freight. Women even, and quite a few were tryin' to disguise themselves.

I ran into a couple of self-styled professors, safe blowers, skilled mechanics and all that. Quite a few boomers were traveling. These people usually had money. When they finished a job, they'd get paid, go on a bender and get rolled. They didn't like the farmer types. And there were quite a few farmers buried.

I'm talkin' about this big dam job out west, this big Hoover Dam. There was a lot of farmers in the concrete. They just shoved 'em in there. They didn't like 'em as job competition. Oh, there were some mean people travelin' around.

Old-time hoboes had a circuit, like a preacher or a salesman. The towns knew 'em. They knew the good jails to spend the winter in. They would associate with each other, clannish. They wouldn't let outsiders in very much. A young boy, somebody they took a fancy to, they'd break him in. There was quite a bit of homosexual down there—wolves, punks and all that. I pushed one guy in the river. I don't know if he came up or not, 'cause I ran.

There was always Sally. While you listened to a sermon, they'd feed you a little something, and then you'd go on your way. The missions are pretty horrible because they pre-judge ya. I wanted a flop so I took it. Once in a while somebody would take a nose dive, profess religion. They'd stick around awhile just to have a roof. The first time they get enough money to get drunk, they did.

If you got lucky and got yourself a package of cigarettes, Camels was the bit, you put 'em in your socks and your Bull Durham was in your shirt pocket. So the ones that didn't have would mooch the Bull Durham instead of the Camels.

These kids amaze me today. I mean, they're smokin' and a bus comes, and they throw away the whole butt. I can't. I gotta clinch it. Put it in my pocket. Some days when I'm ridin' around in buses, I find the next day a half a dozen butts. I put 'em in the ash tray for when I run out of cigarettes.

The locals didn't care for the bums, they wouldn't take to 'em. There were always people bummin'. At back doors, tryin' to get a handout.

Did they know which doors to knock on?
No, this bit about the code that the old bums had broke down. If it was still being used, they weren't letting the newcomers know—the *nouveau paupers.*

Sometimes you'd sleep in a field, if the weather was nice. One time in North Dakota, all I had to cover myself was a road map underneath me and a road map on top of me. I woke up in the morning, there was frost on the road map. It didn't bother me, I slept. Now I'm paying the penalty. Arthritis.

■   ■   ■   ■

Kitty McCulloch

"I'm seventy-one and I can still swim."

THERE WERE MANY BEGGARS, who would come to your back door, and they would say they were hungry. I wouldn't give them money because I didn't have it. But I did take them in and put them in my kitchen and give them something to eat.

This one man came in—it was right before Christmas. My husband had a very nice suit, tailored. It was a black suit with a fine white pinstripe in it. He put it to one side. I thought he didn't like the suit. I said to this man, "Your clothes are all ragged. I think I have a nice suit for you." So I gave him this suit.

The following Sunday my husband was to go to a wake. He said, "Where's my good suit?" And I said, "Well, Daddy, you never wore it. I—well, it's gone." He said, "Where is it gone to?" I said, "I gave it to a man who had such shabby clothes. Anyway, you got three other suits and he didn't have any. So I gave it to him." He said, "You're the limit, Mother."

One elderly man that had white whiskers and all, he came to my back door. He was pretty much of a philosopher. He was just charming. A man probably in his sixties. And he did look like St. Nicholas, I'll tell you that. I gave him a good, warm meal. He said, "Bring me a pencil and paper and I'll draw you a picture." So he sketched. And he was really good. He was an artist.

(Laughing.) A man came to my door, and I could smell liquor a little. He said, "You don't suppose you could have a couple of shirts you could give me, old shirts of your husband's?" I said, "Oh, I'm so very sorry, my husband hasn't anything but old shirts, really. That's all he has right now and he wears those." He said, "Lady, if I get some extra ones, I'll come back and give them to you." I said, "Go on, mind your own business."

And another one, I smelled liquor on *his* breath, too. He wanted to know if he could have a few pennies. I said, "Are you hungry?" He said, "I haven't had any food. I'd like some money to buy some food." I said, "I'll make you a nice sandwich." So I made him a sandwich with mayonnaise and chicken and lettuce, a double sandwich, put it in wax paper. He gave me a dirty look and he started down the alley. I watched him when he got, oh, two or three doors down, he threw it down the street.

■　■　■　■

Dawn, Kitty's Daughter

I REMEMBER THAT OUR apartment was marked. They had a mark, an actual chalk mark or something. You could see these marks on the bricks near the back porch. One mark signified: You could get something at this apartment, buddy, but you can't get anything up there. We'd be out in the alley playing, and we'd hear comments from people: "Here's one." They wouldn't go to the neighbors upstairs, 'cause they didn't give them anything. But ours was marked. They'd come out from Chicago and they'd hit our apartment, and they knew they'd get something. Whatever the mark meant, some of them were like an X. They'd say, "You can't get money out of this place, but there's food here anyway." My mother was hospitable to people, it didn't matter who they were.

■　■　■　■

Louis Banks

From a bed at a Veterans' Hospital, he talks feverishly; the words pour out. . . .

"My family had a little old farm, cotton, McGehee, Arkansas. I came to Chicago, I was a little bitty boy, I used to prize-fight. When the big boys got through, they put us on there."

I GOT TO BE fourteen years old, I went to work on the Great Lakes at $41.50 a month. I thought: Someday I'm gonna be a great chef. Rough times, though. It was the year 1929. I would work from five in the morning till seven at night. Washing dishes, peeling potatoes, carrying heavy garbage. We would get to Detroit.

They was sleepin' on the docks and be drunk. Next day he'd be dead. I'd see 'em floatin' on the river where they would commit suicide because they didn't have anything. White guys and colored.

I'd get paid off, I'd draw $21 every two weeks and then comin' back I'd have to see where I was goin'. 'Cause I would get robbed. One fella named Scotty, he worked down there, he was firin' a boiler. He was tryin' to send some money home. He'd work so hard and sweat, the hot fire was cookin' his stomach. I felt sorry for him. They killed 'im and throwed 'im in the river, trying to get the $15 or $20 from him. They'd steal and kill each other for fifty cents.

1929 was pretty hard. I hoboed, I bummed, I begged for a nickel to get somethin' to eat. Go get a job, oh, at the foundry there. They didn't hire me because I didn't belong to the right kind of race. 'Nother time I went into Saginaw, it was two white fellas and myself made three. The fella there hired the two men and didn't hire me. I was back out on the streets. That hurt me pretty bad, the race part.

When I was hoboing, I would lay on the side of the tracks and wait until I could see the train comin'. I would always carry a bottle of water in my pocket and a piece of tape or rag to keep it from bustin' and put a piece of bread in my pocket, so I wouldn't starve on the way. I would ride all day and all night long in the hot sun.

I'd ride atop a boxcar and went to Los Angeles, four days and four nights. The Santa Fe, we'd go all the way with Santa Fe. I was goin' over the hump and I was so hungry and weak 'cause I was goin' into the d.t.'s, and I could see snakes draggin' through the smoke. I was sayin', "Lord, help me, Oh Lord, help me," until a white hobo named Callahan, he was a great big guy, looked like Jack Dempsey, and he got a scissors on me, took his legs and wrapped 'em around me. Otherwise, I was about to fall off the Flyer into a cornfield there. I was sick as a dog until I got into Long Beach, California.

Black and white, it didn't make any difference who you were, 'cause everybody was poor. All friendly, sleep in a jungle. We used to take a big pot and cook food, cabbage, meat and beans all together. We all set together, we made a tent. Twenty-five or thirty would be out on the side of the rail, white and colored. They didn't have no mothers or sisters, they didn't have no home, they were dirty, they had overalls on, they didn't have no food, they didn't have anything.

Sometimes we sent one hobo to walk, to see if there were any jobs open. He'd come back and say: Detroit, no jobs. He'd say: they're hirin' in New York City. So we went to New York City. Sometimes ten or fifteen of us would be on the train. And I'd hear one of 'em holler. He'd fall off, he'd get killed. He was tryin' to get off the train, he thought he was gettin' home there. He heard a sound. (Imitates train whistle, a low, long, mournful sound.)

And then I saw a railroad police, a white police. They call him Texas Slim. He shoots you off all trains. We come out of Lima, Ohio . . . Lima Slim, he would kill you if he catch you on any train. Sheep train or any kind of merchandise train. He would shoot you off, he wouldn't ask you to get off.

I was in chain gangs and been in jail all over the country. I was in a chain gang in Georgia. I had to pick cotton for four months, for just hoboin' on a train. Just for vag. They gave me thirty-five cents and a pair of overalls when I got out. Just took me off the train, the guard. 1930, during the Depression, in the summertime. Yes, sir, thirty-five cents, that's what they gave me.

I knocked on people's doors. They'd say, "What do you want? I'll call the police." And they'd put you in jail for vag. They'd make you milk cows, thirty or ninety days. Up in Wisconsin, they'd do the same thing. Alabama, they'd do the same thing. California, anywhere you'd go. Always in jail, and I never did nothin'.

A man had to be on the road. Had to leave his wife, had to leave his mother, leave his family just to try to get money to live on. But he think: my dear mother, tryin' to send her money, worryin' how she's starvin'.

The shame I was feeling. I walked out because I didn't have a job. I said, "I'm goin' out in the world and get me a job." And God help me, I couldn't get anything. I wouldn't let them see me dirty and ragged and I hadn't shaved. I wouldn't send 'em no picture.

I'd write: "Dear Mother, I'm doin' wonderful and wish you're all fine." That was in Los Angeles and I was sleeping under some steps and there was some paper over me. This is the slum part, Negroes lived down there. And my ma, she'd say, "Oh, my son is in Los Angeles, he's doin' pretty fair."

And I was with a bunch of hoboes, drinkin' canned heat. I wouldn't eat two or three days, 'cause I was too sick to eat. It's a wonder I didn't die. But I believe in God.

I went to the hospital there in Los Angeles. They said, "Where do you live?" I'd say, "Travelers Aid, please send me home." Police says, "O.K., put him in jail." I'd get ninety days for vag. When I was hoboing I was in jail two-thirds of the time. Instead of sayin' five or ten days, they'd say sixty or ninety days. 'Cause that's free labor. Pick the fruit or pick the cotton, then they'd turn you loose.

I had fifteen or twenty jobs. Each job I would have it would be so hard. From six o'clock in the morning till seven o'clock at night. I was fixin' the meat, cookin', washin' dishes and cleaning up. Just like you threw the ball at one end and run down and catch it on the other. You're jack of all trade, you're doin' it all. White chefs were gettin' $40 a week, but I was gettin' $21 for doin' what they were doin' and everything else. The poor people had it rough. The rich people was livin' off the poor.

'Cause I picked cotton down in Arkansas when I was a little bitty boy and I saw my dad, he was workin' all day long. $2 is what one day the poor man would make. A piece of salt pork and a barrel of flour for us and that was McGehee, Arkansas.

God knows, when he'd get that sack he would pick up maybe two, three hundred pounds of cotton a day, gettin' snake bit and everything in that hot sun. And all he had was a little house and a tub to keep the water. 'Cause I went down there to see him in 1930. I got tired of hoboing and went down to see him and my daddy was all gray and didn't have no bank account and no Blue Cross. He didn't have nothin', and he worked himself to death. (Weeps.) And the white man, he would drive a tractor in there. . . . It seems like yesterday to me, but it was 1930.

'33 in Chicago they had the World's Fair. A big hotel was hirin' colored fellas as bellboys. The bellboys could make more money as a white boy for the next ten or fifteen years. I worked as a bellhop on the North Side at a hotel, lots of gangsters there. They don't have no colored bellboys at no exclusive hotels now. I guess maybe in the small ones they may have some.

Jobs were doing a little better after '35, after the World's Fair. You could get dishwashin' jobs, little porter jobs.

Work on the WPA, earn $27.50. We just dig a ditch and cover it back up. You thought you was rich. You could buy a suit of clothes. Before that, you wanted money, you didn't have any. No clothes for the kids. My little niece and my little kids had to have hand-down clothes. Couldn't steal. If you did, you went to the penitentiary. You had to shoot pool, walk all night and all day, the best you could make was $15. I raised up all my kids during the Depression. Scuffled . . . a hard way to go.

Did you find any kindness during the Depression?
No kindness. Except for Callahan, the hobo—only reason I'm alive is 'cause Callahan helped me on that train. And the hobo jungle. Everybody else was evil to each other. There was no friendships. Everybody was worried and sad-looking. It was pitiful.

When the war came, I was so glad when I got in the army. I knew I was safe. I put a uniform on, and I said, "Now I'm safe." I had money comin', I had food comin', and I had a lot of gang around me. I knew on the streets or hoboing, I might be killed any time.

I'd rather be in the army than outside where I was so raggedy and didn't have no jobs. I was glad to put on a United States Army uniform and get some food. I didn't care about the rifle what scared me. In the army, I wasn't gettin' killed on a train, I wasn't gonna starve. I felt proud to salute and look around and see all the good soldiers of the United States. I was a good soldier and got five battle stars. I'd rather be in the army now than see another Depression.

POSTSCRIPT: *On recovery, he will return to his job as a washroom attendant in one of Chicago's leading hotels.*
"When I was hoboin' through the Dakotas and Montana, down there by General Custer's Last Stand, Little Big Horn, I wrote my name down, yes, sir. For the memories, just for the note, so it will always be there. Yes, sir."

■ ■ ■ ■

Peggy Terry and Her Mother, Mary Owsley

It is a crowded apartment in Uptown. * *Young people from the neighborhood wander in and out, casually. The flow of visitors is constant; occasionally, a small, raggedy-clothed boy shuffles in, stares, vanishes. Peggy Terry is known in these parts as a spokesman for the poor southern whites. . . . "Hillbillies are up here for a few years and they get their guts kicked out and they realize their white skin doesn't mean what they always thought it meant."*

* A Chicago area in which many of the southern white émigrés live; furnished flats in most instances.

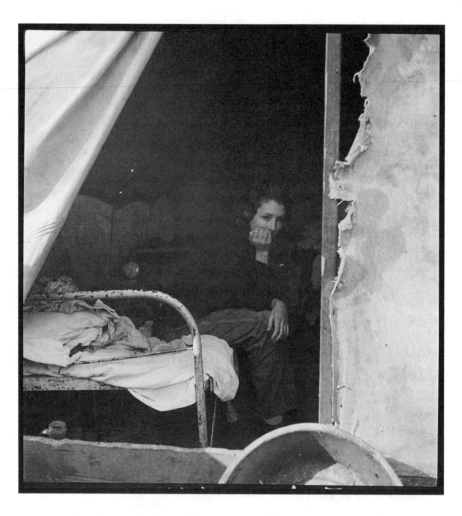

Daughter of migrant Tennessee coal miner. Living in the
American River camp near Sacramento, California

DOROTHEA LANGE, 1936

Mrs. Owsley is the first to tell her story.

Kentucky-born, she married an Oklahoma boy "when he came back from World War I. He was so restless and disturbed from the war, we just drifted back and forth." It was a constant shifting from Oklahoma to Kentucky and back again; three, four times the route. "He saw the tragedies of war so vividly that he was discontented everywhere." From 1929 to 1936, they lived in Oklahoma.

THERE WAS THOUSANDS OF people out of work in Oklahoma City. They set up a soup line, and the food was clean and it was delicious. Many, many people, colored and white, I didn't see any difference, 'cause there was just as many white people out of work than were colored. Lost everything they had accumulated from their young days. And these are facts. I remember several families had to leave in covered wagons. To Californy, I guess.

See, the oil boom come in '29. People come from every direction in there. A coupla years later, they was livin' in everything from pup tents, houses built out of cardboard boxes and old pieces of metal that they'd pick up—anything that they could find to put somethin' together to put a wall around 'em to protect 'em from the public.

I knew one family there in Oklahoma City, a man and a woman and seven children lived in a hole in the ground. You'd be surprised how nice it was, how nice they kept it. They had chairs and tables and beds back in that hole. And they had the dirt all braced up there, just like a cave.

Oh, the dust storms, they were terrible. You could wash and hang clothes on a line, and if you happened to be away from the house and couldn't get those clothes in before that storm got there, you'd never wash that out. Oil was in that sand. It'd color them the most awful color you ever saw. It just ruined them. They was just never fit to use, actually. I had to use 'em, understand, but they wasn't very presentable. Before my husband was laid off, we lived in a good home. It wasn't a brick house, but it wouldn't have made any difference. These storms, when they would hit, you had to clean house from the attic to ground. Everything was covered in sand. Red sand, just full of oil.

The majority of people were hit and hit hard. They were mentally disturbed you're bound to know, 'cause they didn't know when the end of all this was comin'. There was a lot of suicides that I know of. From nothin' else but just they couldn't see any hope for a better tomorrow. I absolutely know some who did. Part of 'em were farmers and part of 'em were businessmen, even. They went flat broke and they committed suicide on the strength of it, nothing else.

A lot of times one family would have some food. They would divide. And everyone would share. Even the people that were quite well-to-do, they was ashamed. 'Cause they was eatin', and other people wasn't.

My husband was very bitter. That's just puttin' it mild. He was an intelligent man. He couldn't see why as wealthy a country as this is, that there was any sense in so many people starving to death, when so much of it, wheat and everything else, was being poured into the ocean. There's many excuses, but he looked for a reason. And he found one.

My husband went to Washington. To march with that group that went to Washington . . . the bonus boys.

He was a machine gunner in the war. He'd say them damn Germans gassed him in Germany. And he come home and his own government stooges gassed him and run him off the country up there with the water hose, half drownded him. Oh, yes *sir*, yes sir, he was a hell-raiser (laughs—a sudden sigh). I think I've run my race.

PEGGY TERRY'S STORY:

I first noticed the difference when we'd come home from school in the evening. My mother'd send us to the soup line. And we were never allowed to cuss. If you happened to be one of the first ones in line, you didn't get anything but water that was on top. So we'd ask the guy that was ladling out the soup into the buckets—everybody had to bring their own bucket to get the soup—he'd dip the greasy, watery stuff off the top. So we'd ask him to please dip down to get some meat and potatoes from the bottom of the kettle. But he wouldn't do it. So we learned to cuss. We'd say: "Dip down, God damn it."

Then we'd go across the street. One place had bread, large loaves of bread. Down the road just a little piece was a big shed, and they gave milk. My sister and me would take two buckets each. And that's what we lived off for the longest time.

I can remember one time, the only thing in the house to eat was mustard. My sister and I put so much mustard on biscuits that we got sick. And we can't stand mustard till today.

There was only one family around that ate good. Mr. Barr worked at the ice plant. Whenever Mrs. Barr could, she'd feed the kids. But she couldn't feed 'em *all*. They had a big tree that had fruit on it. She'd let us pick those. Sometimes we'd pick and eat 'em until we were sick.

Her two daughters got to go to Norman for their college. When they'd talk about all the good things they had at the college, she'd kind of hush 'em up because there was always poor kids that didn't have anything to eat. I remember she always felt bad because people in the neighborhood were hungry. But there was a feeling of together. . . .

When they had food to give to people, you'd get a notice and you'd go down. So Daddy went down that day and he took my sister and me. They were giving away potatoes and things like that. But they had a truck of oranges parked in the alley. Somebody asked them who the oranges were for, and they wouldn't tell 'em. So they said, well, we're gonna take those oranges. And they did. My dad was one of the ones that got up on the truck. They called the police, and the police chased us all away. But we got the oranges.

It's different today. People are made to feel ashamed now if they don't have anything. Back then, I'm not sure how the rich felt. I think the rich were as contemptuous of the poor then as they are now. But among the people that I knew, we all had an understanding that it wasn't our fault. It was something that had happened to the machinery. Most people blamed Hoover, and they cussed him up one side and down the other—it was all his fault. I'm not saying he's blameless, but I'm not saying either it was all his fault. Our system doesn't run by just one man, and it doesn't fall by just one man, either.

You don't recall at any time feeling a sense of shame?
I remember it was fun. It was fun going to the soup line. 'Cause we all went down the road, and we laughed and we played. The only thing we felt is that we were hungry and we were going to get food. Nobody made us feel ashamed. There just wasn't any of that.

Today you're made to feel that it's your own fault. If you're poor, it's only because you're lazy and you're ignorant, and you don't try to help yourself. You're made to feel that if you get a check from Welfare that the bank at Fort Knox is gonna go broke.

Even after the soup line, there wasn't anything. The WPA came, and I married. My husband worked on the WPA. This was back in Paducah, Kentucky. We were just kids. I was fifteen, and he was sixteen. My husband was digging ditches. They were putting in a water main. Parts of the city, even at that late date, 1937, didn't have city water.

My husband and me just started traveling around, for about three years. It was a very nice time, because when you're poor and you stay in one spot, trouble just seems to catch up with you. But when you're moving from town to town, you don't stay there long enough for trouble to catch up with you. It's really a good life, if you're poor and you can manage to move around.

I was pregnant when we first started hitchhiking, and people were really very nice to us. Sometimes they would feed us. I remember one time we

slept in a haystack, and the lady of the house came out and found us and
she said, "This is really very bad for you because you're going to have a baby.
You need a lot of milk." So she took us up to the house.

She had a lot of rugs hanging on the clothesline because she was doing
her house cleaning. We told her we'd beat the rugs for her giving us the food.
She said, no, she didn't expect that. She just wanted to feed us. We said, no,
we couldn't take it unless we worked for it. And she let us beat her rugs. I
think she had a million rugs, and we cleaned them. Then we went in and
she had a beautiful table, full of all kind of food and milk. When we left,
she filled a gallon bucket full of milk and we took it with us.

You don't find that now. I think maybe if you did that now, you'd get arrested. Somebody'd call the police. The atmosphere since the end of the
Second War—it seems like the minute the war ended, the propaganda
started. In making people hate each other.

I remember one night, we walked for a long time, and we were so tired
and hungry, and a wagon came along. There was a Negro family going into
town. Of course, they're not allowed to stop and eat in restaurants, so they'd
cook their own food and brought it with 'em. They had the back of the wagon
filled with hay. We asked them if we could lay down and sleep in the wagon,
and they said yes. We woke up, and it was morning, and she invited us to eat
with 'em. She had this box, and she had chicken and biscuits and sweet potatoes and everything in there. It was just really wonderful.

I didn't like black people. In fact, I hated 'em. If they just shipped 'em all
out, I don't think it woulda bothered me.

*She recalls her feelings of white superiority, her discoveries. "If I really knew
what changed me . . . I don't know. I've thought about it and thought about it.
You don't go anywhere, because you always see yourself as something you're
not. As long as you can say I'm better than they are, then there's somebody
below you can kick. But once you get over that, you see that you're not any
better off than they are. In fact, you're worse off 'cause you're believin' a lie.
And it was right there, in front of us. In the cotton field, chopping cotton, and
right over in the next field, there's these black people—Alabama, Texas, Kentucky. Never once did it occur to me that we had anything in common.*

*"After I was up here for a while and I saw how poor white people were
treated, poor white southerners, they were treated just as badly as black people
are. I think maybe that just crystallized the whole thing."*

I didn't feel any identification with the Mexicans, either. My husband and
me were migrant workers. We went down in the valley of Texas, which is

very beautiful. We picked oranges and lemons and grapefruits, limes in the Rio Grande Valley.

We got a nickel a bushel for citrus fruits. On the grapefruits you had to ring them. You hold a ring in your hand that's about like that (she draws a circle with her hands), and it has a little thing that slips down over your thumb. You climb the tree and you put that ring around the grapefruit. If the grapefruit slips through, you can't pick it. And any grapefruit that's in your box—you can work real hard, especially if you want to make enough to buy food that day—you'll pick some that aren't big enough. Then when you carry your box up and they check it, they throw out all the ones that go through the ring.

I remember this one little boy in particular. He was really a beautiful child. Every day when we'd start our lunch, we'd sit under the trees and eat. And these peppers grew wild. I saw him sitting there, and every once in a while he'd reach over and get a pepper and pop it in his mouth. With his food, whatever he was eating. I thought they looked pretty good. So I reached over and popped it in my mouth, and, oh, it was like liquid fire. He was rolling in the grass laughing. He thought it was so funny—that white people couldn't eat peppers like they could. And he was tearing open grapefruits for me to suck the juice, because my mouth was all cooked from the pepper. He used to run and ask if he could help me. Sometimes he'd help me fill my boxes of grapefruits, 'cause he felt sorry for me, 'cause I got burned on the peppers. (Laughs.)

But that was a little boy. I felt all right toward him. But the men and the women, they were just spies and they should be sent back to Mexico.

I remember I was very irritated because there were very few gringos in this little Texas town, where we lived. Hardly anybody spoke English. When you tried to talk to the Mexicans, they couldn't understand English. It never occurred to us that we should learn to speak Spanish. It's really hard to talk about a time like that, 'cause it seems like a different person. When I remember those times, it's like looking into a world where another person is doing those things.

This may sound impossible, but if there's one thing that started me thinking, it was President Roosevelt's cuff links. I read in the paper how many pairs of cuff links he had. It told that some of them were rubies and precious stones—these were his cuff links. And I'll never forget, I was setting on an old tire out in the front yard and we were poor and hungry. I was sitting out there in the hot sun, there weren't any trees. And I was wondering why it is that one man could have all those cuff links when we couldn't even have enough to eat. When we lived on gravy and biscuits. That's the first time I remember ever wondering why.

And when my father finally got his bonus, he bought a secondhand car for us to come back to Kentucky in. My dad said to us kids: "All of you get in the car. I want to take you and show you something." On the way over there, he'd talk about how life had been rough for us, and he said: "If you think it's been rough for us, I want you to see people that really had it rough." This was in Oklahoma City, and he took us to one of the Hoovervilles, and that was the most incredible thing.

Here were all these people living in old, rusted-out car bodies. I mean that was their home. There were people living in shacks made of orange crates. One family with a whole lot of kids were living in a piano box. This wasn't just a little section, this was maybe ten miles wide and ten miles long. People living in whatever they could junk together.

And when I read *Grapes of Wrath*—she bought that for me (indicates young girl seated across the room)—that was like reliving my life. Particularly the part where they lived in this government camp. Because when we were picking fruit in Texas, we lived in a government place like that. They came around, and they helped the women make mattresses. See, we didn't have anything. And they showed us how to sew and make dresses. And every Saturday night, we'd have a dance. And when I was reading *Grapes of Wrath* this was just like my life. I was never so proud of poor people before, as I was after I read that book.

I think that's the worst thing that our system does to people, is to take away their pride. It prevents them from being a human being. And wondering why the Harlem and why the Detroit. They're talking about troops and law and order. You get law and order in this country when people are allowed to be decent human beings. Every time I hear another building's on fire, I say: oh, boy, baby, hit 'em again. (Laughs.)

I don't think people were put on earth to suffer. I think that's a lot of nonsense. I think we are the highest development on the earth, and I think we were put here to live and be happy and to enjoy everything that's here. I don't think it's right for a handful of people to get ahold of all the things that make living a joy instead of a sorrow. You wake up in the morning, and it consciously hits you—it's just like a big hand that takes your heart and squeezes it—because you don't know what that day is going to bring: hunger or you don't know.

POSTSCRIPT: (*A sudden flash of memory by Peggy Terry, as I was about to leave.*) "*It was the Christmas of '35, just before my dad got his bonus. We didn't get anything for Christmas. I mean nothing. Not an orange, not an apple— nothing. I just felt so bad. I went to the church, to the children's program, and*

I stole a Christmas package. It was this pretty box and it had a big red ribbon on it. I stole it off the piano, and I took it home with me. I told my mother my Sunday school teacher had given me a Christmas present. When I opened it, it was a beautiful long scarf made out of velvet—a cover for a piano. My mother knew my Sunday school teacher didn't give me that. 'Cause we were living in one room, in a little shack in what they called Gander Flat. (Laughs.) For a child—I mean, they teach you about Santa Claus and they teach you all that stuff—and then for a child to have to go to church and steal a present . . . and then it turned out to be something so fantastic, a piano scarf. Children shouldn't have to go around stealing. There's enough to give all of them everything they want, any time they want it. I say that's what we're gonna have."

■   ■   ■

Kiko Konagamitsu

He is a Japanese-American (nisei), living in a Midwestern city.

MY FATHER HAD A farm in southern California. I remember the *Grapes of Wrath* kind of people. They used to work for us, pick crops. It amazed me. They'd say, "Let the Jap boy count it." They'd come in from the fields, and I'd tally up the totals for the day. I'd weigh them on the scale. I didn't feel I was qualified. I was just a little kid. But I could count. They would honor my counting. It was a tremendous trust. It seems the less affluent you are, the more you are able to trust people, the more you are able to give others.

My father had many old-type Oriental feelings about things. If one of his friends had trouble and couldn't afford to have anyone working for him, my father would ask me to go over. I remember once feeling badly. I had worked all day for this man, cleaning lettuce, stacking vegetables. He didn't pay me. My father gave me a real tongue-lashing: "You're not expected to get paid. He didn't ask you to go. *I* asked you to go."

The communal spirit of the nisei is less today than it was in the Depression. The second-generation Japanese has become the most so-called American.

Someone laughingly told: Maybe the war—and the internment camp*
—was good for us. How else could we have gotten out of California? There were hundreds of nisei Ph.D.s working on the family's farm or fruit stands.

* Thousands of Japanese families living on the West Coast were interned in relocation camps during World War II.

Farm boy with sack full of boll weevils, which he has picked off
of cotton plants, Macon County, Georgia.

DOROTHEA LANGE, 1937

Their parents would live in shacks so their sons and daughters could go to college. (Laughs.)

Thousands of us—after Pearl Harbor—were assembled at the Santa Anita racetrack. We were assigned to camps or contracted out to farmers. My brother and I signed up to pick sugar beets for a farmer in Idaho. Here we worked on a sugar beet farm, but we couldn't get any sugar coupons. I didn't know the taste of sugar. (Laughs.)

■　■　■　■

Cesar Chavez

Like so many who have worked from early childhood, particularly in the open country, he appears older than his forty-one years. His manner is diffident, his voice soft.

He is president of the United Farm Workers of America (UFWA). It is, unlike craft and industrial unions, a quite new labor fraternity. In contrast to these others, agricultural workers—those who "follow the crops"—had been excluded from many of the benefits that came along with the New Deal.

OH, I REMEMBER HAVING to move out of our house. My father had brought in a team of horses and wagon. We had always lived in that house, and we couldn't understand why we were moving out. When we got to the other house, it was a worse house, a poor house. That must have been around 1934. I was about six years old.

It's known as the North Gila Valley, about fifty miles north of Yuma. My dad was being turned out of his small plot of land. He had inherited this from his father, who had homesteaded it. I saw my two, three other uncles also moving out. And for the same reason. The bank had foreclosed on the loan.

If the local bank approved, the government would guarantee the loan and small farmers like my father would continue in business. It so happened the president of the bank was the guy who most wanted our land. We were surrounded by him: he owned all the land around us. Of course, he wouldn't pass the loan.

One morning a giant tractor came in, like we had never seen before. My daddy used to do all his work with horses. So this huge tractor came in and began to knock down this corral, this small corral where my father kept his horses. We didn't understand why. In the matter of a week, the whole face of the land was changed. Ditches were dug, and it was different. I didn't like it as much.

We all of us climbed into an old Chevy that my dad had. And then we were in California, and migratory workers. There were five kids—a small family by those standards. It must have been around '36. I was about eight. Well, it was a strange life. We had been poor, but we knew every night there was a bed *there*, and that *this* was our room. There was a kitchen. It was sort of a settled life, and we had chickens and hogs, eggs and all those things. But that all of a sudden changed. When you're small, you can't figure these things out. You know something's not right and you don't like it, but you don't question it and you don't let that get you down. You sort of just continue to move.

But this had quite an impact on my father. He had been used to owning the land and all of a sudden there was no more land. What I heard . . . what I made out of conversations between my mother and my father—things like, we'll work this season and then we'll get enough money and we'll go and buy a piece of land in Arizona. Things like that. Became like a habit. He never gave up hope that some day he would come back and get a little piece of land.

I can understand very, very well this feeling. These conversations were sort of melancholy. I guess my brothers and my sisters could also see this very sad look on my father's face.

That piece of land he wanted . . . ?
No, never. It never happened. He stopped talking about that some years ago. The drive for land, it's a very powerful drive.

When we moved to California, we would work after school. Sometimes we wouldn't go. "Following the crops," we missed much school. Trying to get enough money to stay alive the following winter, the whole family picking apricots, walnuts, prunes. We were pretty new, we had never been migratory workers. We were taken advantage of quite a bit by the labor contractor and the crew pusher.* In some pretty silly ways. (Laughs.)

Sometimes we can't help but laugh about it. We trusted everybody that came around. You're traveling in California with all your belongings in your car: it's obvious. Those days we didn't have a trailer. This is bait for the labor contractor. Anywhere we stopped, there was a labor contractor offering all kinds of jobs and good wages, and we were always deceived by them and we always went. Trust them.

Coming into San Jose, not finding—being lied to, that there was work. We had no money at all, and had to live on the outskirts of town under a bridge and dry creek. That wasn't really unbearable. What was unbearable was so many families living just a quarter of a mile. And you know how kids

* "That's a man who specializes in contracting human beings to do cheap labor."

are. They'd bring in those things that really hurt us quite a bit. Most of those kids were middle-class families.

We got hooked on a real scheme once. We were going by Fresno on our way to Delano. We stopped at some service station and this labor contractor saw the car. He offered a lot of money. We went. We worked the first week: the grapes were pretty bad and we couldn't make much. We all stayed off from school in order to make some money. Saturday we were to be paid and we didn't get paid. He came and said the winery hadn't paid him. We'd have money next week. He gave us $10. My dad took the $10 and went to the store and bought $10 worth of groceries. So we worked another week and in the middle of the second week, my father was asking him for his last week's pay, and he had the same excuse. This went on and we'd get $5 or $10 or $7 a week for about four weeks. For the whole family.

So one morning my father made the resolution no more work. If he doesn't pay us, we won't work. We got in a car and went over to see him. The house was empty. He had left. The winery said they had paid him and they showed us where they had paid him. This man had taken it.

Labor strikes were everywhere. We were one of the strikingest families, I guess. My dad didn't like the conditions, and he began to agitate. Some families would follow, and we'd go elsewhere. Sometimes we'd come back. We couldn't find a job elsewhere, so we'd come back. Sort of beg for a job. Employers would know and they would make it very humiliating. . . .

Did these strikes ever win?
Never.

We were among these families who always honored somebody else's grievance. Somebody would have a personal grievance with the employer. He'd say I'm not gonna work for this man. Even though we were working, we'd honor it. We felt we had to. So we'd walk out, too. Because we were prepared to honor those things, we caused many of the things ourselves. If we were picking at a piece rate and we knew they were cheating on the weight, we wouldn't stand for it. So we'd lose the job, and we'd go elsewhere. There were other families like that.

Sometimes when you had to come back, the contractor knew this . . . ?
They knew it, and they rubbed it in quite well. Sort of shameful to come back. We were trapped. We'd have to do it for a few days to get enough money to get enough gas.

One of the experiences I had. We went through Indio, California. Along the highway there were signs in most of the small restaurants that said

"White Trade Only." My dad read English, but he didn't really know the meaning. He went in to get some coffee—a pot that he had, to get some coffee for my mother. He asked us not to come in, but we followed him anyway. And this young waitress said, "We don't serve Mexicans here. Get out of here." I was there, and I saw it and heard it. She paid no more attention. I'm sure for the rest of her life she never thought of it again. But every time we thought of it, it hurt us. So we got back in the car and we had a difficult time trying—in fact, we never got the coffee. These are sort of unimportant, but they're . . . you remember 'em very well.

One time there was a little diner across the tracks in Brawley. We used to shine shoes after school. Saturday was a good day. We used to shine shoes for three cents, two cents. Hamburgers were then, as I remember, seven cents. There was this little diner all the way across town. The moment we stepped across the tracks, the police stopped us. They would let us go there, to what we called "the American town," the Anglo town, with a shoe shine box. We went to this little place and we walked in.

There was this young waitress again. With either her boyfriend or someone close, because they were involved in conversation. And there was this familiar sign again, but we paid no attention to it. She looked up at us and she sort of—it wasn't what she said, it was just a gesture. A sort of gesture of total rejection. Her hand, you know, and the way she turned her face away from us. She said: "Wattaya want?" So we told her we'd like to buy two hamburgers. She sort of laughed, a sarcastic sort of laugh. And she said, "Oh, we don't sell to Mexicans. Why don't you go across to Mexican town, you can buy 'em over there." And then she turned around and continued her conversation.

She never knew how much she was hurting us. But it stayed with us.

We'd go to school two days sometimes, a week, two weeks, three weeks at most. This is when we were migrating. We'd come back to our winter base, and if we were lucky, we'd get in a good solid all of January, February, March, April, May. So we had five months out of a possible nine months. We started counting how many schools we'd been to and we counted thirty-seven. Elementary schools. From first to eighth grade. Thirty-seven. We never got a transfer. Friday we didn't tell the teacher or anything. We'd just go home. And they accepted this.

I remember one teacher—I wondered why she was asking so many questions. (In those days anybody asked questions, you became suspicious. Either a cop or a social worker.) She was a young teacher, and she just wanted to know why we were behind. One day she drove into the camp. That was quite an event, because we never had a teacher come over. Never. So it was, you know, a very meaningful day for us.

This I remember. Some people put this out of their minds and forget it. I don't. I don't want to forget it. I don't want it to take the best of me, but I want to be there because this is what happened. This is the truth, you know. History.

■   ■   ■   ■

Blackie Gold

A car dealer. He has a house in the suburbs.

WHATEVER I HAVE, I'M very thankful for. I've never brought up the Depression to my children. Never in my life. Why should I? What I had to do, what I had to do without, I never tell 'em what I went through, there's no reason for it. They don't have to know from bad times. All they know is the life they've had and the future that they're gonna have.

All I know is my children are well behaved. If I say something to my daughters, it's "Yes, sir," "No, sir." I know where my kids are at all times. And I don't have no worries about them being a beatnik.

I've built my own home. I almost have no mortgage. I have a daughter who's graduating college, and my daughter did not have to work, for me to put her through college. At the age of sixteen, I gave her a car, that was her gift. She's graduating college now: I'll give her a new one.

We had to go out and beg for coal, buy bread that's two, three days old. My dad died when I was an infant. I went to an orphan home for fellas. Stood there till I was seventeen years old. I came out into the big wide world, and my mother who was trying to raise my six older brothers and sisters, couldn't afford another mouth to feed. So I enlisted in the Civilian Conservation Corps. The CCC. This was about 1937.

I was at CCC's for six months, I came home for fifteen days, looked around for work, and I couldn't make $30 a month, so I enlisted back in the CCC's and went to Michigan. I spent another six months there planting trees and building forests. And came out. But still no money to be made. So back in the CCC's again. From there I went to Boise, Idaho, and was attached to the forest rangers. Spent four and a half months fighting forest fires.

These big trees you see along the highways—all these big forests was all built by the CCC. We went along plain barren ground. There were no trees. We just dug trenches and kept planting trees. You could plant about a hundred an hour.

Mexican mother in California: "Sometimes I tell my children
that I would like to go to Mexico, but they tell me
'We don't want to go, we belong here.'"

DOROTHEA LANGE, 1935

I really enjoyed it. I had three wonderful square meals a day. No matter what they put on the table, we ate and were glad to get it. Nobody ever turned down food. They sure made a man out of ya, because you learned that everybody here was equal. There was nobody better than another in the CCC's. We never had any race riots. Couple of colored guys there, they minded their business; we minded ours.

I came out of there, enlisted in the navy. I spent five and a half years in the United States Navy. It was the most wonderful experience I've ever had. Three wonderful meals a day and my taxes paid for. I had security.

I came up the hard way, was never in jail, never picked up and whatever I've done, I have myself to thank for. No matter how many people were on relief in those days, you never heard of any marches. The biggest stealing would be by a guy go by a fruit store and steal a potato. But you never heard of a guy breaking a window. In the thirties, the crimes were a hundred percent less than they are now. If a guy wants to work, there's no reason for being poor. There's no reason for being dirty. Soap and water'll clean anybody. Anybody that's free and white in a wonderful country like these United States never had any wants, never.

In the days of the CCC's, if the fella wouldn't take a bath, we'd give 'im what we call a brushing. We'd take this fella, and we'd take a big scrub brush and we'd give 'em a bath, and we'd open up every pore, and these pores would get infected. That's all he needed was one bath. I imagine we gave a hundred of 'em. A guy'd come in, he'd stink, ten guys would get him in the shower, and we'd take a GI brush. If a guy come in, he wanted to look like a hillbilly—no reflection on the boys from the South—but if he wanted to look like the backwoods, we'd cut his hair off. Yeah, we'd keep him clean.

You know, in the CCC's or in the navy, you're sittin' amongst thirty guys in one room, and you're not gonna take that smell.

Did you have a committee that decided . . . ?
No, we'd just look at each other and we'd say, "Hey, look at this rat, he's dirty." Then we say, "O.K., he's ready for one. . . ." We'd tell him, "You got until today to take a bath." He'd say, "You're not gonna run my life." We'd say, "You got twenty-four hours." And if he didn't, I guarantee you we grabbed him. We never heard of a goatee. . . .

The guys pretty much conformed?
Absolutely, CCC or navy. I liked that very much. We didn't have to worry where our next three meals were coming from, what the hell. . . .

And in the orphan home . . . ?

Sure. And high school. We had a woodshop teacher, and he would tell you what to do. You give him any back talk, he'd pick up a ruler and crack across the rear end. You settled down. In those days, when I went to school, you said "Yes, sir" and "No, sir." You never gave 'em back talk. They had a parental school, Montefiore, that made a man out of you. You learn to keep yourself clean, I'll tell you that. Obedience. Today, they're giving kids cars when they're sixteen. Another thirty years from now, these kids graduating high school, one may be president, another may be up there buying a planet.

The Big Money

William Benton

During various phases of his life: United States senator from Connecticut; assistant secretary of state; vice president of the University of Chicago; publisher of Encyclopaedia Britannica; *(a founder of the Committee for Economic Development . . . "We organized studies in three thousand American towns . . . planning for conversion to peace time production . . . born out of Depression experiences. . . .").*

His ambition was to retire as a millionaire at the age of thirty-five. He did so, at thirty-six.

In 1929, he was the assistant general manager of Lord and Thomas, headed by Albert Lasker, "the most successful advertising agency man ever developed."

I LEFT CHICAGO IN June of '29, just a few months before the Crash. Chester Bowles* and I started in business with seventeen hundred square feet, just the two of us and a couple of girls. July 15, 1929—this was the very day of the all-time peak on the stock market.

As I solicited business, my chart was kind of a cross. The left-hand line started at the top corner and ended in the bottom of the right-hand corner. That was the stock market index. The other line was Benton & Bowles. It started at the bottom left-hand corner and ended in the top right-hand corner. A cross. As the stock market plummeted into oblivion, Benton & Bowles went up into stardom. When I sold the agency in 1935, it was the single biggest office in the world. And the most profitable office.

My friend Beardsley Ruml was advocate of the theory: progress through catastrophe. In all catastrophes, there is the potential of benefit. I benefited

---

* At one time, governor of Connecticut; later, American ambassador to India.

out of the Depression. Others did, too. I suppose the people who sold red ink, red pencils and red crayons benefited.

I was only twenty-nine, and Bowles was only twenty-eight. When things are prosperous, big clients are not likely to listen to young men or to new ideas. In 1929, most of your Wall Street manipulators called it the New Era. They felt it was the start of a perpetual boom that would carry us on and on forever to new plateaus.

That year, the sales of Pepsodent were off fifty percent. Dentists talked about Pepsodent teeth. It was too abrasive, took the enamel off teeth, they said. None of the old-type advertising seemed to work. I was still in Chicago, with Lord and Thomas. Pepsodent was our account.

In May of 1929, I left my office in the new Palmolive Building* . . . we were its first tenants. I walked home to my apartment. It was a hot muggy night. All the windows were open, and I heard these colored voices leaping out into the street, from all the apartments. I turned around and walked back up the street. There were nineteen radios on and seventeen were tuned to *Amos and Andy*. This is probably the first audience research survey in the history of radio broadcasting.

I went in to see Mr. Lasker the next morning and said we ought to buy *Amos and Andy* for Pepsodent right away. We bought them on the spot, and I went east to Benton & Bowles.

Pepsodent went on the air, and within a series of weeks it was the greatest sensation in the history of American show business. The only thing that's been more famous than *Amos and Andy* was Lindbergh's flight across the Atlantic. Pepsodent sales skyrocketed.

The Crash never hurt Pepsodent. Pepsodent sales doubled and quadrupled. It was sold to Lever Brothers at an enormous price, giving Lasker part of his great fortune. Benton & Bowles plunged into radio in a big way for our clients.

We didn't know the Depression was going on. Except that our clients' products were plummeting, and they were willing to talk to us about new ideas. They wouldn't have let us in the door if times were good. So the Depression benefited me. My income doubled every year. When I left Benton & Bowles, it must have been close to half a million dollars. That's the kind of money great motion picture stars weren't earning. That was 1935. The Depression just passed me right over. I'm not a good man to talk to about the Depression.

---

* It is now the *Playboy* Building.

I had nothing to do with the creation of *Amos and Andy,* just had the judgment to buy it. But I contributed enormously to the *Maxwell House Show Boat,* which later became the Number One program in broadcasting. The show gave a quality of illusion to the radio audiences so perfectly that in its early weeks ten thousand and fifteen thousand people would come down to the docks in Memphis and Nashville, where we said the *Show Boat* was going to tie up.

Show Boat went on in 1933, really the bottom of the Depression. Maxwell House Coffee went up eighty-five percent within six months. And kept zooming. Thus, Maxwell House didn't know there was a Depression. The chain stores were selling coffee that was almost as good—the difference was indetectable—for a much lower price. But advertising so gave glamor and verve to Maxwell House that it made everybody think it was a whale of a lot better. It doubled and quadrupled in sales.

In *Show Boat* we did something nobody had ever done before. We cast two people in one role. We'd get a sexy singer, who might not be a good actress, then we'd get the sexiest actress we could find and we'd give her the speaking lines, softening the audience up, getting it warm and ready to melt. Then the girl would come in and sing.

People in the theater never thought of such an idea. Radio made it possible. It took new men coming into radio to think of new ideas. Hollywood fought it, Ziegfeld was no good at it. The advertising men made radio. We weren't inhibited. We didn't know you couldn't put two people in one part.

We went on to put out other shows like it. And they became big hits. *The Palmolive Beauty Box.* I picked up an unknown member of the Metropolitan chorus, Gladys Swarthout, and we made her a big star. We put a $100-a-week gifted actress with her to speak the lines, while Gladys sang in that seductive voice of hers. They told me I couldn't use her because she was no soprano and the parts were too high. I just coolly said: rewrite the parts; write them lower. Nobody in opera would have thought of this. . . . We succeeded in radio because none of us knew any better.

These were the new techniques of the Depression. As their sales went off, the big advertisers looked around and said: Who are these new young men that have these new ideas that appeal to these new young people? We looked like college boys, and yet they paid us a great deal of money. This is why Chet Bowles and I escaped the Depression.

The type of men that largely dominated advertising, before the Depression, faded, the ones who played golf with their accounts. The Depression speeded up greatly the use of research in marketing. I developed new techniques, working for Lasker, which I took East with me. George Gallup brought in new standards. He once referred to me as his grandfather, because I pioneered in the advertising field . . . finding out what the consumers wanted.

The Maxwell House Coffee program was, to my eternal regret, the stimulus that changed the commercials. When we had Captain Andy drink coffee and smack his lips, you heard the coffee cups clinking and the coffee gurgling as it was poured. It put action and actors into commercials. That was a revolution, the full import of which we didn't suspect at the time. It inevitably led to the singing commercial and all the current excesses. As Bob Hutchins said, when he introduced me at a dinner in my honor at the University of Chicago—I invented things that I now apologize for.

I presumably lost $150,000 in the depression of 1937—on my one stock investment—because I did everything Lehman Brothers told me. I said, well, this is a fool's procedure . . . buying stock in other people's businesses. I'll have to buy my own company. I won't work at operating it, I'll just own it. I'll set the policies. I looked around and bought the Muzak Corporation. I never could have bought it except in a Depression. It was a busted, run-down company. That would be around '38.

Muzak was then only heard in hotels and restaurants in New York. It was only thought of as a substitute for live music. Jimmy Petrillo cursed it as the Number One enemy of musicians. I said to myself: This music ought to be in other places.

I went down to see the five salesmen—we only had five then. They said to me: "We have eighty percent of all the business you can get in New York. There isn't any other place to sell it." I said, "Why don't you put it in barbershops and doctors' offices?" "Oh, you can't put Muzak in places like that!" I said: "Do you all five think that way?" There was a young man, who had only worked there six weeks, he said, "No, I think it's a good idea." I said, "Well, the other four of you guys had better quit and get some other jobs, and I'll make this young man the sales manager. We'll take Muzak into new areas."

Of course, this made a big wonderful business out of Muzak, now earning $2 million a year. And no extra money has ever gone into it. The Depression put me into it.

The first installation outside the customary public for music was a bank in New York. The manager said, "My people who work at night, it's very depressing in these electric-lit offices. They wanted a radio, but I didn't want them to have it. I told them I'd give them Muzak. Now it's all over the bank." There

Under the elevated railway, Chicago, Illinois

John Vachon, 1940

was a girl sitting as a receptionist in the personal loan department. That's where people would borrow money in small units and never come back unless they couldn't pay the installments. The girl said to me: "The music makes this place less gruesome."

I invented the phrase: "Music not to be listened to." That was my commercial phrase with which I sold Muzak. It was the first music deliberately created to which people were not supposed to listen. It was a new kind of background music. That's why my mother, who was a fine musician, held it in contempt. She wouldn't have it in her apartment. Anybody who knows anything about music holds Muzak in contempt.

I have a tin ear. That's why my ear was so good for radio. Most people in the United States have a tin ear like mine. A totally tin ear. I really like Rudy Vallee and Bing Crosby and the stars that were developed by radio.

I owned Muzak for twenty years and sold it for a profit of many millions . . . when I ran out of my first million and needed some more.

Muzak's habit-forming. The man who bought it from me gave me four installations for my homes and my offices. I always have it on. 'Cause I notice it when it's not on and don't notice it when it's on. That's how it's music not to be listened to. And that's how it's habit-forming.

Every businessman wants a product that is habit-forming. That's why cigarettes, Coca-Cola and coffee do so well. Even soap is habit-forming. Soaps were my biggest products when I was in the agency business.

I always thought—at Benton & Bowles—just six more months, three more, and it would all be behind me. But our business doubled every year. Every year, I would say: As soon as I get this new client, I won't be working like this. No intelligent man would put up with what I put up with, even to get a million dollars, if he could have foreseen the six years.

In the fall of '37, I became vice president of the University of Chicago. My day changed enormously, because I started to read and consort with economics professors, and to interest myself in educational broadcasting . . . to produce and guide the "University of Chicago Round Table." However, the habits of hard work were ingrained in me. I didn't lacerate myself in the same way. But I worked the long, hard week. My evenings, though, were different.

The Depression was very seriously affecting the university . . . great deficits run up by its expensive medical school and its clinics. Contributions were less.

When Mr. Walgreen withdrew his niece claiming she was being taught communism, almost every paper in this great city attacked, pilloried the university. The Depression added to the feeling about communism.

I called on Mr. Walgreen to talk to him about this. Nobody from the university had done this. The trustees were startled by Walgreen's charges—and offended. I went to a former client, who introduced me to Mr. Walgreen. I said: "Mr. Walgreen, these great institutions live off the beneficences of people like you. Why don't you help the university teach courses on American institutions, as you think they should be taught?" Hutchins gave me the idea. I said to him: "What can we do to fix things up with Mr. Walgreen?" He said, "Why it's easy. Get him to give some money to the university." The next day, after my talk, Mr. Hutchins went around and collected a half a million dollars from him. That fixed the Walgreen case up right away.

Do you feel the Depression has adversely affected people in the matter of installment buying?
The Encyclopaedia Britannica lives off installment buying, this is our whole business. We don't think about credit as a problem, particularly when we think about a Depression. With more men out of work, we'd have an easier time finding good salesmen. The more men out of work, the more applicants we have. By multiplying our salesmen, we'd have an offset to the fact that there are fewer people to whom to sell. Progress through catastrophe.

■ ■ ■ ■

Arthur A. Robertson

His offices are on an upper floor of a New York skyscraper. On the walls are paintings and photographs. A portrait of President Johnson is inscribed "To my friend, a patriot who serves his country." Another, of Hubert Humphrey—"To my friend, Arthur Robertson, with all my good wishes." Also, a photograph of Dwight Eisenhower: "To my friend, Arthur Robertson." There are other mementos of appreciation from Americans in high places.

He recounts his early days as a war correspondent, advertising man and engineer. "We built a section of the Sixth Avenue subway. I've had a peculiar kind of career. I'm an industrialist. I had been in Germany where I picked up a number of porcelain enamel plants. I had a hog's hair concession from the Russian government. I used to sell them to the outdoor advertising plants for brushes. With several associates, I bought a company nineteen years ago for $1,600,000. We're on the New York Stock Exchange now and recently turned down $200 million for it. I'm chairman of the board, I control the company, I built it.

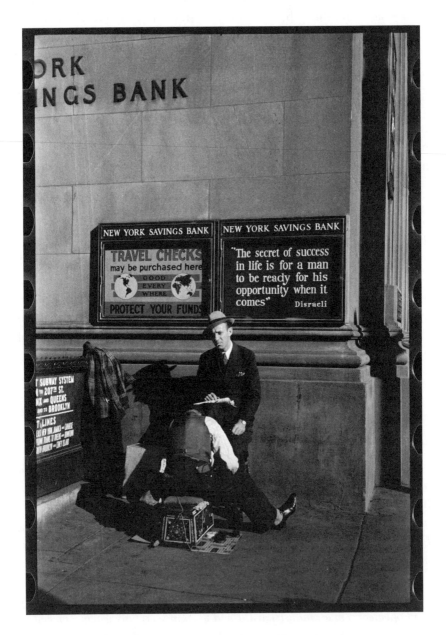

Bootblack, Fourteenth Street and Eighth Avenue,
New York, New York

Arthur Rothstein, 1937

*"I thought seriously of retiring in 1928 when I was thirty. I had seven figures
by the time I was twenty-four."*

IN 1929, IT WAS strictly a gambling casino with loaded dice. The few sharks
taking advantage of the multitude of suckers. It was exchanging expensive
dogs for expensive cats. There had been a recession in 1921. We came out
of it about 1924. Then began the climb, the spurt, with no limit stakes. Frenzied finance that made Ponzi* look like an amateur. I saw shoeshine boys
buying $50,000 worth of stock with $500 down. Everything was bought on
hope.

Today, if you want to buy $100 worth of stock, you have to put up $80
and the broker will put up $20. In those days, you could put up $8 or $10.
That was really responsible for the collapse. The slightest shake-up caused
calamity because people didn't have the money required to cover the other
$90 or so. There were not the controls you have today. They just sold you
out: an unwilling seller to an unwilling buyer.

A cigar stock at the time was selling for $115 a share. The market col-
lapsed. I got a call from the company president. Could I loan him $200
million? I refused, because at the time I had to protect my own fences, including those of my closest friends. His $115 stock dropped to $2 and he
jumped out of the window of his Wall Street office.

There was a man who headed a company that had $17 million in cash.
He was one of the leaders of his industry and controlled three or four situations that are today household words. When his stock began to drop, he
began to protect it. When he came out of the second drop, the man was
completely wiped out. He owed three banks a million dollars each.

The banks were in the same position he was, except that the government
came to their aid and saved them. Suddenly they became holier than thou,
and took over the businesses of the companies that owed them money.
They discharged the experts, who had built the businesses, and put in their
own men. I bought one of these companies from the banks. They sold it to
me in order to stop their losses.

The worst day-to-day operators of businesses are bankers. They are great
when it comes to scrutinizing a balance sheet. By training they're conservative, because they're loaning you other people's money. Consequently, they
do not take the calculated risks operating businesses requires. They were

* A Boston financier of the twenties. His "empire" crashed, many people were ruined. He
went to prison.

losing so much money that they were tickled to get it off their backs. I recently sold it for $2 million. I bought it in 1933 for $33,000.

In the early thirties, I was known as a scavenger. I used to buy broken-down businesses that banks took over. That was one of my best eras of prosperity. The whole period was characterized by men who were legends. When you talked about $1 million you were talking about loose change. Three or four of these men would get together, run up a stock to ridiculous prices and unload it on the unsuspecting public. The minute you heard of a man like Durant or Jesse Livermore buying stock, everybody followed. They knew it was going to go up. The only problem was to get out before they dumped it.

Durant owned General Motors twice and lost it twice . . . was worth way in excess of a billion dollars on paper, by present standards, four or five billion. He started his own automobile company, and it went under. When the Crash came, he caved in, like the rest of 'em. The last I heard of him I was told he ended up running a bowling alley. It was all on paper. Everybody in those days expected the sun to shine forever.

October 29, 1929, yeah. A frenzy. I must have gotten calls from a dozen and a half friends who were desperate. In each case, there was no sense in loaning them the money that they would give the broker. Tomorrow they'd be worse off than yesterday. Suicides, left and right, made a terrific impression on me, of course. People I knew. It was heartbreaking. One day you saw the prices at a hundred, the next day at $20, at $15.

On Wall Street, the people walked around like zombies. It was like *Death Takes a Holiday*. It was very dark. You saw people who yesterday rode around in Cadillacs lucky now to have carfare.

One of my friends said to me, "If things keep on as they are, we'll all have to go begging." I asked, "Who from?"

Many brokers did not lose money. They made fortunes on commissions while their customers went broke. The only brokers that got hurt badly were those that gambled on their own—or failed to sell out in time customers' accounts that were underwater. Of course, the brokerage business fell off badly, and practically all pulled in their belts, closed down offices and threw people out of work.

Banks used to get eighteen percent for call money—money with which to buy stock that paid perhaps one or two-percent dividends. They figured the price would continue to rise. Everybody was banking on it. I used to receive as much as twenty-two percent from brokers who borrowed from me. Twenty-two percent for money!

Men who built empires in utilities would buy a small utility, add a big profit to it for themselves and sell it back to their own public company. That's how some like Samuel Insull became immensely wealthy. The thing that caused the Insull crash is the same that caused all these frenzied financiers to go broke. No matter how much they had, they'd pyramid it for more.

I had a great friend, John Hertz. At one time he owned ninety percent of the Yellow Cab stock. John also owned the Checker Cab. He also owned the Surface Line buses of Chicago. He was reputed to be worth $400 to $500 million. He asked me one day to join him on a yacht. There I met two men of such stature that I was in awe: Durant and Jesse Livermore.

We talked of all their holdings. Livermore said: "I own what I believe to be the controlling stock of IBM and Philip Morris." So I asked, "Why do you bother with anything else?" He answered, "I only understand stock. I can't bother with businesses." So I asked, "Do men of your kind put away $10 million where nobody can ever touch it?" He looked at me and answered, "Young man, what's the use of having ten million if you can't have big money?"

In 1934—after he went through two bankruptcies in succession—my accountant asked if I'd back Livermore. He was broke and wanted to make a comeback in the market. He always made a comeback and paid everybody off with interest. I agreed to do it. I put up $400,000. By 1939, we made enough money so that each of us could have $1,300,000 profit after taxes. Jesse was by this time in the late sixties, having gone through two bankruptcies. "Wouldn't it be wise to cash in?" I asked him. In those days, you could live like a king for $50,000 a year. He said he could just never get along on a pittance.

So I sold out, took my profits, and left Jesse on his own. He kept telling me he was going to make the killing of the century. Ben Smith, known as "Sell 'Em Short Ben," was in Europe and told him there was not going to be a war. Believing in Smith, Livermore went short on grain.* For every dollar he owned, plus everything he could pyramid.

---

* "Selling short is selling something you don't have and buying it back in order to cover it. You think a stock is not worth what it's selling for, say it's listed as $100. You sell a hundred shares of it, though you haven't got the stock. If you are right, and it goes down to $85, you buy it at that price, and deliver it to the fellow to whom you sold it for $100. You sell what you don't have." Obviously, if the stock rises in value, selling short is ruinous. . . . Ben Smith sold short during the Crash and made "a fortune."

When I arrived in Argentina, I learned that Germany invaded Poland. Poor Jesse was on the phone. "Art, you have to save me." I refused to do anything, being so far away. I knew it would be throwing good money after bad.

A couple of months later, I was back in New York, with Jesse waiting for me in my office. The poor fellow had lost everything he could lay his hands on. He asked for a $5,000 loan, which, of course, I gave him. Three days later, Jesse had gone to eat breakfast in the Sherry-Netherlands, went to the lavatory and shot himself. They found a note made out to me for $5,000. This was the man who said, "What's the use of having ten million if you can't have big money?" Jesse was one of the most brilliant minds in the trading world. He knew the crops of every area where grain grew. He was a great student, but always overoptimistic.

Did you sense the Crash coming in 1929?
I recognized it in May and saved myself a lot of money. I sold a good deal of my stocks in May. It was a case of becoming frightened. But, of course, I did not sell out completely, and finished with a very substantial loss.

In 1927 when I read Lindbergh was planning his memorable flight, I bought Wright Aeronautic stock. He was going to fly in a plane I heard was made by Wright. I lived in Milwaukee then. My office was about a mile from my home. When I left my house, I checked with my broker. By the time I reached my office, I had made sixty-five points. The idea of everything moving so fast was frightening. Everything you bought just seemed to have no ceiling.

People say we're getting a repetition of 1929. I don't see how it is possible. Today with SEC* controls and bank insurance, people know their savings are safe. If everybody believes, it's like believing in counterfeit money. Until it's caught, it serves its purpose.

In 1932 I came to New York to open an office in the Flatiron Building. Macfadden, the health faddist, created penny restaurants. There was a Negro chap I took a liking to that I had to deal with. He agreed to line up seventy-five people who needed to be fed. At six o'clock I would leave my office, I'd march seventy-five of 'em into the Macfadden restaurant and I'd feed 'em for seven cents apiece. I did this every day. It was just unbelievable, the bread lines. The only thing I could compare it with was Germany in 1922. It looked like there was no tomorrow.

* Securities and Exchange Commission.

I remember the Bank Holiday. I was one of the lucky ones. I had a smart brother-in-law, an attorney. One day he said to me, "I don't feel comfortable about the bank situation. I think we ought to have a lot of cash." About eight weeks before the bank closings, we decided to take every dollar out of the banks. We must have taken out close to a million dollars. In Clyde, Ohio, where I had a porcelain enamel plant, they used my signature for money. I used to come in every Saturday and Sunday and deliver the cash. I would go around the department stores that I knew in Milwaukee and give them thirty-day IOUs of $1.05 for a dollar if they would give me cash.

In 1933, the night Jake Factor, "The Barber," was kidnapped, an associate of mine, his wife, and a niece from Wyoming were dancing in a nightclub. Each of us had $25,000 cash in our socks. We were leaving the following morning for Clyde, and I was supposed to bring in $100,000 to meet bills and the payroll. We were all dancing on $25,000 apiece. In the very place where Jake Factor was kidnaped for $100,000. The damn fools, they could have grabbed us and had the cash.

■　■　■　■

Sidney J. Weinberg

Senior partner, Goldman Sachs Company, a leading investment house. He served during Roosevelt's first two administrations as an industrial adviser.

OCTOBER 29, 1929—I REMEMBER that day very intimately. I stayed in the office a week without going home. The tape was running, I've forgotten how long that night. It must have been ten, eleven o'clock before we got the final reports. It was like a thunderclap. Everybody was stunned. Nobody knew what it was all about. The Street had general confusion. They didn't understand it any more than anybody else. They thought something would be announced.

Prominent people were making statements. John D. Rockefeller, Jr., announced on the steps of J. P. Morgan, I think, that he and his sons were buying common stock. Immediately, the market went down again. Pools combined to support the market, to no avail. The public got scared and sold. It was a very trying period for me. Our investment company went up to two, three hundred, and then went down to practically nothing. As all investment companies did.

Overspeculation was the cause, a reckless disregard of economics. There was a group ruthlessly selling short. You could sell anything and depress the market unduly. The more you depressed it, the more you created panic. Today we have protections against it. Call money went up—was it twenty percent?

No one was so sage that he saw this thing coming. You can be a Sunday morning quarterback. A lot of people have said afterwards, "I saw it coming, I sold all my securities." There's a credibility gap there. There are always some people who are conservative, who did sell out. I didn't know any of these.

I don't know anybody that jumped out of the window. But I know many who threatened to jump. They ended up in nursing homes and insane asylums and things like that. These were people who were trading in the market or in banking houses. They broke down physically, as well as financially.

Roosevelt saved the system. It's trite to say the system would have gone out the window. But certainly a lot of institutions would have changed. We were on the verge of something. You could have had a rebellion; you could have had a civil war.

The Street was against Roosevelt. Only me and Joe Kennedy, of those I know, were for Roosevelt in 1932. I was assistant treasurer of the Democratic National Committee. I did not support him after the first two terms. I had a great argument with him. I didn't think any man should serve any more than two terms. I was getting a little tired, too, of all the New Deal things. When I was asked to work with the War Production Board in 1940, he delayed initialing my employment paper. Later on, we had a rapprochement and were friendly again.

Confidence ended the Depression in 1934. We had a recession in 1937. People got a little too gay on the way up, and you had to have a little leveling off. The war had a great deal of stimulus in 1939.

A Depression could not happen again, not to the extent of the one in '29. Unless inflation went out of hand and values went beyond true worth. A deep stock market reaction could bring a Depression, yes. There would be immediate government action, of course. A moratorium. But in panic, people sell regardless of worth. Today you've got twenty-odd million stockholders owning stock. At that time you had probably a million and a half. You could have a sharper decline now than you had in 1929.

Most of the net worth of people today is in values. They haven't got it in cash. In a panic, values go down regardless of worth. A house worth $30,000, the minute you have a panic, isn't worth anything. Everybody feels good because the stock they bought at fifty is now selling at eighty. So they have a good feeling. But it's all on paper.

■   ■   ■   ■

John Hersch

He is the senior partner in a large brokerage house in Chicago. From his LaSalle Street office, on this late afternoon we can see the crowds below, worrying toward buses and parking lots, heading home.

"It's been a fascinating business for me right from 1924 to 1968. I've been in it a long time, and I'm very proud of it. It's entirely different than it was in the twenties. The canons of ethics are extremely strict. There are still bad episodes once in a while, but it's a big society."

His is an air of worldly weariness.

I CAME INTO THE business, out of the University of Chicago, about Christmas, 1924. I had about $3,000 in the stock market, which was all the money I had. On Black Friday—Thursday, was it?—that margin account went out of the window. I may have had about $62 left.

My wife had a colossal $125-a-week job with a Shakespearean theater company. That night, she came home to our little apartment, and she said, "Guess what happened today?" I said, "What?" She said, "I quit." I was making about $60 a week and she was making $125. Two-thirds of our income and all of our savings disappeared that day.

I was a margin clerk. He's a man who keeps the figures on individual accounts, if they're carrying stocks on margin—that is, if they're carrying stocks without paying for them.

When the break started, you had a deluge of selling, from weakened margin accounts. We had to stay up all night figuring. We'd work till one o'clock and go to the LaSalle Hotel and get up about five and get some breakfast and continue figuring margin accounts. 'Cause everybody was in trouble. But everybody.

The guy I worked for was sitting in the wire room, watching the tape. The tape was something to see, because Radio Corporation, let's say, would be ninety-five on the tape . . . they'd flash you sixty on the floor. The floor was a madhouse. I said to him: "Are we solvent?" He says, "I won't know till about twelve tonight." He was half-serious. It was brutal.

The Crash—it didn't happen in one day. There were a great many warnings. The country was crazy. Everybody was in the stock market, whether

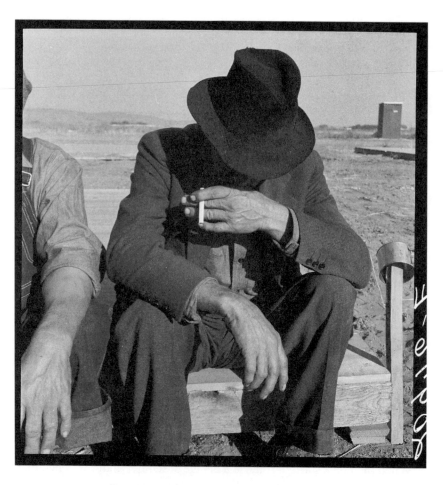

Was Nebraska farmer, now migrant farmworker in the West,
Merrill, Klamath County, Oregon

DOROTHEA LANGE, 1939

he could afford it or not. Shoeshine boys and waiters and capitalists. . . . A great many holding company pyramids were unsound, really fictitious values. Mr. Insull was a case in point. It was a mad dream of get-rich-quick.

It wasn't only brokers involved in margin accounts. It was banks. They had a lot of stinking loans. The banks worked in as casual a way as the brokers did. And when they folded . . .

I had a friend in Cincinnati who was young and attractive. He had a wife and children and he was insured for $100,000. Life was over as far as he was concerned. He took a dive, to take care of his wife and kids. There was a number who took the dive, to collect on insurance policies. It's unthinkable now, when you know how many people have been able to come back.

There were others that impress me. I kept hearing about town that their businesses were in trouble. But they never lowered their standard of living a bit. They lived like kings, right through the Depression. I've never been able to figure this out. I knew some people who maintained their Lake Shore Drive apartments and cars, and everybody knew they were in trouble. I never knew how they did it, and I didn't care particularly. My friends and I were all broke, and we had no pretensions.

You had no governmental control of margins, so people could buy on a shoestring. And when they began pulling the plug . . . you had a deluge of weakness. You also had short-selling and a lack of rules.* There were many cases of staid, reputable bankers making securities available on special deals—below the market price—for their friends. Anything went, and everything did go.

Today, there are very few bankers of any repute who have objected to the Securities Exchange Commission. They believe that the regulation in 1933 was a very, very sound thing for our business.

In '32 and '33, there was no securities business to speak of. We played a lot of bridge in the afternoons on LaSalle Street. There was nobody to call or see. It was so quiet, you could hear a certificate drop. (Laughs.) Nobody was making a living. A lot of them managed to eke out $40, $60 a week, but mostly we played bridge. (Laughs.)

I found a certain obtuseness about what's going on in the country. Even after it happened. Of course, at the beginning of the New Deal, the capitalists embraced Franklin Roosevelt as a real savior of our system. The *Chicago*

---

* "Now under SEC rules, you can only sell if the stock goes up an eighth. You can't sell it on the downtake."

Tribune wrote laudatory articles about him. Editorials. As soon as things got a little better, the honeymoon was over. You know all those old stories about guys getting on the train at Lake Forest: they were always looking for one headline every morning, that black headline about F.D.R. These people. . . .

It took this guy with the long cigarette holder to do some planning about basic things—like the SEC and the WPA and even the lousy Blue Eagle. It put a new spirit in the country.

The Bank Holiday of 1933 brought a certain kind of joyous, devil-may-care mood. People were just gettin' along somehow. It was based on the theory: Good grief, it couldn't get much worse. They bartered things for things.

The Irish Players were in Chicago, and everybody took potatoes to get in. People were taking vegetables to the box office. And they had big audiences.

I'm not trying to detract from the fact that there was wholesale misery in the Depression, 'cause you knew there were people living under the Michigan Avenue Bridge. Gentlemen in old $200 suits were selling apples. There was plenty of misery. I never want to see another. . . .

I don't find that people remember the Depression or think about it. I don't find it coming up in conversations. I also discover that a great many people, even professors, who might have gotten $300 a month during the Depression—some of them are worth a hundred, a hundred fifty thousand bucks today. You've never seen so much money around in history as there is today. Never. It's happened in the last twenty-three years . . . the development of industry and the creation of equities in business.

Another remarkable thing about the Depression—it never resulted in revolution. I remember that out in Iowa some place, there was a fellow named Reno,* who led a small following. There were some trucks turned over, and sheriffs weren't allowed to foreclose. But when you consider what was going on in the country—the whole country was orderly: they just sat there and took it. In retrospect, it's amazing, just amazing. Either they were in shock or they thought something would happen to turn it around. . . . My wife has often discussed this with me. She thinks it's astonishing, the lack of violent protest, especially in 1932 and 1933.

■　　■　　■　　■

---

* Milo Reno, leader of the Farm Holiday Association.

Dr. David J. Rossman

A psychiatrist. He had studied with Freud. His patients are upper middle class. He has been practicing since the twenties.

MILLIONAIRES WOULD COME TO me for treatment of anxiety attacks. In 1933, one of them said to me, "I'm here for treatment because I have lost all my money. All I have left is one house on Long Island which is worth $750,000. I don't know what I'd get for it if I tried to sell it." He was a very aristocratic-looking man. "I've always had a feeling of guilt about the money I've made."

I asked him, "Why do you feel guilty about it?" He said he was a floor trader and when he saw the market begin to fall, he would give it a big shove by selling short. At the end of the day, he had made $50–$75,000. This went on for a long time. He said, "I had always felt as if I had taken this money out of the mouths of orphans and widows."

He felt guilty after the walls caved in. He began to feel what it was like not to have any money. To give you an idea of the importance of this man: he was in a secret meeting at the J. P. Morgan bank, when they were trying to stop the decline. He had an appointment at five o'clock, and he said, "I won't be here today. But when I see you later, I'll have an important message for you."

If I had bought General Motors and Chrysler where it was in March, 1933, I could have been a multimillionaire on the investment of $10,000. But that wasn't his message. He said, "We have decided to close the Bank of the United States because the president was truculent and insisted upon an enormously inflated price for his stock." This was a very small bank in New York. They decided to let him go to the wall. The bank failed.

This man told me to go to the bank and take all my money and get gold notes. They were yellowbacks that said on the back: Redeemable in demand at the U.S. Treasury for gold in bars. I got $10,000 in gold. I said, "What the hell am I going to do with this?" It was heavy as hell. In gold bullion. I put it in a safety deposit box. Two days later, I had to take it out because the president declared the possession of gold to be illegal. I gave it back to the bank, and they credited me with $10,000.

I learned about the crack in our economy long before the stock market crash of '29. I had a patient who was the biggest kitchen utensil distributor in America. He had a huge plant. He said: suddenly, without notice, his orders just stopped. May and June, 1929.

All of us believed a new era in finance dawned. How long was I in the stock market? From '26 to '29. I had doubled my money. I remember some of the stocks I bought. I bought Electric Bond and Share, for example. I bought it at $100 a share and sold it at $465.

That was the only way you could make any real money. Income was piddling. Physicians were the greatest amateur financiers in the world. The way in which doctors, some of my friends, became interested was they had patients in high finance. They told them which stocks to buy. They were heading for a fall.

I began to invest in 1926. At the time I was working for Veterans Administration, and I think every doctor there had his finger in some kind of stocks. Some did better than others. I was too timid. Until a couple of years later, when I got a tip to buy Montgomery Ward, and within ten days I'd made $1,000.

In May of 1929, I personally pulled out of the market. I took my money out of the house I was dealing with and entrusted it to a man who was the backer of one of the wealthiest men in the country. Thinking he was infallible. He began buying stocks. He bought me Johns-Manville, for example. It was selling at $112. He bought a hundred shares at a bargain, 105. I sold it at 50.

This man embezzled stocks in the spring of 1929, something like $3 million worth. He was in very deep trouble. He died of a coronary. There was no prosecution. He was a pawn. The man whose manager he was was worth about a hundred million. He was not injured in the Crash. He made vast fortunes in dealing with devaluating currencies in Europe. He passed tips along to his friends. A good many of them made $6–$8 million. $6 million is a lot of money. They were cashing in on the decline in European currency.

What was happening to humans . . . ?
Nothing much. You wouldn't know a Depression was going on. Except that people were complaining they didn't have any jobs. You could get the most wonderful kind of help for a pittance. People would work for next to nothing. That's when people were peddling apples and bread lines were forming all over the city. But on the whole—don't forget the highest unemployment was less than twenty percent.

Your patients, then, weren't really affected?
Not very much. They paid fairly reasonable fees. I just came across a bankbook that I had between 1931 and 1934, and, by God, I was in those days making $2,000 a month, which was a hell of a lot of money. Then in 1934,

1935, 1936, they began coming in droves, when things began to ease up. People were looking for help. All middle class. Money loosened up. At the outbreak of the war, all psychiatrists in New York were just simply drowned with work. I saw my first patient at seven in the morning and I worked till nine at night.

He dwells on the recession of 1937, his interest in the Spanish Civil War, the disappointment in Roosevelt's embargo on Spain, the fall of Barcelona. . . . A good many of his patients were liberals, some interested in Marxism as a solution; others were "the hard core of the big merchants."

Did you have contact with the lower . . . ?
The lower classes? No. Let's take the lower middle class, a contractor. He built me a ten-room stone house for $8,500. I would pay him five cents a square foot for knotty pine that would cost you $1.50 today. Same thing. No laborer that worked in my house got more than $5 a day. I asked the contractor what he got out of it. He said, "I ate for six months." It was catch as catch can. Undersell yourself, do good work, on the hope that you would be recommended to somebody else.

In those days everybody accepted his role, responsibility for his own fate. Everybody, more or less, blamed himself for his delinquency or lack of talent or bad luck. There was an acceptance that it was your own fault, your own indolence, your lack of ability. You took it and kept quiet.

A kind of shame about your own personal failure. I was wondering what the hell it was all about. I wasn't suffering.

An outstanding feature of the Depression was that there were very few disturbances. People mass-marching, there was some. People marched in Washington and Hoover promised everything was going to be all right. People hoped and people were bewildered.

Big business in 1930 and later in '32 came hat in hand, begging Roosevelt. They have never gotten over their humiliation, and they have never forgiven him for having the wits to do something about it. Priming the pump.

Now people think it's coming to them. The whole ethos has changed. There is a great deal more hatred and free-floating aggression all over the country. We have reached unprecedented prosperity. Everybody says: "Why not *me*?" The affluent society has made itself known to people . . . how the better half lives. It's put on television, you can see it. And everybody says, "Who the hell are they? What's the matter with me? My skin is black, so what?" You don't accept responsibility for your own fate. It's the other fellow who's to blame. It's terrible. It could tear our country apart.

Do you think there might be a revolution if the Depression came upon us again?

It would be an inchoate affair. It wouldn't be organized.

Today nobody is permitted to starve. Now they think it's coming to them. As a matter of fact, it was the government that brought this idea to the people, in the thirties. The people didn't ask the government. They ask the question they can't answer themselves: Why am *I* the goat? Why *me?* They want pie in the sky. . . .

God Bless' the Child

Daisy Singer

A photographer.

I WAS SIX WHEN the Crash came. Of classic, upper-middle-class Jewish, you know, second-generation American. My father was sort of self-made.

He was something of a phony. He could always appear to be richer than he was. A lot of his friends were richer than he was, but he was the most flamboyant. He made what he had go a long way. Like he wasn't terribly intelligent, but he was fantastic at giving advice. People would come to him when they were contemplating suicide.

Headwaiters instantly knew he was someone to contend with. Like if he was on a transatlantic voyage, he would meet, at one time, Cardinal Spellman and, at another time, Al Capone. He was that kind of man.

We lived on Park Avenue before the Depression, like in eleven or four-teen rooms. One of those big apartments which are essentially very dreary. But they're what people hoped to achieve. After the Crash, we moved to Central Park West which wasn't such a terrible comedown. Except my grandparents moved in with us: keep up appearances and double in brass.

I remember vaguely family conferences, which took place behind closed doors. Like loans negotiated and things like that. The front would have to be maintained because I've learned that in business if people smell failure in you, you've had it.

I always had governesses. I had one I really loved when I was young, until I was seven. Then I had a succession of ones I loathed.

I remember going to the park with the one I really liked. There was a shanty town. Like a Hooverville. It was for me the palpable memory of the other side of the tracks. Ever since, when I encounter poverty, it is this memory . . . holding the hand of one's governess. For years, I felt exempt. I grew up feeling immune and exempt from circumstance. One of the things I suffered from was that I never felt adversity. I was confirmed in a sense of unreality. I never saw a real bread line. I saw it in the movies.

The outside world was so far from us, one didn't expect to encounter it. The doors were shut, as if there were some kind of contagion out there. I guess it was innocence, but I don't think of it as anything pretty as all: the less you experience, the better.

When my father was dying of cancer, he would hallucinate. Some of them were businessmen's hallucinations. He had an imaginary pocket with imaginary papers. He kept stashing them away. In a gesture that was famil-iar to him. Important papers. He always had a brief case or something and he had millions of papers. . . .

■   ■   ■   ■

Robin Langston

He is a social worker by day, a jazz musician by night. He is forty-three years old. He lived in Hot Springs, Arkansas, until he was seventeen.

". . . there are so many places that would have been worse. Suppose I had come up, say, in Mississippi . . . ?"

I KNEW THE DEPRESSION had really hit when the electric lights went out. My parents could no longer pay the $1 electric bill. The kerosene lamps went up in the home. And in the business. My father had a restaurant. This did something to me, because it let me know that my father was not the greatest cat in the world. I always thought he was.

My father couldn't read or write. If an airplane wrote his name in the sky, he wouldn't be able to read it. But he had a thirst for knowledge. It was our task, my sister and I, to read to him. He was the type of cat who would keep the radio on all day, just to listen to the news.

I remember that kerosene lamp, because for Christmas, '30, around in there, I got a little book that pictured Lindbergh's flight. My mother was telling me how great Lindbergh was. She told me I would fly a plane like that. But she didn't tell me about my chances of flying. That was the point, you see. 'Cause they were trying to shield me.

My mother was a teacher. She never did teach, because my father never did want her to work. He was the person to wear the pants in the family. He wanted to be the strong one. I was exposed to a lot of books: Pushkin, Frederick Douglass, Raymond Moley, *Time* magazine. No Booker T. Washington. He was anathema in my home.

My father taught us how to adjust to situations. We were fortunate compared to others. We always had food. Very little money, but there was so much spiritual guidance. I don't mean this Billy Graham type. I mean this thing that develops in a family where you anticipate the other's needs. I can kiss my father and not feel ashamed that I kissed a man. This is the type of thing we had going.

One time, my father and I tore a wall down to enlarge the business. I must have been around eight or nine. I could see blood coming from his hands, from using the crowbar, and I kissed his hand.

The restaurant was in the black community. But we made as much money off white people as we did off blacks. White people wanted to come in and get fried chicken. He had them fooled that there was something mystical about the batter he used. Another device he would use: they say that colored people like watermelon. Well, he raised the price of watermelon when white folks came in. All these survival techniques. . . .

I started washing dishes in the restaurant about five. My father didn't start me, I insisted. I'd get up on a Coca-Cola box to bend over the dish trough. My mother worked the cash register, and my sister was the waitress. It was a family type.

During the Depression, my father bought most things cash. The biggest thing we bought was a car and a refrigerator. I remember distinctly he paid on this in cash, because he didn't want to keep going back up to the store and taking this white man money and receipt book. My father did not like hat-in-hand situations.

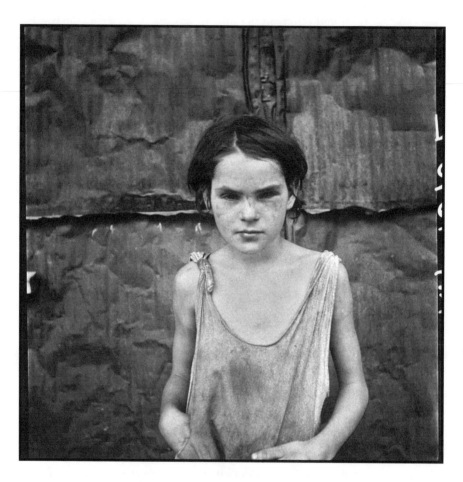

Child living in Oklahoma City shacktown

DOROTHEA LANGE, 1936

My family always had a lot of white friends because there was always some food. A white friend would forget his supposedly superior attitude if there's food involved. They were going to get some of my father's mystical fried chicken.

There was a unique thing about this black community. It wasn't like Chicago. There were Caucasians in the community. The police chief lived right in the heart of it. I guess there must have been ten white families within fifty feet of us. I remember feeding snotty-nosed white kids. It was the Depression because no white and no blacks were working. The *whites* not working made it official. Father and Mother did that thing out of the goodness of their hearts.

I remember when times got so hard, this sheriff pawned a radio to my father for $10. He had come to the black man to get $10. He really needed the ten. He had some people out of town, he wanted to bring them there to eat some chicken. So he told my father he didn't have the money. Dad told him he had to have some collateral. So he brought the radio.

My father carried black people on the tab during the Depression. We had a basement in our home and people who would come there, down and out, my father let them live there as long as they would keep it up, work around the garden, keeping up the roses and things. This is how I learned to gamble and shoot dice, from these guys. We got in a couple of boxers there. One of them became a champ.

The schools were segregated. I doubt if we had one teacher who had a bachelor's degree. These were tremendous people, black people. One lady's been teaching there over fifty years. I doubt if she's finished tenth grade. You'd go to a sandbox, she'd show you how to make a pond in the sandbox by taking a mirror, putting it in the sand and letting the mirror shine through.

It might have been in eighth or ninth grade. It was in one of the English classes. We didn't have a library in the black school. We depended on what people who came in would give us. We were reading *Time* magazine. There was an article on Raymond Moley on economics. We were supposed to get this article and make a report on it. I had to go to the white high school.

A frowsy Caucasian woman opened a crack in the door and threw the book on the floor. I tried to determine what's more important: this affront or getting Raymond Moley? My immediate thing was to get Raymond Moley. But my father always told me never to stoop. So I left the book on the floor. It hurt. I cried because I wanted the article so bad.

Hot Springs was a unique place. It was a health resort. It depended on rich people coming in. They came to the racetrack with their women.

There was a sort of sophistication. A sort of *Encyclopaedia Britannica* attitude. It was cosmopolitan and yet semirural. A rurban area.

They had one mayor. It seemed like he stayed in office a million years.
He would ride around in his carriage with two black ponies. He lived in
the black ghetto. Only he was on top of the hill. He would visit all the
gambling places in the community. White people came down and shot
dice. They'd come down looking for women, too. The red-light district was
always in the black area. The only white prostitutes you would find would
be in the hotels. They would be the high-priced ones. They would go with
the Negro bellhop. Say, if the bellhop caught a politician, maybe she made
a couple of hundred bucks. She'd give him some money, plus she'd go to
bed with him.

The church I knew was controlled by City Hall: "Every Christmas we'll
get these niggers some turkeys. We'll send somebody from the white school
board to talk to them. We might let one of you come to our church, sing." To
keep us quiet like that. It was easy to control the black community in Hot
Springs, because everything was geared toward money. "O.K., you don't
give us any problems, we'll let your gambling houses stay. We'll let you play
policy. We'll let the black racketeer who's in charge of everything, we'll let
him get the nigger out of jail on Saturday night. You can fight and whip your
woman on Saturday night, just don't bother us over here. We'll give you
a break, a suspended thirty-day sentence. We'll let you go home and be a
good boy."

We'd get the Chicago *Defender*. They had one edition for the North and
another for the South. That's how we heard about the Scottsboro case. One
of the people defending the boys came and spoke at the black church there.
Oh yes, we knew about this case and this white woman, Ruby Something—

Ruby Bates.
This was during the time when a lot of young people wanted to get a job
and venture out and go places, and they were afraid to hobo because they
didn't want to get caught up in a Scottsboro case.

The *Defender* was read openly. It was brought down on a white railroad
and thrown off a white boxcar. It was sold in the black community on the
newsstands.

During the Depression, they had a transient bureau in my hometown.
Poor whites and poor blacks. This bureau would have them do work in the
mountain area, say, cutting vines or shrubbery. This was in Roosevelt's time.
They would go down and show people how to farm this no-good land. They
would also give them a dole. I would see a line waiting to get beans. Boll

weevils in them. It's almost an impossibility that some people lived through. Eating those beans and separating the bugs from the beans.

Roosevelt touched the temper of the black community. You did not look upon him as being white, black, blue or green. He was President Roosevelt. He had tremendous support through his wife. Yet the immediate image is "Great White Father."

The WPA and other projects introduced black people to handicrafts and trades. It gave Negroes a chance to have an office to work out of with a typewriter. It made us feel like there was something we could do in the scheme of things. I don't remember any serious black opposition to Roosevelt. When you see a blithe spirit, naturally you're attracted to it.

I think the powers-that-be missed the boat, during the Depression. There was a kind of integration of poverty. But even though everybody was poor, we still had this stiff-collar, white-shirted Puritanical Wilson thing going. So even though we were all in the same boat, I'm still white and you're still black, and so we don't need to get together. Things are going to get better for the white folks, and you black folks will have to . . .

Do you think a Depression of that depth could come again?
I think it could. But it would behoove the federal government not to let it come. Because you're dealing with a different breed of cat now. If they really want anarchy, let a Depression come now. My sixteen-year-old son is not the person I was when I was sixteen. He has manly responsibilities. And he doesn't want any shit. When I was sixteen, I wasn't afraid to die. But the kid, sixteen now, is not afraid to kill.

■ ■ ■ ■

Dynamite Garland

In the old hotel, once elegant, where she is the most popular guest, from whom elderly widows and male pensioners ask advice and solace, her apartment flows over with paperbacks, artwork, her own and others', oddments, indicative of varied and passing interests. . . .

She is an attractive forty-five-year-old waitress at an Italian-style restaurant in Chicago's Loop.

She comes from Cleveland, "a working-class family." Her father, before the Depression, had been a railroad man. "He's now seventy-eight and one of the roller skating experts in the country. He and my mother used to dance in marathons."

I REMEMBER ALL OF a sudden we had to move. My father lost his job and we moved into a double-garage. The landlord didn't charge us rent for seven years. We had a coal stove, and we had to each take turns, the three of us kids, to warm our legs. It was awfully cold when you opened those garage doors. We would sleep with rugs and blankets over the top of us. Dress under the sheets.

In the morning, we'd get out and get some snow and put it on the stove and melt it and wash around our faces. Never the neck or anything. Put on our two pairs of socks on each hand and two pairs of socks on our feet, and long underwear and lace it up with Goodwill shoes. Off we'd walk, three, four miles to school.

My father had owned three or four homes. His father left them to him. He lost these one by one. One family couldn't pay the rent. They owned a bakery shop. They used to pay him off half in money, half in cookies. We lived on cracked cookies and those little bread things. So my father was pretty sharp in a way.

He always could get something to feed us kids. We lived about three months on candy cods, they're little chocolate square things. We had these melted in milk. And he had a part-time job in a Chinese restaurant. We lived on those fried noodles. I can't stand 'em today. He went to delivering Corn Flake samples. We lived on Corn Flake balls, Rice Krispies, they used to come out of our ears. Can't eat 'em today either. Can't stand 'em. My mother used to make the bread, put it under a blanket to raise. Oh, that was tasty. I never tasted such good bread since.

Every Sunday we used to go house hunting. That was a recreation during the Depression. You'd get in the Model A with the family and go look at the houses. They were all for sale or rent. You'd go look and see where you could put this and where you could put that, and this is gonna be my room. I knew where I was gonna have my horse in the barn. My mother'd go down in the basement, saying, "Oh, this is well constructed. This is where we're gonna put the potato bin, this is where we're gonna put the onions." We knew just where everyone was gonna be. (Laughs.)

My mother was raised in a lace curtain Irish family and went to a finishing school. We had our napkin rings even during the Depression. My mother'd set up everything just so and so. I used to go to my girlfriend's to eat. They used to have a pile of Italian food on the table. She'd come over to my place to eat, because she liked the way everything was set up.

Some of the kids seemed a little better off at the Catholic school. I used to spend most of my time under the desk, lookin' at the nun's black-top shoes. It seems I always was doin' somethin' to get punished. I was gonna bite her in

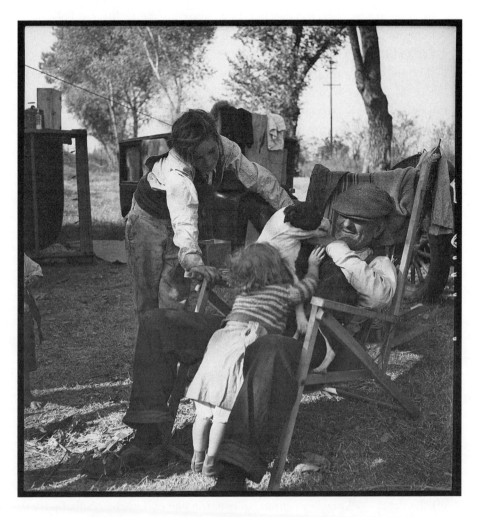

Destitute family. American River camp, Sacramento, California.
Five children, aged two to seventeen years

DOROTHEA LANGE, 1936

the knee one time. (Laughs.) I wanted to be a nun. I was in awe of those lovely ladies. So I wound up bein' a strip dancer. (Laughs.)

They made you put your name on the collection envelope. All my mother could put in was two, three cents. Gold stars on the wall for scholastic achievements. I know doggone well I did better than some of 'em. They got a star and I never got one.

My mother always picked a school where the other children were far better off than we were. She would work at a cleaning store, managed the tuition and books. We could have gone to a free public school.

It was status with my mother. She used to walk around and my father used to call her "Queenie." She always had grandiose ideas.

My father did the best he could. He used to stuff in the mailboxes those little sheets, "Pink Sheets for Pale Purses." I think it was for a left-wingish organization. My father disagreed with whatever philosophy was on there. He got $3 a week for this.

'Cause he got a job in Akron, delivering carry-out food, we moved there. That was a dandy place: dirt, smoke, my mother scrubbing all the time. We lived right on the railroad tracks. They used to throw us watermelons and things like that. When the trains slowed down, he used to jump on and have us kids pick up the coal.

I was about fourteen when I joined the NYA.* I used to get $12.50 every two weeks. Making footlockers. I gave half to my mother. This was the first time I could buy some clothes. After I bought some nice clothes, I decided I didn't want to be a nun. (Laughs.)

My girlfriend's father was in a new movement, Technocracy,† I used to wear a badge with her 'cause it was my girlfriend. I remember the circular sort of thing on the badge.

I worked part-time in a bakery. I used to slide plastic papers under those nice chocolate eclairs. You'd be surprised how many times you picked 'em off the floor. Cockroaches runnin' all over the place. (Laughs.) Nobody got sick. You'd just kick 'em out of the way. They were big roaches, too.

I finished high school and got sort of engaged. I thought maybe if I got married I could eat hamburgers and hot dogs all night, have a ball, play the guitar and sing. I was singing with a hillbilly band and married the guitar

* National Youth Administration.
† A movement popular in the early days of the Depression. It was based upon a price system measured in units of energy rather than dollars and cents. The society envisioned was to be run by engineers and scientists. Founded by Howard Scott, a young engineer, it was the subject of much discussion. With the election of Roosevelt, it fell out of public grace and memory.

player. Anything would be better than coming home and sleeping on the floor.

Trains along the Illinois Central tracks, just outside the hotel, are heard. "I miss those low train whistles. I'd like to take off like my grandfather did. He was a hobo, not a bum. He was an able-bodied seaman. He'd go maybe to China, bring back gifts, tell us fantastic stories. We didn't have a place for him, so he ensconced himself in the bathtub. He had a nice little pillow and bed right in the bathtub. He was an alcoholic. We used to hide all the silver, because he'd take it out and hock it to get a little mist. . . ."

Eleven months later, I had a baby. I was pregnant with another when war was declared. When we got married, my husband was making $14 a week. Seven of it went each week into the coat and suit we bought for the marriage. From $14 a week, we jumped to $65 a week, working in a defense plant. It sort of went to my head. Wow! Boy, we were rich. First thing I did was to get me one of those red fur chubbies. I had to have a fur with that amount of money. Oooooh, those things looked awful. With my red hair, it looked like I was half orangutan. Then I had to get the shoes with the crisscross straps and balls hanging down, and the skirt with the fringe. Ick!

They say if you're raised poor, you'll know how to handle money. We were raised poor as church mice. But when I get it, I blow it. It's a personality thing. I don't regret any of it. But still. . . .

■　　■　　■　　■

Slim Collier

A bartender.

"I was born in Waterloo. A great deal of Iowa, southern Iowa, particularly, didn't have electricity until the end of World War II. I was eleven years old before I lived in a house with running water. That was 1936.

"My people are Manx. The island between Scotland and Ireland. The first Collier came here in chains off a British warship. 1641. He was known as a white nigger. He was a political prisoner. He was sentenced to seventeen years for sedition. After ten years of servitude, he was granted a king's pardon. Nope, my people didn't come here on the Mayflower.

"Every Collier would go back to the Isle of Man to get himself a wife. My father broke the tradition. He married the daughter of a German immigrant

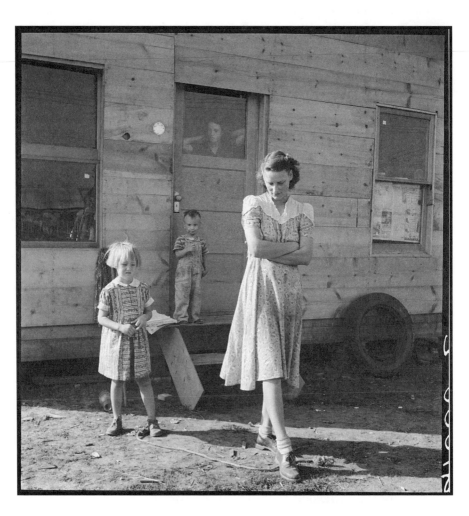

Young mother of twenty five says "next year we'll be painted and have
a lawn and flowers"; rural shacktown, near Klamath Falls, Oregon

DOROTHEA LANGE, 1939

living in the Dakotas. My mother was really a snot-nosed big sister. She was only fourteen years older than I was. . . ."

MY FATHER WAS SORT of a fancy Dan. A very little man, five feet two. He was a tool-and-die maker in addition to being a farmer. The kind of man that would get up in the morning and put on a white shirt and tie, suit, camel hair coat, gloves, get in his late model Chrysler, drive from the farm into the city, park his car in the parking lot, get out, take off his coat, put his suit in the locker and put on those greasy overalls to be a tool-and-die maker. He had a lot of pretensions. When the Depression hit him, it hit hard.

He was the kind of man that would put a down payment on a place, get a second mortgage, put a down payment on another place. The Depression wiped out his houses. The anger and frustration he experienced colored my whole life. He was the kind of man, if somebody went broke he was pleased. Now it happened to him.

It was a 160-acre farm, primarily corn. My brother farms the same 160 acres today. He does it in an hour, two hours, with automation. But my father was a stubborn old cuss. I ran off because he wouldn't buy a tractor. I was fourteen in 1938, when I ran away from home. My last day's work that I did for the old man was taking logs out of the woods, with oxen. He bought a tractor in 1939. (Laughs.)

My father was laid off in the fall of '31 as a tool-and-die maker. He worked at the John Deere tractor plant. I was seven, and I just barely started school. All of a sudden, my father, who I saw only rarely, was around all the time. That was quite a shock. I suddenly became disciplined by him instead of my mother. The old woodshed was used extensively in those days.

Fear and worry was the one thing that identified the people. John Paul's was a furniture store in Westfield, near Waterloo—I suppose you'd call it a suburb today. It was sort of a village where roosters wake you up in the morning, where people kept cows and pigs. Parts of it had street lights, but it was rural enough to have farm animals. We kids would patronize the store, too, because it carried candy and a few school supplies.

I remember men congregating in the store. One man bragged how he had never been on welfare and wasn't going to be on welfare. Quite a few people there resented it, because most people in Westfield were on welfare.

This short temper was a characteristic of the time. Men who were willing to work couldn't find work. My father was the kind of man who had to be active. He'd invent work for himself. A child who was playing irritated him. It wasn't just my own father. They all got shook up.

My old man went back to work in '33, part-time. Nevertheless, he was earning cash money. That term, "cash money," impressed itself on my childhood. A dime was a weekly event. It brought me a bag of popcorn and a seat in the third row of the theater where I could see Bob Steele shoot off the Indians. On Saturday—buffalo nickel day, they called it. It provided conversation to my schoolmates for the rest of the week.

Cash was extremely rare. I remember having found a dollar and my father gravely taking charge of it and doling it out to me a dime at a time.

When he was hired back, we went to the 160 acres that the finance company had. Because he was able to make payments, they waived the foreclosure. They were so hard up for cash money themselves.

There was a family that experienced a farm foreclosure. It was the first of March when they were forced off, and all their household goods were sold. Even family pictures. They went for five cents, ten cents apiece. Quite a few of the kids were brought there by their parents, partly by morbid fascination, partly by sympathy, partly—well, there was something going on. In those days of no TV, no radio in some places, an event was an event.

It was a hilarious thing for us kids. We got together, there were lots of new kids. Games. . . . Gradually, I was aware, slightly, of the events. Overhearing the adults talk. The worry and the relief they expressed: it hadn't happened to them. The anticipation that it might . . . the fascination with catastrophe. I recall this undertone, horror, but also fascination. It dominated the conversation for weeks.

The dominant thing was this helpless despair and submission. There was anger and rebellion among a few but, by and large, that quiet desperation and submission.

The phrase, "Prosperity is just around the corner," was something we kids would repeat. But we didn't quite dig what prosperity meant. (Laughs.) Iowa is traditionally Republican. When my father was voting Democrat and announced it ahead of time—he voted for Roosevelt—it was something of a shock: "Collier is turning radical." (Laughs.) Well, Hoover got blamed for the Depression.

"When I quarreled with my father and left home, I worked as an itinerant farmer for $16 a month and found. It was understood that a hired man went to church with the family. He didn't sit with 'em. The hired help all sat in the back row. Your hired men and hired girls would sit at the table and eat with*

---

* An archaic rural phrase: "That was your board. If you got sick, the farmer paid the doctor bill. The wife washed your clothes and saw you had a clean shirt on Sunday for church."

the family. But in public you had certain amenities you had to observe. You held the door open and let every member of the family walk in before you came in. Oh yes, we had social classes in those days."

Among his other jobs: theater usher, bellhop, truck helper, coal loader. Finally, at the age of seventeen, the army. Out of the entire company, only he and another had completed eighth grade; they were made medics.

In 1939, I went out an itinerant farm worker. I got a job cutting asparagus, fifteen cents an hour, as fast as you could move. I remember standing up once to rub my aching back, 'cause you worked in a crouch almost at a running pace, and the straw boss yelling: "See those men standing by the road? They're just waiting to get you fired. If I catch you straightening up once more, one of them will be working and you won't."

We'd gather at a certain site at four in the morning. And stand there waiting for the truck to come by, and they'd yell the terms off: fifteen cents an hour. If you wanted work, you'd come to these intersections in Waterloo. Men would be standing there, smoking and talking, bragging, joking as men talk when they get together and don't know each other. They'd decide: I'm not gonna work for fifteen cents an hour. After all, I got $2 cash money at home. The rest of us would pile on the truck, and a man would say: That's enough.

They were bringing people out of town to work in the country. The people in the country were getting up in arms, refusing to work at these wages. At that time, I didn't realize the exploitation, and the competitiveness of workers.

Was there talk of organizing?
Not in Iowa, not in that east central part. The people were too conservative. I was past forty years of age before I joined a union. I was conditioned—to join a labor union would take away your ability to stand on your own two feet. It would mean surrendering yourself. I probably picked up a great deal more of my father's arrogance than I realize. I was too arrogant to join a union. Hell, I'd work for less money just to be my own self.

To be a union man had some sort of shameful label to it. There was a man in our neighborhood, whose wife was a part-time prostitute. This was known. He smoked tailor-made cigarettes, as opposed to Bull Durham roll-your-owns. The man had very little respect. In the same way, being a union man wasn't quite respectable.

POSTSCRIPT: *"Back then, a woman by the time she was forty or fifty was an old woman. When I was back in Iowa last September, some of these forty-five- and fifty-year-old chicks are better lookin' than their twenty-year-old daughters. Labor-saving devices, cosmetics . . . and they're health conscious: vitamins. I have noticed a peculiar number of people my age wear dentures. We didn't get the right vitamins. We didn't get the minerals."*

∎　∎　∎　∎

Phyllis Lorimer

"I was unaware of what was happening. I knew what happened to me. I did hear of people jumping out of windows. It didn't mean anything personally to me.

"I grew up in Greenwich, Connecticut, a lovely house. My family was extremely well off, but I always thought I was poor. All my cousins, everybody's father was a millionaire. My best friends had their own island. They each had their boat, and all had their jumping horses.

"My mother and father were divorced. My father was a successful motion picture producer in California. My mother took me out there. Came the Crash, and we all stayed."

WHEN IT HAPPENED, I was in a boarding school which I loved. At Glendora. It was the best boarding school in California at that time. A beautiful school in the middle of orange trees. I was about to be president of the student body and very proud of myself. Suddenly I couldn't get any pencils and went to the principal to find out why. She was embarrassed because we were old friends. She said, "I'm sorry, the bills just haven't been paid." She complimented me, saying, "Were there scholarships, you could have it." And, "I couldn't be sorrier."

I was mortified past belief. It was hard for the principal. I called my mother and said, "Come and pick me up." Which she did. I went back home which wasn't much of a home because we were living with a stepfather whom I detested.

It was rough on me, the thirties. I wasn't aware of it being with everyone else. I thought it was just personal. I was in no way aware that it was a national thing. Having grown up in some affluence, I was suddenly in a small court in Hollywood with a stepfather who was drunk and ghastly.

My brother was still at Dartmouth, where he was fortunate enough not to know what was going on at home. Whatever money there was went to keep brother at Dartmouth. We were living on a form of relief. We had cans of tinned bully beef. And we had the gas turned off. My mother was an engaging lady who made everything a picnic. We cooked everything on an electric corn popper, so it was gay in certain aspects. (Laughs.) My mother had humor and charm, so I didn't know it was a desperate situation. When there wasn't any money, she'd buy me a china doll instead of a vegetable. (Laughs.) She was an eccentric, and everybody stared at her. I was the little brown mouse.

My father was still holding up his pride. He had been successful, and then things went. Two houses with everything in it. His own career had nothing to do with the Depression. He blew it. Lots of times bills weren't paid when there was no Depression.

I had come from this terribly wealthy family, with cousins who still had so much that, even during the Depression, they didn't lose it. Suddenly I had four great white horses. They were given to me by my cousins. I was a very good horsewoman. (Laughs.) I rode at all the shows and steeplechases and all that. And went home to canned bully beef at night. (Laughs.)

My brother was socially oriented, a tremendous snob. While we were eating bully beef, he was living extremely well at Dartmouth. Nobody told him how bad things were. He lived magnificently, with a socialite friend, in a house with a manservant. He came back and found the truth, and the truth was ghastly.

He was five years older, a male, facing the fact that he had to go out and do it. It set for him a lifelong thing: he was never going to be caught in the same trap his parents were—never, ever going to be the failure his father was.

His first job was carrying rubber at the Firestone factory, and he got the white tennis clothes smelly and he violently hated the whole thing. He came home reeking of it and hating himself.

It was unbearable. He wouldn't tell the people with whom he played tennis on the weekends. He had an old Ford with no door, but if you held on, there was a door. When he would take me out in the car, I would be the one that held the door on. It was that kind of Ford.

He was going to get somewhere and he fixed himself a little black book: what he was going to do by such and such a date. And he did it—to make up for his parents' failures. He wished to be in color photography. He studied every night he came home from Firestone. Within a year, he was manager of the New York office of Technicolor. He had such determination. . . .

Now it was necessary for me to make some money because the stepfather was drunk all the time and the father was pretending it hadn't happened. Having gone to a proper lady's finishing school, I didn't know how to do anything. I spoke a little bad French, and I knew enough to stand up when an older person came into the room. As far as anything else was concerned, I was unequipped.

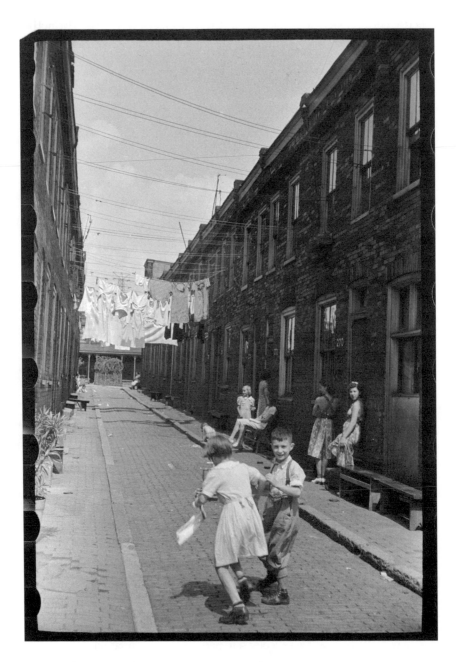

Housing conditions in Ambridge, Pennsylvania,
home of the American Bridge Company

ARTHUR ROTHSTEIN, 1938

I heard there was a call for swimmers for a picture called *Footlight Parade*. At Warner Brothers. The first big aquacade picture.* I went, terrified, tried out the high-diving thing and won. I couldn't have been more stunned. I truly think this is where I got a lifelong point of view: respect for those who *did*, no respect for those who *had* . . . just because their father had done something and they were sitting around.

I loved the chorus girls who worked. I hated the extras who sat around and were paid while we were endangering our lives. I had a ball. It was the first time I was better than anybody at something. I gained a self-respect which I'd never had.

In the midst of my suddenly getting $7.50 a day for risking my life daily on the high boards and stunt work, falling out of wagons, and no overtime, I discovered what a good union could mean. I had spent most of my childhood alone. Now I came to respect those who worked for each other and for others. I got a great respect for the Screen Actors' Guild, who were protecting us who were working underwater for $7.50 a day.

It was the big thing in my life at that moment. I had been a brown wren in uniform in a lot of proper girls' schools. My mother was an exhibitionist, and I wanted just that nobody ever look at me. I just wanted to disappear. I was fond of my mother, who was of no world. She could have lived in any era. I never got from her what was going on. I did from my brother, because he was undone by it.

Always having felt slightly rejected by Westhampton society, Greenwich society, Great Neck society, I had the feeling we weren't "it," whatever "it" was. I was sure my relatives were "it." I knew my mother was a loon, wore fishnet and rode bicycles. We were odd.

All of a sudden I found another group with whom I belonged. The ex-Olympic stars who were diving and swimming and the chorus girls who worked like mad. Suddenly I didn't care about my brother's friends, the socially important. He kept saying, "When they ask what you're doing, don't say you're a chorus girl." I said, "I'm proud to be a chorus girl." That used to destroy him.

In Westhampton, Greenwich and Great Neck, my only knowledge of what people do about anything was to keep Polacks from moving in. I truly believed, as a child, the bridge across the canal from Southampton was to keep Jews out of the country club. (Laughs.) Suddenly I'm a wild labor enthusiast. I'm here with the chorus girls and the grips.

---

* Busby Berkeley's extravaganza, starring Ruby Keeler, Dick Powell and James Cagney.

Bonnie Laboring Boy

I've worked in the Susquehanna yard
I've got one dollar a day
Toiling hard to make a living, boys,
I hardly think she pays.
They said they will raise our wages
If they do, I won't complain.
*If they don't, I'll hoist my turkey**
And walk the road again.

—Traditional Folk Song

Larry Van Dusen

Fifty-five years old, he's been a labor union organizer most of his life. "I was nine-teen when I left home and never went back. Bummin' around on the road—Colorado, Texas—hitchhiking, ridin' boxcars . . . oh, coming back home once in a while and finding the family on relief. Checking out. . . ."

He was a social worker in Kansas City during the early thirties; organized unemployed councils; participated in strikes; was arrested several times. . . .

I STILL PLAY A little game with myself, shaving. To get shaved before I'm picked up by the cops. Once I was picked up and I had a two-day beard on my face, and three days in a hundred-degree weather in a Kansas City jail, I developed a terrific rash on the neck. It still comes back once in a while. So that's just a little gimmick you work . . . if they're gonna get you this time, you're gonna go to jail clean-shaven. When I want to entertain myself now, I still think: I'm gonna get shaved before the knock on the door.

---

* A bindle: possessions wrapped in a handkerchief.

The brutality in the jails, the treatment of the unemployed, especially Negroes—I remember this cursing crash of some new arrival. They were dragging a big Negro into a cell next to ours. The din and the hell-raising we made to try to get him medical attention. We assumed, because nobody came, and he was taken out pretty stiff the next morning, that he died in the cell.

In those days, Chicago was quite a place to be arrested in. They had a system of moving you from precinct station to precinct station, so that it might be two or three days before your lawyer could find out where you were at. It was rougher than I had been accustomed to in Kansas City. Police stations at the time had these gimmicks, like seats with electric shocks. We were kept six or eight to a cell. Arrests of this sort were common enough for people who were organizing.

Unemployed councils, in my opinion, laid the basis for much of the New Deal legislation. . . . They attracted people who subsequently became labor organizers, particularly in the CIO. They were youthful in character and in ideas. They were not hidebound as left-wing political parties were in that period, although Communists and Socialists took part. They sort of threw away the rule book and just organized people to get something to eat.

The unemployed council people out in St. Louis were responsible for the first strike I ever saw—a tiff* miners' strike in southern Missouri. The housing was primitive. It was a miserable existence—literally, digging one out from the ground. They were trying to get better prices, so there was a strike. They tried to withhold their product from the market. I watched the meeting of the miners broken up by the local police and vigilantes.

Like most strikes of that period, it made more of a political than an economic point. There was a lot of publicity in the *St. Louis Post-Dispatch* and other papers. It pointed up the miserable conditions of the miners. It put into focus right on Park Avenue and Grosse Pointe and Winnetka . . . what was really going on. All the left-wing groups had a part in dramatizing it. And this reflected itself later in Roosevelt's New Deal measures.

One of the most common things—and it certainly happened to me— was this feeling of your father's failure. That somehow he hadn't beaten the rap. Sure things were tough, but why should I be the kid who had to put a piece of cardboard into the sole of my shoe to go to school? It was not a thing coupled with resentment against my father. It was simply this feeling of regret, that somehow he hadn't done better, that he hadn't gotten the breaks.

---

* "Tiff is a material used in making paint, comparable to white lead. It was dug out of straight shafts, like little wells. The miners didn't own the land, of course. They were simply sinking these wells, getting the tiff out and selling it to big companies."

Also a feeling of uneasiness about my father's rage against the way things are.

My father was very much of an individualist, as craftsmen usually are. He would get jobs he considered beneath his status during this period. Something would happen: he'd quarrel with the foreman, he'd have a fight with the boss. He was a carpenter. He couldn't be happy fixing a roadbed or driving a cab or something like that. He was a skilled tradesman and this whole thing had him beat. I think it bugged the family a lot.

Remember, too, the shock, the confusion, the hurt that many kids felt about their fathers not being able to provide for them. This reflected itself very often in bitter quarrels between father and son. I recall I had one. I was the oldest of six children. I think there was a special feeling between the father and the oldest son.

We had bitter arguments about new ideas. Was Roosevelt right in making relief available? Was the WPA a good idea? Did people have the right to occupy their farms and hold them by force? The old concept that there was something for everybody who worked in America went down the drain with the Great Depression. This created family strains. A lot of parents felt a sense of guilt, a feeling of shame that they had to be rescued by WPA and building a dam. A craftsman like my father felt pretty silly pouring concrete for a wall on the bluffs around the K.C. railroad yards . . . when the nation needed houses and his craftsmanship could have been used. Men like him suffered indignity, working at projects they considered to be alien to the American concept of productive labor.

My father led a rough life: he drank. During the Depression, he drank more. There was more conflict in the home. A lot of fathers—mine, among them—had a habit of taking off. They'd go to Chicago to look for work. To Topeka. This left the family at home, waiting and hoping that the old man would find something. And there was always the Saturday night ordeal as to whether or not the old man would get home with his paycheck. Everything was sharpened and hurt more by the Depression.

Heaven would break out once in a while, and the old man would get a week's work. I remember he'd come home at night, and he'd come down the path through the trees. He always rode a bicycle. He'd stop and sometimes say hello, or give me a hug. And that smell of fresh sawdust on those carpenter overalls, and the fact that Dad was home, and there was a week's wages—well, this is something you remember, too. That's the good you remember.

And then there was always the bad part. That's when you'd see your father coming home with the toolbox on his shoulder. Or carrying it. That meant

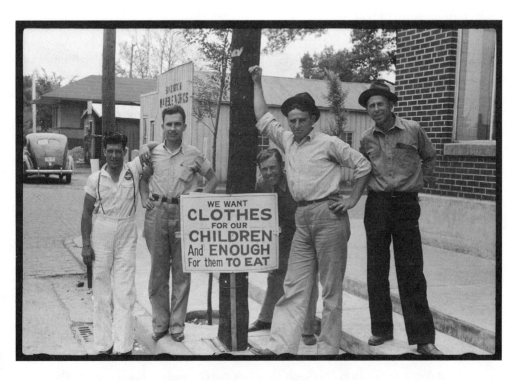

Employees of Coca-Cola plant on strike, Sikeston, Missouri

JOHN VACHON, 1940

the job was over. The tools were home now, and we were back on the tread-mill again.

I remember coming back home, many years afterwards. Things were better. It was after the Depression, after the war. To me, it was hardly the same house. My father turned into an angel. They weren't wealthy, but they were making it. They didn't have the acid and the recriminations and the bitterness that I had felt as a child.

I remember coming back that day. My mother had roast beef. It was very good, and there was plenty of it. There was meat left over on the table when we finished. During the Depression, one day a week, if we were lucky enough, we got round steak. I was nineteen or twenty before I knew there was any kind of steak except round steak. I can remember all the kids sitting around, eyeing that meat, hands on forks, poised and ready. Depend-ing on which way my father started that meat: that decided who got the first choice. There was one piece of meat per kid, and you were still hungry after the meal was over. I think of this very often when I see my wife trying to force food down my children's throats.

I don't think most children escape this. The oldest son, like me—it had the effect of getting me out of the home earlier. It's not a question of dis-owning your family. Any great economic upheaval, I think, alters patterns. Children develop doubts about their parents. They leave home early, out of necessity. They must find jobs quicker and quicker. Different from the cur-rent generation.

It comes through clearly these days when old labor leaders like myself try to talk to young workers who come into the shop. You try to talk to them about what we've been through, when we were organizing a plant—the blacklist, how we'd go under other names . . . you tell them about the Me-morial Day Massacre . . . you tell them about the troops in Flint and sit-down strikes and the revolution this represented in the auto industry. . . . Well, they listen, if they're polite. But it doesn't really touch them, these things. These things that mean so much to us.

The young worker comes into the plant very often having the same values as his parents. The parents were a Depression couple. But years have passed, fights have been won, and this couple now has a suburban home, a child or two to college or high school. So the youngster comes into a plant where the workers are much more middle class than we were.

The Depression left a legacy of fear, but also a desire for acquisition—property, security. I now have twenty times more shirts than I need, be-cause all during that time, shirts were something I never had.

■ ■ ■ ■

Jose Yglesias

Author. Among his works are The Goodbye Land, In the Fist of the Revolution *and* An Orderly Life.

"*Ybor City is a ward of Tampa. Spanish-speaking. I didn't learn English until I started public school.*"

It was built in the 1880s by Cuban cigar manufacturers, seeking a hot, damp climate and freedom from labor troubles. "*Within two months, there were strikes. (Laughs.) Cigar makers are the most radical workers you could find. Wages were bitterly fought for. They had many, many strikes.*" *There was no union recognition until the beginnings of World War II.*

"*People date their lives from various strikes in Tampa. When they refer to a scab, they say: 'It's no surprise he's trying to break this strike since his mother did it in 1921.' In my hometown, strikes were passionate affairs. Nobody considered it outrageous to make the life of a strikebreaker totally miserable. It was a stigma never forgotten.*

"*Women beat up women scabs. Women worked in cigar factories from the very beginning. Their pay was equal to that of the men. Oh yes, the women were very militant.*"

IN THE SUNLIT TOWN, the Depression came imperceptibly. The realization came to me when Aunt Lila said there's no food in the house. My aunt, who owned the house we lived in, would no longer charge rent. It would be shameful to charge rent with $9 a week coming in.

The grocery man would come by and take a little order, which he would bring the next day. When my mother would not order anything because she owed, he'd insist: Why are you cutting down on the beans?

There was a certain difference between the Depression in my hometown than elsewhere. They weren't dark, satanic mills. The streets were not like a city ghetto. There were poor homes, that hadn't been painted in years. But it was out in the open. You played in the sunlight. I don't remember real deprivation.

Ybor City was an island in the South. When an American got mad at any Latin, he called him a Cuban nigger. This was one of the first feelings I remember: I want to be an American. You become ashamed of the community. I was an ardent supporter of Henry Ford at the age of twelve.

The strike of 1931 revolved around readers in the factory. The workers themselves used to pay twenty-five to fifty cents a week and would hire a man to read to them during work. A cigar factory is one enormous open area, with tables at which people work. A platform would be erected, so that he'd look down at the cigar makers as he read to them some four hours a day. He would read from newspapers and magazines and a book would be read as a serial. The choice of the book was democratically decided. Some of the readers were marvelous natural actors. They wouldn't just read a book. They'd act out the scenes. Consequently, many cigar makers, who were illiterate, knew the novels of Zola and Dickens and Cervantes and Tolstoy. And the works of the anarchist Kropotkin. Among the newspapers read were *the Daily Worker* and the *Socialist Call.*

The factory owners decided to put an end to this, though it didn't cost them a penny. Everyone went on strike when they arrived one morning and found the lecture platform torn down. The strike was lost. Every strike in my hometown was always lost. The readers never came back.

The Depression began in 1930, with seasonal unemployment. Factories would close down before Christmas, after having worked very hard to fill orders throughout late summer and fall. Only the cheaper-grade cigars would be made. They cut off the more expensive type. Regalia.

My uncle was a foreman. He was ill-equipped for the job because he couldn't bear to fire anybody. He would discuss it with his wife: We have to cut off so many people. What am I going to do? My aunt would say: You can't fire him. They have twelve children. You'd hear a great deal of talk. You knew things were getting worse. No more apprentices were taken in. My sister was in the last batch.

The strike left a psychological scar on me. I was in junior high school and a member of the student patrol. I wore an arm band. During the strike, workers marched into the schools to close them down, bring the children out. The principal closed the gates, and had the student patrols guard them. If they come, what do I do? My mother was in the strike.

One member of the top strike committee was a woman. That day I stood patrol, she was taken off to jail. Her daughter was kept in the principal's office. I remember walking home from school, about a block behind her, trying to decide whether to tell her of my sympathies, to ask about her mother. I never got to say it. I used to feel bad about that. Years later, in New York, at a meeting for Loyalist Spain, I met her and told her.

Everybody gave ten percent of their pay for the Republic. It was wild. The total community was with Loyalist Spain. They used to send enormous

amounts of things. It was totally organized. The song "No pasarán" that was taken to be Spanish was really by a Tampa cigar maker.

It was an extraordinarily radical strike. The cigar makers tried to march to City Hall with red flags, singing the old Italian anarchist song "Avanti popolo," "Scarlet Banner." I thought it was Spanish because we used to sing "Avanca pueblo." You see, the bonus march made them feel the revolution was here.

It was a Latin town. Men didn't sit at home. They went to cafes, on street corners, at the Labor Temple, which they built themselves. It was very radical talk. The factory owners acted out of fright. The 1931 strike was openly radical. By then, there was a Communist Party in Ybor City. Leaflets would be distributed by people whom you knew. (Laughs.) They'd come down the street in the car (whispers) with their headlights off. And then onto each porch. Everybody knew who it was. They'd say, "Oh, *cómo está*, Manuel." (Laughs.)

During the strike, the KKK would come into the Labor Temple with guns, and break up meetings. Very frequently, they were police in hoods. Though they were called the Citizens' Committee, everybody would call them Los Cuckoo Klan. (Laughs.) The picket lines would hold hands, and the KKK would beat them and cart them off.

The strike was a ghastly one. When the factories opened, they cut off many workers. There was one really hated manager, a Spaniard. They would say, "It takes a Spaniard to be that cruel to his fellow man." He stood at the top of the stairs. He'd hum "The Scarlet Banner": "You—you can come in." Then he'd hum "The Internationale": "You—you can come in." Then he'd turn his back on the others. They weren't hired. Nobody begged him, though.

When the strike was lost, the Tampa paper published a full page, in large type: the names of all the members of the strike committee. They were indicted for conspiracy and spent a year in jail. None of them got their jobs back.

The readers' strike lasted only a couple of weeks: *La huelga de los lectores.* I just don't know how they kept up their militancy. There were, of course, many little wildcat strikes. Cigar makers were just incredible. If they were given a leaf that would crumble: "Too dry—out!" When cigar makers walked out, they didn't just walk out at the end of a day. They'd walk out on the day the tobacco had been moistened, laid out The manufacturer lost a few hundred dollars, in some cases, a thousand.

There were attempts to organize the CIO. I remember one of my older cousins going around in a very secretive manner. You'd think he was planning

the assassination of the czar. He was trying to sign people up for the CIO.
The AF of L International was very conservative and always considered as
an enemy. They never gave the strike any support. It was considered the
work of agitators.

People began to go off to New York to look for jobs. Almost all my family
were in New York by 1937. You'd take that bus far to New York. There, we
all stayed together. The only place people didn't sleep in was the kitchen. A
bed was even in the foyer. People would show up from Tampa, and you'd
put them up. We were the Puerto Rican immigrants of that time. In any
cafeteria, in the kitchen, the busboys, the dishwashers, you were bound to
find at least two from Ybor City.

Some would drift back as jobs would open up again in Tampa. Some
went on the WPA. People would put off governmental aid as long as possible. Aunt Lila and her husband were the first in our family, and the last, to
go on WPA. This was considered a terrible tragedy, because it was charity.
You did not mention it to them.

That didn't mean you didn't accept another thing. There was no payday
in any cigar factory that there wasn't a collection for anyone in trouble. If a
father died, there was a collection for the funeral. When my father went to
Havana for an operation, there was a collection. That was all right. You yourself didn't ask. Someone said: "Listen, so and so's in trouble." When Havana
cigar makers would go on strike, it was a matter of honor: you sent money to
them. It has to do with the Spanish-Cuban tradition.

Neighbors have always helped one another. The community has always
been that way. There was a solidarity. There was just something very nice. . . .

People working in the cigar industry no longer have the intellectual hori-
zons that my parents had, and my aunts and uncles. They were an extraordinarily cultivated people. It makes it very difficult for me today to read
political analysts, even those of the New Left, who talk in a derogatory way
of the "glorification" of the working class. The working class I knew was just
great.

POSTSCRIPT: *"My family thought very highly of Roosevelt, except my grandfather. As a young man, he had known José Martí, the Cuban liberator. He'd
say, 'We learned to eat stones and survived on it.' He'd say, 'Hoover was just a
mean old skinflint and Roosevelt is just another Mussolini.' But the New Deal
did become the basis of a new union drive. And people did find jobs. . . ."*

■   ■   ■   ■

Hank Oettinger

A linotype operator. Much of his spare time is devoted to writing "Letters to the Editor." "I like to throw barbs into my political opponents. I hang around bars in the Loop. I like arguments and I get into dillies. Even Birchers look toward my coming into the place. When I don't show up, they get worried: 'Where the hell ya been?'

"I go to work late in the afternoon, get through at midnight. See my friends at the taverns. Agitate. Get my sleep. I wake up, and it's nice and warm and it's light. I go down and maybe have a couple of arguments before I go to work."

I CAME FROM A very small town in northern Wisconsin. It had been ravaged by the lumber barons. It was cut-over land, a term you hear very often up there. It was a one industry town: tourist business. During the winter, there was nothing.

A lot of people who suffered from the Depression—it was new to them. It wasn't new to me. I was number ten in a family of eleven. My father, who had one leg, worked in a lumber mill for a while. Lost it, held a political job for a while, registrar of deeds. Lost it. Ninety-two percent of the people in the county were on welfare in the early years of the Depression.

We could have gone on relief, but my father refused. Foolish pride. He would not accept medical care, even. I had, oh God, a beautiful set of teeth. To have one filled was $2 at the time, I think. Oh, my gosh, my teeth just went. Eventually, I got to work and saved most of them. But the fact that he wouldn't even accept medical relief—stubborn Dutchman!

He was a great admirer of Bob La Follette. He liked the idea of Bob's fighting the railroads and being against our entering the First World War. I came from German stock, that was a factor. People up here loved old Bob. They had been so downtrodden and knew they had been misused by the lumber companies. In 1924, my mother said to my father, "You know La Follette isn't going to win the presidency. Why don't you vote for somebody who can win it?" He said, "I vote for what I believe in."

I remember seeing a hunger march to City Hall. It was a very cold, bitter day. My boss was looking out of the window with me. I didn't know what the hell it was. He says, "They ought to lock the bastards up." I thought to myself: Lock them up for what? All of a sudden, the printing business like everything else went kerplop. I was laid off in '31. I was out of work for over

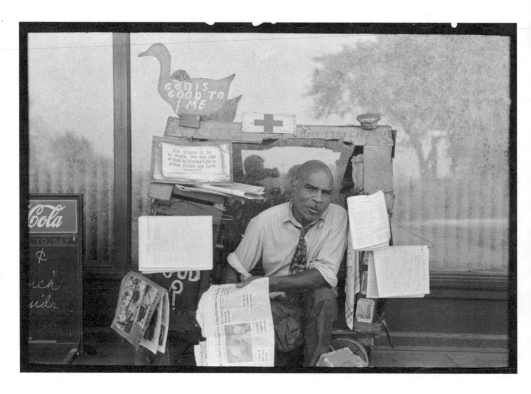

Newsstand, Memphis, Tennessee

RUSSELL LEE, 1938

two years. I'd get up at six o'clock every morning and make the rounds. I'd
go around looking for work until about eight thirty. The library would open
at nine. I'd spend maybe five hours in the library.

The feeling among people was beautiful. Supposing some guy was a
hunter. He'd go out and get ahold of some ducks or some game, they'd have
their friends over and share it.

I can remember the first week of the CWA* checks. It was on a Friday.
That night everybody had gotten his check. The first check a lot of them
had in three years. Everybody was out celebrating. It was like a festival
in some old European city. Prohibition had been repealed, of course. You'd
walk from tavern to tavern and see people buying ponies of beer and sharing it. They had the whole family out. It was a warm night as I remember.
Everybody was so happy, you'd think they got a big dividend from Xerox.

I never saw such a change of attitude. Instead of walking around feeling
dreary and looking sorrowful, everybody was joyous. Like a feast day. They
were toasting each other. They had money in their pockets for the first
time. If Roosevelt had run for president the next day, he'd have gone in by
a hundred percent.

I had it drilled in me: there are no such things as classes in America. I
awoke one day. I was, by this time, working for a newspaper in Waukesha.
They had a picture of this farm woman, standing in the window of her home
and the dust had completely covered everything, and there was a dead cow.
And here, at the bottom of the same page, they had a picture of Bernard
Baruch. He had made some big deal in the stock market and was on some-
body's yacht. I looked at one picture and then the other. No classes in
America.

I was making sixty-seven cents an hour as a linotype operator. At about
$27 a week, I was a big shot. I was rolling. And gradually got involved in the
union movement. The printers played a big role in the early days of the CIO.
This may seem unusual, a high-class craft union went along with John L.
Lewis against the old aristocracy of labor.

The union man today under forty knows absolutely nothing about
the struggles. They don't want to upset the wonderful applecart they have.
We used to sing, in the organizing days of the CIO, "Solidarity Forever." The
Communists were active in it. Hell, we'd even sing "The Internationale" on
occasion. Could I get a young printer today, who drives a big Buick, who has
a home in the suburbs—could I get him to sing "Arise, ye prisoners of starvation . . ."? It's like when I was in the civil rights marches of 1965, they'd

* Civil Works Administration. It presaged the WPA.

start chanting, "We want freedom." Here I am, a printer making $200 a week. It sounds silly as I chant, "I want freedom now." I know it's theirs I'm asking for, and, in a way, it's mine. But it does sound silly, as *I* say it.

During the Depression, the La Follette movement grew, with Bob, Junior, and Phil. When the New Deal came in, they worked with Roosevelt. By this time, my father was getting pretty old and bitter. Being an extreme strict Catholic, he fell for Coughlinism.

It was quite a deal between him and his favorite son. He even wanted to sell *Social Justice.* I hated to do it, but I had to tell him: If *Social Justice* is quartered in this home, I'm not quartered in this home.

How do you explain the switch from Bob La Follette to Father Coughlin?
Even in the Depression, he wasn't able to accept the idea that there were different classes in America. The same as I couldn't when I was a child. And he was violently anti-Red. He objected to a lot that was going on: that's why he liked La Follette. But it was still the Great America. So there had to be some other reason for all the injustice.

He had great respect for the priestly collar, for one thing. While he was for Roosevelt in the beginning, he felt he was now in the hands of the Jews. The latent anti-Semitism had always been there.

Well, the rise of Hitler comes along the same time as the rise of Roosevelt. And after all, Hitler certainly took care of the Communists in Germany. I think it was his anti-Communism more than his rigid Catholicism that was the cause.

When Father Coughlin's silver market manipulations were uncovered, my father felt it was another plot. He just couldn't bring himself to believe that Coughlin was in it for anything except to help the poor people who were at the mercy of Roosevelt and the Jews. He was about eighty-two at the time and never gave up his belief. He followed Coughlin until the end.

When Coughlin was on, Sunday afternoons, everything in the house had to be absolutely quiet, not a whisper. You could walk down the street and every single Catholic house—it was Coughlin. To hell with the ball game or going out for a ride. . . .

Every time Coughlin would mention the name of a movie actor who was of Jewish extraction, and add his real name after his stage name, my father would gloat. And yet, my father was a good and kind man, and suffered along with his neighbors.

At the same time, he didn't see any benefits in social legislation: giving people something they didn't deserve, he felt. He liked Bob La Follette because he could see with his own eyes what Bob was fighting. He was for Workmen's Compensation. Oh, my father was full of contradictions. . . .

In 1938, I threatened *The Freeman*—the Waukesha paper I was working on—to pull the boys out on strike, if they wouldn't raise our wages from ninety cents an hour to ninety-five. We finally got it up to $1 an hour. I was making forty bucks a week. I'm reading *Esquire*, seeing what kind of shoes I should buy, suits and stuff. I was really a big shot. I'd go out drinking on Saturday night, sometimes I'd spend as much as seven or eight dollars. Tavern keepers would welcome me with open arms. He's a big spender.

∎ ∎ ∎ ∎

E. D. Nixon

For twenty-five years, he had been president of the Montgomery (Alabama) branch of the Brotherhood of Sleeping Car Porters.

"A Pullman porter can always get into a conversation anywhere. He walked into a barbershop, somebody'd say, 'I didn't see you around here,' or maybe they'd notice his pants with the stripe. Everybody listened because they knowd the porter been everywhere and they never been anywhere themselves.

"In cafes where they ate or hotels where they stayed, they'd bring in papers they picked up, white papers, Negro papers. He'd put 'em in his locker and distribute 'em to black communities all over the country. Along the road, where a whole lot of people couldn't get to town, we used to roll up the papers and tie a string around 'em. We'd throw these papers off to these people. We were able to let people know what was happening. He did know a whole lot of things."

I WORKED FOR THE Pullman Company from 1928 to 1964. It was a hard job. We had a rest period: 10 P.M. to 2, for one porter, and 2 to 6, for the other. During that time, one man guarded two cars. From 6 in the morning to 10 at night, he was plenty busy with his one car: touch it up all the time, clean up, call a man at a certain time. You get that man off, you run back and tidy up the place, you run back and bring a new man in. By that time, they holler "All aboard!" you got to get that step up. You have to touch up the men's room, the ladies' room, the vestibule. You carried a mop and a broom and the Company said: just bring me the handle back.

When I first went to work, they had a cuspidor set between every section. That means you had six on each side and three in the men's room and two in the ladies' room. Seventeen, they had to shine like gold. Twelve lowers and

Pullman porter at the Union Station, Chicago, Illinois

JACK DELANO, 1943

twelve uppers and three beds in the drawing rooms. Twenty-seven, they had to be made up all the time.

Maximum sleep was four hours a night. And some trips were Chicago to Los Angeles, Chicago to Miami. Before the Brotherhoood, we had to cover 11,000 miles a month. No established time. Sometimes it took four hundred hours to make it.

Passengers wrote up complaints. Sometimes conductors wrote up complaints. Newsboys could write up complaints, just so he's white. Here a man could leave his pocketbook at home. He'd swear he had it on the train: "That nigger porter took it." A whole lot of porters were searched and humiliated, and they found the man left it at home.

I was in New Orleans one day. The supervisor came in ahead of me. I had four bags, one in each arm and one in my hand. He opened the drawing room door. I said, "Thank you." He turned around and said in a rough manner, "I didn't open 'at door for you." I said, "Thank you again."

We got $62.50 a month. We had to depend a lot on tips. Some of the passengers would get hot about something. He wouldn't give you nothing and run down and tell the other passengers not to give you anything. "Didn't shine my shoes right. . . ." "Didn't get my pillow." They said it loud for other people to hear.

The porter instructor was a Negro man. The permanent inspector was a white man. They would have a mimeographed sheet. All he had to do was put a cross opposite any rule. The porter instructor would set there and watch you and write down when you turned your back. They turned in plenty on me because I was active in the Brotherhood. They were stool pigeons. They watched me my every move. They'd turn in what I said. A lot of men were scared off. But in spite of all that, we had a few here, there—kept the Brotherhood alive.

"The Brotherhood was born after several attempts by porters who were fired for it. The Company set up a Pullman Porter Benefit Association. Controlled by the Company. Three of the men were walkin' down the street one day and heard Randolph speakin' on a soapbox.* These three porters heard him and said, 'This is the man we need.'

"They didn't have any salary to offer him. Randolph took the chance. We had a women's auxiliary. They would have fish fries and raise some money. He stuck it out for twelve long years without a salary. Never knew when he'd come back to a place, because he didn't have the money to get there."

* A. Philip Randolph, founding president of the Brotherhood of Sleeping Car Porters.

When Pullman fought the Brotherhood, almost all the Negro papers sold out to the Company. I think the *Pittsburgh Courier* was an exception. And *we* carried these papers. They'd have big red headlines lambasting Randolph. They'd point out that the Pullman Company been good to the Negro: decent jobs, opening schools for children, all that kind of stuff. Don't bite the hand that feeds you.

When I heard Randolph speak, it was like a light. Most eloquent man I ever heard. He done more to bring me in the fight for civil rights than anybody. Before that time, I figure that a Negro would be kicked around and accept whatever the white man did. I never knew the Negro had a right to enjoy freedom like everyone else. When Randolph stood there and talked that day, it made a different man out of me. From that day on, I was determined that I was gonna fight for freedom until I was able to get some of it myself. I was just stumblin' here and there. But I been very successful in stumblin' ever since that day. It was in 1928.

Shortly after, he became president of the Montgomery branch of the NAACP. His was the first private home that was bombed. In the late thirties, "I got a call about a sheriff who beat a woman to death. I got a telephone call about two o'clock in the morning from a white man: 'I don't like what happened. I can't tell you on the phone. Come see me.'

"It was pouring rain. You might think I was crazy, but I drove forty miles out there. I walked on the front porch. Knocked on the door. Would I get a shotgun blast? I hear a man's voice, 'Is that you, Nixon?' He opened the door and told me what had happened. But he wouldn't sign anything. I don't blame him. If he did, they would've done something to him.

"The grand jury met. Same man called and said, 'You ought to have her sons there. They saw it.' I got ahold of the dean at Miles College: 'Put them boys on the train. I'll get your money for you.' I met the train. I said to the clerk, 'I want these boys to testify before the grand jury.' She almost fell dead. 'The sheriff issues subpoenas,' she said. 'He's the man who done the killin'.'

"I walked into his office. A short, fat fellow with hobnailed boots, two pistols, handcuffs, bullets around his belt, blackjack in back pants pocket, shirt all open. I said, 'You Sheriff White?' He said, 'I'm Sheriff White.' I said, 'My name is E.D. Nixon. I represent the NAACP.' You oughta seen him when I said that. 'I'm here to ask you to subpoena these boys. They got a grand jury at three o'clock about the killin' of their mother.' He looked at me. He didn't know what to say.

"He pulled out a pencil. He licked it. He took him so long to trace out the boys' names. I said, 'You know the state pays eight cents a mile for travel. Both *these boys are entitled to transportation.' He said, 'It's a hundred miles from here to Birmingham!' I said, 'That's correct. And thirteen from Montgomery to where the case is, and three miles from the college to the station. So you got 116 miles.' He said, 'Yeah, that's right.'*

"He started figurin' on a piece of paper. I could see he didn't know what he was doin'. So I figured it out ahead of time. I wrote the figure and I said, 'I believe when you get through figurin' yours up, this'll tally.' He grabbed my sheet and said, 'Yeah, that's right, that's right.' He wrote a voucher. I got the money.

"Of course, he was acquitted. The woman died 'from causes unknown.' But he couldn't believe his eyes. He just couldn't believe a Negro had the courage to challenge him. I had nothing on me. If I had a pocket knife and had been arrested, that's all they needed."

I was in St. Louis when Randolph spoke that Sunday in '28. He says, "If you stick with me, the day will soon come when you'll be making $150 a month." I couldn't see a man raising my salary from $62.50. But I put a dollar in the collection anyway.

When I got home the next morning, the manager met me as I stepped off the train. "I understand you attended a meeting of the Brotherhood yesterday." A stool pigeon had told him. I said, "That's right." He said, "If you continue to go, you won't have no job." Well, I won't let nobody push me around. I said, "I *joined* the Brotherhood yesterday. I think I got enough money to carry any so-and-so to jail who messes with my job." I never had any trouble after that.

In the course of my speaking, I got into hot water quite a bit. I took care of grievances. The southern white man couldn't see why he had to abide by a contract that was agreed upon by the Company. Despite the fact that Randolph started the Brotherhood in 1925, they were not recognized as a bonafide union until 1938. During that time, a whole lot of us were gettin' fired. Any time the Company felt you'd done *anything*—if you had anything to do with the Brotherhood, they got rid of you. Or punished you. . . .

I was once called in. The supervisor wrote me up, said I was talkin' to "some woman." The woman was my wife. I said, "Mr. Maloney, that woman is Mrs. Nixon. And I'm gonna demand you respect her as Mrs. Nixon, just as you would expect me to respect Mrs. Maloney as Mrs. Maloney. And I want my statement in the record." It knocked him for a deck of tombstones.

They found me guilty of dereliction of duty. They gave me eight days on the ground. You get no pay for that time. The Chicago office of the Company said eight days. The local man made it read: eighteen days. So I said to my wife, "They're askin' for a fight and they're gonna get it."

The Brotherhood appealed it to the Relations Board.* I was found not guilty, and the Pullman Company had to pay me for all the time lost. And that my record be clear of all charges.

We had a porter named Cooley. He was extremely large and weighed close to three hundred pounds. The Company wanted to get rid of him. The superintendent got on the train at Montgomery. He weighed three hundred and some odd pounds. Cooley gave him a pillow. He stretched out on the sofa and shut the door. When he got to Atlanta, he wrote a statement saying Porter Cooley failed to shut the toilets between Montgomery and Atlanta.

He told the conductor to write up Cooley as no good. The superintendent's letter was May 31st. The conductor dated his letter June 6th. And the superintendent quoted the conductor in his letter.

At the hearing, I said he must be a fortune-teller. He could read what the conductor wrote seven days before he wrote it. I wonder if he would read my hand. I'd like to have him tell my fortune if he's that good.

What won the case, though, was weight and width. The superintendent stated that Porter Cooley didn't lock the toilet doors from Montgomery to Atlanta. There were seventeen stops between. That means the superintendent would have to get out of that drawing room and walk to the other end of the car and back thirty-four times. He'd have to pass Cooley each time. If he weighed three hundred and some odd pounds and Cooley weighed close to three hundred, together they weighed close to six hundred pounds. You know the aisle of a Pullman car, it's about thirty inches. It just wasn't wide enough. He couldn't pass him once, let alone thirty-four times. I pointed this out. We won the case.

Sure, there are fewer Pullman porters today. That's because railroads are goin' downhill. The plight is much of its own fault. No regard for passengers. What a railroad sells is service. When a man bought a ticket, it was service he bought along with transportation: cordial treatment, sanitation, ticket claims all that. They ran away a whole lot of passengers. I wanted to go to New Orleans last week. There was only one train, leaving at 11:50 at night. My God, there used to be a train out of here every three hours. . . .

* The National Labor Relations Board. An election was held in 1938, under the supervision of the federal government. "There were sealed ballots, and the Brotherhood won. We got a closed shop. Plenty folks didn't want to join the union, but they wanted the gains that the union got for them."

POSTSCRIPT: *He was a key figure in the Montgomery bus boycott. Mrs. Rosa Parks, the lady who was arrested for refusing to move to the back of the bus, was his secretary at the NAACP. It was he who issued the call to all the black preachers of the city. It was he who suggested the young pastor Martin Luther King Jr. as head of the Montgomery Improvement Association. The rest is history. . . .*

■ ■ ■ ■

Gordon Baxter

Attorney. An alumnus of Yale University and Harvard Law School, '32. "Children in eighth grade today have more knowledge of what's going on in the world than I had all during college. I was sitting there listening to William Lyon Phelps lecturing about Tennyson and Browning, the most terrible crap in the world, but I didn't have the judgment to know it was a lot of crap.

"Those times, people went through school insulated from everything except the immediate environment. Very few people doubted their ability to make a living. Success was measured by income: to get ahead fast in the business world. If people thought of going into teaching, they didn't say anything about it. They were regarded as kind of nuts.

"It was really in my last year at law school that I noticed something was going on. At the New Haven football games, I met Yale graduates, who a couple of years before were claiming it was easy on Wall Street. Now the market crashed, and they were back at school, out of jobs. The world rushed in on us suddenly. . . ."

In 1937, at the age of thirty-two, he became general counsel and vice president of a large company, employing ten thousand. It was engaged in the making of die castings, appliances and automotive parts.

THERE WAS A WAVE of sit-down strikes. Newspapers and respectable people said it was bad enough to have strikes, but it was clearly immoral as well as unlawful to seize property. In those days, strikes were broken by the importation of strikebreakers. Sitting down in a factory kept strikebreakers from getting in. It was a new technique. When suddenly the rules of the game, which the unions had always lost, were altered by the sit-downs, there was an outcry.

You hear the same kind of talk about student demonstrators today. It's all right for them to protest peacefully, but they must do it in accordance to the rules.

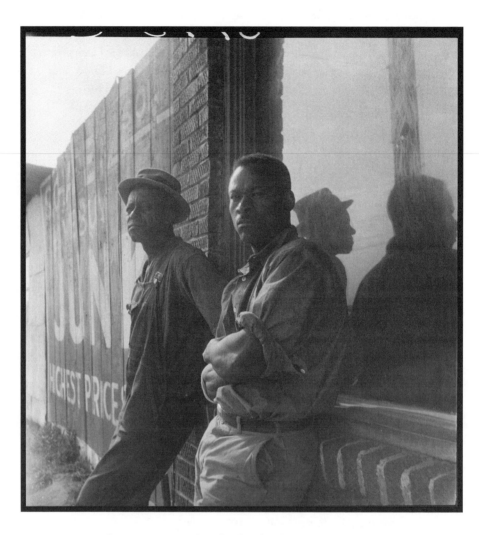

In Memphis, Tennessee, hundreds of colored laborers congregated near the bridge every morning at daylight in hopes of work chopping cotton on a plantation. They are hauled to and from work on trucks. Reduced cotton acreage has made employment scarce for this class of seasonal labor in all towns. "You can't live the commonest way on six bits a day. Not alone nor no way. A man like me can't get no foothold. It's a mighty tough old go. The people here in the morning are hungry, raggedy, but they don't make no hungry march."

DOROTHEA LANGE, 1938

There was a sit-down strike at one of our plants. We had a plant manager who dealt with these labor troubles. In his way, he was a nice guy, but his appearance was that of a cartoon factory boss: cigar in the corner of his mouth, a big square face and a big square frame. He had ways of beating the strikers that were not generally published, but known to manufacturers.

There was a police detail in Chicago known as the Industrial Squad,* in charge of a lieutenant, Make Mills. When a strike occurred, Mills would arrange to arrest the leaders. They'd beat them up, put them in jail, make it pretty clear to them to get the hell out of town. Mills got tips, $1,000, or if it was a was a serious thing, $5,000. He made a hell of a lot of dough to get the agitators, as they were called.

These were organizers, some of whom didn't work in the factory. With his plainclothesmen, Mills would get them in a saloon. They'd have free drinks, then a fight would break out.

His uniformed men would come in and arrest the organizer, beat hell out of him, put him in jail. They got a lot of people out of town. There was an awful lot of rough stuff going on.

The factory was shut down. I was drawn into it. The union had filed a complaint with the National Labor Relations Board.† The issue was union recognition. The complaint: blacklisting.

The company sent letters out in very fancy language: we will pay the best wages, we will always discuss grievances with employees, but will allow no outside intervention. Newspaper editorials were urging employees to return to work. Each day of the strike was costing them money they'd never recover.

I was handed a stack of cards to take downtown to our attorneys. Some of those I examined had notations: "Union agitator, do not rehire." Others were marked with little round dots. The employment manager told me they indicated a union sympathizer. Many of them had been or were to be fired. If any prospective employer were to ask about them, he'd be told: "Don't hire him—troublemaker, agitator." The word "Communist" wasn't used much at the time. "Red," though, was a common term.

I took the cards to Twynan, Hill and Blair. The operating head of the thing, Blair, came out of the Northwest as a successful railroad attorney. He represented many big companies and was a member of our board. A

---

* It was popularly known as "The Red Squad."
† With the passage of the Wagner Act, the National Labor Relations Board came into being. It became illegal to fire or blacklist any employee on the grounds of union activities.

tremendous bore, a funny little guy, about five feet four, small mustache. All his clients were saints, under attack. He was about seventy at the time.

When he'd get agitated, it would upset his stomach, he'd bounce up and down in his leather chair and reach for mineral water. Then he'd run out in the hall, holler for his secretary and relieve himself by dictating letters.

He had a special phrase he liked: "This presents a situation pregnant with danger." Of course, it's a great sustenance for a lawyer. If a danger is pregnant, he's got to come to the rescue. The annual retainer doesn't quite cover this. He got a hell of a lot of fees out of this operation.

Blair told me the cards were harmless. It dawned on me that he didn't know of the existence of the Wagner Act. When I told him, he said, "There cannot be any such law. And if there were, I would not hesitate to advise you it would be unconstitutional because it would be an impingement upon the freedom of contract." I said, "There is such a law. It's sometimes called the Wagner Act." He said, "I never heard of it." And I said, "It was adjudicated in the Supreme Court and its validity was upheld." He howled, "That is impossible!" He swiveled around and grabbed for his mineral water.

He called in an associate. "This young man tells me there is a law by the name of the Watson Act." "The Wagner Act." The other nodded. "There is? This young man goes further and claims the United States Supreme Court declared it constitutional." The other nodded. "That, sir, is impossible!" His associate said it was so. "It's a fine thing!" With that, Blair slapped the stack of cards on his desk, bang. "Well that's one more of these left-wing New Deal activities. Respectable citizens who built up this country can come in and testify, and their testimony won't be believed." The other said, "That's the way it would go." Blair said, "We sent the president of the company to deny these charges, and he wouldn't be believed?" I said, "Mr. Blair, one of the reasons he wouldn't be believed is because it would be a lie."

"What do you mean a lie?"

"Look at these cards. It identifies union men."

"Is something wrong with that?"

"Yes, it's prohibited."

"That has to be adjudicated."

"It was adjudicated. And all these people who were fired. It says on the face of it: Don't rehire."

"But they are *former* employees."

Well, this is the way it went. He called in a detective, who was on the company payroll and said, "Take these cards. I don't ever want to see them again. I don't want to know what happened to them, and I don't want you to ever know anything about them."

The National Labor Relations Board did find the company engaged in unfair labor practices. The union was recognized. A large sum of money was awarded in back wages to employees who were fired. There were tremendous legal fees, of course.

There was a curious aftermath. The people went back to work. But there persisted an attitude of bitterness and resentment. A continuing hostility. Each side wished the worst of the other.

During the ten years I stayed on, this feeling existed. Finally, the company sold its die-casting plant. They couldn't make any money out of it. It's a difficult business, but there are companies that do make it. I've often wondered whether the failure here wasn't due to this long, sustained bitterness. Every negotiation became a war, bitterness begetting bitterness, violence begetting violence.

Most people don't become vice presidents until their late fifties. I was one of the few college-educated men in the company. There was a lot of suspicion of me: I had to be watched. But a great many of the older men would take me out to lunch and ask me to tell them something.

This was at a time when people who went to Yale or Harvard went into brokerage, not into manufacturing. In contrast to now, the industrialists were basically men who came up from the bench. The hard way, they called it.

That had a lot to do with their tone and attitude. If anybody has the impression that a man who had come up the hard way had an easy way of looking at the working man, he's completely mistaken. His view was: I got ahead. Why can't you?

There's a parallel in this race business today. Look, my family came from the Old Country, and my grandfather sold pots and pans off his back, and I've moved out to the suburbs, and if my grandfather could do it, what the hell's the matter with these niggers?

The people who made it were very impatient with the agitators. Agitators were parasites, trying to tear down the structure. There was no law of agreed principles. It was nothing but a contest of staying power. It was a jungle.

People would regard a depression today as man-made. In the past, depressions fell in the same category as earthquakes and bad weather. An act of Providence or God. I don't think there'd be the acquiescence of the thirties. I think there'd be a rebellion. I think even in these suburbs out here you'd get a rebellion. Exactly what they'd do about it, I don't know. I think there'd be a vigorous and, ultimately violent, insistence: if not my measure, then some other measure. Something and soon.

There was some of this in the thirties, the left wing. Some were called Communists; some were Communists. They pointed up, as they called it, the contradictions: people starving, with farmers being told to kill off their pigs. There was anger and frustration with the inability to put the productive capacity to work to meet the needs of the people. There wasn't much of this talk in the thirties—these were the nuts, the fringe. They wouldn't be the fringe today. . . .

Three Strikes

Bob Stinson

THE SIT-DOWN

"Everybody has to have something they're really sold on. Some people go to church. If I'd had anything I'm really sold on, it's the UAW."

Regularly, he visits the regional headquarters of the United Automobile Workers union in Flint, Michigan. He's a small-boned man, in specs, sports shirt and a business suit.

"I started working at Fisher Body in 1917 and retired in '62, with 45 and 8/10 years service. Until 1933, no unions, no rules: you were at the mercy of your foreman. I could go to work at seven o'clock in the morning, and at seven fifteen the boss'd come around and say: you could come back at three o'clock. If he preferred somebody else over you, that person would be called back earlier, though you were there longer.

"I left the plant so many nights hostile. If I were a fella big and strong, I think I'd a picked a fight with the first fella I met on the corner. (Laughs.) It was lousy. Degraded. You might call yourself a man if you was on the street, but as soon as you went through the door and punched your card, you was nothing more or less than a robot. Do this, go there, do that. You'd do it.

"We got involved in a strike in Detroit, and we lost the strike. Went back on our knees. That's the way you learn things. I got laid off in the fall of '31. I wasn't told I was blackballed, but I was told there was no more jobs at Fisher Body for me. So I came to Flint and was hired right off the bat. I'm positive my black marks in Detroit followed me later. (Laughs.)

"We had a Black Legion in this town made up of stool pigeons and little bigoty kind of people. They got themselves in good with the management by puttin' the finger on a union organizer. On the same order as the Klan, night riders. Once in a while, a guy'd come in with a black eye. You'd say, 'What *happened?' He'd say, 'I was walking along the street and a guy come from be-hind and knocked me down.'*

"The Black Legion later developed into the Flint Alliance. It was supposed to be made up of the good solid citizens, who were terrorized by these outside agitators, who had come in here to take over the plant. They would get schoolkids to sign these cards, housewives. Every shoe salesman downtown would sign these cards. Businessmen would have everyone in the family sign these cards. They contended they had the overwhelming majority of the people of Flint.

"Most people in town was hopin' to hell the thing'd get solved. They had relatives and friends that they knew working in the plant was no bed of roses. They did accept some of this outside agitator stuff that got in the paper. I think anybody who reads this stuff day after day accepts a little bit of it. The great majority of the people was neutral.

"There was fear. You kept your mouth shut when you was in strange com-pany. Every time you put a union button on, you were told to leave the plant. You were fired so fast, it made your head spin.

"We'd meet in an old ramshackley building. No doubt, stool pigeons came. Frenchie was exposed. Somebody got up on the platform and said, 'I know this guy's a stool pigeon, 'cause I gave him information and it passed right from him to the foreman!' They trapped the guy. Nobody touched him. He just walked down the stairs."

He tells of constant betrayals by the AFL International to which they had belonged, and of the subsequent organization of the CIO, led by John L. Lewis.

THE FLINT SIT-DOWN HAPPENED Christmas Eve, 1936. I was in Detroit, playing Santa Claus to a couple of small nieces and nephews. When I came back, the second shift* had pulled the plant. It took about five minutes to shut the line down. The foreman was pretty well astonished. (Laughs.)

The boys pulled the switches and asked all the women who was in Cut-and-Sew to go home. They informed the supervisors they could stay, if they stayed in their office. They told the plant police they could do their job as long as they didn't interfere with the workers.

We had guys patrol the plant, see that nobody got involved in anything they shouldn't. If anybody got careless with company property—such as sitting on an automobile cushion without putting burlap over it—he was talked to. You couldn't paint a sign on the wall or anything like that. You used bare springs for a bed. 'Cause if you slept on a finished cushion, it was no longer a new cushion.

---

* The men who worked from 4:30 P.M. to 12:30 A.M.

Governor Murphy* said he hoped to God he would never have to use National Guard against people. But if there was damage to property, he would do so. This was right down our alley, because we invited him to the plant and see how well we were taking care of the place.†

They'd assign roles to you. When some of the guys at headquarters wanted to tell some of the guys in the plant what was cookin', I carried the message. I was a scavenger, too.

The merchants cooperated. There'd be apples, bushels of potatoes, crates of oranges that was beginnin' to spoil. Some of our members were also little farmers, they come up with a couple of baskets of junk.

The soup kitchen was outside the plant. The women handled all the cooking, outside of one chef who came from New York. He had anywhere from ten to twenty women washing dishes and peeling potatoes in the strike kitchen. Mostly stews, pretty good meals. They were put in containers and hoisted up through the window. The boys in there had their own plates and cups and saucers.

Didn't the guys want a drink now and then . . . ?
That was one of the hard ones. Even though you had strict discipline in there, anybody wanted to climb through the window, you couldn't stop him. He could leave any time he wanted. There was always some of the boys who would take a day off, go out and see how the old woman was doing. When they'd come back in, if somebody didn't search 'em, why, there'd be a pint.

The plant police would start bringin' in some women. That was damn quickly stopped.

We had 'em outnumbered. They may have been anti-union at the time, but it wasn't more than three or four years later before the plant guards' union was organized. I don't blame 'em. They were dependent on their supervisors for jobs just like we were.

Most of the men had their wives and friends come down, and they'd stand inside the window and they'd talk. Find out how the family was. If the union supplied them with enough coal. . . .

We had a ladies' auxiliary. They'd visit the homes of the guys that was in the plant. They would find out if there was any shortage of coal or food. Then they'd maneuver around amongst themselves until they found some place to get a ton of coal. Some of them even put the arm on Consumer Power if there was a possibility of having her power shut off.

---

* Frank Murphy. He subsequently became a Supreme Court justice.
† See Harry Norgard's interpretation in the sequence "Strive and Succeed," p. 405.

Any of the wives try to talk the guys into coming out?

Some of 'em would have foremen come to their homes: "Sorry, your hus-band was a very good operator. But if he don't get out of the plant and away from the union, he'll never again have a job at General Motors." If this woman was the least bit scared, she'd come down and cry on her husband's shoulder. He'd more than likely get a little disturbed, get a hold of his strike captain. . . . Maybe we'd send a couple of women out there. Sometimes you just had to let 'em go. Because if you kept them in there, they'd worry so damn much over it, that'd start ruinin' the morale of the rest of the guys.

Morale was very high at the time. It started out kinda ugly because the guys were afraid they put their foot in it and all they was gonna do is lose their jobs. But as time went on, they begin to realize they could win this darn thing, 'cause we had a lot of outside people comin' in showin' their sympathy.

Time after time, people would come driving by the plant slowly. They might pull up at the curb and roll down the window and say, "How you guys doin'?" Our guys would be lookin' out the windows, they'd be singin' songs and hollerin'. Just generally keeping themselves alive.

Sometimes a guy'd come up to you on the street and say, "How the guys doin'?" You say, "They're doin' all right." Then he'd give ya a song and dance: "I hear the boys at Chevrolet are gonna get run out tonight."* I'd say, "Hog-wash." He'd end with sayin': "Well, I wish you guys the best of luck because, God damn, when I worked there it was a mess." The guy'd turn around and walk away.

Nationally known people contributed to our strike fund. Mrs. Roosevelt for one. We even had a member of Parliament come from England and ad-dress us.

Lotta things worked for the union we hadn't even anticipated. Company tried to shut off the heat. It was a bluff. Nobody moved for half an hour, so they turned it back on again. They didn't want the pipes to get cold. (Laughs.) If the heat was allowed to drop, then the pipes will separate—they were all jointed together—and then you got a problem.

---

* Several other General Motors plants in Flint were the scenes of similar sit-downs. "At Chevrolet Four, there was a knock-down and drag-out fight. That's where the Battle of Bull Run happened. The boys took it over, and the city police and the sheriff's men decided they were gonna throw 'em out. Between the tear gas the police used and the nuts and bolts the strikers used, there was hell to pay. We run 'em off. When the tear gas got in the plant, the women's brigade smashed every damn window they could find to let the air in. It was vi-cious. (Laughs.) Hans Larson, he was shot in the Battle of Bull Run."

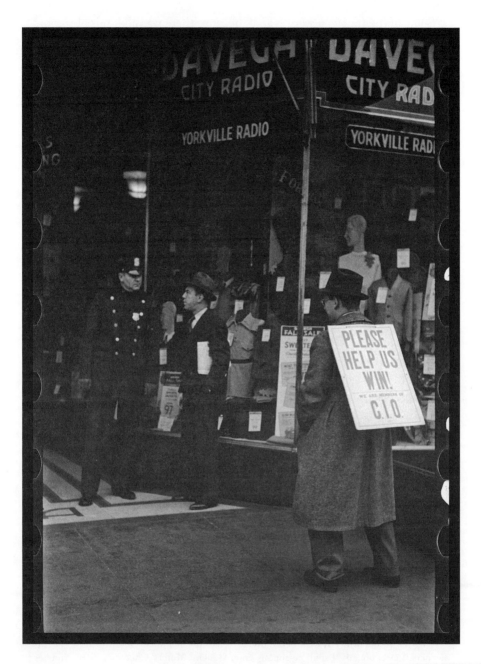

Strike pickets, New York, New York

Arthur Rothstein, 1937

Some of the time you were scared, because there was all kinds of rumors going around. We had a sheriff—he came in one night at Fisher One and read the boys the riot act. He told 'em they had to leave. He stood there, looked at 'em a few minutes. A couple of guys began to curse 'im, and he turned around and left himself.

National Guard troops were there. Some from Pontiac, some from Detroit. I lived within a block where they camped. I would pass these young fellas every day. One boy, pretty young, he had a union button on. Was it his union button or was it his dad's? I walked up to him. "Your captain allow you to wear that button?" He says, "I don't know, but I'm gonna find out." (Laughs.) They were twenty-year-olds. Well-behaved boys. No rough stuff, nothing untoward happened.

The men sat in there for forty-four days. Governor Murphy—I get emotional over him (laughs)—was trying to get both sides to meet on some common ground. I think he lost many a good night's sleep. We wouldn't use force. Mr. Knudsen was head of General Motors and, of course, there was John L. Lewis. They'd reach a temporary agreement and invariably the Flint Alliance or GM headquarters in Detroit would throw a monkey wrench in it. So every morning, Murphy got up with an unsolved problem.

John L. was as close to a Shakespearean actor as any I've ever listened to. He could get up there and damn all the adversaries—he had more command of language. He made a speech that if they shoot the boys out at the plant, they'd have to shoot him first.*

There were a half a dozen false starts at settlement. Finally, we got the word: THE THING IS SETTLED. My God, you had to send about three people, one right after the other, down to some of those plants because the guys didn't believe it. Finally, when they did get it, they marched out of the plants with the flag flyin' and all that stuff.

You'd see some guys comin' out of there with whiskers as long as Santa Claus. They made a rule they wasn't gonna shave until the strike was over. Oh, it was just like—you've gone through the Armistice delirium, haven't you? Everybody was runnin' around shaking everybody by the hand,

* When Governor Murphy was being urged to use the National Guard to oust the sit-downers, Lewis orated: "I shall personally enter General Motors' Chevrolet Plant Number Four. I shall order the men to disregard your order, to stand fast. I shall then walk up to the largest window in the plant, open it, divest myself of my outer raiment, remove my shirt and bare my bosom. Then, when you order your troops to fire, mine will be the first breast that those bullets will strike. And, as my body falls from the window to the ground, you will listen to the voice of your grandfather as he whispers in your ear, 'Frank, are you sure you are doing the right thing?'"

sayin', "Jesus, you look strange, you got a beard on you now." (Laughs.) Women kissin' their husbands. There was a lotta drunks on the streets that night.

When Mr. Knudsen put his name to a piece of paper and says that General Motors recognizes the UAW–CIO—until that moment, we were non-people, we didn't even exist. (Laughs.) That was the big one. (His eyes are moist.)

■ ■ ■ ■

Mike Widman

THE BATTLE OF DETROIT

A Preface

Justin McCarthy quit college in 1933. He was working at a Ford assembly plant in an industrial suburb, near Chicago.

"*I sandpapered all the right-hand fenders. I was paid $5 a day. The parts were brought in from the River Rouge plant in Detroit. When I went to work in January, we were turning out 232 cars a day. When I was fired, four months later, we were turning out 535. Without any extra help and no increase in pay. It was the famous Ford speed-up.*

"*The gates were locked when you came in at eight o'clock in the morning. They weren't opened again until five o'clock in the evening. People brought their own lunch. No commissary wagons were permitted on the grounds. Nobody bothered to tell me. So I didn't eat that first day. You were supposed to buy your own gloves. Nobody bothered to tell me that, either. Imagine my hands at five o'clock that first day.*

"*I was aware of men in plain clothes being around the plant, and the constant surveillance. I didn't learn till later these were the men of Ford's service department. Many of them, ex-cons.*

"*If you wanted to go to the toilet, you had to have permission of the foreman. He had to find a substitute for you on the assembly line, who could sandpaper those two right fenders as they went by. If he couldn't right away, you held it. (Laughs.)*

"*If you didn't punch that clock at 8:00, if you came in at 8:02, you were docked one hour's pay. There wasn't any excuse. If you did this two or three times, you got fired.*

Street corner, South Second Street, Camden, New Jersey

Arthur Rothstein, 1938

"I made the mistake of telling the foreman I had enrolled at Northwestern University night school. He said, 'Mr. Ford isn't paying people to go to college. You're through.'"

A longtime associate of John L. Lewis, Mike Widman was appointed director of the campaign to organize the Ford Motor Company, the automobile industry's last holdout against the UAWU.

WE STARTED OUT ON the sixteenth day of October, 1940. The three plants in Detroit, Hamtramck and Dearborn had about a hundred thousand men. We immediately zoned the town and located the Ford workers. The milkmen helped. There were about seven hundred of them, members of the CIO. They told us who their Ford worker customers were. But we had to shake the bushes to get them. There was great fear in the hearts of these men.

This was three years after Reuther and Frankensteen were beaten up by the service department.* This department was made up of men who served time in prison. They could be paroled to someone who ensured them employment. Ford readily gave them jobs. It made him a fine espionage system. Bennett built it.†

As fast as the men signed application blanks, they were fired. We couldn't figure how the company found out so fast. So we tightened our security. I kept the cards in my safe until it got too small for all the cards coming in. There were hundreds of John Doe applications. They were just scared to death.

They'd come into our office when it first opened, they'd walk three, four times around the vestibule, look in all directions. Finally, they'd jump in the door and ask you to take them in the back room.

The life of a Ford worker was quite miserable. These service men were everywhere. The way they'd throw men out . . . today, anybody that wore a blue shirt got laid off. Tomorrow, if you had brown hair, black hair, anything. No recourse.

If they caught some of our people on the street, they slapped 'em around. When some of our boys first wore union buttons or UAW baseball caps, they were given the works. Some of our boys got fed up, and next thing a

* Shortly after GM had signed with the UAWU, Walter Reuther and Dick Frankensteen were assaulted at the overpass, near Detroit's River Rouge plant, while in the act of passing out union handbills. The La Follette Civil Liberties Committee confirmed the charge that the assailants were members of Ford's service department.
† Harry Bennett, chief of the service department.

couple of service men were slightly hurt. That ended their parading in public. But this was later. . . .

Within sixty days after the campaign started, we challenged Ford, through Bennett, to have an election. Bennett refused to meet any "outsider," but he agreed to meet with employees on grievances. Bennett and I exchanged blasts through Jim Dewey, the federal conciliator, who acted as go-between. We blasted each other in newspapers. The more stories got in, the more cards we signed. It was $1 initiation fee and $1 dues. In February, we took in $88,000 plus.

The first meeting I addressed, some thirty days after my arrival, had a grand total of twenty-three in the audience. Now we were having meetings of more than thirty thousand at the fairgrounds. We had broken down this fear.

We had forty organizers on the outside. Those were the men Ford had fired, so we put 'em on the staff. But the real secret of our success were the ones Ford paid for himself—the six thousand volunteers inside the plant.

We bought an old abandoned school building. This was lined up as cur soup kitchen. We didn't want any strike, but we knew sooner or later, Ford would force us into one. We were prepared just in case. . . .

On April 1, it happened. The five men on our grievance committee had permission from the foreman to leave their job and see the division superintendent. He said, "Talk to the employment office." At the employment office, they were told, "You left your jobs. You're fired."

We asked the company, through the conciliator, to arbitrate this matter. The answer was: They're fired, and we don't care what you do. The word spread in the plant like wildfire. . . .

We called the strike for 12:15, just after midnight. The boys on the day shift stayed in the plant until four o'clock. Now both shifts were inside. We were still trying to get the five men reinstated. Again the company refused. So we let the midnight shift come in. Ford had about eighty-nine thousand workers in that plant all at the same time. What everybody said was impossible was about to happen.

We had organized a band.* The boys came marching out to the sound of music. We had surveyed the fourteen highways that led into the plant. It would take at least two thousand cars on each of 'em as a picket line to tie

* Efforts were made from the beginning by the UAWU to interest the young workers. Bowling leagues, baseball teams and bands were organized. "We hoped for about eight teams, we ended up with ninety." There were five hundred applicants for the eighty-piece band. Uniforms, caps and shirts with UAWU insignia were issued.

things up. One of the boys got the idea: We'll pull the trolley pole off the first streetcar coming in from Detroit. So we had the streetcars clear downtown for about six miles all stopped. The boys stacked up rubbish and cars and anything they could find. Everything was tied up.

Word came from the governor. He wanted the highways opened up. We agreed, if Ford would keep the plant shut down while mediation was going on. At the insistence of the governor, Ford agreed. We had fourteen picket lines, and I made fourteen speeches that morning. I explained what was happening. We opened up the highways and set up skeleton picket lines.

All the workers were out, except about five thousand Negroes. Ford was lenient in hiring Negroes at that time.* This was their first chance to work in the industry, and they were fearful of losing their jobs. They weren't really scabbing. It was just fear. They weren't doing any work. They were sitting there making all kinds of homemade weapons, short pieces of iron and rubber pipe. They were afraid somebody was gonna come in and get 'em. But we weren't trying to get them out Ford was keeping them in there twenty-four hours a day. They never went home. Keeping them around the clock for five or six days was costing him a pretty penny.

Bennett went to the conciliator and said, "We want those fellows out of the plant." I called my pickets over to the east side. Dewey, the conciliator, had arranged with Bennett to get the Negroes on city buses, on the west side of the plant. So that's how it worked. There was no trouble.

Then comes the A F of L sticking their nose in, at Ford's insistence. I happened to meet their director, a teamster from Boston. I said, "Where the hell are you goin'?" He said, "I'm goin' to compete with you." I said, "You're too damn late. I've got the barn door locked." He said, "I've been ordered to do it."

Do you think Ford made a deal with the A F of L to keep the CIO out?
Exactly. They had never touched this place before. They weren't interested. They opened up six offices: one for white workers, who numbered more than seventy thousand; and five in Negro areas with less than ten thousand workers. With one purpose: If they couldn't win, they'd create a race riot or damage the CIO. Among our militants were many southern white workers, who were incensed. But they were disciplined.

The strike continued until the eleventh of April. It lasted about nine or ten days. When the company consented to the election, the boys all went

* "I think be brought them in to show a philanthropic attitude. He also brought in a lot of deaf and dumb people and other handicapped. I signed up a good number of them. We had somebody who could talk on his fingers to them."

back, without discrimination. But Ford wouldn't put those five men back. Rather than delay the return of the workers, I put 'em on my staff.

On May 21, 1941, we had the election. It took that long to get things straightened out. We carried seventy-two percent of the vote. We were certified. So negotiations started. They went on for about thirty days.

Ford, through Bennett and Capizzi, his lawyer, agreed to just about everything we asked for. He'd match what the rival companies were paying, and more. He was out to top them. He suspected—in his wild imagination—that they had put us up to this strike. (Laughs.)

I was dumbfounded when Capizzi said, "Mr. Ford doesn't want any dues collection in the plant. Would you accept the check-off?" We said, "That could be arranged." (Laughs.) He asked if we'd take in, without recrimination, the twenty percent who voted against us. We said, of course. They'll all be treated alike. He asked, "Do you have a union label you could put on the cars?" We offered to get one designed. For a while we put 'em on, but didn't keep it up.

Bennett surprised me by going completely overboard. He gave workers the right to vote on who they wanted as their foreman. (Laughs.) When I found this out, I hit the roof. "What the hell are you doing?" He said, "Your boys are gonna work for the foreman they like and won't work for the one they won't like." This was his reasoning. I said, "Do you think we'd let you appoint our committeemen? Appoint your own damn foremen." There'd be no stability. If the foreman says, "Hey, you're not performing your end of the work," the guy could say, "We'll vote you out at noon."

My union experience taught me that the direction of the working force is vested in management. The union shall not abridge the right, so long as there is no discrimination or unfairness. Ford was abridging his own right.

How do you explain this 180-degree turn in the attitude of Ford and Bennett?
I think Bennett was a realist. He saw he couldn't fight us any more. He told me: "I want to see this thing work out, and Mr. Ford wants me to make it work." I've a hunch Ford put him on trial: make this work or get out. And that was the end of the Ford service department.

It was a little tough for some of the fellows to accept at first. They were suspicious. There was a rash of wildcat strikes. I think it came out of this newborn freedom. Each little thing, they'd pull the pin in that department until the grievance was settled. I got a call. Bennett offered to send over a chauffeured car for me. That's all I needed was a car with a chauffeur, provided by the Ford Motor Company. (Laughs.) For a while, I handled each of the grievances.

From a very tough anti-union position, the company now tries to get along. In the old days, every time we saw a Ford go by, we'd say, "There's another tin lizzie." After the strike, we said, "Doggone, isn't that a nice little buggie?"

■   ■   ■   ■

Dr. Lewis Andreas

MEMORIAL DAY, 1937

In 1932, he was a founding member of Chicago's first medical center: group practice and low fees. Sympathetic to labor, he found himself involved. . . .

THE WAGNER ACT HAD become the law—the right of labor to picket, to organize. Professionals, social workers, theological students—all kinds of people got into the thing. Some of the workers didn't like this. They must have wondered what we were doing there. But they didn't mind me, because I was a doctor and trouble was brewing.

A few days before Memorial Day, 1937, some steel workers picketed Republic Steel on the Far South Side. I received a call: "We've got a very nasty situation here. There're probably going to be some injuries. There's not a hospital for miles around, not even a drugstore. Would you come and get a few first aid stations started?"

There was a tavern called Sam's Place. I took a few supplies and got a first aid station started. The men who picketed that day got clobbered. There were a few split skulls and a few fractures. Everybody got mad and then decided to try it again on Memorial Day.*

It was a holiday, so we had them from Indian Harbor and Gary and all kinds of places. Some were looking for trouble, but for many it was simply a family picnic sort of thing: little kids, people dressed up in their Sunday shirts. Many came just for the fun of it; they weren't expecting anything.

The police were standing in line in front of Republic Steel, quite a distance from the others. It was a hell of a hot day, about ninety. They had their winter uniforms on. The sun was strong, and all I could see were their stars glittering.

The people began wandering out. A long line. This was a mixed bunch. Some of them may have been planning to use the sticks they were holding

---

* The circumstances of the Republic Steel Massacre were re-created by Meyer Levin in *Citizens*, a novel in which Dr. Andreas is the principal character.

the signs on for other purposes, for clobbering somebody. Nobody was armed. But the police got the idea these people were armed. At least, they were told so by Captain Mooney and Lieutenant Kilroy, who were managing this thing. Mayor Kelly was out of town.

I stayed behind. All of a sudden, I heard some popping going on and a blue haze began rising. I said: My God, tear gas. What do you do for that? I couldn't remember what the medical books said. I ran back to Sam's Place. About three minutes later, they started bringing in the wounded, shot. There were about fifty shot. Ten of them died. One little boy was shot in the heel. I took care of him. One woman was shot in the arm. They were lying there, bleeding bullet wounds in the belly, in the leg and all over. All sorts of fractures, lacerations. . . . I had absolutely no preparation at all for this. I was there alone, except for one guy sent by the party. He tried to take over.

The Communists didn't like the idea. I seemed to be doing what they wanted to be doing. I had no sympathy with them, I couldn't get along with them. I couldn't tolerate their dogmatism, their lack of tolerance and, worst of all, their lack of humor. They were so grim. I couldn't understand this blind business of apologizing for everything—for all the Russian business. That I couldn't swallow.

We all wanted a better society, but I didn't want to deal with these boys, and they kind of resented my intrusion into their business. One of them helped me a little bit, but I was practically alone.

I jumped on a chair and said: Get all the gun shots out of here right away to the nearest hospital. I can't handle them. Some of them had been taken to Bridewell and to other hospitals by the police.

Were many shot in the back?
I made charts of these gun shots. A great majority of them were shot from behind. Mel Coughlin, the assistant state's attorney, asked me, "Can you define the back?" In the courtroom, I just got up and turned around and said, "What you're looking at now—that's the back."

What happened was this: There were a few rocks thrown at the police when the shooting started. Or even before. They all turned and ran. I said in my testimony before the La Follette Committee: like the shutters of a venetian blind. As they were running, the police shot into them.

The police weren't all bad. Some of them quit the force because of the incident. They couldn't stand what happened. I know this as a fact because some of the guys came up here as patients and told me.

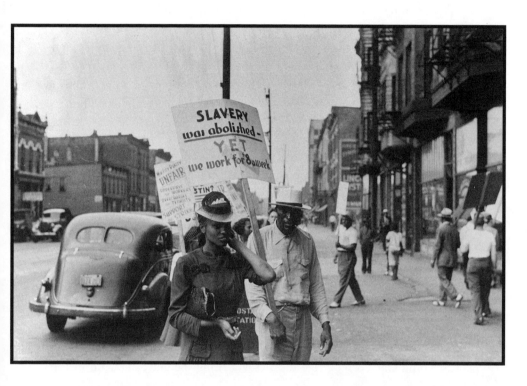

Picket line at Mid-City Realty Company, South Chicago, Illinois

JOHN VACHON, 1941

There was a break in the trial at the Criminal Court. I had been testifying. I went out for a smoke. There were about sixty cops in the corridor, and I was nervous. Some big guy comes up to me and I thought: Oh-oh, here it comes. I prepare myself for the blow. He came up very close and said, "Every day I get a pain up here in my stomach. What do you think it is, Doc?" (Laughs.) I wasn't hostile to all these guys. They committed a brutal act. They were told to do this thing. They were told these people were armed. They were scared, they were trembling and they were shooting, at whom they didn't know.

Mayor Kelly tried to get me, when he heard about this. I had an excited call from Wesley Hospital: There are people going all over your records. What's the matter? I said, "They're trying to find out how many abortions I did during the last few years." I wasn't scared. A friend of Kelly's told him to lay off, he'd be disappointed. I had a pretty clean record. He quit.

The misrepresentation in the newspapers was so great. There was a picture in the back page of the *Tribune,* for instance: a little old guy lying on the prairie in his white shirt, blood streaming down his face and Lieutenant Kilroy beating the hell out of him with his club. The caption said: "Striker Beats Up Police at Republic Steel Riot." A few of us said this will be called a historical fact some day unless we do something about it. So we decided to have a mass meeting at the Civic Opera House.

Paul Douglas was the chairman. Robert Morss Lovett* and Carl Sandburg and A. Philip Randolph came. I described the wounds and an organ was playing and almost everyone in the place was crying. Lovett got up and said, "Captain Mooney is a killer." Carl Sandburg got mesmerized by A. Philip Randolph and started chanting the words: "The Brotherhood of Sleeping Car Porters." He didn't say a thing; he got caught up in the rhythm.†

It's the tableau I remember: people walking out on the prairie and the police shooting them down.

He recounts the struggles of his group; editorials in the AMA journal labeling them subversive, un-American; the denial of hospital facilities. "All through

* A professor at the University of Chicago. He was an outspoken dissenter on many issues of the day.
† I sat in the gallery that evening. During Sandburg's incantation, in which he seemed to be improvising a poem, a few of my neighbors, among whom were steel workers, became impatient: "Get goin', get goin', for Chrissake!" They were shushed by others, in shocked stage whispers: "That's Carl Sandburg. Quiet, please!" Came the response, low and hurt: "I don't give a fuck who it is, he's holdin' up the works."

the thirties, it was difficult. We had no way of calling peoples' attention to our work, because we were opposed to advertising as much as the AMA."

In medicine, people were having a hell of a hard time. Doctors themselves were pressed, particularly the younger ones. Doctors coming out now are almost sure to find a place. The kids coming up in medicine now have absolutely no conception. You talk Depression to these boys, nonsense. They're met on all sides with delightful offers. Their biggest job is to find which piece of French pastry to choose.

In the bad days of the Depression, there was really almost nothing. Competition with the older generation was terrific. One found oneself with a lot of training, knowledge, skills, ready to spring forth on the world—no customers. They weren't going to doctors because they couldn't afford it.

The poor got some care, could go to free dispensaries. The rich got good care because they could afford it. There was this big middle class that was not getting any care. The middle class got very much in the position of the poor people. . . .

The poor people would not hesitate to go to free clinics, there was no loss of self-respect for them. They were used to this business. But the middle class couldn't drag itself to that point.

People fairly well off suddenly found themselves without funds. Insull-destroyed teachers, they were in a heck of a fix. A lot of teachers had been actively assaulted by the Insull sales force and lost all their savings. Particularly older teachers who were soon to retire. We had many teachers among our patients.

They couldn't afford to get medical care, and they couldn't bring themselves to sitting in a dispensary. They put off care until things got real bad. They probably lost their lives.

The spirit of the free hospital and the spirit of the free clinic was the spirit of the alms house. I was working at the Northwestern dispensary in '30, '31. We noticed a lady coming to us rather frequently. She'd come in a Cadillac, park three blocks away and walk over. She belonged to a class I used to call the well-dressed destitute. She had the clothes, she had the Cadillac, but she didn't have any money. She'd come over and get her care for nothing. If she had come up in the Cadillac, and the social worker saw her, she would have been excluded. People of that status would find it very difficult to accept charity.

"These simple things we stood for—group medicine and prepayment—have been achieved. I read some of the arguments for Medicare. They were almost

verbatim the arguments we used thirty years ago, the same damn thing. With an innocent air of discovery they're just finding out about this stuff. This has been the habit of the AMA. They sing the praises today of what they condemned yesterday."

All of a sudden, I find myself taking care of an ex-president of a university. And there was a widow of the curator of an art museum, well dressed, white hair, genteel. We were surprised. The kind of people we expected to find were the dispensary-goers. . . . It was a mixture of people, with one common denominator: difficulty in paying their medical bills.

And people starved on the street and on streetcars. I knew a resident at People's Hospital. Every day, he told me, somebody would faint on a streetcar. They'd bring him in, and they wouldn't ask any questions. They'd look the patient over briefly. The picture was familiar, they knew what it was. Hunger. When he regained consciousness, they'd give him something to eat. People were flopping on the streets from hunger.

They would just sit there. This was a kind of incoherent, senseless structure we were facing. Some of us figured it was collapsing. We decided we were gonna reconstruct the thing. This was sort of unique medical care in the new society. We were kidding around, really. Chewing the rag.

But there *was* a feeling of creativeness. We belonged to a thing called New America. Our outlook was socialism. The leadership was mostly from the Union Theological Seminary. It was up to us to create a substitute for the society that was disappearing. (Laughs.) We were arrogant, perhaps, but this was the feeling. Splendid ideas about what we could accomplish.

There was a feeling of perplexity. Unless something like the New Deal happened, people might have become violent. I remember an ominous march down Michigan Avenue one day. It was about '34. A very silent, scraggly march of the unemployed. Nobody said anything. Just a mass of people flowing down that street. In their minds, I think a point was reached: We're not gonna take it any more. I remember it particularly because of the silence. No waving of banners, no enthusiasm. An undercurrent of desperation.

It was the hopeful voice of F.D.R. that got this thing out of the swamps. He didn't have much to offer, but it was enough. He was a guy flexible enough to understand the need for experiments, for not being rigid and for making people feel there was somebody who gave a damn about them.

In the late thirties, I'd say our society was saved again. By Hitler. Because the stopgap wasn't working, and things were sliding back. The war, in a sense, ended the Depression. It's like an incurable disease in which there is a remission. Like Hodgkin's disease. Everybody is happy, the gland gets smaller. And then the guy dies. The war stopped the second slide, which might have gone as far as violent upheaval. You see, people now undergo improvement with leukemia. They feel good, but they all die.

But there is something important about this treatment, about stopgaps: the hope that if the patient keeps on living, somebody will come up with something new. We saw this with pernicious anemia. A doctor friend had it. We kept him going for months and months with transfusions. His daughter said: Why do you guys keep this poor man living and suffering? I said: Because there's always a chance somebody will come up with something. This man died. But three months later, Murphy and Minot came out with Vitamin B_{12}. If this fellow had been kept alive with transfusions, he would probably be alive today. I'm in favor of stopgaps for a man or for a society.

Those were terrible days, remarkable days. We had achieved goals. We wanted to promote the interests of labor. Outsiders like myself and Bob Lovett and the rest felt their interests were along with ours. The Social Security laws, Unemployment Compensation, all that was connected with the labor movement. Some of these goals—largely achieved. Today, I think, it is much more terrible. This terrible sense of wondering how we're going to get out of things. Then, we got out. And we felt good.

My habit of life has been changed by the Depression. I'm sitting here in this office . . . these wounds are permanent. My father was a doctor, and his life's savings were in one piece of property. It was foreclosed on him by the University of Chicago, and he lost every cent he had. They simply took it away because they had the legal right to take it away. And he taught at Rush Medical College* for twelve years for nothing. (Laughs.) So there was no help from Papa any more. I had planned research work, but the Depression got me into this—I don't have too many regrets. I would have been a nice rich guy probably, with a practice . . . I would have been one of many other fellows. As it is, I'm myself, unique, as they say. (Smiles.) I have no regrets. . . .

* An adjunct of the University of Chicago at the time.

Book Two

High Life

Life is just a bowl of cherries,
Don't make it serious,
Life's too mysterious.
You work, you save, you worry so,
But you can't take your dough when you go—go—go,
So keep repeating it's the berries.
The strongest oak must fall.
The sweet things in life,
To you were just loaned,
So how can you lose what you've never owned.
Life is just a bowl of cherries,
    So live and laugh at it all.

—WORDS BY LEW BROWN, MUSIC BY RAY HENDERSON*

Sally Rand

A dancer.

"I was twenty-six in 1930. A good age to start savoring things. I was born in the last naïve moment America was ever to enjoy . . . between the Spanish-American War and the First World War. Things were S.S.&G.—Sweet, Simple and Girlish."

Hers was a rural Missouri childhood and a Kansas City adolescence. When she arrived at the age to be giggly, her father, a West Point graduate, said, "the giggly girl causes grief." She was raised according to the old homilies: Virtue triumphant, Honesty prevailing. . . . "It poorly prepared us, who grew up in this innocent way, for the thirties.

"Suddenly, all the copybook maxims were turned backwards. How could it be that a man who had been at his job thirty years couldn't have a job? How could it be that a business that had been in business for a lifetime suddenly isn't any more? Friends of mine who had been to Harvard, Yale and Princeton jumped out of windows. With accuracy. The idea of the stock market quittin' was unbelievable. Only naïveté permitted us to believe this could go on forever. . . .

"For those who lived with little money, it didn't make much of a difference. I never saw money until I was nine or ten years old. On $100 a month, my father supported us. We were clothed, sheltered, well fed. There was always enough of everything—except love."

When she was six, she saw Pavlova dance. "I sat up and wept uncontrollably. At that moment, there was born this true knowledge: I was going to be a dancer, a ballerina." She traveled with Adolph Bolm's ballet company throughout the Midwest, "bringing culture to the masses." (Laughs.)

In Hollywood, she worked as a Mack Sennett girl and was under contract to Cecil B. DeMille. "I followed him every waking minute. I was at story conferences, I saw every rush, I was a little ghost. When he went to the men's room, I waited outside." Her stage name had been Billie Bett. "DeMille took Rand off of a Rand McNally map."

A close friendship developed with Mary Pickford. "Later when Doug Fairbanks achieved a more sophisticated marriage with Lady Ashley, Mary turned to religious contemplation. She wrote a book, Why Not Try God? Subsequently, she married Buddy Rogers."

Sally Rand traveled the Orpheum circuit with her company, Sally and Her Boys. The impact of the Depression caused canceled bookings. Her wealthy friends went broke.

THESE BEAUTIFUL YACHTS THAT cost a half million dollars were sitting around with barnacles on them. These are the people who had jumped out of windows. Who's gonna buy a yacht? A man came up to me and said, "Hey, any of these yachts for sale?" I said, "Are you kiddin'? They're all for sale." This guy was a bootlegger. So I sold half-million-dollar yachts to bootleggers. For five or ten thousand dollars. And took my six percent commission on them. Beautiful.

They used to have their own fast boats, to go beyond the three-mile limit, or eight-mile limit or whatever it was, to pick up their booze. By now, all the federal agents knew their boats. So they took these yachts and decorated them with pretty girls in bathing suits, like going out for a little sail. Load up and come back.

The interiors of those boats were done in rosewood, gold handles on the toilets and all that jazz, great oil painting in the salons. They're now jammed up with loads and loads of wet alcohol. The interiors of them were gutted and ruined.

Every hotel in the Loop was in 77-B. This was being in bankruptcy to Uncle Sam—legitimately. I couldn't pay my bill. I didn't have any food or whiskey or anything. I went to the management and said, "I never ran out on a hotel bill in my life. I don't have a job, but I'll get one. Meanwhile, I can't pay what I owe you." They said, "Don't worry. Nobody's in the hotel anyway."

One of the boys in the show, Tony, said, "Don't worry. All my uncles are stagehands and the rest of 'em are bootleggers. Pick out a nightclub you want to work, we'll work." I looked at these freaks, with these little postage-stamp stages. . . .

Up to this time, the most sexy thing I'd ever done is Scheherazade in the ballet. I thought a girl who went on the stage without stockings was a hussy. (Laughs.) I got a job, $75 a week, only because Tony's uncles were delivering alky to Frankie, the owner.

Now I've got to find a number to do. I can't do a toe dance there. I went down to Maybelle Shearer's costume shop. She had a lot of old fans laying on the counter. I'd been wanting to do "White Birds Fly in the Moonlight" for a long time. I used to see these white herons come down on my grandfather's farm. I'm harking back to Pavlova and her bird dance, "The Swan." As a youngster, I tied wings on my shoulders. I'm glad I had the good taste even then to know this wasn't it. Then I saw pictures of Isadora Duncan. I may have been a fine dancer, but I wasn't ready to create. So, necessity being the mother of invention . . .

I picked up a pair of these feathered fans that prima donnas used to hit the high note with. Any time any female puts a fan in her hand, she instantly becomes a *femme fatale*. A coquette. I've seen this happen down in the Ozarks at Baptist revival meetings. The lady in a poke bonnet and calico picks up a palmy fan and instantly becomes the Queen of Sheba. So I picked up the fan and looked in the mirror. I immediately tried my inscrutable smile and the whole thing. Suddenly I saw the fans did exactly what I wanted.

I ordered a beautiful pair from New York. The fans came C.O.D. and I couldn't spring them, having no money whatsoever. Ollie, a girl I knew, who was running a floating crap game, said, "Don't worry about a thing. Petey's

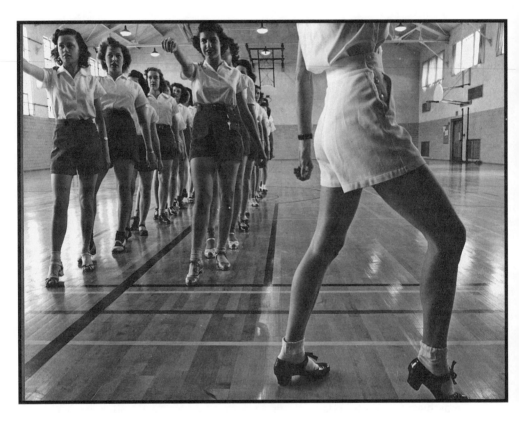

Tap dancing class in the gymnasium at
Iowa State College, Ames, Iowa

JACK DELANO, 1942

coming in from Canada with a load. He'll be loaded." When Petey came
back, the rear end of his Buick looked like a sieve. He'd been hijacked and
no money to spring the fans. But he hocked his rings, and they sprung the
fans for me.

I went to the club for my opening, but Frankie didn't remember me: "Who
the hell are you?" So I called Tony: "He won't let me open." So Tony, Petey
and another boy came into Frankie: "It'd be a terrible thing if this place got a
stink in it." Frankie was horrified: "Wha-wha-wha-what?" So I rehearsed the
whorehouse piano player, and Tony went over and clouted two of the Chez
Paree's* best blue spotlights. So there I stood. . . . I intended to take my chif-
fon nightgown and make a classic little Grecian tunic out of it à la Isadora
Duncan. I was saving that nightgown for an occasion, but it hadn't come yet.
I didn't have a chance to get back to the hotel. . . . I was announced!

So I stood on the threshold of decision, in a pair of slippers and a pair of
fans, period. Either I went on or Frankie would have every excuse to fire me.
So I rationalized, I said, "All righty, who's gonna know what's behind these
fans anyway?" And they didn't. That night I proved the Rand is quicker than
the eye.

No one was vaguely interested. They were waiting for the table singers.
These were the folk who went around with a little push-around piano and
sang sad songs while customers cried in their beer. It was weeks before
anybody discovered I wasn't wearing anything. It was economically sound,
because I didn't have any money to buy anything.

It's now the spring of '33. I'd met Charlie Weber, who was county commissioner for forty years. Charlie had the beer concession at the Streets of
Paris.†

Meanwhile, they had the Beaux Arts Ball at the Congress Hotel. There
were bread lines, and people were starving. Yet women in Chicago had the
bad taste to have themselves photographed in gowns they were going to wear
at the ball. One was made of thousand-dollar bills. People went to Paris o
get these gowns that cost thousands of dollars, wearing jewels, while people
are starving in the streets, and people are marching in Washington and being
shot at. It was such bad taste.

A friend was doing press work for me. We were socially conscious. She
said, "Why don't you have your picture taken in the costume *you're* going to
wear at the Beaux Arts Ball?" I didn't have a costume. She said, "How about
Lady Godiva?" She sent out a blurb to all the papers.

* For many years one of Chicago's leading nightclubs.
† One of the features of A Century of Progress (Chicago's world's fair), 1933 and 1934.

We had to hire a horse. So I had a picture taken as Lady Godiva. It was like saying: How dare you have a dress of thousand-dollar bills when people are hungry? The girl sponsoring the ball was a little upset because of all the publicity my pictures got. So I went to the Congress, and they wouldn't let the horse in because he didn't have rubbers on his shoes. They put me and the horse on a table, and all the guys carried us in: Lady Godiva's riding into the ballroom floor on a white tabletop. The Hearst papers came out the next day with the whole double column, front page. All righty.

Now I'm harassing Charlie Weber for that job at the world's fair, and he's not coming up with it. Because the Streets of Paris was sponsored by the high and mighty of this town, the social set. It was all French entertainment. Mr. Weber just didn't swing it big enough to get a job for me there. He suggested I crash the preview, the night before it opens. Mrs. Hearst was giving one of her famous Milk Fund dinners: "You'll get your foot in the door. . . ."

I hired the horse again, but the gates of the fair were closed. No wheeled vehicle could come in until the next day when Mrs. Roosevelt would be there and the ribbon, cut. I took the horse out of the truck: "O.K., no wheeled vehicle, it's a horse." But no animals were allowed. O.K. Back into the trailer, we go up to the Wrigley docks. The Streets of Paris had a yacht landing there. The clientele is so posh, huh.

So I paid $8 for the tickets to the boat. He said, "Who's going with you?" I said, "Just a friend." So I brought the horse on the boat, and the man demurred. I said, "What do you care if it's a horse or a human?" At the yacht landing of the Streets of Paris, there was a little Frenchman who spoke no English. He figured that a broad that arrives in a boat with a horse is *supposed* to be there. So he opened the gate. The master of ceremonies, poor soul, figured: God, here's a woman with a horse and nobody told me about it.

Up to this time, the party'd been pretty dull. They had two bands. It kind of takes people's appetite away at a hundred dollars a plate. The fanfare sounded and the MC announced: Now, Lady Godiva will take her famous ride. Music played. Every photographer in the business, especially the Hearst ones, were there. Flashlights went off and the music played, and everybody was happy. They said: do it again. So I did it again. I had to get back to the show at the club.*

---

* The Paramount Club. "Mildred Harris Chaplin was playing there with me. She said one night, 'I want you to meet a sweet and lovely man.' In the ladies' room, a girl said, 'You're certainly in high society tonight Machine Gun Jack McGurn.' I left my coat and ran back to the hotel and locked myself in. Wow!"

The next day I went down to the Streets of Paris to importune some-body for a job. I couldn't get in. There was a riot. All the people were wait-ing to tell them when Sally Rand was going to appear. You see, the fair had opened. To hell with the cutting of the ribbon. Every newspaper in America came up that morning with Lady Godiva opening the fair. The place was jammed. When does she go on? Nobody knew. (Laughs.)

A poor soul was walking the floor: "Nobody's gonna come in unless Sally Rand's gonna be here." I said, "I'm Sally Rand." Whaaat? They hired me at $90 a week. I had to go home immediately and get the fans. They had no piano, just a xylophone. That's how we got started.

They planned this fair to bring business to Chicago, into the Loop. But you could have fired a cannon down State Street and hit nobody, because everybody was out at the fair sleeping in their Fords. No business in the Loop. They figured they'd better get a fair attraction down there. It wasn't easy to bring the Streets of Flags or the Hall of Science. I was the most mobile. So they hired me in the Chicago Theater.

There was a big scandal on in City Hall. A reporter got a hold of this tax business that Mayor Kelly was stealing. Taking property for taxes and hadn't even sent out tax notices. It hit the front pages. So City Hall had to do something to attract attention away from their own nefarious business. They got an old jim-dandy slogan: Clean Up the Loop for Fair Visitors.

Their first net brought in a little prostitute who wasn't paying the right madam. And a guy selling rubber goods in a back alley. Everybody else was protected. They paid. Well, you're not gonna get a headline that way. You gotta get a hold of somebody big.

So on my opening night, this enormous policewoman, a giantess, came crashing through the scrim curtain. I thought she was a sex maniac. She came screaming. . . . Here I am locked in my dressing room with a tiny little reporter trying to get a story. The police sirens are going, and the whole detective squad is out there. It's the biggest thing since sliced bread. Finally, John Balaban* had to get his firm of lawyers to get me to come out of my dressing room. Why . . . I'm arrested!

By this time, it's all on the radio, and the lines are beginning to queue up. I went down to the police station, signed the necessary papers, came back, did my show. I was arrested again. Four times that day. Finally, a little police-woman said, "Honey, don't worry about it. It wouldn't make any difference if you were wrapped up in the back drop. They'd still arrest you." I was trying to conform to whatever the hell they wanted, but nobody would say.

---

* Of Balaban & Katz, owners of a chain of movie theaters.

That was the point. They had to get headlines to distract away from the tax thing. That was the whole bag. The lines queued up for eleven solid weeks, four deep. I was doing seven shows a day at the Chicago Theater and seven shows a day at the Streets of Paris. I got my first $1,000 a week that week, and the first thing I bought with it was a tractor for my stepfather.

In June '33, $1,000 a week was a lot of money. I did the fair again in '34. On the eleventh of November, 1934, mass hysteria took over. They completely demolished the Century of Progress. They tore down flags, they tore down street lights, they tore down the walls. It started out being souvenir hunters, but it became mass vandalism. Anybody who witnessed it had this terribly frightening feeling. . . .

When we say "our society," it has a smug kind of ring to it. We seem to be a people who can't get out of our childhood. We don't believe what we see, what we hear. . . .

The rich still eat rich and wear mink coats, while people in Chicago literally freeze to death in the streets.* When I first went to India and saw dead in the streets, I couldn't eat. When I think of the garbage that goes into our garbage can, and here are people dying in the streets. And it's happening in our country, too. And I'm wearing a mink coat. Yeah.

I truly believe we shall have another Depression. I think people will just go out and take what they need. I don't think there will be any more people queueing up on bread lines waiting to be fed by charity, God damn it. I'm not condoning this, but we've let it happen. Take the television. It isn't food they're hungry for now, it's a different kind of food. Not only the Negroes. All the poor.

The middle class look upon the deprived smugly: the poor we'll have with us always. Oh yeah?

■ ■ ■ ■

Tony Soma

New York restaurateur. In his early days as a young immigrant from Italy, he suffered privation. As a waiter in a Cincinnati hotel, during the nomination of William Howard Taft, 1908, "I got a black eye from a tall red American. He said I had no business being in America because I was a wop." Later, in New York, he became Enrico Caruso's waiter . . . "he was a bad tipper."

---

* "I read of the Negro girl, found in the alley, frozen to death. They brought her back to life after her heart had stopped beating."

Homemade swimming pool for steelworkers'
children, Pittsburgh, Pennsylvania

ARTHUR ROTHSTEIN, 1938

*In the late twenties and early thirties, he was known as "Broadway Tony."
His speakeasy was a favorite watering place for members of literary and theater
circles.*

THE DEPRESSION MEANT THE glorification of Tony's. I had three leases,
three blocks east of Sixth Avenue. I sold them for $104,000. In '29. So for
me, '29 was the biggest year I had in my American life. Glorification,
moneywise and in friends, too. I had the greatest friends and from both
continents, Europe and Hollywood.

Didn't some of them go broke?
They didn't went broke—they went crazy. They were still rich. Americans
never broke. It's a question of figures. Oh yes, I had stock. Paper went into
paper. City Bank stock when I bought it, $518. Went down to $35. The same
stock, the same people. It was the figures that changed. To me, money was
paper. My ego is meant all the moneys in the world. I am an egotist.

I am a capitalist myself, but I think money rules too many human beings.
No, I am not enlightened, I'm just a capitalist. After all, this is a capitalist
country, and I am entitled to live like a capitalist. But I know the propertied
classes, the conservative element kept the Depression going. Roosevelt
changed the country back into the United States today. We are still adven-
turous today. I would give credit not to F.D.R., but to Mrs. Roosevelt. She
was the genius of that family. He was a vain man.

I thought I was going to be well protected, but I had at that time a lawyer—he did not understand the procedures of business. It was on the night
of repeal, the vestibule of Seventy-Seven* was piled up with cases of liquor,
which we were not supposed to have. The name Seventy-Seven brand. A
retailer was not supposed to have a wholesaler's license. Only one license.
So I had a retail license, that was enough. But the Seventy-Seven Corporation could be many things. I always thought what I did was responsible. I
should have had for myself a corporation. Today that's why they are millionaires. Double standard of laws being made for the protection of money and
not for the protection of human beings. Still today.

My business was better than ever in the Depression. Never changed my
mode of life. I'm a very humble man. Many, many of my customers were in
the paper. They were my friends: Wolfe, Fitzgerald, any of the big names. I
never suffered economically because I never looked at economics. To have

---

* A celebrated club, bearing another name.

credit in an individual like Robert Benchley and to have credit in a bank—Benchley was better than a bank.

I give you an instance. I met him at Seventy-Seven to settle certain matters. In those days, they were the place you had to meet certain people that was of value to my business. We had a little contract, it was in four figures. He gave to me, he says, "Tony, if I die today, you can collect." Just a piece of paper. That's the type of customer. It was a kind of mutual sympathy.

Were you ever raided?
Raided? No, never. A visitor was here. They wanted to know what business we had to be open with liquor. Well, I don't do anything here, I'm drinking here. It was not by the authorities considered bad, unless you had bad liquor, unless you had dope, unless you had prostitution. My place was a place where you could go and sit down and have liquor with a bottle on the table. I never measured it. They were my guests and they had their friends. Absolutely, there was no crime.

I never suffered. Life is not to suffer. The Depression is still here for some peoples. Depression is a disease, a mental disease. There's bread lines today, but they're getting money. Paid by people that works.

In the old days, the poor were more ignorant. They didn't have television. They had to work sixteen hours a day, and they didn't have time. The Plaza Hotel, where I used to work sixteen hours a day, my pay used to be a dollar a day. The Knickerbocker; I was frisked when I walked out, whether I had something in my pocket. They found out once I had a box of candy, so they fired me.

Today the poor are not guilty, just sick, mentally sick. Poverty is always a sign of laziness.

During those days, did you ever notice homeless men?
No. I always lived between Forty-third Street and Fifty-ninth Street. I never bumped into slums.

Ever see apple sellers?
I was busy. I worked.

POSTSCRIPT: *Immediately following the conversation, he, a devoted follower of the Yoga philosophy, stood on his head and sang "La donna è mobile."*

■   ■   ■   ■

Alec Wilder

Composer. Among the more than five hundred songs he has written are "It's So Peaceful in the Country," "While We're Young," "I'll Be Around," "Trouble Is a Man," "The Winter of My Discontent," "Good-bye, John." Among his instrumental compositions, woodwind octets, concerti, and concert band music. He has lived at the Algonquin Hotel, New York, off and on, since pre-Depression days.

I KNEW SOMETHING WAS terribly wrong because I heard bellboys, everybody, talking about the stock market. At the Algonquin they were grabbing as much as they could—horse betting, anything—and running to put this money on margin. It sounded nutty to me. About six weeks before the Crash, I persuaded my mother in Rochester to let me talk to our family adviser. I wanted to sell stock which had been left to me by my father, who was president of a Rochester bank. Maybe that's why I became a musician. I certainly didn't want to be a banker. Anything but a banker.

I talked to this charming man and told him I wanted to unload this stock. Just because I had this feeling of disaster. He got very sentimental: "Oh, your father wouldn't have liked you to do that." He was so persuasive, I said O.K. I could have sold it for $160,000. Six weeks later, the Crash. Four years later, I sold it for $4,000. John Balcom was his name, I'd never seen a face as red as his. It turned out he'd been an alcoholic. So all this advice came to me through the fumes of gin. He'd finally killed himself. Oh, gentle John Balcom! Solid citizen and everything. He cost me about $155,000. I could have done nicely with that. The sage old gentleman. So I did know something was wrong.

I wasn't mad at him, strangely enough. But I wanted nothing to do with money. The blow had fallen, and it was over. I was very skeptical and never invested. I became tired of people telling me: "Oh, there's a marvelous thing happening—and if you should have any extra money . . ." I'd say, "Don't talk to me about the market." I would have nothing to do with it.

I didn't even take money to a bank. I kept it all in my pocket. I didn't have a bank account for years. The money was drifting in. Taxes weren't as bad in those days, so you didn't have to keep track of what you spent. So I just kept the money in my pockets. It was crazy. To walk around with three or four thousand dollars and not be able to pay any bills by check. Just crazy.

I carried thousand-dollar bonds around in my pocket, and whenever I would run out of money, I'd cash one. Again, I was reinforced by money. It was a counter-active against any feeling of Depression.

I met a very beautiful girl just outside a speakeasy, on the sidewalk. She was reading the funny paper about midnight. It was all very romantic. She wanted to appear in a play a friend of hers had written. So I sold my New York Central stock for $12,000. I don't think the play cost more than ten or twelve thousand dollars to produce. Had I waited five years, I could have gotten—oh, $100,000. Of course, the play was a perfect mess. That was about '30 or '31. So I did know a little bit about the Depression. (Laughs.)

I loved speakeasies. If you knew the right ones, you never worried about being poisoned by bad whiskey. I'd kept hearing about a friend of a friend who had been blinded by bad gin. I guess I was lucky. The speaks were so romantic. A pretty girl in a speakeasy was the most beautiful girl in the world. As soon as you walked in the door, you were a special person, you belonged to a special society. When I'd bring a person in, it was like dispensing largesse. I was a big man. You had to know somebody who knew somebody. It had that marvelous movie-like quality, unreality. And the food was great. Although some pretty dreadful things did occur in them. I saw a man at the door pay off a gentleman in thousand-dollar bills to keep from being raided.

I recall the exact day Prohibition ended. I went into a restaurant that started serving booze. It was such a strange feeling, 'cause I started drinking in speaks. I didn't know about open drinking, to go in off the street and order a drink without having an arm on your shoulder. I'd gotten used to the idea of being disreputable. A friend of mine took me to some dump up in Rochester and gave me my first glass of beer. I don't think I'd have drunk it if it had been legal.

A very rich family up in Connecticut, before taking off for Europe, said to their children: No liquor in this house. So, under the rhododendron bush, the gin; under the hawthorn bush, the bourbon. It was all scattered just outside the house. No liquor *in* the house. All the drinking had to be done on the porch.

Roosevelt came in, and that was a cheery moment. Everybody seemed to know it. Even politically uninformed kids. I'm so sick of hearing how devious he was politically. So was Abraham Lincoln, for heaven's sake. To be a politician in a country like this, you've got to be devious.

His miraculous quality seemed to hit everybody. His fireside chats. It was very odd to me. Although his wit and speeches were beautiful, I never could understand how the public could pick up on his voice. It wasn't the kind of voice you hear on the street. But it grabbed them. They all mocked him, and the comedians kept doing imitations of "My friends." Yet the moment he said it—bang!—you were home. It was really a very extraordinary experience.

My mind doesn't move in political ways, 'cause I'm fixed on music. Away from the seamy side. Maybe it's cowardice. That could have been part of it. I wouldn't go up to a Hooverville and look at those shacks. I didn't want to know too much about it, because it depressed me too much and I couldn't write any music. That's no excuse, but . . .

■ ■ ■ ■

Doc Graham

A mutual acquaintance, Kid Pharaoh, insisted that we meet. Doc Graham had obviously seen better days.

"*My introduction to Chicago was when a guy got his head blowed off right across from where I went to stay. In that neighborhood where I gravitated, there was every kind of character that was ever invented. Con men, heist men, burglars, peet men: you name it, they had it.*

"*These are highly sophisticated endeavors. To be proficient at it—well, my God, you spent a lifetime. And then you might fall, through not being sophisticated enough. You may have committed a common error, leaving fingerprints. . . .*"

I WAS A CAGED panther. It was a jungle. Survival was the law of the land. I watched so many of my partners fall along the way. I decided the modus operandi was bad. Unavailing, nonproductive. After spending ten Saturdays in jail, one right after another, I changed my modus operandi.

What were you in jail for?
Various allegations. All alleged. I been a con man, a heist man—you name it.

How does a heist man differ from a con man?
One is by force and the other is by guile. Very few people have encompassed both. I was very daring. When I came to the city and seen groceries on the sidewalk, I swore I'd never be hungry again. My family was extremely poor. My father was an unsuccessful gambler, and my mother was a missionary. Not much money was connected with either profession.

A family conflict . . . ?
Yes, slightly. He threw the Bible in the fire. He was right, incidentally. (Laughs.) My mother didn't see it that way.

I'm sixty-one, and I have never held a Social Security card. I'm not knocking it. I have been what society generally refers to as a parasite. But I don't think I'd be a nicer fellow if I held two jobs.

My teacher was Count Victor Lustig. He was perhaps the greatest con man the United States has ever known. Lustig's outstanding achievement was getting put in jail and paying a Texas sheriff off with $30,000 counterfeit. And the sheriff made the penitentiary also. He got to be a believer. And he went into the counterfeit profession.

Another teacher was Ace Campbell.* He was the greatest card mechanic that ever arrived on the scene. Nick the Greek† wouldn't make him a butler. A footman. He couldn't open the door for him. Ace played the crimp. A crimp is putting a weave in a card that you'd need a microscope to see it. I know the techniques, but having had my arm half removed, I had to switch left-handed, deal left-handed. I'm ambidexterous.

An accident . . . ?
With a colored North American. The twenties and early thirties was a jungle, where only the strong survived and the weak fell by the wayside. In Chicago, at the time, the unsophisticated either belonged to the Bugs Moran mob or the Capone mob. The fellas with talent didn't bother with either one. And went around and robbed both of 'em.

We were extremely independent. Since I'm Irish, I had a working affiliate with Bugs Moran's outfit. In case muscle was needed beyond what I had, I called on Moran for help. On the other hand, Moran might use me to help him in one of his operations.

The nature of one operation was: if you had a load of whiskey hijacked, we went over and reloaded it on a truck, while several surrounded the place with machine guns, sawed-off shotguns, et cetera.

Did you find yourself in ticklish situations on occasion . . . ?
Many of them. You see this fellow liquidated, that fellow disposed of. Red McLaughlin had the reputation of being the toughest guy in Chicago. But when you seen Red run out of the drainage canal, you realized Red's modus operandi was unavailing. His associates was Clifford and Adams. They were set in Al's doorway in his hotel in Cicero. That was unavailing. Red and his partners once stole the Checker Cab Company. They took machine

* A pseudonym for a celebrated gambler of the twenties and early thirties. He is still alive.
† Another renowned gambler of the time.

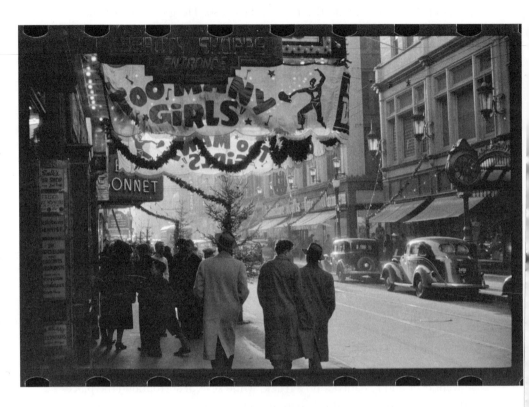

Crowds in downtown section of Providence, Rhode Island

JACK DELANO, 1940

guns and went up and had an election, and just went and took it over. I assisted in that operation.

What role did the forces of law and order play?
With a $10 bill, you wasn't bothered. If you had a speaking acquaintance with Mayor Thompson,* you could do no wrong. (Laughs.) Al spoke loud to him.

There was a long period during the Depression where the police were taking scrip. Cash had a language all of its own. One night in particular, I didn't have my pistol with me, and the lady of the evening pointed out a large score to me. (Laughs.) A squad car came by, which I was familiar with. A Cadillac, with a bell on it. I knew all the officers. I borrowed one of their pistols and took the score. Then I had to strip and be searched by the policemen, keeping honest in the end, as we divided the score. They wanted the right count. They thought I might be holding out on 'em. They even went into my shoes, even.

Oh, many policemen in that era were thieves. Legal thieves. I accepted it as such and performed accordingly. We didn't have no problems. It was an era where there was no bread on the table. So what was the difference whether I put the bread on the table by my endeavor or they put the bread? I performed with a hundred policemen in my time. I can't say nothin' for 'em, nothin' against 'em. I would say they were opportunists. I would say that they were merely persons that didn't perhaps have the courage to go on and do what I did. Nevertheless, they were willing to be a part of it. A minor part, that is.

The era of the times led into criminality, because of the old precept and concepts were destroyed against everyday reality. So when a policeman or a fireman was not being paid, how in the name of God could you expect him to enforce what he knew as the concept of law and order, when you see the beer barons changing hundred-dollar bills, and the pimp and the whorehouse guy had hundred-dollar bills, and the guy digging the sewers couldn't pay his bills? So how could you equate these things?

A good example is Clyde Barrow and Bonnie Parker. They were a product of the era. Dillinger—it wasn't that he was really a tough. No, he was just a product of survival. Actually, Dillinger was a country bumpkin. He realized the odds were stacked against him and performed accordingly. I knew Dillinger. Yeah, I met him on the North Side. And Dillinger was nothing like people wrote about him. The times produced Dillinger. Pretty Boy Floyd. Baby Face Nelson.

* William Hale Thompson, three-term mayor of Chicago.

They were dedicated heist men and in the end were killed, to achieve their purpose. By themselves, they didn't need an army.

Al Capone sublet the matter. Capone quickly removed himself from the danger zone, aside from murdering Anselmi and Scalisi with a baseball bat. Bugs Moran to the end—he died for a bank heist in Ohio. They were from two different bolts of cloth. One was a dedicated thief. And one was an intriguing Mediterranean product of guile, et cetera. So you'd have to say that Moran was dedicated while Capone was an opportunist.

How did you get along during those hard times?
By every way known to the human brain. All my brothers were in the penitentiary. I had one brother in Jefferson City, another one in San Quentin, another one in Leavenworth, another one in Louisiana. At that time, I am a fighter. I started boxing in 1925. Fourteen years till 1939. And it's a bloodthirsty thing.

How'd you become a boxer?
Gravitation. Being on the road simulated that fate, trying to grab a buck and so forth. Five different years, *Ring* magazine rated me the most devastating puncher in the profession, pound for pound.

What was it like, being a boxer in those days . . . ?
Survival. If it worked out that you were on top, you made a living. And if you were three or four shades below the top, you scuffled for a buck. Fighters were very, very hungry.

I made some pretty big scores. But I spent it practically all on getting my brothers out of penitentiaries around the country. At that time, the one in San Quentin stood me thirty thousand, the one in Jefferson City stood me twenty-five thousand. Those were big give-ups in those days.

I lived from the bottom to the top. I lived as good as you could live. I run the gamut of having a butler and a chauffeur to a flop joint, into an open car overnight.

He describes the boxing "combination" of those days; the fix; the refusal of his manager and himself to "play ball"; the boxer as an investment, cut up "like a watermelon."

I had many injuries in between. My hands, you can see. (He holds out his gnarled, broken knuckles.) In the meantime, I had to step out and make a dollar otherwise. It was never within the law.

I've switched craps, I've run up the cards, I do the complete bit. Every way known to the human brain. I'm probably a rare species that's left.

Was muscle always involved?
Muscle if you hope to leave with the money. Muscle everywhere, yes. Because for some unknown reason, muscle has been going on since the Roman army conquered the field with a way of life.

When you enter an endeavor unsuccessfully, then the planning was incorrect. The risk was above the gains, and you stumble along the way. And the windup is a rude awakening with numbers strung out over your back. Unsuccessful in your modus operandi. Sagacity, ingenuity, planning . . . it involves much weighing, odds against failure, odds against gain—if you care to be in a free society.

I spent much time in jail. That's why I'm a student of the matter.

(At this point, Kid Pharaoh and he conducted a vigorous and somewhat arcane debate concerning the relative dishonesty of Hoover and Roosevelt. The Kid insisted it was Hoover who, by clout, was saved from "the bucket." Doc was equally certain it was F.D.R. who should have had "numbers strung out over his shoulders.")

Do you recall your biggest haul during the thirties?
It was alleged—

Who alleged . . . ?
The newspaper report came out as $75,000. We took eight and were happy about the whole thing.

What was your role during Prohibition?
I was a cheater. After studying under Count Lustig and Ace Campbell, I considered it beneath my dignity delivering a barrel of beer. Although I drink beer. I hustled with crap mobs, on the crimp, the weave, the holdout—the reason I didn't do the rum running is you can hire a mooch with muscle. But can you hire brains? Big firms have not succeeded in doing this.

I have met only several proficient men in my time. One of them was Jack Freed. (Cups hand over mouth, whispers.) D–e–a–d. He worked right up to the edge of his demise. This is in the evening, when you are not at home. He was dedicated to his labor. He spent half his lifetime in the penitentiaries. One of my closest friends. I, of course, assisted him, from time to time. He accused me of rattling my coat one night, making entrance. I, who have endeavored in every participation known to the human brain, where art, subterfuge and guile is involved.

I take it you were caught a few times—
Incarcerated. Nothing proven substantially. I was a victim of circumstances. What they were, I didn't say. Yes, I spent a year in Salinas, California, amongst other places. The highlight was when I was nineteen. If I get convicted, I'm going out to join my brother in San Quentin. My brother was doing twenty years there. If I'm not convicted, I'm going up to visit him. I'm going to San Quentin, one way or the other.

And you did?
I did. As a free man. I was fortunate enough in having one of the greatest criminal lawyers of all time defending me.

For someone engaging in your varied skills, do you sense a difference between the thirties and today?
It's so different today, it's unfathomable. You can't conjure what the difference is. Today everything is a robot. Today everything is mechanical. There is very little ingenuity. Everything today is no-personal, there is no personality whatsoever. Everything today is *ipso facto, fait accompli.* In my era they had to prove their point. Today, you don't have to prove your point.

Back then Ace Campbell steered Arnold Rothstein,* with Nigger Nate Raymond, into one of maybe the biggest card games was ever involved. I was a small feature of it in the Park Central Hotel in New York. Ace changed the weave (laughs), and when Rothstein wound up a half-a-million loser, he said he was cheated. Rothstein became jaded after he lost the half a million, no longer had any interest. No interest in life. After the card game broke up, he said he was no longer interested in this, that or the other. He refused to pay off. So Nigger Nate Raymond held court with him. And that was the end of that.

Held court . . . ?
The S & W people† had the implements that they held court with. That's all. Rothstein didn't have to pay off. You understand what I mean? I know,

---

* A gambler and fixer of reknown. He was involved in the Black Sox scandal of 1919.
† Smith & Wesson, revolver manufacturers.

because I assisted in the operation with Ace. But let that be as it may. It was unfortunate, yes. But that was his demise.

Were the S & W people popular those days?
Naturally, it was part of your wearing apparel.

Aren't some of the survivors in legitimate enterprises today?
One of the fellows who was a pimp in Chicago is the boss of one of the grandest hotels in Las Vegas. I assisted him in a few small matters. But true to all pimping, he forgot me entirely as he advanced into the autumn of life.

After Prohibition, what did the guys do?
The ones that were adroit enough branched into other fields. If they didn't have any knowledge, they fell by the wayside. I achieved some small success in racetracks. Machine Gun Jack McGurn* couldn't stand the traffic. He got his brains blowed out, branching into other fields.

The night Prohibition was repealed, everybody got drunk. It was the only decent thing Roosevelt ever did in his administration. I was not one of his admirers. I tried to fire him on four different occasions. If I ever had a person work for me that displeased me, it was Roosevelt. I voted against him four times.

What was it about him you didn't like?
Him being a con man, taking advantage of poor, misguided, gibbering idiots who believed in his fairy tales. The New Deal, the various gimmicks, the NRA . . . the complete subterfuge, artifice and guile. . . .

Some say Roosevelt saved our society. . . .
I dare say it would have been saved if Roosevelt's mother and father had never met.

Many people were on relief . . . on WPA. . . .
I didn't have a thing to do with that, because I was above that. Nevertheless, the people that were involved in it did it merely to get some meat on the plates, some food in the kitchen. It was no more, no less. Survival.

---

* It was alleged that he was one of Capone's executioners in the St. Valentine's Day Massacre. He was killed in a bowling alley in 1936, on the day after St. Valentine's Day.

None of the connotations of social dissent that has crept in since then. Merely an abstract way of eating. . . .

What do you think would happen if there were a big Depression today?
Very simple. They'd commit suicide today. I don't think they're conditioned to stand it. We were a hardier race then. We'd win wars. We didn't procrastinate. We'd win them or lose them. Today we're a new race of people. They'll quit on a draw—if they see any feasible way to see their way out to quit with any dignity, they'll quit. Back then, you had a different breed of people. You got $21 a month going into the army or the navy. So them guys, they went to win the war. There's been an emancipated woman since the beginning of the war, also.

KID PHARAOH *interjects: "The American woman during the Depression was domesticated. Today, as we move into the late sixties, if you go into any high school, you don't see any classes of cooking any more. You don't see any classes at all in sewing. None of them can boil water. They're all today in business in competition to the male animal. Why should a Playboy bunny make $200 a week? If a veteran goes to war, puts his life up . . . can't raise a family."*

DOC: *". . . a lot of country bumpkins in the city wanting to look at poor, misguided, gibbering idiot waitresses. That they've stripped down like a prostitute, but hasn't sense enough to know that it's on her alleged sex allure that the poor misguided chump is in the place. In the end it amounts to absolutely nothing. A hypothesis of silly nothingness . . . undressed broads serving hootch, that cannot fulfill . . ."*

KID PHARAOH: *". . . his dick directs him, like radar, to the Playboy Club. In a high moral society—in Russia—guys like Hugh Hefner would be working in the library."*

During the Depression . . . if a guy had a few drinks with a girl . . . ?
If she had two drinks with him, and she didn't lay her frame down, she was in a serious matter. She could have one, and explain she made a mistake by marrying some sucker that she was trying to fulfill her marriage commitment. But in the thirties, if you had a second drink and she didn't make the commitment where she's going to lay her frame down for you, the entire matter was resolved quickly to the point and could end in mayhem. She was in a serious matter.

In the thirties, then, the individual con man, the heist man, had an easier time with it—all around?
Oh yes, it was much easier then. The federal government now has you on practically anything you do. They make a conspiracy whether you accomplish the matter or not. Today, it's fraught with much peril, any type of endeavor you engage in. A nefarious matter. It constantly comes under the heading of a federal statute. The federal government then collected taxes, and just a few interstate things, as white slavery, and that was about it.

Today, the federal government has expanded into every field. If you use a telephone, as an example, and you put slugs in it, that's a penitentiary offense. Strange as that may seem. So that will give you an idea how far the federal government has encroached on a citizen's prerogative.

You think Roosevelt had a role to play in this?
Definitely. He was perhaps the lowest human being that ever held public office. He, unfortunately, was a despot. I mean, you get an old con man at a point in high office, he begins to believe the platitudes that are expounded by the stupid populace about him.

What about the young people, during the Depression . . . ?
The young people in the Depression respected what laws there were. If they'd steal, they tried to do it with dignity. And whatnot. They respected the policeman. They looked at him with forbearance, that he was a necessary part of society. But, nevertheless, he didn't impede the mere fact of gain.
No, he didn't stop 'em.
The young today are feminized, embryo homosexuals. Stool pigeons.

What about the young dissenters?
If you gave 'em a push, they'd turn into a homosexual. When the German hordes fifty years ago surrounded Paris, Marshal Pétain brought out the pimps, whores, thieves, underground operators, he says: Our playground is jeopardized by the German Hun. Well, all Paris, every thief, burglar, pimp, he come out and picked up a musket. Stopped the German hordes.

Today you don't see any kind of patriotism like that. They're trying to tear down the courthouse, they try to throw paint on Johnson's car. How can you compare that era, coming into this? Those were men, and today you've got to question whether they're homosexual or whether they're not.

Since the Depression, manhood has been lost—the manhood that I knew. Where four or five guys went on an endeavor, they died trying to take the endeavor off. It was no big deal if they did die. If it didn't come off right, there was no recrimination. Everybody put skin off what they set on.

Today, the foible of our civilization is to attack the policeman with a rotten egg, throwing it at him. Or walking around with a placard, that they're against whatever the present society advocates as civilized. Those people today—the Fall of Rome could be compared with it. Because they were the strongest nation on earth, and they disinterrogated into nothing. Through debauchery, through moral decay.

They need a narcotic to do anything, they can't do it on their own. They need a drug. Back in my era, we could cold-bloodedly do it.

Sixteen Ton

You load sixteen ton and what do you get?
Another day older, and deeper in debt.
St. Peter, don't you call me, because I can't go.
I owe my soul to the company store.

—MERLE TRAVIS

Buddy Blankenship

A West Virginian émigré, living in Chicago. Illness has kept him jobless. Children, ranging wide in age from late adolescence to babyhood, stepchildren, son-in-law, grandchild and a weary wife are seated or wandering about the apartment: trying to keep cool on this hot, muggy summer afternoon. Hand-me-down furniture is in evidence in all the rooms.

I'VE BEEN IN A depression ever since I've been in the world. Still, it's better and worse. '31, '32, that's about the worst we ever been through.

I told my dad I wasn't going to school any more. He said: Why, you just come on and go work with me. I went in the mines, and I went to work. From '31 to about the last of '32. The Depression got so bad, we went to farming, raising our own stuff. He worked in the mines fifty-one years. He was sixty-three when he got killed. A boy shot him.

We lived eight miles from the mine, and we had to ride it horseback. I was riding behind my dad. Many times I'd have to git off and hammer his feet out of the stirrups. They'd be froze in the stirrups. It was cold, you know. When you come out of the mines, your feet would be wet of sweat and wet where you're walking on the bottom. And get up on those steel stirrups, while you're riding by eight miles, your feet'd be frozen and you couldn't git 'em out of the stirrups. I'd have to hammer 'em out. His feet were numb, and they wouldn't hurt till they started to get warm, and then they would get to hurtin'.

We got up at five in the mornin', start at six. We got out at ten that night. We'd work about sixteen hours a day, seventeen hours. The boss said we had to clean up. We didn't clean it up, the next morning there'd be another man in the mine to clean it up. The motor man would say: How many cars you got? Five more. Well, hurry up, we want to get out of here.

They was gettin' a dollar seventy-five a day. We'd get sixty to sixty-five ton a day—that is, both us, me and Dad. Then they changed me off and let me get a dollar and a half a day. I was trappin'.

Trappin'? The trap door was shut so the air would circulate through the mine. Then the motor come along, I'd open it up. I had to stay there till everybody quit. Then we'd walk about two miles and a half till we got outside. We walked about a mile before we got to where we could get our horses. We got down to the horses, why we rode about eight miles before we got to home. Summertimes it wasn't too bad. But in wintertime, boy, it was rough. You'd get snowbound and it would get so you couldn't get in and out. Ice'd be so bad . . . an' dangerous. Of course, we had to go to work. We didn't eat if we didn't go.

They had what they called safety devices, but it wasn't real safety. They had an axe and a saw and you cut your own timbers. You brought 'em in, strapped on your back. You went out on the mountain with your one-man saw. You sawed down a bush or whatever size prop you wanted and you tuck 'em in on your back. On Sunday, I packed timbers on my back, about two miles to the place . . . to set 'em on Monday. Company furnished the timber but you had to cut 'em. You had to lay your own track. . . .

I've seen several accidents. I've had to take four out of the mines dead. I didn't think about nothin' like that, though. I packed one for seven miles, and he got up and walked better'n I could. I was gonna give out, and he wasn't hurtin' any bit. There was some rock on him, and I took a jack and lifted it up and pulled 'im out. Just his breath knocked out of 'im. . . .

About '32, it got so they wouldn't let us work but two days a week. We saved $20 in the office. They laid us off two weeks till we traded that $20 in the store. We had to trade it out in the store, or we didn't get to work no more. It was a company store. What we made, we had to go next evening and trade it off. If we didn't, they'd lay us off. They didn't let you draw no money at all. It was scrip. They had a man top of the hill who took your tonnage down, how many tons you loaded, and it was sent up to the scrip office. If you made $20 over your expenses—for house, rent, lights and all—why, then they laid you off till you spent that $20.

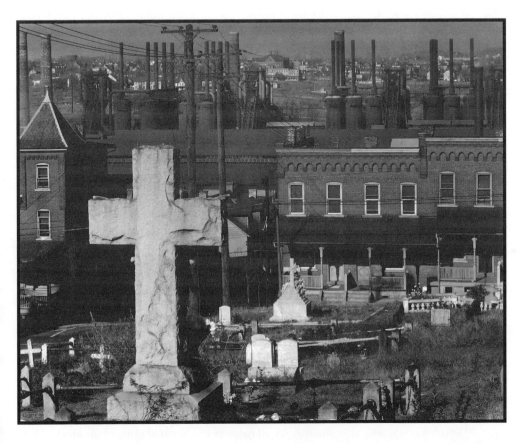

Bethlehem graveyard and steel mill, Pennsylvania

WALKER EVANS, 1935

This town you lived in . . .

It was a cave, a coal cave. Thirty-two families lived in the caves. It was nice buildings, built up inside, but they was just rough lumber. The company was the landlord, too. They owned it all. They still got company houses yet.

I worked about two years on the mines, then we went back to the farm from '32 to '37. It seemed like you lived a lot better on the farm than today. The works was bad, but you didn't have to pay some big price for the stuff. You raised your own hogs, you could have your own cattle. And you had your own meat, your own bacon, lard. You didn't have to buy nothin' but flour and meal. You raised your own potatoes. You never had money because you didn't make it to have it. It was a pretty bad time. It seemed just like a dream to me, the Depression did. I was young and didn't pay no attention to it. I didn't get the clothes or the underwear or stuff like that, but the eatin' part was good. I'd rather be back on the farm than anything I ever done.

Then we went to camp—minin'—in '37. The same mines. Roosevelt brought the mines a-rolling again. Things got to moving, and money got to circulating through. I worked the mine from '37 up to '57. Then it was a lot different. They had the union there and we worked just seven hours and fifteen minutes. We didn't work as hard as when the Depression was on. And they wouldn't let us stay no overtime, 'cause they didn't want to pay the overtime. I guess. We made some good money, me and my dad, both. He worked up to '41 and they cut him out. Age. He never did get a pension. He never worked long enough in the union to get a pension.

I took part in four strikes. They fined us one time for takin' a strike. A wildcat, that's what they called it. I helped organize about six mines. Now the company didn't like this, and they was kickin' on us all at the same time. They'd do anything, they'd kill and everything else. One place in West Virginia, they was shootin' us all to pieces. They had guns of all kinds there.

They had three hundred state troopers there. They was on the labor's side, and they took a lot of smoke bombs out of the men's pockets, the scabs. They said: "If you fellows wants to sign up or not wants to sign up . . . but go to carryin' no guns. You fellas ain't paid to carry 'em and ain't paid to use 'em, we're paid to use 'em. If you want to sign 'em up, you go ahead and sign 'em up." And they signed up.

It surprised everyone that these three hundred state police come—on our side. The captain said: If they don't want to organize, shut 'em down. He walked into the bathhouse and, boy, they had guns hanging out all around, the scabs. See, the company furnished 'em guns. They had machine guns and everything. They took the state police in there to take all them guns

out. I know the name of the governor if I could think of it—he was on labor's side.* That was '42.

*As he remembers, past and present fuse. . . . "The mines were runnin' out, ex-
cept this little wagon of a mine, and it didn't have no tracks. You had to get on
your knees, coal was so low. Coal was just twenty-eight inches. Panther Creek,
West Virginia. We drove tunnels clear through the mountain to the other side.
We'd drive up as far as we could go without air, and we'd come back and get a
sniff and drive it up again as far as we could again without air. We could get
breakthroughs to the other place and get air, you see.*

*"They cut one tunnel there was twelve miles long one way and twenty-eight
miles long the other way, 'cause it was a ridge one way. They took twenty-eight
inches of rock from the top, make it high enough for the men to work. I traveled about seven miles a day back and forth on my knees. They'd be knots on
'em big as your double fist. . . ."*

I liked the mines till it got so I couldn't work no more. My wind was too
short, and there was too much dead air and I just choked up and couldn't do
no good. I went to work for a dollar an hour . . . on the roads. Till that run
out. And I come to Chicago.

■   ■   ■   ■

Mary Owsley

*Before setting off with his family for Oklahoma in 1929, to follow the oil
boom, her husband was a dynamite man in Kentucky mines.*

ONE DAY HE NOTICED on the side of the boiler a place as big as a saucer.
They call it a breather—it's a weak place on the boiler. He told the boss that
had to be fixed, because he didn't want to get killed. Monday morning, I
saw him comin' back home. They hadn't fixed it, hadn't done a thing about
it. He told 'em in less than three weeks there'll be an explosion. Sure enough,
there was. Killed three men and two mine mules from that very thing. He
left.

We lived in a company house. We had to buy every bucket of water we
used, 'cause the company undermined things so bad, they ruined all the
water wells. I bought my food from the company store, and we bought our

* M. M. Neely, governor of West Virginia, 1941–1945.

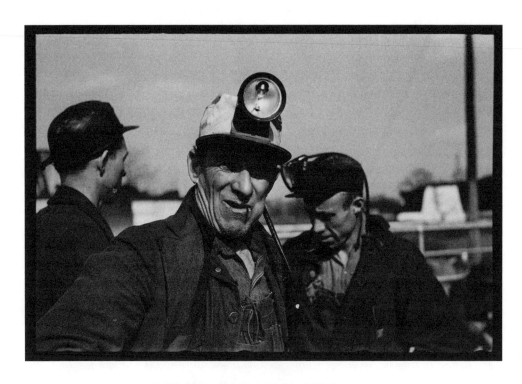

Coal miners, Birmingham, Alabama

ARTHUR ROTHSTEIN, 1937

furniture from the company store, and we paid three prices on it. I've seen my husband have to borry from his next pay check—what they call scrip—to buy just medicine and things like that. And we didn't live extravagant either. We paid over 260 some odd dollars for furniture from the coal company. We paid it all back but $20. And when he went and got another job, he bought a truck down there for the furniture. And they took the whole thing away from us. They wouldn't let us pay the $20.

Because he was a troublemaker . . . ?
No, because he quit that job there where the breather was on that boiler. That's the kind of troublemaker he was, you're mighty right he was. He wanted to live.

We lived in this coal mine camp, this next one, and there was a pump out in the middle between four houses. The four families of us shared that one pump. In the wintertime, that thing would get covered up with ice a foot thick. Us women had to keep a tub of water on our coal stove hot. The men would have to get up at three in the morning to get out there and melt the ice off the pump before they went to work. Just for the simple want of a shed built over a water pump. It might deflate the company's bank account.

■   ■   ■   ■

Aaron Barkham

"I'm too young to retire and too old to work in the coal mines. When a man gets to be up around thirty-five, forty years old, been in a mine ten or twelve years, they want somebody younger. When they get the chance, they'll replace him."

He is from West Virginia. His father, a miner all his life, died in a coal camp. "Silicosis wasn't even heard of. He died of hardened arteries.* Dad belonged to the Oddfellows, and they paid Mother about $11 a month. We had a cow and a hog. When things got tight, we let loose of that. We had a hard-scrabble farm, worn-out ground, not worth much. From the time I was four years old, that's all I knowed, hard times."

PEOPLE WORKED FIFTEEN HOURS a day, loaded a four-ton car, they got a dollar out of it. If the company could, it'd take that. (Laughs.) I think they

---

* "Several hundred autopsies have confirmed that many miners die of heart failure when coal dust clamps the small arteries in their lungs in a stiff unyielding cast which eventually puts a critical load on their hearts." Robert G. Sherrill, *The Nation*, April 28, 1969, p. 533.

made about $2 a day, most of 'em. We had boarders from the coal camp, others weren't that lucky. My oldest brother, he was fifteen, he went to work as a breaker boy at the tipple.

Years before, he and my other brother, who was twelve, got the idea of sellin' moonshine. We'd pay a dollar a gallon and sell it for twenty-five cents a pint. So that worked all right. We sold sometimes three gallons a day. During Prohibition, and after, people that got the relief checks was the ones that bought the whiskey. We'd get it in half-gallon jars and put it in pint bottles.

That's where a playful little boy comes in. A little boy—I was about six, seven—could get aholt of somethin' and carry it right along the road where a man could get arrested. 1931 was when that started and come to about 1936. That was 'bout the only family income. The only obstacle I had, I had with my own second cousin. He was a deputy sheriff. He was big and fat, and I could get around him. He chased me miles through the thickets.

Nine revenuers were split up into three bunches. Work in the woods, lookin' for stills. They'd put down a marker. It was my job to switch the markers. And they'd get all confused. Everybody bootlegged. It kind of got to be a legitimate business. You had to be foxier than the foxes, that's all.

That second cousin, he was on the political side of the fence. So when WPA come in, we didn't get any relief from the local politicians. My mother was a Republican. I think it was her pride that wouldn't change our politics. Not much use complainin' about somethin' like that. We had enough to eat from the bootleg. About four out of five was unemployed in the county till 'bout 1938.

I never did get a whole year of school—maybe five or six months. I started workin' when I was thirteen. In a sawmill at ten cents an hour. I worked for the guy that had all the timber monopoly for the company. I worked for the bulldozers. I finally got twenty-five cents an hour, but he raised the board to seventy-five cents a day. Get up at four o'clock in the mornin', we clumb on a big truck and was hauled about fifteen miles. We started about a quarter to five and worked till we couldn't see. Then we'd quit. It was nearer sixteen hours than it was eight hours. I know we'd get into bed and turn over one time, and they'd be yellin' for breakfast.

It got bad in '29. The Crash caught us with one $20 gold piece. All mines shut down—stores, everything. One day they was workin', the next day the mines shut down. Three or four months later, they opened up. Run two, three days a week, mostly one. They didn't have the privilege of calling their souls their own. Most people by that time was in debt so far to the company itself, they couldn't live.

Some of them been in debt from '29 till today, and never got out. Some of them didn't even try. It seem like whenever they went back to work, they owed so much. The company got their foot on 'em even now.

When the Crash come, they got about ten cents an hour—that is, if they begged the supervisor for a job. They had to load a seven-ton car for fifty cents. If they found three pieces of slate as big as your hand, they took that car, and you didn't get paid. That's what they called the dock. A man couldn't predict what's gonna fall on that car, goin' through maybe a couple of miles of tunnel, and everything fallin' anyhow.

One time they hauled a mule out. They fired the guy that got that mule killed. They told him a mule's worth more'n a man. They had to pay $50 for a mule, but a man could be got for nothin'. He never had worked another day since. Blackballed for costin' 'em that money.

I remember one time, the Red Cross shipped in about four ton of flour in twenty-four-pound bags. Unloaded it in the company warehouse. It was a Red Cross gift. But the company said they have to work a day to get a sack of flour. That started it. Pretty much like walkin' the inferno.

An old woman, about sixty years, she come down from Canyon Creek. One time she was makin' a speech near a railroad track. She was standin' on a box. The strikebreakers shot her off with a shotgun. So she come down to Logan County where we was and made speeches and helped get them organized. But they had a time.

The county sheriff had a hundred strikebreakers. They were called deputies. The company paid him ten cents a ton on all the coal carried down the river, to keep the union out. He was beaten in the election by T. Hatfield of the feudin' Hatfields. He was for the union. They had pretty much a full-scale war out there for about three years.

They brought the army in. The county was under martial law, stayed till about '31. What strikes me is the soldiers along the company road, dispersin' people. When people'd gather together, they couldn't talk. Two guys could, but three couldn't.

About that time, a bunch of strikebreakers come in with shotguns and axe handles. Tried to break up union meetings. The UMW deteriorated and went back to almost no existence. It didn't particularly get full strength till about 1949. And it don't much today in West Virginia. So most people ganged up and formed the Ku Kluck Klan.

The Ku Klux was the real controllin' factor in the community. They was the law. It was in power to about 1932. My dad and my older brother belonged to it. My dad was one of the leaders till he died. The company called in the army to get the Ku Klux out, but it didn't work. The union and the Ku Klux was about the same thing.

The superintendent of the mine got the big idea of makin' it rougher than it was. They hauled him off in a meat wagon, and about ten more of the company officials. Had the mine shut down. They didn't kill 'em, but they didn't come back. They whipped one of the foremen and got him out of the county. They gave him twelve hours to get out, get his family out.

The UMW had a field representative, he was a lawyer. They tarred and feathered 'im for tryin' to edge in with the company. He come around, got mad, tryin' to tell us we were wrong, when we called a wildcat. He was takin' the side of the company. I used the stick to help tar 'im. And it wasn't the first time.

The Ku Klux was formed on behalf of people that wanted a decent living, both black and white. Half the coal camp was colored. It wasn't anti-colored. The black people had the same responsibilities as the white. Their lawn was just as green as the white man's. They got the same rate of pay. There was two colored who belonged to it. I remember those two niggers comin' around my father and askin' questions about it. They joined. The pastor of our community church was a colored man. He was Ku Klux. It was the only protection the workin' man had.

Sure, the company tried to play the one agin' the other. But it didn't work. The colored and the whites lived side by side. It was somethin' like a checkerboard. There'd be a white family and a colored family. No sir, there was no racial problem. Yeah, they had a certain feelin' about the colored. They sure did. They had a certain feelin' about the white, too. Anyone come into the community had unsatisfactory dealin's, if it was colored or white, he didn't stay.

I remember one family moved in from acrost us. They had a bunch of women. I remember where I saw out the window, it didn't look right. The Ku Klux warned 'em once. Gave 'em twenty-four hours. They didn't take the warning. The next night they whipped Hughie (that was the man), his wife and his niece, his uncle and his aunt, and whipped six more that was a-crowdin' around. They whipped 'em with switches and run 'em out, all of 'em. They was white; they wasn't niggers.

One time a Negro slapped a white boy. They didn't give him no warning. They whipped 'im and run 'im out of town. If a white man'd slapped a colored kid, they'd a done the same thing. They didn't go in for beatin' up niggers because they was niggers. What they done was kept the community decent to live in. What they did object to was obscenity and drinkin'.

What about bootlegging?

Oh, they objected to raisin' a fuss in town. What you do private, that's your business. You're talkin' about mountain people now. This ain't the Deep South.

People'd get their temper rubbed off quick. In organizin' the union, we didn't go through the Labor Relations Board. We went through what we called "mule train." We'd figure how many people were workin' at that certain mine, and we'd just tell 'em to organize it or we'd close 'em. We'd give 'em three days. Sometimes they'd stand at the mouth of the mine with a club. There was seventeen thousand in the whole district. I have knowd every one of them to come out on account of one man bein' called out. And join the UMW.

At a UMW meeting, they'd iron it out themselves. I had to pull out a .38 once to get out of a union meetin'. Our chairman of the local was thick with the superintendent of the mine, and I made mention of it in the meeting. Some guys didn't like it: they followed him close. We was in a school building. I was up next to the blackboard, and the door was on the other end of the room. So they blocked the door. My wife's half brother was sittin' about halfway back. So he pulled out his gun and throwd it to me. I told 'em I'm goin' out and anybody stops me, I'm gonna shoot. They followed me outside, there was about fifty. They blocked the gate. So I told 'em I'm gonna shoot the first six gets in my way.

The next day I went back to work. I took my gun with me. They cooled off. It took 'em a week, they cooled off.

In my life, I've found people won't take anything. If things get real bad again, I'm afraid there'd be some millionaires made paupers because they'd take their money. They'd take it the rough way. The people are gonna take care of their families, if they'd have to shoot somebody else. And you can't blame 'em for that. You think I wouldn't take what you got if you had a million dollars and I had to protect my family? I sure would. I'd take your money one way or the other. Some people don't have courage enough to fight for what they have comin'. Until 1934, more than half the people of Logan County were scabbin'. Gives you an idea how they don't know. . . .

Explosions? Had one back in '35, killed a few men. They had one in Bartley, killed 136 men. In Macbeth the same year—when was that?—a fire and explosion killed eighteen and twenty men. Then in 1947, they had an explosion that killed a couple of men.

They sent me for a job in Virginia. Shaft was fifteen hundred feet deep. I went down and looked it over and went up and didn't go. Gas and dust.

That was 1965. Supposed to have been the most safest mine in the world. They had an explosion about four months after that. Killed two men, injured nine more. . . .

POSTSCRIPT: *Suddenly, a light laugh: "I remember the first radio come to Mingo County, next to Logan. Wayne Starbuck, a cousin to me, brought that in 1934. That was a boon. It was a little job, got more squeals and squeaks than anything else. Everybody came from miles around to look at it. We didn't have any electricity. So he hooked up two car batteries. We got* Grand Ole Opry *on it."*

The Farmer Is the Man

Oh, the farmer is the man, the farmer is the man
Lives on credit till the fall.
With the interest rate so high
It's a wonder he don't die
For the mortgage man's the one
That gets it all.

—POPULIST SONG, 1896

Harry Terrell

His Quaker forebears moved westward early in the nineteenth century. A South Carolina ancestor was hanged by the British, following the Battle of Cowpens; he would not betray the guerrillas. . . . "But he wasn't quite dead. His wife revived him, and he lived to a ripe old age to tell the tale."

It is a rainy Saturday in Des Moines. As he recalls the late twenties and early thirties—in this plastic-oriented room of a large motel chain—he feels alien, though he has lived in this region all his life, seventy-seven years.

He had worked as a YMCA secretary, but "I had naturally been a farmer, 'cause I never went off the farm until I went to college when I was twenty-two years old."

320 ACRES OF FARM LAND, fine land, that my uncle owned and cleared, he lost it. 'Cause they foreclosed the mortgage. Some of the best in the state, and he couldn't borrow a dime.

The farmers didn't have anything they could borrow on. He came down here to see me, because he knew that a fellow that had a job could get credit. He wanted to borrow $850. I knew my banker would give it to me. So I told him I'd get it.

He said, "Harry, I want to give you a mortgage to support this loan." I said I'd never take a mortgage from my mother's brother. But here's what he put up: a John Deere combine and tractor, about sixteen head of cattle, a team of mules and wagons and farm implements. For $850. So you can see how far this had gone. He couldn't get a loan, a man who lived in this state from the time he was two years old.

I was born across the road from the farm of Herbert Hoover's uncle. I knew the Hoover family, distant cousins of the president. My folks sold hogs for 'em, thoroughbred, pure Chester White hogs at two cents a pound. Even people like them, they had times just like the rest of us. That's the way it was going. Corn was going for eight cents a bushel. One county insisted on burning corn to heat the courthouse, 'cause it was cheaper than coal.

This was at the time that mortgaging of farms was getting home to us. So they was having ten cent sales. They'd put up a farmer's property and have a sale and all the neighbors'd come in, and they got the idea of spending twenty-five cents for a horse. They was paying ten cents for a plow. And when it was all over, they'd all give it back to him. It was legal and anybody that bid against that thing, that was trying to get that man's land, they would be dealt with seriously, as it were.

That infuriated all the people that wanted to carry on business as usual. It might be a bank or an implement dealer or a private elevator or something like that. They had their investments in this. The implement dealer, he was on the line, too. The only place he had of getting it was from the fellow who owed him. And they'd have a sheriff's sale.

The people were desperate. They came very near hanging that judge. Because they caught this judge foreclosing farm mortgages, and they had no other way of stopping it. He had issued the whole bunch of foreclosures on his docket.

It all happened in Le Mars. They took the judge out of his court and took him to the fairgrounds and they had a rope around his neck, and they had the rope over the limb of a tree. They were gonna string him up in the old horse thief fashion. But somebody had sense enough to stop the thing before it got too far.

They had marches, just like we have the marches nowadays. They came from all over the state. That was the time of the Farm Holiday. There was a picket line. The Farm Holiday movement was to hold the stuff off the market, to increase the price. It saw its violence, too.

They stopped milk wagons, dumped milk. They stopped farmers hauling their hay to market. They undertook to stop the whole agriculture process. They thought if they could block the highways and access to the packing plants, they couldn't buy these hogs at two cents a pound.

They'd say: we're gonna meet, just east of Cherokee, at the fork of the road, and so on. Now they spread it around the country that they were gonna stop everything from going through. And believe me, they stopped it. They had whatever was necessary to stop them with. Some of 'em had pitchforks. (Laughs.) You can fix the auto tire good with a pitchfork. There were blockades.

The country was getting up in arms about taking a man's property away from him. It was his livelihood. When you took a man's horses and his plow away, you denied him food, you just convicted his family to starvation. It was just that real.

I remember one man, as devout a man as I ever met, a Catholic. He was mixed up in it, too—the violence. His priest tried to cool him down. He says, "My God, Father, we're desperate. We don't know what to do." He was the most old, established man you could find. He was in the state legislature.

I remember in court when they were going to indict a Norwegian Quaker, when they were offering them lighter sentences if they'd plead guilty, his wife said, "Simon, thee must go to jail."

Did they ever talk about changing the society . . . ?
No, the nearer to the ground you get, the nearer you are to conservative. His land is his life. And he's not for anything that might alter the situation. I never found anything in the Iowa farmer to indicate he would accept any form of government but his own. If my family, grandfather, great-grandfather, ever heard my political beliefs, why, they'd turn over in their graves. I don't think that without the Depression this farm country would be anything but McKinley Republican.

You know, Hitler's men were awfully interested that I'd been through a farm strike in northern Iowa. I was in Germany, with my wife, as a tourist in 1937. I had been to Geneva for a disarmament conference. I met Hitler's agricultural attaché in Berlin. They were just putting controls on their farmers. He wanted to know how this violence was handled. He kept getting madder and madder. I said: "What do you do with these people?" He said: "They've got to come to terms with the government or well just wipe them out."

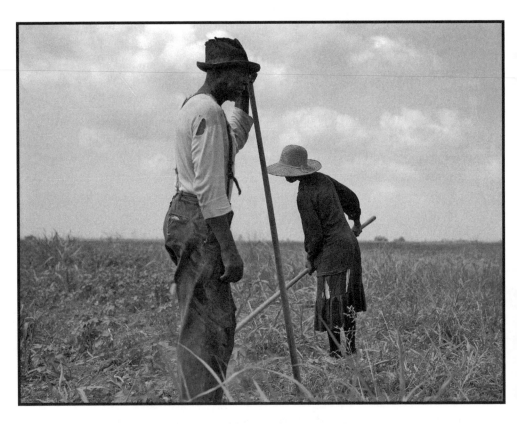

Cotton sharecroppers. Greene County, Georgia.
They produce little, sell little, buy little.

Dorothea Lange, 1937

The New Deal came along . . .
The progress was very slow, though. Of course, Henry Wallace and his ever-normal granary was the man who saved the farmer. The farmer would have passed clear out of the picture. They took this corn and paid for it and stored it. They put a price on it that was above the miserable going price. It wasn't allowed for no eight cents a bushel.

The farmers broke the laws, as a last resort. There was nothing else for them to do. To see these neighbors wiped out completely, and they would just drift into towns and they would have to be fed.

Oh, these towns are pathetic. Today, I mean. You'll pass through towns and if you get off the highway a little ways, and went down the main street, it's one vacant building after another. Little ghost towns with an elevator and a service station.

It's an abject depression now for the small farmer. My brother-in-law still has the farm that his father took when he came out here as a young man. The reason he can stay in business is that he turns everything he got on that farm into cattle feed and turns it into beef. Beef prices are decent because beef is used by factory workers. But the grain farmer, the farmer who gets cash out of his crop, he's feelin' the pinch of poverty.

Many of the farm families can't get any of their family to farm it. The children are goin' to the cities. The farm is just going on the block and is added to some other big land holding in the community. The individual farmer is becoming a thing of the past. Larger and larger holdings, fewer and fewer people. Even a fellow farming eight hundred acres now, which he doesn't own, is right up against the buzz saw.

The war economy is not helping the farmer . . . ?
No, it isn't. Not the small farmer. He's getting the worst of it all the time. You never see a war help the farmer, except temporarily. Much as I hate to say it, the Second World War *did* end the Great Depression. I think we solve our problems by killing our boys and others.

But I can see a Depression ahead right now. If we go to pot, it would make that one look like a Sunday school picnic. A Depression today would cut deep, quick. Today, in the machine age, like everything—it would be sudden.

In the thirties, my sister's family lived on their own production. They had gardens, they had eggs, they had flocks of chickens. Now the eggs are all produced in these large establishments. Machines turn out thousands of dozens. Then, they had their own and were more self-sufficient. Today, the milk is supplied by the same company that supplies this dining room here. They didn't have money to buy new clothes or cars or machinery. But they had enough to keep body and soul together. Today, the money would be gone. They wouldn't have the food. . . .

People today have been taught violence, the denial of humanity under money pressure. People are going in that direction. I don't think they'd tolerate those conditions that we came through. The younger people wouldn't take it, because they know it isn't necessary. But you can't have a lot of people in Congress that you got today.

■   ■   ■

Oscar Heline

For all his seventy-eight years, he has lived on this Iowa farm, which his father had cultivated almost a century ago. It is in the northwestern part of the state, near the South Dakota border. Marcus has a population of 1,263.

On this drizzly October Sunday afternoon, the main street is deserted. Not a window is open, nor a sound heard. Suddenly, rock music shatters the silence. From what appeared to be a years-long vacant store, two girls and a boy emerge. They are about thirteen, fourteen.

I ask directions. They are friendly, though somewhat bewildered. "An old man?" They are eager to help. One points north; another, south; the third, west. Each is certain "an old man" lives somewhere in the vicinity.

Along the gravel road, with a stop at each of three farmhouses; no sign, no knowledge of "an old man," nor awareness of his name. At each is a tree bearing the identical sticker: "Beware the Dog." One trots forth, pauses warily and eyes the stranger in the manner of Bull Connor and a black militant. The young farmers are friendly enough, but innocent of Oscar Heline's existence.

At the fourth farm, an elderly woman, taken away from the telecast of the Tigers–Cardinals World Series game, knows. . . . Several gravel roads back I find him.

THE STRUGGLES PEOPLE HAD to go through are almost unbelievable. A man lived all his life on a given farm, it was taken away from him. One after the other. After the foreclosure, they got a deficiency judgment. Not only did he lose the farm, but it was impossible for him to get out of debt.

He recounts the first farm depression of the twenties: "We give the land back to the mortgage holder and then we're sued for the remainder—the deficiency

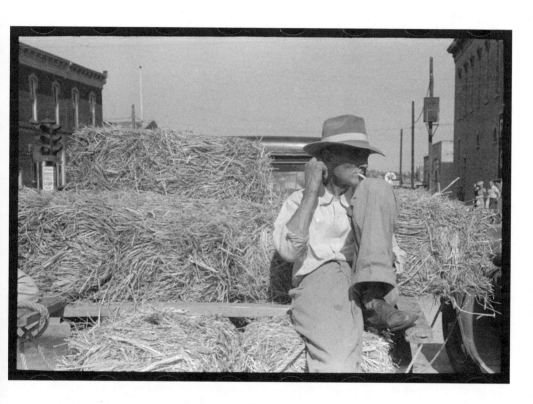

Farmer on a load of hay, farmers' market,
Weatherford, Texas

RUSSELL LEE, 1939

judgment—which we have to pay." After the land boom of the early twenties,
the values declined constantly, until the last years of the decade. "In '28, '29,
when it looked like we could see a little blue sky again, we're just getting
caught up with the back interest, the thirties Depression hit. . . ."

The farmers became desperate. It got so a neighbor wouldn't buy from a
neighbor, because the farmer didn't get any of it. It went to the creditors.
And it wasn't enough to satisfy them. What's the use of having a farm sale?
Why do we permit them to go on? It doesn't cover the debts, it doesn't liquidate the obligation. He's out of business, and it's still hung over him. First,
they'd take your farm, then they took your livestock, then your farm machinery. Even your household goods. And they'd move you off. The farmers
were almost united. We had penny auction sales. Some neighbor would bid
a penny and give it back to the owner.

Grain was being burned. It was cheaper than coal. Corn was being
burned. A county just east of here, they burned corn in their courthouse all
winter. '32, '33. You couldn't hardly buy groceries for corn. It couldn't pay
the transportation. In South Dakota, the county elevator listed corn as
minus three cents. *Minus* three cents a bushel. If you wanted to sell 'em a
bushel of corn, you had to bring in three cents. They couldn't afford to
handle it. Just think what happens when you can't get out from under. . . .

We had lots of trouble on the highway. People were determined to withhold produce from the market—livestock, cream, butter, eggs, what not. If
they would dump the produce, they would force the market to a higher level.
The farmers would man the highways, and cream cans were emptied in
ditches and eggs dumped out. They burned the trestle bridge, so the trains
wouldn't be able to haul grain. Conservatives don't like this kind of rebel
attitude and aren't very sympathetic. But something had to be done.

I spent most of my time in Des Moines as a lobbyist for the state cooperatives. Trying to get some legislation. I wasn't out on the highway fighting this
battle. Some of the farmers probably didn't think I was friendly to their cause.
They were so desperate. If you weren't out there with them, you weren't a
friend, you must be a foe. I didn't know from day to day whether somebody
might come along and cause harm to my family. When you have bridges
burned, accidents, violence, there may have been killings, I don't know.

There were some pretty conservative ones, wouldn't join this group. I
didn't want to particularly, because it wasn't the answer. It took that kind of
action, but what I mean is it took more than that to solve it. You had to do
constructive things at the same time. But I never spoke harshly about those
who were on the highway.

Some of the farmers with teams of horses, sometimes in trucks, tried to get through. He was trying to feed his family, trying to trade a few dozen eggs and a few pounds of cream for some groceries to feed his babies. He was desperate, too. One group tried to sell so they could live and the other group tried to keep you from selling so they could live.

The farmer is a pretty independent individual. He wants to be a conservative individual. He wants to be an honorable individual. He wants to pay his debts. But it was hard. The rank-and-file people of this state—who were brought up as conservatives, which most of us were—would never act like this. Except in desperation.

There were a few who had a little more credit than the others. They were willing to go on as usual. They were mostly the ones who tried to break the picket lines. They were the ones who gained at the expense of the poor. They had the money to buy when things were cheap. There are always a few who make money out of other people's poverty. This was a struggle between the haves and the have-nots.

The original bankers who came to this state, for instance. When my father would borrow $100, he'd get $80. And when it was due, he'd pay back the $100 and a premium besides that. Most of his early borrowings were on this basis. That's where we made some wealthy families in this country.

We did pass some legislation. The first thing we did was stop the power of the judges to issue deficiency judgments. The theory was: the property would come back to you someday.

The next law we passed provided for committees in every county: adjudication committees. They'd get the person's debts all together and sit down with his creditors. They gave people a chance. People got time. The land banks and insurance companies started out hard-boiled. They got the farm, they got the judgment and then found out it didn't do them any good. They had to have somebody to run it. So they'd turn around and rent it to the fella who lost it. He wasn't a good renter. The poor fella lost all his capacity for fairness, because he couldn't be fair. He had to live. All the renters would go in cahoots. So the banks and companies got smart and stopped foreclosing.

Through a federal program we got a farm loan. A committee of twenty-five of us drafted the first farm legislation of this kind thirty-five years ago. We drew it up with Henry Wallace. New money was put in the farmers' hands. The federal government changed the whole marketing program from burning 10-cent corn to 45-cent corn. People could now see daylight and hope. It was a whole transformation of attitude. You can just imagine . . . (He weeps.)

It was Wallace who saved us, put us back on our feet. He understood our problems. When we went to visit him, after he was appointed secretary, he made it clear to us he didn't want to write the law. He wanted the farmers themselves to write it. "I will work with you," he said, "but you're the people who are suffering. It must be your program." He would always give his counsel, but he never directed us. The program came from the farmers themselves, you betcha.

Another thing happened: we had twice too many hogs because corn'd been so cheap. And we set up what people called Wallace's Folly: killing the little pigs. Another farmer and I helped develop this. We couldn't afford to feed 45-cents corn to a $3 hog. So we had to figure a way of getting rid of the surplus pigs. We went out and bought 'em and killed 'em. This is how desperate it was. It was the only way to raise the price of pigs. Most of 'em were dumped down the river.

The hard times put farmers' families closer together. My wife was working for the county Farm Bureau. We had lessons in home economics, how to make underwear out of gunny sacks, out of flour sacks. It was cooperative labor. So some good things came out of this. Sympathy toward one another was manifest. There were personal values as well as terrible hardships.

Mrs. Heline interjects: "They even took seat covers out of automobiles and reused them for clothing or old chairs. We taught them how to make mattresses from surplus cotton. We had our freedom gardens and did much canning. We canned our own meat or cured it in some way. There was work to do and busy people are happy people."

The real boost came when we got into the Second World War. Everybody was paying on old debts and mortgages, but the land values were going down. It's gone up now more than ever in the history of the country. The war. . . . (A long pause.)

It does something to your country. It's what's making employment. It does something to the individual. I had a neighbor just as the war was beginning. We had a boy ready to go to service. This neighbor one day told me what we needed was a damn good war, and we'd solve our agricultural problems. And I said, "Yes, but I'd hate to pay with the price of my son." Which we did. (He weeps.) It's too much of a price to pay. . . .

In '28 I was chairman of the farm delegation which met with Hoover. My family had always been Republican, and I supported him. To my disappointment. I don't think the Depression was all his fault. He tried. But all his plans failed, because he didn't have the government involved. He depended on individual organizations.

It's a strange thing. This is only thirty-five years ago—Roosevelt, Wallace. We have a new generation in business today. Successful. It's surprising how quickly they forget the assistance their fathers got from the government. The Farm Bureau, which I helped organize in this state, didn't help us in '35. They take the same position today: we don't need the government. I'm just as sure as I'm sitting here, we can't do it ourselves. Individuals have too many different interests. Who baled out the land banks when they were busted in the thirties? It was the federal government.

What I remember most of those times is that poverty creates desperation, and desperation creates violence. In Plymouth County—Le Mars— just west of us, a group met one morning and decided they were going to stop the judge from issuing any more deficiency judgments. This judge had a habit of very quickly O.K.'ing foreclosure sales. These farmers couldn't stand it any more. They'd see their neighbors sold out.

There were a few judges who would refuse to take the cases. They'd postpone it or turn it over to somebody else. But this one was pretty gruff and arrogant: "You do this, you do that, it's my court." When a bunch of farmers are going broke every day and the judge sits there very proudly and says: "This is my court . . ."; they say: "Who the hell are you?" He was just a fellow human being, same as they were.

These farmers gathered this one particular day. I suppose some of 'em decided to have a little drink, and so they developed a little courage. They decided: we'll go down and teach that judge a lesson. They marched into the courtroom, hats on, demanded to visit with him. *He* decided he would teach *them* a lesson. So he says: "Gentlemen, this is my court. Remove your hats and address the court properly."

They just laughed at him. They said, "We're not concerned whose court this is. We came here to get redress from your actions. The things you're doing, we can't stand to have done to us any more." The argument kept on, and got rougher. He wouldn't listen. He threatened them. So they drug him from his chair, pulled him down the steps of the courthouse, and shook a rope in front of his face. Then, tarred and feathered him.

The governor called out the National Guard. And put these farmers behind barbed wire. Just imagine . . . (he weeps) . . . in this state. You don't forget these things.

■   ■   ■   ■

Emil Loriks

*On a farm in Arlington, South Dakota. He had served in the state senate from
1927 through 1934.*

*"In 1924, our grain elevator went broke. Farm prices collapsed. I remember
signing a personal note, guaranteeing the commission company against loss. I
didn't sleep very good those nights. The banks were failing all over the state.
The squeeze was beginning to be felt. The stock market panic didn't come as
any surprise to us. Our government had systematically done everything
wrong. . . . We were going to take the profits out of war. The only thing we did
was put a ceiling on wheat. We passed high protective tariffs, other countries
retaliated. . . ."*

THERE'S A SAYING: "DEPRESSIONS are farm led and farm fed." That was
true in the thirties. As farmers lost their purchasing power, the big tractors
piled up at the Minneapolis-Moline plant in the Twin Cities. One day they
closed their doors and turned their employees out to beg or starve. My
cousin was one of them. I took my truck to Minneapolis and brought him
and his family out to my farm for the duration. They stayed with us until
the company opened up again, two or three years later.

During my first session in the state senate, in 1927, five hundred farmers
came marching up Capitol Hill. It thrilled me. I didn't know farmers were
intelligent enough to organize. (Laughs.) They stayed there for two days. It
was a strength I didn't realize we had.

The day after they left, a senator got up and attacked them as anarchists
and bolsheviks. (Laughs.) They had a banner, he said, redder than anything
in Moscow, Russia. What was this banner? It was a piece of muslin, hung
up in the auditorium. It said: "We Buy Together, We Sell Together, We Vote
Together." This was the radical danger. (Laughs.) They'd been building cooperatives, which the farmers badly needed.

I was the first man to answer him from the senate floor. Eleven others
took turns. He never got reelected. In the lower house, we had about thirty
or forty members of the Farmer's Union. It was quite an education for me.

Among the members of our Holiday Association were bankers, businessmen, the president of the Farm Bureau, of the Chamber of Commerce.
(Laughs.) They didn't stick their necks out very far, but the meetings were
always jammed. People were hanging out of windows. Our slogan was:
"Neither buy nor sell and let the taxes go to hell." (Laughs.)

Melons on Frank Tengle's porch. Hale County, Alabama

WALKER EVANS, 1936

Oh, the militancy then! At Milbank, during a farm sale, they had a sheriff and sixteen deputies. One of them got a little trigger-happy. It was a mistake. The boys disarmed him so fast, he didn't know what happened. They just yanked the belts off 'em, didn't even unbuckle 'em. They took their guns away from 'em. After that, we didn't have much trouble stopping sales.

Thirteen highways to Sioux Falls were blocked. They emptied the stockyards there in a day or two. There was some violence, most of it accidental.

I'll never forget a speech by a Catholic priest at a Salem meeting, straight south of here about forty miles. It was the most fiery I ever heard. He said, "If you men haven't got the guts to picket the roads and stop this stuff from going to market, put on skirts and get in the kitchen and let your wives go out and do the job." (Laughs.) The boys used the police stations as their headquarters. (Laughs.) The police couldn't do much. The sheriffs and deputies just had to go along.

That judge situation in Iowa was a warning. In Brown County, farmers would crowd into the courtroom, five or six hundred, and make it impossible for the officers to carry out the sales. (Laughs.)

Deputies would come along with whole fleets of trucks and guns. One lone farmer had planks across the road. They ordered him to remove them. They came out with guns. He said, "Go ahead and shoot, but there isn't one of you S.O.B.s getting out of here alive." There were about fifteen hundred farmers there in the woods. The trucks didn't get through. It was close in spirit to the American Revolution.

One incident stands out in my memory. It was a mass meeting in the city park at Huron. Ten thousand farm folks were in attendance. I had invited Governor Warren Green to appear. He stressed law and order. He seemed frightened. Then came the surprise of the evening: John A. Simpson, president of the National Farmers Union. He electrified the crowd with his opening remarks, which I remember verbatim: "When constitutions, laws and court decisions stand in the way of human progress, it is time they be scrapped." When the meeting was adjourned, the crowd did not move. In unison came a mighty roar: "We want Simpson! WE WANT SIMPSON!" They didn't budge until he was called back to the platform.

The Holiday Association was fairly conservative. There was a United Farmers League that was leftist. In the northern part of the state. The business community welcomed us to head off the extreme leftists, the Commies. We didn't have anything to do with 'em.

The situation was tense in ten or eleven states. You could almost smell the powder. When Governor Herring of Iowa called out the militia, Milo Reno said, "Hold off. I'll not have the blood of innocent people on my

hands." He suggested they picket the farmyards instead of highways. We
had a heck of a time getting the farmers off Highway 75. There were probably a thousand of them out there. Reno called a meeting at Sioux City.
About thirty thousand farmers showed up. We decided to go to Washington
and settle for a farm program.

If Roosevelt hadn't come in in '32, we'd a' been in real trouble. I'll never
forget our meeting with him. He came to Pierre on a special train. He appeared on the rear platform. Next thing I know, we were ushered into a
private room, some of us leaders of farm and labor. We had about an hour
with the president.

He pointed to the Missouri River and said, "This is the greatest resource
of your state. It's got to be developed." He told us how Sweden had developed their power resources for the benefit of the people—the low rates of
electricity and so forth. He was extremely well informed.

I resigned from the state senate in 1934 to become president of the
South Dakota Farmers Union. We had many battles. Before that, I'd introduced a bill to cut penalty interest in delinquency payments from twelve
percent to six. So I was attacked. The local editor said my radical legislation
would destroy the state. (Laughs.)

Reactionary forces have controlled South Dakota since statehood. Corporation interests like the gold mine out here. That's the first time I heard
the word "communist." I stayed at the Waverly Hotel, so they called that a
Communist headquarters. They started to use that word about everything
they didn't like. I had to look it up in the dictionary. (Laughs.)

We have the world's richest gold mine out here, in the Black Hills. While
in the legislature, I was one of the promoters of a tax on ore. The mine was
owned by the Hearst interests. It was very difficult. We took the matter to
the people by the route of a referendum. We won. We passed the tax. Our
slogan was: "Tax gold, not Russian thistles." These thistles, thorny, hateful
things, were stacked, during the drought of '33, and fed to our livestock. They
have lots of proteins.

It was in '35—we had this campaign to raise a million tax dollars. In the
town of Phillips, one evening, during a blizzard, I was met by a crowd of miners. They were given the day off and a stake to attend this meeting. They
surrounded me and said this tax would cost six hundred of them their jobs.
They were busted farmers and fortunately found a job in these Home Stake
mines. I went back home feeling worried. But the tax was passed, and not a
single miner lost his job.

They had been stirred up by the mining interests. They made grants to
colleges all over the state. When the tax was on the verge of passing, they'd

write the alumni, send along a check and a message: Wire your senator to oppose this vicious, discriminatory tax. (Laughs.) Today, they're in a squeeze like us farmers, because the price of gold is fixed and the cost is going up. But they get a moratorium on taxes. We don't.

In 1938, I ran for Congress. I carried the votes in the cities and lost the straggling farm precincts. A week before election, Senator Case, Governor Bushfield and my opponent asked the Dies Committee to investigate me. A night or two before election, they put out a picture of me and the Farmers Union Board meeting with CIO people. Here was proof that I was a Communist.

After I lost the election, Senator Case apologized to me. He said his name was used without his consent. The papers also broke their neck apologizing— after the election. I had served papers on some of them. One said I had marched in a Communist parade. I've never seen a Communist parade.

Whimsically, he recalls the names of prominent and wealthy Dakotans, big grain men, who were members of the Holiday Association in the thirties. "They're millionaires today and a lot of these have gone reactionary."

Once in a while I'll meet a farmer who'll thank me. He'll say: "You sure helped me out. I was busted, and I got that loan." But it doesn't happen too often. A lot of fellows that were rescued became Roosevelt haters and extremely conservative.

Today, corporations are moving in. Agribusiness. Among their clients are movie stars and doctors. Good investments.

This cattle operation is like a crap game. They can write off their losses, charge depreciation. . . . The small farmer doesn't stand a chance.

■   ■   ■   ■

Ruth Loriks, His Wife

ONE TIME WE WERE driving up to Aberdeen. It was during the grasshopper days in 1933. The sun was shining brightly when we left home. When we were about halfway, it just turned dark. It was the grasshoppers that covered the sun.

We had a large garden. The chickens would go in there and pick what little grass which they'd find. Our neighbors said: "The grasshoppers have come in, they'd taken every leaf off our trees, they're even starting to eat the fence posts." I thought that was a joke. Well, the next day they moved

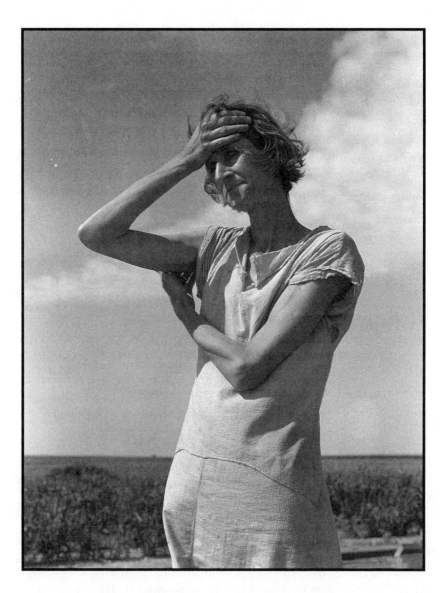

Wife of a migratory laborer with three children,
near Childress, Texas (Nettie Featherston)

DOROTHEA LANGE, 1938

on here, and they did line up the fence posts. My faithful hen sort of kept them off the tomatoes (laughs), but they were moving in.

One day at noon, we had one of our worst dust storms. I never want to see one again! The air was so filled. We could just see it float in, and we had good, heavy storm windows. A year before, we heard of the dust storms to the south. They were collecting wheat to send down there by the carloads. Some of the good folks said, "Better share, because we never know when we may have a drought." The next year, we finally did. I'm surprised to think we lived through it.

This neighbor woman lost her husband, and, of course, he was owing in the bank. So the auctioneers come out there, and she served lunch, and she stood weeping in the windows. "There goes our last cow. . . ." And the horses. She called 'em by names. It just pretty near broke our hearts. They didn't give her a chance to take care of her bills. They never gave her an offer. They just came and cleared it out. She just stood there crying. . . .

■   ■   ■   ■

Clyde T. Ellis

Former congressman from Arkansas. For twenty-five years, he was general manager of the National Rural Electric Cooperative Association.

THE DIRTY THIRTIES—the phrase was coined where we had the dust storms. My people came from Arkansas, where the years of drought coincided with the hard years of the Depression. Even the one good year was no good. Everything dried up . . . the springs, the wells, the ponds, the creeks, the rivers.

We saw bank failures everywhere. In my county, all but three of perhaps a dozen failed. The most valuable thing we lost was hope. A man can endure a lot if he still has hope.

Mountain people are more rigorous than others. We lived a harder life. We had to grow or make most of the things we needed. The country never did lend itself to mechanization . . . still doesn't. Rock. We had relatives who just gave up. Broke up homes, scattered to different states. From down in my county, many would go to what we called *De*-troit. Then they started to go to California, any way they could. Thumbing rides . . . I thumbed rides when I was peddling Bibles. It was during a summer, while still in high school.

I became a schoolteacher. It didn't pay much, but it was decent work. I taught in a one-room country school. By the time Roosevelt was elected, I'd

Inhabitants of Nethers, Virginia, in front of
post office

Arthur Rothstein, 1935

been to law school. A group of us there decided if we were going to hell, we might just as well get active in it. We ran for office ourselves.

I ran for the state legislature. I didn't ask the machine. So I was viciously attacked at county meetings. The political and economic establishment were one. But I was elected. The majority in the House were new fellows who had beaten the sitting candidates. We called it the Revolution of 1932, and organized ourselves as Young Turks.

I'd been talking about electricity for the people. The little towns hardly had any—just a putt-putt plant that wasn't reliable. The rural people had nothing. We could see the fogs rise over the White River, and when the river was up big, we heard the roar. We knew there was tremendous power going to waste. We had read about hydroelectric plants elsewhere in the world. We talked about it, but there wasn't much we could do. The power companies were against it. Arkansas is probably the state most completely dominated by a power company.

We tried to do something about flood control—and in the process do something about electrification—because the TVA had come to be and it was multipurpose: flood control and power.

We set to form electric co-ops, hoping to buy power from the companies. It would be too long to wait on the dams. They demanded an outrageous price. They were determined to fight the cooperatives all the way.

In 1934, I was elected to the state senate, and introduced another rural electrification bill. It was passed in '35, but it was still a struggle. It became a model for the REA* and other states used it around the country. In 1936, we got some electric co-ops organized.

Today, there are dams up and down the White River, and others along the Arkansas. Industry has come into the state and development is encouraged. And yet, there are some areas that have never recovered from the Depression.

"What I'm about to tell you is related to poverty. In 1942, I ran for the U.S. Senate on the issue of rural electrification—but just at that time, Bataan fell. There was only one thing our people were interested in—the lives of our boys. Almost all the boys were in National Guard units. These were the children of the poor, who joined immediately because it gave them a few dollars. My baby brother, Harold, had no work. He quit school, volunteered. He was killed. . . .

"They were the first to go. Our whole county was cleaned out of young boys in Corregidor. . . ."

* Rural Electrification Administration.

I wanted to be at my parents' house when electricity came. It was in 1940. We'd all go around flipping the switch, to make sure it hadn't come on yet. We didn't want to miss it. When they finally came on, the lights just barely glowed. I remember my mother smiling. When they came on full, tears started to run down her cheeks. After a while, she said: "Oh, if we only had it when you children were growing up." We had lots of illness. Anyone who's never been in a family without electricity—with illness—can't imagine the difference.

From there, I went to my grandmother's house. It was a day of celebration. They had all kinds of parties—mountain people getting light for the first time.

There are still areas without electricity. Coal oil lamps are used, with the always dirty chimneys. But there are more and more electric co-ops, which first sprang out of the New Deal. And the power companies are still fighting us. . . .

Editor and Publisher

Fred Sweet

During the last years of the Depression, he was editor and publisher of the Mount Gilead Union-Register. *The town in central Ohio had a population of 2,500.*

OH, GOD, ONE OF the reasons I went broke is that a farmer would say: "I want to put an ad in the paper. I had to sell the place off." He had so many head of Jersey cattle and a baler and a tractor and wagon and this and that. At the bottom of the ad, there was always the line: "And other articles too numerous to mention."

You'd go to the auction and what would you see among the "articles too numerous to mention"? A doll, a couple of books, a basket with the Bible in it, the kids' wagon. . . . Here you had the whole history of the family in all this junk. People pawing over it and buying it for a penny on the dollar.

I never had the heart—the guy wanted a forty-inch ad. Twenty-five cents an inch. That's ten bucks, isn't it? And he always wanted about fifty or a hundred handbills to put on telephone posts and fences. How could you charge a guy who's dead broke for those extra handbills? You'd feel funny about charging for the ad in the first place.

The paper had 843 subscribers when I took over. When I left, it had about 2,780. It was a great success editorially. But I was running a New Deal paper in a Republican town. The two other papers got the legal advertising. I didn't have a share of that stuff.

You see, the judge of the Probate Court is a Republican. The law says he's got to publish certain kinds of ads in two newspapers of general circulation. If he'd been a Democrat, I would've gotten a piece of the business, see? But that was only one of the reasons I went broke.

There's one factory in Mount Gilead at the time. It's making hydraulic presses for airplane fuselages. 1940—the war's coming, but it's still Depression down here. Highly skilled mechanics are working for sixty, seventy cents an hour. In Cincinnati, Cleveland and Toledo, they're making $2.50.

Into town one day comes a walking delegate from the union. He says, "I find there's nobody around here wants to be seen even talking to me. Everybody's scared." I said, "The back end of the shop is yours any time you want a bunch of guys to come down here. We'll pull the shades down and you can sit behind the press down there and nobody will see you." So our little newspaper office became the center where the plot was laid to organize the company.

The president of the company was the superintendent of the Presbyterian Sunday school. He dominated the whole town. But the men in the plant responded. Pretty soon, the paper was covering the organizing drive. I'm trying to play it right down the middle in the news columns. Every time the union's got something to say, I'd call up this guy: "Have you got anything to say?" I'd print 'em side by side. But in my own column, I'd express my personal thoughts.

Pretty soon, the head of the town's biggest department store comes over. "Fred, you gotta get off this union kick." I said, "It would be a good thing for this town to have a union." A couple of weeks later, he jerks his ad. Biggest advertiser. (Laughs.)

Pretty soon we've got the Legion with ax handles and all the rest of it. The county sheriff lets the highway repair trucks haul the Legionnaires with their Legion caps. The highway department supplies the ax handles, and they beat up the pickets.

Eventually, the place gets organized. On a Saturday night, this department store man comes in, takes me to his place, and puts me near the cash register. He says, "I want you to stand here and watch for a while." Here are these machinists coming in with their paychecks bigger than they ever had in their lives. They're payin' bills they've been runnin' for six months or a year, two years.

The guy's amazed. He says, "I shouldn't have taken the ad out. You were right. I was wrong." But it was too late. I haven't got any money. I'm consistently overdrawn at the bank. One day it's gotten to the point where the kid linotype operator is sitting on the front porch with a knife about this long in his lap. He's also got the paycheck he tried to cash at the bank. "I want my $15." Well, I simply failed in the country newspaper business. . . .

■   ■   ■   ■

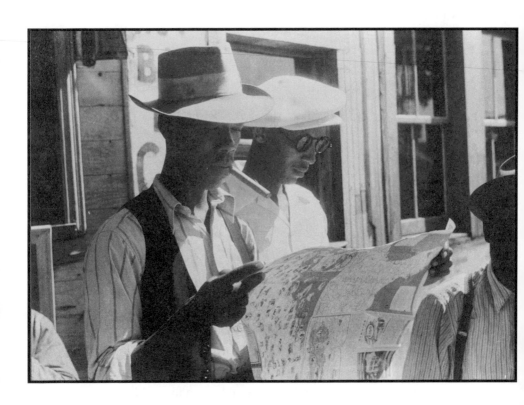

Florida migrants studying road map before leaving Elizabeth City,
North Carolina for the state of Delaware

Jack Delano, 1940

W. D. (Don) Maxwell

He recently retired as editor of the Chicago Tribune. *As much as any living journalist, he reflects the thoughts and spirit of the paper's singular publisher, Colonel Robert R. McCormick.*

"*The first interview I really had was on a Saturday. I got a call from the Colonel's office. His first question was: 'How far is it from Vladivostok to Shanghai?' I said, 'Colonel, that's one of the few things I don't know. But if you'll excuse me, I'll run downstairs and look it up.' I called him back in five minutes and told him how many miles it was. He was pleased that I didn't bluff it.*

"*He had a push button on his desk. Whenever he'd use it, his secretary knew he wanted to get rid of the visitor. On one occasion, the head of the UP had come up to tell of an interview he had with MacArthur. He had a cropped haircut, like the boys used to wear in college. He talked and he talked, and the Colonel was listening intently. I heard the button, so the man had to go. The Colonel said, 'Don, I want to talk with you.' I assumed it was something important concerning MacArthur. He looked at me and said, 'Why does he wear his hair like that?'*

"*The Colonel and MacArthur were very good friends. He admired military men very much. You know, he wrote the life of Grant and all kinds of treatises. When he visited Russia as a boy, he went around with the Grand Duke Nicholas. He wrote about the efficiency of the Russian army. It didn't prove to be valid later on, but at that time . . .*"

What was the Colonel's reaction to the Crash of '29?
I KNOW HE BOUGHT a lot of cattle downstate, so he'd be sure to have steaks (laughs), if things went completely to pieces. He also had money in different lock boxes in New York, so he'd have plenty when he went there.

Did he ever say anything when Roosevelt's name was mentioned?
I don't think anybody would mention it. (Laughs.) The way to get along with the Colonel was very simple. When he proposed something, you'd say: "That's interesting. I'd like twenty-four hours to think it over." If you came back with more arguments against it than for it, he'd say, "I think you're right." He wasn't infallible.

Hardly anybody ever got fired. An exception was Bob Jones, who quit. It was silly. The Colonel asked him to put a map in the paper. He was great on maps. During the war, we were probably the best mapmaking paper in the

United States on battles and so forth. Well, Jones told the Colonel, "We just had it three days ago." That was not the right thing to say. The Colonel hadn't seen it (laughs), and if he hadn't seen it, why . . .

. . . It wasn't there.
That's right. Anyway, I became the news editor. That's in '30. You see, he was a patrician. So was Roosevelt. They weren't going to push around, either by the other one. The Colonel had control of his paper, and no boss could tell him: I like Roosevelt, don't print that. He hated Roosevelt's hypocrisy.

He was friendly to Roosevelt at the start. So was Patterson.* But when F.D.R. tried to wreck the Supreme Court and shove through the NRA, the Colonel was against him. It was an attempt to impose upon people something you could get by with in Russia. When a delegation of merchants came over and demanded the *Tribune* quit attacking the NRA, the Colonel listened to them, ushered them out and ordered a front-page cartoon. It had a great big barbed-wire fence, with poor people trying to get through. The caption was: "No Relief Anywhere. NRA."

Did the Colonel think up the cartoons himself?
He had an editorial conference every day, which the cartoonists and writers attended. He did all the talking. There wasn't much discussion. He'd have something he wanted written about or cartooned. John McCutcheon never paid much attention to that.† Orr was a kind of hatchet man that would be the political cartoonist.

He fought Roosevelt from that time on. Not very successfully. We had a candidate named Landon that got nowhere. We had Willkie, though the Colonel wasn't sold on him. He fought hard for Taft two times. The Illinois delegation stayed right in line. He liked to have a state delegation that went down the *Tribune* line all the way.

At one time, the Colonel was so irritated with the New Deal, he ordered a star taken out of our flag. It was on a standard in the lobby of the Tribune Tower. The Rhode Island Supreme Court had upheld some New Deal measure. He wanted the star representing that state removed from the flag.

I called up our law firm. They said: "You better put it right back or you'll all be in jail. You can't deface the American flag." Now they let 'em burn it

---

* Captain Joseph Patterson, the Colonel's cousin, publisher of the New York *Daily News.*
† His were primarily nonpolitical cartoons. His most celebrated, "Injun Summer," has been reprinted every season for many years.

on the streets, like Spock and those other fellows. The Colonel would have taken after those kids that burn and desecrate flags.

There were numerous anti-WPA cartoons, as I recall. . . .
He didn't believe in this WPA. He thought it was a waste of money. Guys that should be doing something useful were sweeping leaves. We never fought relief as relief. We fought this boondoggling.

And those cartoons portraying New Deal professors in mortarboard hats. . . .
There's nothing that proved him more right. A lot of people agree with him today. If he was against professors, it was the kind that today join these rebels in destroying these universities. It's about as silly as joining with the rebels in the Civil War when you wanted to protect the North.

I'm thinking about the Brain Trusters. . . .
He was against Tugwell. As it happened, everybody else turned on Tugwell, too. The Colonel was against Wallace. He was against Ickes. Ickes hated him, and he hated Ickes. When they showed their animus and tried to get the Colonel, he counterattacked. The first thing you know, we're on the aggressive and they're on the defensive.

Did those protest marches in the thirties bother him?
Not too much. He'd be against 'em, but there's nothing like this stuff today. When Episcopal ministers led a rabble from down here to Georgia or something like that.

All of the Colonel's behavior fits in with the pattern of the patrician. I gave him the title "The Duke of Chicago." As a duke, he was kind to the peasants and fought for their rights. You might say he treated his subjects very well.

■   ■   ■   ■

Carey McWilliams

Author; editor, The Nation.
"I had been conditioned for the 1929 Crash. My father was a prosperous cattleman in northwest Colorado. In 1919, in the wake of World War I, the cattle market fell apart. From 1914 to 1918, western cattlemen had experienced a bonanza. They continued to expand. They thought it was going on forever. It didn't. They all went to the wall, including my father. It had a tremendous impact on my family.

"My mother took my brother and myself to live in California, which is where you go under these circumstances. . . ."

THE LATE TWENTIES AND early thirties was a time of innocence.

After the stock market crash, some New York editors suggested that hearings be held: what had really caused the Depression? They were held in Washington. In retrospect, they make the finest comic reading. The leading industrialists and bankers testified. They hadn't the foggiest notion what had gone bad. You read a transcript of that record today with amazement: that they could be so unaware. This was their business, yet they didn't understand the operation of the economy. The only good witnesses were the college professors, who enjoyed a bad reputation in those years. No professor was supposed to know anything practical about the economy.

It was a mood of great bewilderment. No one had anticipated it, despite the fact that we had many severe panics in the past. The innocence of the business leaders was astonishing. There were groups pictured at the time as being vicious, arch-reactionary and so forth . . . the Liberty League, for instance. There was a bit of truth in it, but by and large, they were babes in the wood or comedians.

There were obvious symptoms before the Crash . . . ?
Oh, yes. There was a runaway stock market. The value of stocks was all out of relation to earnings. There was indication of severe trouble in Europe. Reparations had gone from bad to worse in Germany. Hitler was beginning to make noises in the early twenties. Mussolini in Italy . . .

Could the Depression have been avoided?
In '29 I'm sure it could. If you started back at some point well before 1929, with modern fiscal management, with an understanding of the business cycle.

As a result of my father's experience in Colorado in 1919, and my own during the Great Depression, my confidence was destroyed in the operation of this economy. I've tried—unsuccessfully—not to acquire any property. I didn't have confidence in stocks and bonds. The whole thing was put together in a way that didn't inspire my confidence. And it doesn't now. This may be an unreasonable attitude on my part, nonetheless. . . .

There was a delayed reaction to the events of October, 1929. I was practicing law in Los Angeles. In a year or two, I saw the impact on clients—the kind of widows who are legion in southern California. Who had brought money out from the Middle West and had invested it in fly-by-night real estate promotions. They began to lose their property. I was bugged when I saw what was happening. There was a feverish activity in foreclosures.

When I got out of law school in 1927, I was not a political person. I was an H. L. Menckenite character. My interests became increasingly social and political as the thirties began to unfold.

My first reaction to Roosevelt was very adverse. I remember particularly my great disappointment in a 1932 speech he made at the Hollywood Bowl. I thought it was fatuous. He didn't have a ghost of an idea, really, of what the Depression was all about. He was going to balance the budget, he was going to do all kinds of things, unrelated to the problems he had to face. He, too, was an innocent. He had no program. He was pressured into doing the fine things he did.

The labor movement, the sit-ins, were responsible for the labor legislation. The Farm Holiday movement was responsible for the farm program. Dr. Townsend, Coughlin, Huey Long and company were responsible for the pressures that brought about social security. Roosevelt was responsive, sympathetic. In later years, I became a great admirer.

There were many pension movements in California, aside from Doctor Townsend's. It was fascinating to attend these early meetings. At the same time, you had some apprehensions about their character. They had elements of the demagogic. The Allen Brothers and "Ham and Eggs." The Utopian Society . . .

The critical year, in my own personal experience, was 1934. First, you had the San Francisco General Strike. Then you had Upton Sinclair's campaign for governor. I had known Sinclair. We were good friends. I covered the campaign for the *Baltimore Sun*. It was amazing. He ran as the Democratic nominee and almost won. This man started out a year before the elections with a pamphlet and no resources—and a reputation of being an atheist, a Socialist and a free love advocate. The motion picture industry brought obscene pressure to bear on their employees, threatening to close the studios if Sinclair was elected. He rolled up a vote of 800,000.

He had this passionate conviction that he could in fact end poverty in California.* I remember six or eight years after the '34 campaign, way in the wilds of northern California, written on rocks or on approaches to bridges, you could see this slogan in chalk: "End Poverty In California." It was an enormously educational campaign. I think it would have been a disaster if Sinclair had been elected. He wouldn't have known what to do. But he did have the conviction that poverty was man-made, that you didn't need it.

---

* EPIC (End Poverty In California) was the symbol of Sinclair's candidacy.

Going around the state in those years, you saw California as synony-
mous with abundance. It's so enormously rich, especially in agriculture. Yet
you saw all kinds of crops being destroyed. There were dumps in southern
California, where they would throw citrus fruits and spray them with tar
and chemicals. At a time when thousands of people were in real distress.*
So my Menckenisms began to fade as the thirties progressed.

You could easily romanticize the thirties. The racial attitudes were not
very good. I was intimately involved with these issues, and the attitudes
were incredible. Though there was no categorization of the poor as there is
today—the former doctor, the man who lost his law practice, the businessman, everybody was in on it—there was no feeling that there was a national
race problem.

I was appointed by Governor Culbert Olson in 1938 as chief of the Division of Immigration and Housing. It put me in touch with all the minority
groups in the state: Mexican-Americans, Japanese-Americans, Chinese-
Americans, Hindus, Filipinos. Negroes were not as significant as a group in
California as they are today.

In the second half of the thirties, about 350,000 Dust Bowl refugees
flooded the state. They were promptly stereotyped, exactly like a racial minority. They were called Okies and Arkies: they were shiftless and lazy and
irresponsible and had too many children, and if we improve the labor camps
and put a table in, they would chop it up and use it for kindling. Once I went
into the foyer of this third-rate motion picture house in Bakersfield and I
saw a sign: Negroes and Okies upstairs.

When the war boom began in California around 1939, these Okies and
Arkies were the salvation of the state. They promptly went into shipyards and
defense plants. Within a couple of years, the stereotype began to fade. Now
these people think of themselves as old Californians. Of course, they look
down on the recent migrants from the South. The stereotype is the same.

When they first came in, they had no racist feelings. They were too pre-
occupied with their own distress. At the time of their migration, there were
many Mexicans on public assistance, meager, inadequate. As the Okies
came in, the authorities thought they could get rid of the Mexicans. I was
eyewitness to many deportation trains that left the Southern Pacific station, taking thousands of Mexican-Americans back to Mexico, with their
families and bundles of belongings. Of course, they'd turn right around and
come back. And the process would be repeated.

---

* Dorothy Comingore, a former film actress (*Citizen Kane*), recalls, "I saw heaps of oranges
covered with gasoline and set on fire and men who tried to take *one* orange shot to death."

I inspected labor camps. The conditions were not to be believed. There were no programs of aid for these people. The camps were filthy. We had a labor camp population of 175,000 in August and September, the harvest season. In the spring, they'd force people off relief rolls to take jobs at twenty cents an hour. I induced Governor Olson to let me hold some hearings. We recommended they not be cut off relief unless they were paid twenty-seven and a half cents an hour. The reaction could hardly have been more violent had we bombed San Joaquin Valley. Outrageous, that they should pay twenty-seven and a half cents an hour.

At his request, the La Follette Committee came to California in 1939 to investigate the denial of elementary liberties to farm workers and to probe the role of the Associated Farmers. Earl Warren, then attorney general for the state, refused to cooperate, defending sheriffs in "every rural county of the state." The mass evacuation of Japanese-Americans is recounted. Again, he opposed Warren, who was in its favor. ". . . his education and growth as a civil libertarian were unquestionably acquired in California. I smile when I see these signs: Impeach Earl Warren."

The impulse of the New Deal was over by 1938. Its most creative years were 1934 to 1938. There were a lot of good times, too, because money was not so terribly important. A friend of mine and I had a protégé, a young writer. We rented him a room in Los Angeles and put up $5 a week to sustain him while he was doing a couple of books. He managed to live on $10 a week. On so meager an amount, we were philanthropists, you see. (Laughs.)

If such times were to come again, it would not be the same. Our discontents today are more vague and ill-defined. At the same time, we have an apparatus of police controls that could develop into a kind of American fascism. It would not be European style.

I think the New Deal saved American capitalism. It was a bridge. But it never really solved the problems.

Book Three

Concerning the New Deal

Gardiner C. Means

Co-author (with A. A. Berle) of The Modern Corporation and Private
Property.

"In the summer of '33, I got a call from Rex Tugwell: would I consider
coming down to Washington?"*

*He became economic adviser on finance to Henry Wallace, secretary of
agriculture. Among his other New Deal assignments were his work as a member of the Consumer Advisory Board of the NRA and as director of the Industrial Section of the National Resources Planning Board. During the war, he
was chief fiscal analyst in the Budget Bureau.*

AT THE BEGINNING OF the New Deal, they called it a revolution. Then they
began to say it wasn't a revolution. Our institutions were being shored up
and maintained. What really happened was a revolution in point of view.
We backed into the twentieth century describing our actual economy in
terms of the small enterprises of the nineteenth century.

We were an economy of huge corporations, with a high degree of con-
centrated control. It was an economy that was in no sense described by
classical theory. What Roosevelt and the New Deal did was to turn about
and face the realities.

It was this which produced the yeastiness of experimentation that made
the New Deal what it was. A hundred years from now, when historians look
back on it, they will say a big corner was turned. People agreed that old things

* Rexford G. Tugwell is one of the original members of Roosevelt's "Brain Trust" along with
Dr. Means's colleague Adolph A. Berle.

didn't work. What ran through the whole New Deal was finding a way to make things work.

Before that, Hoover would loan money to farmers to keep their mules alive, but wouldn't loan money to keep their children alive. This was perfectly right within the framework of classical thinking. If an individual couldn't get enough to eat, it was because he wasn't on the ball. It was his responsibility. The New Deal said: Anybody who is unemployed isn't necessarily unemployed because he's shiftless.

Roosevelt was building up new ideas in a milieu of old ideas. His early campaign speeches were pure Old Deal. He called for a balanced budget. When he got into office, the whole banking system collapsed. It called for a New Deal.

I was never told what to do at any time, during those early days. I made my own way. We had meetings that would run into the early morning. A dozen of us sitting around the table, thrashing out problems. They were more than bull sessions, because we were making decisions.

I answered some of the mail for Wallace. Great quantities came pouring in, letters from everywhere. I must have handled some two, three hundred. They were proposals from people, solutions to all sorts of problems. Some of them crackpot, some of them quite good. Everybody had a suggestion. The country was aware, as it never was before, that it was on the edge of something.

Talking a couple of days ago with a couple of old New Dealers, we agreed it was a very exhilarating period. There was no question in our minds we were saving the country. A student of mine remembered how exciting it was to him. He worked in the Department of Labor. He said, "Any idea I had, I put down on paper. I'd send it up and somebody would pay attention to it—whoever it was, Madame Perkins, Ickes or Wallace." This is how it was all the way through.

I remember a request from Mrs. Roosevelt. One of the big corporations had thumbed its nose at a stockholder. The woman had written to Mrs. Roosevelt: Have they a right to do this? She sent the letter to Tugwell, who sent it to me. I wrote an answer for Mrs. Roosevelt to send to her. I remember I did have a suggestion for her.

One of the first things I did was get in touch with Mary Rumsey. She was head of the Consumer Advisory Board of the NRA. It was she who sold Roosevelt on the idea of having the consumer represented. The first thing she did when we met was take me down to her limousine—she was Averill Harriman's sister—and had her chauffeur drive us up and down the countryside as we talked. We spent all morning talking about the needs of the consumer, his protection. She was very perceptive.

Another thing I remember. I brought Leon Henderson into the NRA. We sent him up to discuss some problems with General Hugh Johnson, the chief. He was a blustery, flamboyant person. As Henderson started to talk, Johnson began to ride all over him. Leon swore back at him and pounded the table. Johnson loved it and made him his assistant. (Laughs.) This was the kind of climate in Washington at the time—highly personal and highly charged.

The NRA was one of the most successful things the New Deal did. It was killed when it should have been killed. But when it was created, American business was completely demoralized. Violent price cutting and wage cutting . . . nobody could make any plans for tomorrow. Everybody was going around in circles. The NRA changed the attitudes of business and the public. It revived belief that something could be done. It set a floor on prices and on wages.

Pressures had been coming from business to get free of the antitrust acts and have business run business. Pressure was coming from labor for a shorter workweek to spread jobs. It was a whole institutional matter. Roosevelt put the two together. Mary Rumsey brought in consumers' rights. So there were three advisory boards: Business, Labor and Consumer. Codes of behavior were set up. You couldn't sell below cost. . . . Labor got collective bargaining rights. It was, in a sense, a prelude to the Wagner Act. The wage increases were worked out between business and labor.

Most important, laissez-faire in the nineteenth century manner was ended. The government had a role to play in industrial activity. We didn't move into a fascist kind of governmental control, because we continued to use the market mechanism. In the two years of the NRA, the index of industrial production went up remarkably.

Things had been going downgrade—worse, worse, worse. More than anything else, the NRA changed the climate. It served its purpose. Had it lasted longer, it would not have worked in the public interest. Although toward the end, the consumer group was making progress.

Had the NRA continued, it would have meant dangerously diminishing the role of the market in limiting prices. You see, there was little governmental regulation of the NRA. The government handed industry over to industry to run, and offered some minor protection to others in the form of Labor and Consumer Advisory Boards. Industry became scared of its own people. Too much power was being delegated to the code authorities. It was business' fear of business rather than business' fear of government, though they wouldn't quite put it that way. You might say, NRA's greatest contribution to our society is that it proved that self-regulation by industry doesn't work.

Laissez-faire as such certainly did not come to an end with the New Deal. We still have a tremendous amount of freedom of decision making in the individual corporate enterprise. The new element is the government's positive responsibility for making our economy run.

As for those first New Deal days, much of the excitement came from improvisation. Nothing was fully set in the minds of the people there. They were open to fresh ideas. Always. We wouldn't have been where we are now, were it not for Washington improvisations. . . .

This outflowing of people felt they were somehow on the way—though they were not sure how. A surprising number, we discovered, were sons of ministers, rabbis, missionaries. Yes, there was an evangelical quality, though it was nonreligious. People who were personally concerned about a better world came to Washington, were drawn to it. Even though where we were going was still to be worked out. There was an élan, an optimism . . . an evangelism . . . it was an adventure.

■   ■   ■   ■

Raymond Moley

He is seated, on this Indian summer day, at his desk: one of Roosevelt's original Brain Trust. "I had served him in various ways, from the time he ran for governor. I wrote my first speech for him in '28.

"My interest, as was his, was restoring confidence in the American people, confidence in their banks, in their industrial system and in their government. Confidence was the buoyant spirit that brought back prosperity. This has been, always, my contention."

DURING THE WHOLE '33 one-hundred-days' Congress, people didn't know what was going on, the public. Couldn't understand these things that were being passed so fast. They knew something was happening, something good for them. They began investing and working and hoping again.

People don't realize that Roosevelt chose a conservative banker as secretary of treasury* and a conservative from Tennessee as secretary of state.†

---

* William H. Woodin.
† Cordell Hull.

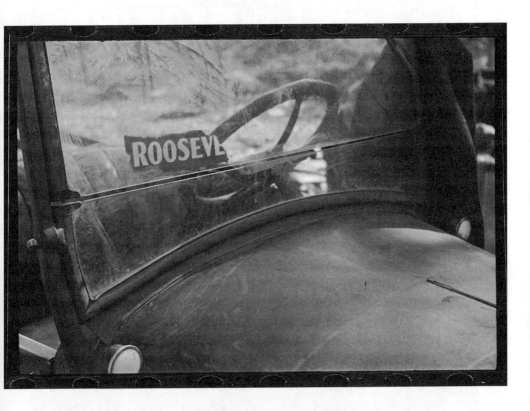

The windshield of a migratory agricultural laborer's car, in a squatter
camp near Sacramento, California

Dorothea Lange, 1936

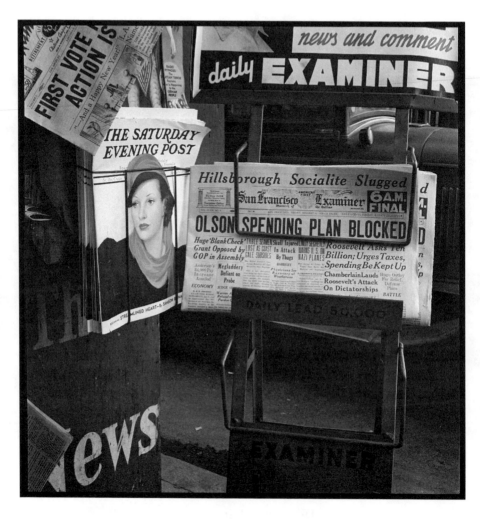

San Francisco, California. After forty-four years of Republican
administration, California gets a Democratic administration.
The California "New Deal" faces same opposition
as the national "New Deal."

DOROTHEA LANGE, 1939

Most of the reforms that were put through might have been agreeable to Hoover, if he had the political power to put them over. They were all latent in Hoover's thinking, especially the bank rescue. The rescue was done not by Roosevelt—he signed the papers—but by Hoover leftovers in the administration. They knew what to do.

The bank rescue of 1933 was probably the turning point of the Depression. When people were able to survive the shock of having all the banks closed, and then see the banks open up, with their money protected, there began to be confidence. Good times were coming. Most of the legislation that came after didn't really help the public. The public helped itself, after it got confidence.

It marked the revival of hope. The people were scared for a little while—a week. Then, Congress passed the bill, and the banks were opened. Roosevelt appealed to them on Sunday night, after the week of the closing. It was his very first fireside chat. They put their money back in the banks, the people were so relieved.

A Depression is much like a run on a bank. It's a crisis of confidence. People panic and grab their money. There's a story I like to tell: In my hometown, when I was a little boy, an Irishman came up from the quarry where he was working, went into the bank and said, "If my money's here, I don't want it. If it's not here, I want it."

The guarantee of bank deposits was put through by Vice President Garner, Jesse Jones (a Texas banker), and Senator Vandenburg—three conservatives. They rammed it down Roosevelt's throat, and he took credit for it ever after. If you can quiet the little fellows, the big fellows pretty much take care of themselves. If you can cover it up to $10,000, all the little fellows are guaranteed. So it's O.K. You didn't have any bank trouble after that.

Now that wouldn't be agreed to by some liberals. But, after all, I was never a real liberal. I was an old-fashioned Democrat. I was a believer in our industrial system. It didn't need a complete rehauling. I thought if we could get it back into operation and normal conditions return, we'd be all right. This happened.

Tugwell thinks we should have gone much further in shaping the economy, but I don't. What we did accomplished its purpose. We don't know what would have happened if something else had been done.

The first New Deal was a radical departure from American life. It put more power in the central government. At the time, it was necessary, especially in the farm area of our economy. Left to itself, farming was in a state of anarchy. Beyond that, there was no need to reorganize in industry. We merely needed to get the farms prospering again and create a market for the industrial products in the cities.

The second New Deal was an entirely different thing. My disenchantment began then. Roosevelt didn't follow any particular policy after 1936. Our economy began to slide downhill—our unemployment increased—after that, until 1940. This is something liberals are not willing to recognize. It was the war that saved the economy and saved Roosevelt.

We had a slight recession in 1937, which was occasioned by his attack on copper prices, specifically, and on business, generally. Of course, his Supreme Court packing plan shocked the people. They resented it. It was his first great defeat. Then he tried to purge Congress in '38. Everyone he tried to purge was reelected, except one congressman in New York.

I think if it weren't for the war, Roosevelt probably would have been defeated in 1940. You would probably have had a more business-minded administration: less centralizing on the part of Washington. More normal conditions would have prevailed.

During those first hundred days, wasn't there a slight fear in some quarters that our society . . . ?
I never had any doubt that our society would survive—and survive in much the way that it had existed before. As Dirksen recently said: our society was not sick, it was mismanaged.

Remember, Roosevelt at the start was a very conservative president. People didn't realize that. In the first place, he was a very prudent governor of New York. He balanced his budget. He was not a spender. We resisted all the efforts of radicals, like La Follette and Tugwell, to spend a lot of money in public works. Roosevelt said: there aren't more than a billion dollars of public works that are worth doing. They wanted five billion dollars. So he compromised on three billion . . . a split between what he said and what they wanted.

What led to Roosevelt's shift from prudence to . . . ?
I think he was tired of reform. He began to bring in the radical elements, who up to that time had not been in support of him. Business went along with him in his early reforms, but after 1937, it began to be nervous about where he was going. He was improvising all the time. Hit or miss.

Unemployment insurance was unsound the way it was financed. When I wrote the original message in '34, the idea was to invest the receipts from the tax in municipal and state bonds and high-grade industrials. Congress created a phony trust fund, which was composed of IOUs of the government. It's unsound. You collect money from the taxes, then you spend it and you put your IOUs in the trust fund. If you did this in private industry, you'd be put in jail.

Unemployment insurance is a welfare measure. It isn't insurance in any sense of the word. More and more people were living off fewer and fewer people. That's when the unsound practices began. Until now, we've got it in a big way . . . even in a period of prosperity.

In 1935, I took a firm stand. I said welfare is a narcotic, because it will never end. We'll have to stop this business and put people to work. The best way to put people to work is to encourage the development of industrial science. The government can't put people to work.

I began to have my doubts in 1935. I had many arguments with him. There were a lot of radicals. I had them in my group. Tugwell, for instance. He expressed sorrow that Roosevelt didn't turn more radical in 1932. As a matter of fact, he doubted very much whether he'd vote for Roosevelt.

The whole city, Washington, began to fill up with these young radicals. They stayed down, many of them there, with Frankfurter. They were scattered all over the lot. Still, it was conservative until '35.

Finally, in '36, in the middle of the year, I quit. I never went back to him again.

Was he trying to persuade you to stick with him?
Yes. He was a proud man, and it was very difficult for him to make the request, yet I couldn't do it. I didn't like the direction in which he was going. He was turning into a demagogue. He was out–Huey Longing Huey Long. He was afraid of Huey.

Huey was a good friend of mine. He was threatening to run for president in 1936. The poll showed that Huey would take ten percent of the vote. I'm sure Farley could confirm this. He would have cut into the Democratic vote all over the country. Roosevelt, in order to counteract that, moved toward the Long program. His tax program in '36 was pure Huey: soak the rich. Roosevelt was using the same demagogic tactics. It's possible Huey Long—if he weren't killed—would have busted open the Democratic Party even then. As George Wallace is doing now.

Of course, Huey had a much finer brain than Wallace. Only he abused his power. He was arrogant and he drank too much. You'd go to see Huey after three o'clock in the afternoon, and he didn't make much sense. He made sense in the morning. He had a rather contemptuous attitude toward Roosevelt. He didn't think Roosevelt was very smart.

I used to go up and see Huey in his apartment at the Mayflower. I said, "Huey, you have a great capacity. Watch out for the people around you." He said, "I haven't got any money. This is the way I live. I live simple." I don't think he enriched himself. But he did have a lot of thieves around him.

He spent himself. He tore his passion to tatters, as Shakespeare would put it. He didn't need to do that. He had too much brains to get violent. But that was his way of dealing with the people down South. One of the things he destroyed was himself. He didn't need to go swaggering around. He was much too good for that. It was one of the great tragedies.

I think Roosevelt was a product of his time, his environment, that sort of thing. He had all that with him. Huey didn't. He came from a poor family, sought power and got it. Roosevelt hated him because he was so different. It was the aristocrat distrusting this farm boy.

POSTSCRIPT: *"Huey Long came up to my office, one hot day in August '33. He said: 'I want you to get a dean for my law school.' I had been teaching Public Law at Columbia. He said: 'I'll pay anything you say. I got a damn good medical school. I want a good law school.' I said: 'I suppose the dean at Harvard gets $15,000.' 'Well, that's nothing.' I thought for a while. I had a student two years before at Columbia. His name was Wayne Morse. He was dean of the Law School at the University of Oregon. 'Call him up,' says Huey. Huey talked to him and said, 'How much you getting? I'll double your salary.'*

"Wayne sent me a telegram: 'What is this all about? Is the senator able to appoint a law school dean?' I sent back a telegram: 'If he offered you the job, you can have it.' So he went to the president of the University of Oregon, who doubled his salary. Now what would have happened had Wayne Morse gone to Louisiana?"

■   ■   ■   ■

C. B. (Beanie) Baldwin

He came to Washington from Virginia in 1933, as an assistant to the secretary of agriculture, Henry Wallace. He served in the administration until the death of Roosevelt in 1945

"When he first met me, Wallace said, 'We've been lookin' for someone with a southern accent in this office.'" (Laughs.)

THE NEW DEAL WAS an uneasy coalition. Fights developed very early between the two factions: one, representing the big farmers, and the other,

Railroad workers, Port Barre, Louisiana

RUSSELL LEE, 1938

the little farmers. The Agricultural Adjustment Administration came into being shortly after I got to Washington. Its purpose was to increase farm prices, which were pitifully low. All the farmers were in trouble, even the big ones. There was a proposal that it be set up independent of the Department. Wallace and Tugwell* were able to thwart that.

You might say there were three interests involved. There was the consumer thing, too. Rex brought Jerome Frank in as general counsel for the Triple-A. To protect them. George Peek, the head of the agency—he resented bein' under Wallace—was only interested in high farm prices. They would never admit it, but George represented the big farmers. And there was the need to protect the sharecroppers and tenant farmers in the South.

Tobacco got down to four cents a pound. Nobody could produce it for that. The Triple-A people reached an agreement with the industry: to more than double the price of tobacco overnight. They wanted no restrictions on the price of cigarettes and smoking tobacco. The net profits would have been greater than the total price paid the small farmers and the labor cost in the manufacture of cigarettes and smoking tobacco, all put together. Naturally, our consumers' group and Jerome Frank raised hell. Wallace decided to turn it down.

Peek, who wanted to see the agreement ratified, went to Roosevelt, undercutting Wallace. The president called the secretary, I happened to be on the phone: "Henry, I'm sorry we've got to make some compromises. I want you to approve this." They argued a little. Finally, Wallace said, "Mr. President, this is your decision." I brought the papers for Wallace to sign. We met in the lobby of the Mayflower. He said, "Beanie, this is the most appropriate place in the country to sign this damned agreement."† (Laughs.)

Wallace was actually opposed to crop restriction. Very few people know this. But we had a problem. Hog prices had just gone to hell. What were they—four, five cents a pound? The farmers were starving to death. They were at the mercy of the packers. We tried to reach an agreement, similar to the tobacco deal—which, despite everything, had worked out fairly well.

They decided to slaughter piggy sows. You know what a piggy sow is? A pregnant pig. They decided to pay the farmers to kill them and the little pigs. Lot of 'em went into fertilizer. This is one of the horrible contradictions we're still seeing.

* Rexford G. Tugwell, undersecretary of agriculture. It was he who suggested Henry Wallace as secretary of agriculture. A political scientist: "Rex was my intellectual mentor."
† The Mayflower Hotel was a favorite gathering place for the lobbyists of various interests.

They lowered the supply goin' to market and the prices immediately went up. Then a great cry went up from the press, particularly the *Chicago Tribune*, about Henry Wallace slaughtering these little pigs. You'd think they were precious babies. The situation was such, you had to take emergency measures. Wallace never liked it.

You had a similar situation on cotton. Prices were down to four cents a pound and the cost of producing was probably ten. So a program was initiated to plow up cotton. A third of the crop, if I remember. Cotton prices went up to ten cents, maybe eleven.

This brought on other complications. The Farm Bureau was pressing for these benefit payments to be made to the land owners. We were fighting for these payments to be made directly to the sharecroppers and the tenant farmers, rather than flowing down through the land owners. In most cases, they'd get very little money.

People like Norman Thomas moved in, highly critical of the Department, and properly, I think. Paul Appleby* and I had meetings with him, told him what we were trying to do. He didn't spare us, either, and I don't blame him. The Southern Tenant Farmers Union picketed the Department of Agriculture. As I look back on it, a very poor job was done in protecting the sharecroppers and the tenant farmers. The bureaucratic process, even in a decent administration, defeats you. And where there's an uneasy coalition of opposing forces . . .

"Roosevelt committed himself in the campaign of '32 to cutting government expenditures. It was the most conservative speech he ever made. So we got started with our hands tied behind our back. A lot of things New Dealers wanted couldn't be done without increasing expenditures.

"He had to shift his position. So he brought Harry Hopkins in. Unemployment had jumped to about sixteen million. Something had to be done. He got a substantial appropriation in '34 for relief and also for public works. The public works thing went to Ickes—the very careful, methodical guy who was gonna be sure that nobody took advantage of the building monies.

"Hopkins persuaded the president that the situation was so desperate that everybody in the country who wanted a job had to have a job. Even with very low pay. Almost overnight, he set up the Civil Works Administration.

"Harry was really a sloppy administrator. Ickes was a very careful guy. Hopkins was impatient and he knew you had to have something to eat on. He was

---

* His associate, the other assistant to the secretary of agriculture.

the kind of guy that seldom wrote a letter. He'd just call and say, 'Send a mil-lion dollars to Arkansas and five million to New York. People are in need.'

"They set up this CWA very hurriedly. There was no means test. Any guy could just walk into the county office—they were set up all over the country—and get a job. Leaf raking, cleaning up libraries, painting the town hall . . . Within a period of sixty days, four million people were put to work.

"There was no real scandal in this thing, but it lent itself to all the reaction-ary criticisms that it couldn't be well managed. With our mores, you just can't dump $20,000 into a county in the Ozarks and say: put people to work. That's contrary to everything our political establishment was brought up to believe.* This lasted only six months. Roosevelt and Hopkins had to end it. They weren't able to get congressional support to continue.

"Roosevelt won another appropriation—three billion—through an omni-bus bill. This brought on another ruckus. Ickes thought it should go for public works: Grand Coulee Dam, Bonneville, projects of this type. They're slow to get under way—wonderful, but they take time. Hopkins thought people should be put to work immediately, even though it might not be done very efficiently."

Among the agencies created was the Resettlement Administration. It was independent of the Department of Agriculture, with Rex Tugwell as head, reporting directly to the president. This was a unique agency and, for that time, fantastic. It was Rex who largely drafted the Executive Order. It had to do with the plight of the small farmer and the migrant worker.

"I was in it from the beginning. Rex brought me in to run the administrative end of it. When he'd delegate authority to someone he trusted, he'd back 'em to the hilt. There were all sorts of bureaucratic battles, but Rex would have nothing to do with 'em. He gave me just absolutely marvelous backing."

Harry Hopkins had established the Rural Rehabilitation Division. It had something to do with urban unemployment. One of the answers was send-ing people back to the farm, even though they had no farm experience. Tugwell objected and he was absolutely right. Farming requires a good deal of skill. These people just would have been lost.

---

* He had an occasion to visit "Cotton Ed" Smith, U.S. senator from South Carolina, a vo-ciferous opponent of many New Deal measures. Apropos of nothing, the senator told him: "You seem like a nice, intelligent young man. I don't know why you work for the govern-ment. Get out where you can make an honest living."

Hopkins recognized it as a mistake fairly early—that this thing ought to be more closely tied to agriculture. So he agreed to transfer the operation to the Resettlement Administration.

"With a paltry $5 million appropriation, the Subsistence Homestead Division was established. A lot of Utopians dreamed of this for years: setting up rural industrial communities. This was given to Ickes originally, but he never had much empathy for Utopians. (Laughs.) All sorts of the craziest ideas came out on how to spend this money. Ickes was glad to get rid of this, so he transferred it to us. Generally, Ickes liked to handle everything, but this was one he wanted out of." (Laughs.)

He describes a project in Hightstown (now called Roosevelt), New Jersey. A group of Jewish ladies' garment workers moved from New York City to this rural community. "The enthusiasm was terrific." It was a cooperative, some working on the farm, others in the garment plant. "They had a hell of a good first year, but you take people out of a highly competitive situation and try to set up a Utopian society, you're gonna have some difficulty. (Laughs.)

"Mrs. Roosevelt tried to get Dubinsky interested,* but he didn't like this co-op nonsense. The garment industry was against it, too. They called it a Social-istic, Communist project. Anyway, it failed."

The Rural Rehabilitation had to do with buying submarginal land. To retire it from cultivation, reforest it and convert it into a state park. Much of the land we were authorized to buy was in the Great Plains area, damaged by dust storms. Tugwell's idea was: These people should be moved to better land, not just kicked off bad land.

This is what Rex and I were most interested in. There were about six million farmers in the country. I think we helped over a sixth of the farm families. A million farms. The most exciting part was the resettlement projects.

Tugwell had a passion for the adjustment of people to the land. But being a good economist, he foresaw what was gonna happen to small farmers, who just couldn't meet the competition. So we set up a certain number of co-op farms, about a hundred of 'em around the country. About twenty thousand families. Everett Dirksen later described it as Russian collectiv-ism. (Laughs.) We were trying to work out cooperatives, where farmers would have their houses grouped, as a matter of convenience. We varied the pattern from place to place—nursery schools for their kids, central markets for their products. . . . Maybe it was Utopian, but I don't think so.

---

* President of the International Ladies Garment Workers Union (ILGWU).

I'll just tell you about one of 'em. We bought this beautiful delta land in Arkansas for about $100 an acre. It's worth about $700 now. We set up this little community of five or six thousand acres. We brought in about fifty young families.* A carefully selected group of young families. . . .

We built these houses, put in a school, nursery . . . they had individual garden plots. It was diversified land—livestock, cotton, fruits, vegetables. They were paid so much a month, and at the end of the year, when the crops were in, they'd divide the profits. It had been operating about two years. They were doin' pretty well. . . .

Will Alexander spent several days on the project visiting with these families. He'd talk to them in the evening, when they were relaxed. They'd say, "Dr. Alexander, this is wonderful. You know, if we're able to stay here four, five years, well be able to go out on our own farm."

It came to us as sort of a shock. See, this hunger for land ownership . . . Although they were happy and more secure than they'd ever been in their lives, they were lookin' forward to gettin' out and ownin' their own land. You have to reckon with this kind of thing.

These projects were all stopped cold, after the death of Roosevelt, all liquidated. Congress saw to it. It's one of the really sad things. They had all sorts of problems, sure—but this certainly would have been an important answer to poverty, as we see it now. Over half the farm families have disappeared. They are contributing to the ghetto problems of the city, black and white.

Almost everything we did became controversial. Hopkins had built a couple of migratory labor camps in California. They were also transferred to us. They were very simple camps—well, *Grapes of Wrath* tells you about them better than I could.

"I got a call from John Steinbeck. He wanted some help. He was planning to write this book on migrant workers. Will Alexander and I were delighted. He said, 'I'm writing about people and I have to live as they live.' He planned to go to work for seven, eight weeks as a pea picker or whatever. He asked us to assign someone to go along with him, a migrant worker. We chose a little guy named Collins, out of Virginia.

"I paid Collins's salary, which was perhaps illegal. He and Steinbeck worked in the fields together for seven or eight weeks. Steinbeck did a very nice thing.

---

* It was now called the Farm Security Administration (FSA). "Rex left, I guess, in '37. He became the chief target of the anti–New Dealers. I think he felt his usefulness had been impaired. I'm also sure he was tired." Dr. Will Alexander succeeded Tugwell.

He insisted Collins be technical director of the film, this little migrant worker. And he got screen credit. . . ."

At these camps, the people ran their own affairs. We had our project manager there to help them.* This became the most controversial thing we ever did. Before we'd build a camp, we'd hold a public hearing. There was a lot of opposition, particularly from groups like the Associated Farmers.

I was on the stand during one of these hearings. A congressman, Al Elliott of California, was cross-questioning me. I had all the information, photographs—the plight of migrant workers. He argued against the camp. The real reason the big farmers didn't want them built is that they were places where the migrants might get together and organize. Think of this guy, Chavez, today—things have changed so little in thirty years, it makes you sick to think of it.

When Elliott finished his slambang cross-examination, I said, "You haven't convinced me not to build the camp. I'm issuing instructions for it to be started." He stormed across the room. He was a heavyweight boxer, about six-three, weighing about 210. I weighed in at 155. (Laughs.) He hollered, "You don't represent the people of my district! *I* represent them!" I said, "I have a national constituency. And a very important part of that are the migrant workers of this big country. I'm telling you again, Congressman Elliott, I'm gonna build this camp." We built it. (Laughs.)

Oh, the battles we had! There were any number of people in Congress who made a career out of it. Senator Byrd of Virginia—my own senator— he was really out to destroy us.† He introduced legislation to abolish the agency.

The Farm Bureau, representing the big farmers, sent a very inexperienced kid into the South to investigate what we were doing. He came back with all sorts of fantastic charges. All of which had been published. I had to answer. I was called on the carpet by Byrd's committee.

There was one thing I had authorized that almost tripped me up. I advised our field workers and county supervisors to include in the rehabilitation loans enough to pay the poll taxes of individuals who couldn't vote.‡ Byrd thought he had me on this one.

---

* See John Beecher, p. 251.
† "He sent me a letter of congratulations when I was appointed administrator of Farm Security."
‡ "In states like Alabama, the tax would amount to as much as $40. It was a bar to poor people voting, particularly Negroes."

He said: "You are using federal money to pay the poll taxes of people in the South, is that true?" I said, "No, it isn't true." He said, "What do you mean?" I said, "We make *loans* to people. Small farmers who can't get credit elsewhere. We make these loans for a variety of reasons. Number one, to buy their seed. Number two, to assure them enough to eat till their crop comes in. Number three, to buy the necessary equipment. Then we have to make sufficient allowance so the kids can at least have decent clothes. And—I have told our supervisors—if these people can register and vote, we should include in the loan enough to pay their poll tax . . . so, Senator, they can become citizens of the United States."

Carter Glass, the senior senator from my state, said I was violating the Virginia Constitution: nobody could pay anybody else's poll tax. I said: "We're not paying them; we're just lending them money as part of a complete operation."

I thought I came out fairly well on it. I was due to go back two days later. The next morning I picked up the *Washington Post*, and here's a front page story: "Baldwin Criticized by Roosevelt for Paying Poll Taxes." Jesus. I knew something had gone wrong. Roosevelt was opposed to the poll tax.

But I knew a guy who was interested in the poll tax question and had entrée to the White House. I said, "Go see Steve Early* and get this message to the president. He's completely misunderstanding what we're doing." He rushed down.

I was back on the stand. And, boy, Byrd was just beamin'! He had me locked. He started out: "Mr. Baldwin, I have a story in the *Washington Post* of yesterday morning saying Roosevelt is opposed to the things you are doing, paying poll taxes." In the meantime, I'm filibustering—took forty minutes with another statement—hoping that guy would show up from the White House. I knew the president was calling a press conference at ten-thirty. I heard a rustle in the back of the room—the place was jammed. This was the hottest story in town. The guy rushed up with a little sheet of paper and handed it to me.

Byrd was really at it now—the president had criticized me and said that I must desist from this activity at once. So I cleared my throat (laughs), and I said: "Senator Byrd, I've just been advised that the president in his press conference, only thirty minutes ago, completely supported my position on poll taxes." Well, my senator from Virginia was the most miserable-looking character you've ever seen. (Laughs.)

* Roosevelt's press secretary.

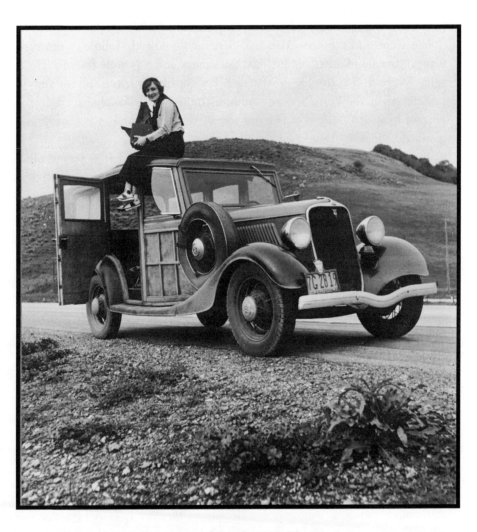

Dorothea Lange, Resettlement Administration
photographer, in California

DOROTHEA LANGE, 1936

Oh, the harassment was constant. It was a colossal job, reorganizing the Resettlement Administration, getting all the agencies to mesh and run smoothly. I had a good staff. But I also knew, in order to save it, we had to have a pretty good people's lobby.

We were under fire in Alabama. Senator Bankhead, Tallulah's uncle, was pretty conservative, but he liked the agency and was quite friendly. He said, "We're in real trouble in Alabama. I've got fifteen letters, all my supporters, sayin' the Farm Security Administration should be abolished. Important men." He looked at me and sort of smiled: "Beanie, what are you gonna do about it?" I said, "Give me two days."

I called our regional director in Alabama and asked him to get all the county supervisors to call all their political friends and get some letters to Senator Bankhead. And I said, "I think you ought to get in at least three thousand letters. Have most of 'em written in pencil. It don't matter what they say, just from the people that we're helpin' 'em."

About ten days went by and Senator Bankhead called me. (Laughs.) He had a little stack of letters, about so high, in opposition. And stacks of letters about *this* high. (Laughs.) He said, "For God's sake, stop these letters. We're safe." (Laughs.)

Under Baldwin's administration of the FSA, photographers were employed to take pictures, showing the plight of the rural poor. Among the people involved were Dorothea Lange, Walker Evans, Ben Shahn and Margaret Bourke-White. "I had to cover up a lot of this—even though we were payin' 'em peanuts— because you know what a reactionary congressman would say: 'Here are these bastards wasting my money. Why are they sending people out to take photographs.'

"We ended up with over a hundred thousand of these photographs. Along about 1940, I had become the most controversial person in the Department of Agriculture. Congress was after me. Because of these projects and because I was a protégé of Tugwell. I knew we weren't going to get by much longer. The only thing we wanted to do was to save these negatives. . . .

"Roy Stryker* got in touch with Archibald MacLeish, who understood the importance of this. He agreed. So we moved all the films quietly into a safe storage space. When MacLeish became Librarian of Congress, we were able to get them in there, where they will always be.

---

* Head of the Historical Division of the Resettlement Administration. "He's the guy responsible for these magnificent photographs."

"I think our most lasting contribution was this collection of photographs. I think it more effectively dramatized the plight of poor people than anything else done in thirty years. It was accidental. We just happened to hit on the medium. . . ."

Pare Lorentz's two documentary film The Plow That Broke the Plains and The River were produced under the auspices of the Farm Security Administration. Again, controversy. "We couldn't get into many movie houses at first. Finally we got into a lot of 'em."

The Depression lessened, but it never really ended until the war. The New Deal was never enough. Looking back, it was a pretty conservative effort. Rex Tugwell once said to me, "Beanie, we were pikers." I'd ask for $800 million, we'd get a couple of hundred million, and we thought we did pretty well. Today, with our war budget. . . .

When Roosevelt's death came, the New Deal was dead as far as I was concerned. I have nothing against Truman, but he simply wasn't up to it. Morgenthau was forced out.* Ickes was forced out. Wallace was fired. It was a whole new game of cards. At this point, my fascination with government was gone.

■　■　■　■

James A. Farley

Postmaster general during Roosevelt's first two administrations. He had been F.D.R.'s campaign manager in the elections of 1932 and 1936.

In 1928, Roosevelt was elected governor of New York by fewer than 30,000 votes.[†] In 1930, "I was chairman of the Democratic State Committee and conducted his campaign for reelection, and he carried the governorship by 750,000 votes."

On the wall, facing his desk, is a large portrait of Franklin D. Roosevelt— youthful, vigorous.

He glances up at the photograph. . . .

IT BRINGS BACK THE last discussion I had with him. I urged him not to run for the third term. I predicted he was in for rough going. The world was in

---

* Henry Morgenthau, Roosevelt's secretary of treasury.
† Alfred E. Smith, in 1928, running for president against Herbert Hoover, failed to carry New York State.

a bad way. He'd break a tradition that shouldn't be broken—that had existed from Washington's time. And he wasn't getting any younger. I predicted that he'd run for a fourth time. I just told him I thought that, if he won, he'd even run for a fifth time. I broke with him on the issue, of course.

I felt very keenly about it. He just didn't think anybody else was big enough to be president. And that's not said unkindly. He did not like to give up power, let's put it that way.

In 1936, I was more optimistic than he was. I predicted he'd carry every state but two: Maine and Vermont. I coined a slogan then: There used to be a phrase: "As Maine goes, so goes the nation." The day after election, at a press conference, I said, "As Maine goes, so goes Vermont."

I went across the country for him in 1931, starting about June 18, if my memory serves me correctly. All by train. I was gone about twenty-odd nights, and I was on the train eighteen nights. When you'd get up in the morning, the sheets were covered with coal dust. It was hot, no air-conditioning. Pretty tough going.

As the train stopped for refueling, say, at Grand Island, Nebraska, or Pocatello, Idaho, I'd get off and walk around the station platform. I'd talk with the railroad men and the others. They didn't know who I was. I'd ask them who they thought was the best man for the Democrats to nominate, and could he win, and so on.

I wrote Mr. Roosevelt a letter—I don't know if it was from Portland or Seattle—in which I said that nearly every governor I met was a candidate for vice president because they were sure he could win.

It's one of those things. You go riding around town and talk to taxi drivers and other people, you can go into lunchrooms. The information is not always accurate, but the sentiment is obvious.

People wanted a change. Unemployment. And then, Prohibition. Arthur Brisbane, who was a great reporter for Hearst, supposedly a very astute newspaperman—and I'm sure he was—made this statement in the lobby of the Congress Hotel in Chicago: What difference does it make what plank the Democrats put in their platform? The Eighteenth Amendment won't be repealed during the lifetime of any person attending this convention. This was in July of '32. It was repealed early in December of '33. Goes to show you how fast public opinion moves.

Mr. Roosevelt showed great leadership. He surrounded himself—one of the best men he had around him in those days was Ray Moley. I was sorry that relationship was broken. And it wasn't Moley's fault, see.

I felt those fellas around Roosevelt—he told me in 1940 that the people around the White House thought he was the only one who could win. I looked at him and said, "Mr. President, you know damn well that they want their jobs, and if you don't run again, they won't be around here the day after the inauguration." I said: "Hull* can make a better race than you can, because the third term won't enter into it." Hull was strong, according to the polls.

Very few presidents have people around them who talk up to them. If they do, they're not around very long. Moley talked up to him, and so did I, at cabinet meetings and otherwise.

I never knew about the court packing, until I read it in the paper. The *Evening Telegram,* that afternoon, the early edition. I wasn't in Washington when he called the cabinet together. I didn't happen to get down to the meeting. So I saw him a few days later. I said, "Why the hell'd you call that meeting without letting me know?" He said, "Well, I tried to get word to you, but it was understood you were in New York and I couldn't reach you." I said, "You probably figured I'd be against it." And he said, "Not necessarily." (Laughs.) It was a mistake. But I did make speeches in favor of the court bill, because I was a member of the administration.

They say that Roosevelt in '32 saved our society. . . .
He saved our free enterprise system, he saved the banks, he saved the insurance companies. There ain't any doubt but what Roosevelt in those first hundred days . . . this was a tremendous job.

What do you think would have happened if he hadn't been elected . . . if his New Deal legislation had not been enacted?
God only knows. I remember, during the inauguration period, you couldn't get a check cashed in Washington. The hotels were afraid to cash a check, so many banks were failing. During the week of inauguration, Roosevelt closed all the banks and then gave orders to move as quickly as they could to open what were known to be definitely solvent banks. A quick survey. They didn't lose any time.

If a Depression came on us today, would the attitude of people be different?
The attitude of people today is bad enough even though they're gainfully employed. It's difficult for me to understand the attitude of youth. I never went to college, but I'd proceed on the theory that if you're not satisfied, resign and go to some other college. If I was a student at Columbia now, I wouldn't be dissenting out around and causing a lot of trouble. I'd go to a

* Cordell Hull, secretary of state during Roosevelt's first three terms.

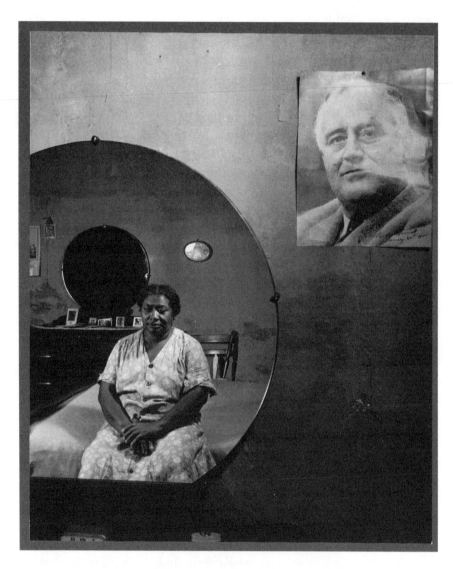

Washington (southwest section), D.C.,
Negro woman in her bedroom

GORDON PARKS, 1942

college where I thought the conditions were ones under which I could labor and graduate and get the education I sought. That's an old-fashioned idea, but that's the way I feel.

What are your memories concerning Mrs. Roosevelt?
I had a very fine relationship with her. She sought my help on many occasions and I tried to help her. She was well intentioned. Despite what may have been said to the contrary, she never interfered with my political activities at all. She'd ask me for my advice and pass on some suggestions, and I'd accept them or reject them. We never had any difficulties.

She really was very kindly disposed toward me. After I left the government, friends of mine would see her, and she'd always say that Franklin—referring to him the way she did—didn't handle my situation properly.

The only thing that annoyed her is what I had in my book.* I quoted her as saying that President Roosevelt was ill at ease with a person who was not his social equal. Well, he *was* a snob. We're all snobs. We're all kinds of snobs, see. Unknowingly, he talked down to others. A lot of them resented it.

You see, he was raised in that kind of patrician society where they looked over their noses. He didn't realize it. He never thanked me for anything I ever did for him. When he was elected governor, he wrote me. But after that, he never wrote me or thanked me for anything. And I did a lot of things. It never affected my relationship with him. I wouldn't let it. Up to the third term, it was as fine a relationship as ever existed between two men. I was sorry it broke up that way.

■   ■   ■

Burton K. Wheeler

Former senator from Montana. In 1924, he was Senator Robert La Follette's running mate on the Progressive Party ticket. They polled nearly five million votes.

I SAW THE DEPRESSION coming. Joe Kennedy came to see me. He said, "I'm afraid I'm gonna wake up with nine kids and three homes and no dough." I said, "Do you want to be safe? Buy gold." He came to me again. "They've taken my gold." I said, "Buy silver bullion." He came down once more. "They're

* *The Jim Farley Story,* by James A. Farley (New York: McGraw Hill, 1948).

taking my silver bullion." I said, "Do you want to be perfectly safe? Go get a farm, where you can raise a cow and a pig and some chickens, and put some of those kids of yours to work. But don't get too big, because we might take it away from you." He said, "Is it as bad as that?" I said, "No, but it might get that bad."

He recounted his experiences as a visitor in Vienna in 1923, as the Depression there affected all classes. "I didn't think it would start as quickly as it did here in the United States."

Hoover was president when they passed the Reconstruction Finance bill. I opposed it. Its purpose was to bail out the bankers, the insurance companies and the railroads. I said, "The pressure's gonna be so great that anybody who's got a sick cow is gonna come to Washington to borrow money." Bob La Follette, Junior, said he's voting for it, because he's afraid there would be a crash. I said, "There would be, but the sooner it comes off, the better." This RFC would only prolong it. The greater our indebtedness, the greater the crash.

Old J. Ham Lewis came up to me.* He used to call me "boy." That made me mad. "Boy, give 'em the devil." I said, "Won't you make a speech on it?" He said, "No, I can't. I represent a damn bunch of thieves. Thieves, I tell you, who want to reach their hand in the public coffers and pull all the money out. My God, if I were a free man, I'd tear this thing limb from limb."

I'd get pretty discouraged when the men in the cloak rooms would come up to me and say, "I agree with you." Then go out and vote the other way. I remember one piece of legislation I was interested in. It involved a challenge to the big money powers. A senator said to me, "I think you're right. I'm gonna vote with you." In the afternoon he said, "I can't." "Why not?" "My bosses called me up." "You have a boss that tells you how you've got to vote?" "Who's your boss? You've got one." I said, "The only boss I've got is the people." He said, "Don't give me that stuff. You've got a boss somewhere."

When Tom Pendergast† was indicted, Harry Truman came up to me. "Should I resign?" I said, "Why should you resign?" He said, "They've indicted the old man. He made me everything I am, and I've got to stand by him."

* J. Hamilton Lewis, pink-whiskered, pearl-gray-spatted fashion plate, was a Democratic senator from Illinois.
† Political boss of Kansas City for many years.

After Roosevelt's election, I introduced a bill to remonitize silver. All the bankers of the country were against it. They were able to control the money much better with the gold standard. Some of the big mining companies out West were interested in my bill. For the wrong reasons. They were interested in raising the price of silver, but not in its use in money. The president of Anaconda Copper thought I was right—better silver than paper. There wasn't enough gold to go around. I said, "Why don't you say so publicly?" He shrugged his shoulders. I said, "You don't dare say so, because you owe the National City Bank so much money."

He recounts his disagreement with Roosevelt in the matter of court packing. During "the hysteria of the First World War, I saw men strung up. Only the federal courts stood up at all, and the Supreme Court better than any of them. Not as well as they should have, but better than the others." The aid of Associate Justice Brandeis and a letter from Chief Justice Hughes helped him in defeating Roosevelt's effort. He nonetheless led the fight for some of F.D.R.'s social legislation.

I handled the Utility Holding Company bill. It was a hard-fought one. I was approached by a fishing companion: "These utility people are gonna destroy anyone who gets in their way." A few days later, two of their chief lobbyists visited me. I said, "Have you got any guns?" They said, "No, your boy frisked us." I said, "I told him to." They said, "How much time you gonna give us?" "One week." "We've got to have a month." "I'll give you a week, and the government a week. If you can't tell what's wrong with the bill in a week's time, that's too bad." They said, "You're pretty cocky." "No," I said, "I'm just tired of crooked lobbyists and crooked lawyers."

He was pressured by colleagues of Roosevelt to accept the candidacy as vice president for the 1940 campaign. "Justice Murphy came from the White House. 'The president will call you up.' 'I won't take it.' 'You're the biggest damn fool I ever met. You'll be president of the United States.' 'I can't take it.'" He was opposed to what he felt were Roosevelt's "war policies."

I had seen Roosevelt in '39. I told him it would be a mistake if he ran for a third term. He agreed. He said to me, "Burt, along about January or February of next year, we'll pick out somebody who can win. I'm tired of supporting some of these old reactionaries." And then he said, "Farley would like to see Hull run, and he'd like to run as vice president. He doesn't think Hull would live through it. That'd make him president. Cardinal Mundelein told me that even though he'd like to see a Catholic president some day, he didn't want to see him come in the back door." That Roosevelt was really a master.

■   ■   ■   ■

David Kennedy

Secretary of the treasury.

"I came to Washington in September of '29 to attend law school. I joined the Federal Reserve Board in April of 1930. Marriner Eccles came in '33 as governor of the board.

"He laughs about that. He said, 'I'm from Utah, too. Did you know me?' I said, 'Yes, I knew you, but you didn't know me. I was a boy, and you were a man in a dark office.' He said, 'Well, I can't be blamed for bringing you.' I said, 'No, but I can be blamed for bringing you.'"

MY FIRST WORK WAS with the story of bank failures. In 1933, when President Roosevelt came in and declared a Bank Holiday, we worked day and night. We had three days in which to license the banks which were solvent. We had to get reports from the various states, Federal Reserve banks, the comptroller of currency and individual banks. From all over the country. I never left the office those three days. I slept on the couch and had sandwiches brought in.

We had a number of very famous cases, considered on a twenty-four-hour basis, as to whether they should open or not open. It was a matter of judgment. Two major banks in Detroit remained closed, because it was determined they were not solvent. Borderline cases were permitted to open.

There were three days of openings. Major banks in large cities were opened one day. The next day, the Reserve cities—the rest of the banks on the third day. In those three days, the field examiners knew the banks and knew their stories. It was not just starting from scratch. They'd been studying them day by day as these problems were developing.

The Bank Holiday was probably the most dramatic happening in the history of the financial world. It shocked many people. What was going to hap-

---

* The conversation took place before his appointment by President Nixon. He was at the time chairman of the board of the Continental Illinois National Bank and Trust Company.

pen? Was this it? But once it was considered in realistic terms, it was accepted by the people on Wall Street and around the country, as a period in which to get your house in order. It gave the bankers themselves a chance to consolidate their resources.

All through the twenties, they were having about six hundred banks a year close. Before the Crash, when conditions were booming. People don't realize that. In '29 and '30, they got into the thousands. Closings every day. There was one bank in New York, the Bank of the United States—in the wake of that closing, two hundred smaller banks closed. Because of the deposits in that bank from the others.

We had the problem of reconstructing the banking laws. In a serious depression or a forced sale in bankruptcy, what is anything worth? It's worth only what somebody will pay you for it. Values just tumble away down. So Marriner Eccles conceived the theory of intrinsic values, whatever that means. There must be some basis, other than paper, on which an examiner can determine whether a bank should stay open.

This was difficult to sell the accountants and the bankers. But the Banking Act of '33 was passed, and they started to follow that theory. It permitted the Federal Reserve to lend on any sound asset. Before, they had the commercial paper theory—you could lend on certain things. And banks ran out of collateral for borrowing purposes.

Then the FDIC* was established. It gave confidence to the man on the street that his bank would not fail, and if it did, he was insured up to $10,000. That was part of the Banking Act of '33.

The Banking Act of '34 was much more fundamental. It gave our whole Federal Reserve System a better basis. This caused a fight between Marriner Eccles and Carter Glass.† They had different philosophies. Marner was one of the original advocates of pump priming. Glass was of the older school. Marriner loves an argument, and he was able to get most of his recommendations approved. It was a great victory for him.

He recounts the defeatist attitude, as he saw it, of the early thirties. "Every one that we talked to, in the schools, in the universities, would have very little vision of what this great country and its resources could do. We had studies going on, in housing, in education, in various public works, in order to stimulate the economy.

* The Federal Deposit Insurance Corporation.
† Senator from Virginia; chairman of the Senate Finance Committee.

"We were all affected by the Crash. My salary was cut fifteen percent. I was supposed to get a raise. There were thirty-five applicants for the job when I was hired. I was promised a substantial increase at the end of my six months' trial period. The man in charge of my division came to me and said: There's a freeze on all salaries in the Federal Reserve. The government had done it, and even though the board was independent,* it'd go along. He said he'd make it up when the crisis was over.

"Finally, when the Banking Act of '33 was passed, he made two exceptions. I was one of 'em. After three years, I got a \$600 increase. I learned what the word 'substantial' means." (Laughs.)

1937 and 1939 were interesting periods. We hadn't come out of the Depression. It was deep-set. The board increased reserve requirements of member banks because they had large excess reserves. We made studies showing that only a very few banks would be affected by this increase in requirements. Then we got a real turn-down.

There was a very, very serious recession in '37. Marriner spent a good share of his time trying to prove to the public that it was not caused by the Federal Reserve action. Critics said it was.

We had a serious break in the market, when war broke out in Europe in 1939. A problem in securities. The Federal Reserve Board said it would buy all the securities that were offered, no matter what the volume, at the market price. That stopped the avalanche of sales. The market settled down, and we got through that.

We really had not made a substantial recovery from the deep Depression of the early thirties. Unemployment was still very high. The New Deal programs were not stimulating the way people thought. There was sort of a defeatist attitude—that the government just had to do all this for the people. It was not until the war, with its economic thrust, that we pulled out of it. The war got us out of it, not the New Deal policies.

As a matter of fact, the policies pursued could have thrown us into real trouble. It was changing our way of life. You're spending money and going into debt, but you're not really finding ways and means to explore new projects. Like today, we're in an explosion of ideas.

---

* "It's completely autonomous. Of course, it's a creation of Congress and its members are appointed by the president, but it has an air of independence few other agencies have, because we're not under the General Accounting Office. There has been a continuous battle. Congressman Wright Patman believes the board should be under governmental control."

Despite all the programs—PWA, WPA, FSA . . . ?
It took care of immediate suffering in part of the areas. I'm not criticizing it
in that sense. But it didn't pull the thing up so that private enterprise could
take its place and replace it.

You applied the word "defeatist" to Roosevelt's as well as Hoover's time. . . .
Roosevelt gave us quite a bit of hope, early. He probably saved us from complete collapse, in that sense. But he did not answer the things. Many of his
programs were turned on and off, started and stopped . . . shifting gears.
Because we had never been in anything like this.

Planning had not been done. So they'd go out and sweep the mountains
and clean up the debris, and then the wind comes along and blows it back
again. It gave some work. But the people that got the money in some ways
were benefited and in other ways were hurt. They didn't like to see the
waste. . . . They had mixed reactions.

We have a ranch in Utah. In 1933, we had a serious drought. Anyone
that lived out there can tell you it nearly broke all the ranches in the area. I
was on the ranch this day with my father. We had cattle coming in from the
range land, thirsty, without food, getting down to the water. We'd gather
these up and sell them to the government. They'd pay from $4 to $20 a
head. If the animal was alive, you'd get $4. If it was a good animal, you'd get
up to $20.

They drove up, the buyers from the agricultural department. There were
seven of them in this one car, on government pay. There was an argument
over the value of one steer, which was as perfect an animal as any I'd ever
seen. They didn't want to give but $16. My father said it was $20 or nothing.
After some argument with the seven men, they gave it. Before the government was in on this, we'd sell all our cattle to a buyer, one man. Here were
seven. The people out there got the feeling this was just Big Government, a
make-work thing. These things tended to create a defeated attitude.

*Do you recall any change in the Washington atmosphere, during the time
you were there, between the last days of Hoover and the early days of
Roosevelt . . . ?*
In the last days of Hoover, it was very gloomy. The financial collapse had
just dampened everything. They didn't know which way to turn. Mr.
Hoover, as a man, took a good deal of this blame personally upon himself.
It was unjustifiable. Roosevelt, with his silver tongue, brought words of
hope. He started many things going, but they were turned on and off. We
had the NRA, the WPA and these things—they'd come and go. You never

could get clear-cut decisions. One day, one thing; the next day, another. It was bedlam and confusion in Washington.

Ickes and those fellows not knowing which way to go. One day, he was in good grace; the next day, it was Morgenthau. And the next day, everybody was questioning Harry Hopkins and those fellows, because they had the ear of the president, and they were getting in there on the side. We'd get stories about tossing a coin in the air to decide the price of gold. . . . Whether it's true or not, I don't know. But we'd get these stories.

I was enthusiastic when Roosevelt came in. I thought: We're in serious trouble. Something has to be done, and here's a man that's going to do it. I voted for him his first term and his second. After that, I voted against him. It wasn't just on the two-term basis, although that was important. The packing of the Supreme Court and the fact that we were not making the progress I thought our country was capable of making. . . . I became terribly disenchanted.

He was a dramatic leader. He had charm, personality, poise and so on. He could inspire people. But to me, he lacked the stick-to-it-iveness to carry a program through.

The private sector was not called upon enough . . . ?
I felt we were relying too much on the government to save us. There was not enough involvement in the private area to carry its share of the burden. I felt people were losing their initiative to get out on their own instead of: Please hand it to me. Of course, we hadn't seen anything then compared to what we have now in this respect. But today, we have all this private involvement that is so interesting and expansive. It offsets the other. I don't want to be too critical of Mr. Roosevelt, because he did, in our period of history, do something.

This is—to use a Rooseveltian phrase—an "iffy" question: Suppose he didn't step in with these programs, what do you think would have happened?
We had to have some of them. If he hadn't done it, someone else could have. In one way, you could say he saved it because he was our leader and he surely had the support.

At the time of the collapse that stunned so many, was there some doubt about our society?
Not as it is today. It is a different sort of thing. It was bewilderment. Of course, we hadn't been used to the affluence we have today. I didn't think our people were poor, many of them. They ate well, and so on. But the unemployment continued on and on and on.

Today, attitudes have changed. There'd be some rebellion that you didn't have then. It was peaceful then. It was law abiding. You could walk down the street and have money in your pocket, and no one would take it from you. You might have a beggar ask you for something. But there wouldn't be the kind of feeling that you'd have it taken away from you. There was more respect for law. Now there is this demanding thing. It's general, it's in all the world now.

POSTSCRIPT: *"When I first came to Washington, Doc Townsend visited me. He was a nice-looking gentleman, gray-headed, thin. A good country doctor, I felt. Well, he had a crazy idea which you couldn't talk him out of: a tax on all the desposits that went through the banks. I said, 'Somebody would have to pay for it.' He said, 'Look at all those billions of dollars. We don't have to take but a small amount of it.' He didn't realize, however, you raise it, it's going to be a burden on somebody. But he was a spokesman for a great lot of older people, and he gave them hope. I thought he was a little daft on this concept. On the other hand, he served a purpose at the time. He gave old people the idea of a pension. And now they're organized." (Laughs.) "I respected the old man."*

■　■　■　■

John Beecher

Poet. Two of his anthologies, To Live and Die in Dixie *and* Hear the Wind Blow, *concern the Depression in the South.*

He is of abolitionist ancestry, a great-grandnephew of Henry Ward Beecher and Harriet Beecher Stowe. His maternal grandfather, an Irish-American coal miner, was a member of the Molly Maguires, terrorist mine organizers in the 1870s. . . . "He was the principal subversive influence in my life. . . .

"My father was a top executive of a southern subsidiary of the United States Steel Corporation. Fortunately for me and possibly fortunately for him, he lost most of his money in the stock market crash of '29. He had a hard time recovering from it, psychologically.

"I remember how, after dinner, he'd just lie on the couch in utter despair, night after night, for hours. A man who was interested in music, read all kinds of literature, novels, plays, history, economics and so on—there was this man so knocked out. We were afraid he was going to commit suicide. His close personal friend did take a header out of the fourteenth-story window. He was still getting an excellent salary, but he felt—up to that time—the measure of a man's success was the amount of money he accumulated.

Flood refugee encampment at Forrest City, Arkansas

WALKER EVANS & EDWIN LOCKE, C. 1937

"But he did recover. He became a kind of coolly critical intelligence. He was ready for any kind of change in the system—perhaps this system was not eternal, perhaps there should be a more cooperative society."

I HAD MY FIRST job in the steel mills, back in the twenties. You could say the Depression commenced in this town, Ainsley, Alabama, a steel mill suburb of Birmingham. We had the first bank to go bust in the early days of the Depression. All the workingmen trusted the banker.

In the fall of 1929, I left my job as metallurgist on the open hearth to teach at the University of Wisconsin. For Alexander Meiklejohn's Experimental College. Of course, the students became turned on very rapidly during the Depression. At commencement, you'd see fellows in caps and gowns selling apples at the doors of the stadiums, where they were handing out the programs. This was kind of a demonstration, just to show . . . highly gifted chaps, you know, going to work in dime stores, after they got their degrees. And lucky to get the work. So they were radicalized by the Depression the way kids are radicalized today by the Vietnam War and the whole drift of our society. . . .

In the summer of '32, I played hookey from the academic rat race. I was doing a doctoral dissertation on the novels of Dickens and hard times back in 1832. I decided to find out what was happening in my own time. In my hometown. I found out with a vengeance. This led, actually, to my going out into the Depression. First, as a volunteer social worker and then as a New Deal administrator.

For eight years, starting in '34, I worked as field administrator all over the South . . . with white and black, rural people, coal miners, steel workers, textile workers, a fertilizer plant people, turpentine camp workers and sharecroppers.

Was theirs an attitude of resignation?
No, indeed. The ferment I discovered in Birmingham was just tremendous. The people were ready, really, to take action. They, of course, didn't know which way to turn. Few people believed, in '32, that Roosevelt was going to be the answer.

I remember passing through Chicago on my way to the South. I stopped off at Hull House to see my literary idol, John Dos Passos.* He thought we were on the road to revolution . . . that Roosevelt would, of course, be re-

---

* Dos Passos was covering the Republican and Democratic conventions for the *New Republic*.

elected, but that he wouldn't rise to the occasion. He seemed to believe some kind of anarcho-syndicalist solution would be found. The American labor unions would lead the way. Of course, they were not leading the way. And Roosevelt surprised everyone by coming up with emergency programs which did take most of the bite out of popular discontent.

I remember in Ainsley that year, in the relief headquarters, a woman had been arguing and arguing to get some milk for her baby. You should have seen the things they were giving babies instead of milk. I remember seeing them put salt-pork gravy in milk bottles and putting a nipple on, and the baby sucking this salt-pork gravy. A real blue baby, dying of starvation. In house after house, I saw that sort of thing.

Well, this woman was determined to get real milk for her baby. She raised all the cain she could, until the top supervisor agreed to let her have a quart. When they handed it to her, she got back as far as she could and threw it up against the wall—pow!—and smashed it. This was the kind of spirit, you see. Not unlike the kind of thing you see today amongst the black people. But it was white people then, principally. They seemed to be the most militant ones—at least down South.

As an administrator, I worked with Rex Tugwell's rural resettlement programs. Rex had written, when he was an undergraduate in Columbia, a poem in praise of socialism. They kept dragging up this undergraduate poem on Poor Rex. You recall how viciously he was attacked? Actually this program, of which I was a charter employee, wasn't as radical as I would have liked it to be.

It was a stopgap, dealing with rural problems. Grants-in-aid, to small farmers, so they could hold on and continue to produce crops. I managed a group of five of these communities.

I switched to the migratory labor program. I set one up in Florida for migratory farm workers, who at the time were poor blacks, displaced share-croppers from Georgia and Alabama. Also displaced whites who had been, largely, packinghouse workers.

We built a hospital, clinics, community centers, schools and a number of temporary camps. They were at least better than the grass huts, tree houses and all those terrible barracks in which they were living.

I was down in the same area last winter, almost thirty years later. I found those "temporary" camps still standing there, deteriorated and disintegrated. In one place the ground had dropped ten feet. These places were way up in the air, on piles, because the land had subsided. In 1968, they were still living in these camps we had built in the thirties.

The migratory workers, then, were not really affected by the New Deal?

No. When the war came along, all the domestic programs were swept under the rug. They turned our migratory camp over to the local communities. The kind of thing we hear so much about today: local control. So the local people got hold of it. . . .

We had built a big hospital in the Everglades for the black people. There wasn't a hospital bed for fifty thousand people, not one. They had all kinds of things wrong with them, and there was nowhere they could go, so we built a hospital. It was the first thing of its kind the administration had ever done. It was designed primarily for the black people.

The minute it was turned over the locals, in the days of the war, they evicted all the black people. They repainted the hospital inside and out and made it a white hospital. I was talking recently to one family in the black camp—in those days they kept everything separate. The black camp is still a black camp, and the white camp is still the white camp—still segregated.

They told me down there, this last winter, they're not allowed to have community meetings any more—or any kind of self-government that they had. They didn't even have dances any more in the community centers we had built for them. They were run by white managers and white deputies and all this sort of thing. The very thing we had been trying to get away from, a generation later had been reinstated.

The migratory labor program was the most advanced thing I encountered in the whole administration. The resettlement communities were more paternalistic. They carefully selected families, according to criteria handed down from Washington. In the camps, we had to rely on the people to do it. So they made all the ordinances, and they ran all the camps and did a much better job than the bunch of bureaucrats.

(*Half-tells, half-muses a poetic remembrance.*) They were living on the canal banks in stinking quarters and barracks, sometimes thirteen people in a room. Or in tarpaper huts, in shelters in the weeds. Every morning before dawn, they climbed onto trucks, bound for the bean fields. Where all day, everybody that could pick, down to five or six years old, picked. Kneeling in the black Everglades mud. It would be dark night again when they got back to quarters. And all night long the gyp joints stayed open, where whiskey, dice and women ate up the earnings of the day.

* See Cesar Chavez, p. 53.

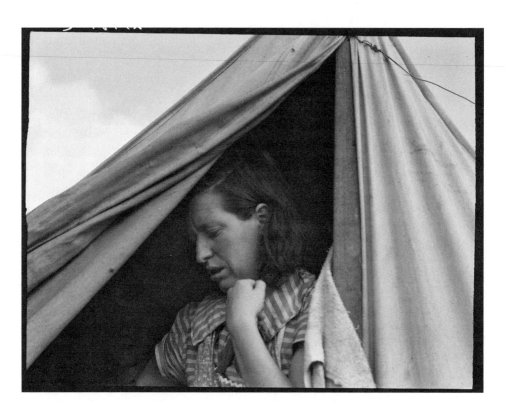

"We made good money in the cherries this year. From then on we made just beans." Merrill, Klamath County, Oregon. Woman in mobile unit of FSA (Farm Security Administration) camp.

DOROTHEA LANGE, 1939

That was the white growers' idea of how to hold labor: Keep the Negroes broke, they said. Instead of a church or a school, the grower would build a gyp joint at the center of his quarters. To get back at night what he paid out in the day.

When the government came in and started to build a model camp for the Negroes, with screened shelters and shower baths and flush toilets, and an infirmary, a community center, a school and playgrounds, laundry tubs and electric irons—the growers raised hell. What was the government's idea anyway, ruining the rental value of their canal bank quarters? And fixing to ruin their labor with a lot of useless luxury? Besides, the Negroes wouldn't use the camp. They liked to be dirty; they liked to be diseased; they liked to be vicious.

When the growers saw the government was going ahead anyway, they said: You'll have to hire a bunch of camp guards, white guards, and have them control the camp with clubs and pistols or the Negroes won't pay the rent. Or they'll stop working entirely and they'll take the camp to pieces.

I was there. I was in charge of the camp. When the day came to open, we just opened the gate and let anybody in that wanted to come in. No hand-picking, no references or anything like that. It was enough for us that a family wanted to live there. We didn't hire white guards, either, and nobody carried a club or a pistol in all that camp that held a thousand people.

We just got them all together in the community center and told them it was their camp. They could make it a bad camp or they could make it a good camp. It was up to them. And there wouldn't be any laws or ordinances, except the ones they made for themselves through their elected council. For a week, they had a campaign in camp with people running for office for the first time in their lives. After it was over, they celebrated with a big dance in the community center. Nobody got drunk or disorderly and nobody cut anybody with a knife. They had themselves a council.

The council made the laws and ordinances. The council said nobody's dog could run around loose, it had to be tied up. The council said a man couldn't beat his wife up in camp. And when a man came in drunk one night, he was out by morning. The council said people had to pay their rent and out of that rent came money for baseball equipment, and it kept up the nursery school.

Finally, the council said: It's a long way to any store. And that's how the co-op started, without a dollar in it that the people didn't put up.

Some of the men and women on that council couldn't so much as write their names. Remember, these were just country Negroes off sharecrop farms in Georgia and Alabama. Just common ordinary cotton pickers, the kind Lowndes County planters say would ruin the country if they had the vote. (*He opens wide his half-shut eyes.*) All I know is: My eyes have seen democracy work.

An Unreconstructed Populist

Congressman C. Wright Patman

The gentleman from Texas is serving his twenty-first term in Congress. He is chairman of the House Banking and Currency Committee. His appearance is that of an ingenuous "country boy." Physically, he bears a remarkable resemblance to actor Victor Moore as Throttlebottom in Of Thee I Sing. Journalist Robert Sherrill has pointed out that appearance, at least in this instance, is quite deceiving.

IN THE LATE TWENTIES, the farmers were in distress because all the money went to Wall Street. They were using it up there, manipulating. They were not using money out in the country. The same thing's happening right now—a repeat performance of the '29 deal. Less than two hundred men are controlling everything—the fixing of interest, bonds, everything. Members of Congress just don't step on the toes of these bankers.

That's why in May 1929, I introduced the first bill to pay three and a half million World War I veterans cash money, direct from the United States Treasury. It took from then till 1936 for these veterans to be paid—$1,015 each, on the average. They were in such distress, we had to agree on bond payments. They wanted to rob 'em on interest rates. The way they treated those men. . . . They didn't want to pay 'em their money. It was adjusted pay, really. Remember, the army only paid $21 a month. In June 1932, the House passed the bonus, but the senators resented the pressure and voted against it. Those poor fellas, instead of doing something rash, why, they'd sing "America." They took it.

You were a hero to the bonus marchers. . . .
Why, certainly. They brought a donkey on top of a freight train from Texas up here to my office. They educated him, they taught him tricks and things. They wanted me to run for president. I said, "No, let's just get this thing paid."

There was twenty thousand here at one time. I addressed them out there on the Capitol steps.

Who were the so-called bonus marchers? They were lobbyists for a cause. Just like the ones in the Mayflower Hotel. They didn't try to evict *them*. When the poor come to town, they're troublemakers. Why, certainly. They step on the grass and they're put in jail for stepping on the grass. The Mayflower crowd, they don't have any problem at all. They're on every floor of every building of Capitol Hill all the time.

The marchers were good, law-abiding citizens. They built these lodgings down here from waste paper and boxes and things. They had lots of streets and everything. Like Resurrection City. Those buildings were burned down by the army, the military, under the direction of Mr. MacArthur and Mr. Eisenhower. Mr. MacArthur was strutting down the street just like it was a big parade.

The next morning, after driving them out, using tear gas, you'd see little babies and mothers on the side of the road. . . . There was never such a horrible thing happen on earth as that. They killed some of the veterans. They all ought to have been charged with murder. These people had as much right to be lobbying here for their cause as the Mayflower crowd.

Andrew Mellon* was opposed to any payment. He said it would unbalance the budget. They always talked that way. Some of them called it the 'boodget' (laughs)—unbalance the boodget. That's what led me to go after him. I'm against a few people taking advantage of privilege, using it for their own selfishness and punishing other folks.

As soon as I returned to Congress, on January 6, 1932, I rose to impeach Andrew W. Mellon for high crimes and misdemeanors. The Republicans were so shocked and confused, they didn't stop me. I got an hour's time on the floor. I spoke of the conflict of interests. He owned banks, stocks and everything else, and here he was heading the treasury. It was made a violation a hundred years ago for a secretary of treasury to even own a government bond.

---

* Secretary of treasury from 1921 to 1932.

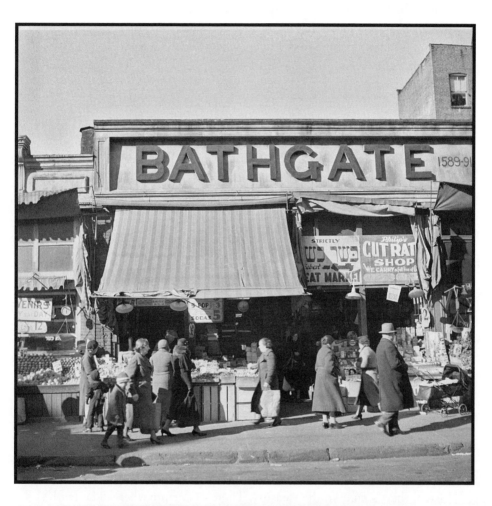

Scene along Bathgate Avenue in the Bronx, New York, a section
from which many of the New Jersey homesteaders have come

ARTHUR ROTHSTEIN, 1936

They voted to refer the proposition to the Judiciary Committee. I sat on one side of the long table by myself and Mr. Mellon and his twelve lawyers sat on the opposite side. The most high-prices lawyers in the United States, the best money could buy. I had a rough time for a couple of weeks. But I was always able to fall on my feet like a cat, because I had the information. I had it documented. I knew what it was. They didn't. See, these high-prices lawyers, the higher they're priced, the less they study. (Laughs.)

At the end of two weeks, it was Mr. Mellon's turn to be on the witness stand. The committee recessed until one thirty that afternoon. Well, about twelve thirty, the papers came out with huge headlines: "Mellon Resigns, Appointed to the Court of St. James." Some members of the committee wanted to impeach him anyway. La Guardia was one. But the argument was made: Why take up time? He's not only out of office, he's out of the country. So they just let it go. They destroyed all the papers.

What papers? Your documents . . . ?
Why, certainly. Stolen from my office. They robbed my office time and time again. They had people up there in corners, where they could see anybody that went in and out of my office. They'd even go in at night. In the morning, I'd find papers piled in the middle of the floor. I'd try to get the officers around here to do something about it, couldn't get them to do it.

Which officers?
The security officers around Washington. The treasury has some. Also the White House and the FBI-type people. . . .

And it's all gone?
Listen, there's none in the treasury. There's none anywhere. The truth is Mellon didn't resign. He didn't want to leave that office. He was willing to buck it. He thought he had enough money to win. But this was the beginning of the campaign where Hoover was gonna face Franklin D. Roosevelt. He knew he had to get Mellon out of office. He accepted a resignation that had not been tendered. It was the most courageous thing Hoover ever did.

While he was taking the oath as ambassador, Mellon told a newspaper friend of mine, "This is not a marriage ceremony; it's a divorce." They put him out. For all effective purposes, he was impeached. Hoover gave him a pardon in the middle of the trial.

Weren't there pressures to defeat you during the thirties?
Why, certainly. About every three or four elections, they'd lower the boom
on me. They could see I was givin' 'em trouble on their city-slicking deals. I
pictured them as money changers and was after them with sharp sticks.
(Laughs.) They come in, spitin' me back. I had a lot of hard races. The big
business fellas didn't need me. They got their own paid people around here.
They threw plenty of money around and begin to get very popular.

We have two governments in Washington: one run by the elected
people—which is a minor part—and one run by the moneyed interests,
which control everything.

Like the farmer down in Texas. He had a few oil wells. He began buying
up all the land around the rivers. Folks got terribly wrought up about it.
Him buying up all the land in the country. He let 'em know he wasn't buying up all the land. He just wanted to buy that land that adjoined his'n.
(Laughs.) That's what we had. A few fellas that was buying up all the property that adjoined theirs.

It was the big ones closing in on the little ones for the kill. At one time,
they thought they'd get a dictatorship here. General Smedley Butler was
picked out to be the leader. He was gonna be their man on the white horse.
They were gonna close in and take this country over. And they come damn
near doing it. They just picked the wrong man.* They'll get this country in
that position again if they can.

You worried about it?
Yeah, I'm worried about that. A dictatorship could spring up here overnight,
if this country got so bad. If another Depression came, we'd have a revolution. People wouldn't take it any more. They have more knowledge. The big
ones, they'd be looking for somebody that'd have the power to just kill

* In his autobiography, John L. Spivak, a journalist, recounts his investigation of the matter.
During his visit to Butler's home, the general . . . "an extraordinary man, described 'what
was tantamount to a plot to seize the Government, by force, if necessary.'" In 1935, "Butler,
on a national radio hookup, denounced the Congressional Committee for suppressing parts
of his testimony, involving the names of important men.

"Roger Baldwin, who did not look with friendly eyes on communists because they denied
free speech and free press, issued a statement as director of the American Civil Liberties
Union: 'The Congressional Committee investigating un-American activities has just reported
that the fascist plot to seize the government . . . was proved; yet not a single participant will be
prosecuted under the perfectly plain language of the federal conspiracy act making this a high
crime. Imagine the action if such a plot were discovered among Communists!'

"Which is, of course, only to emphasize the nature of our government as representative
of the interests of the controllers of property. Violence, even to the seizure of government,
is excusable on the part of those whose lofty motive is to preserve the profit system. . . ."
From *A Man in His Time*, by John L. Spivak (New York, Horizon Press, 1967), pp. 329–30.

people, if they didn't agree. When John Doe begins to get up, they'd just go
down and shoot him. . . .

What were your relations with Roosevelt during the Depression?
I liked him very much. There was an air of optimism. When he got in—
getting the fat cats out, getting the money changers out. But he was wrong
on the veterans' pay. He was against it, too, Roosevelt. I didn't bother him
because I knew Congress was gonna have to pass it.

They had a leadership conference at the White House. The *New York
Times* had a headline: "Patman at White House on Program." They had a
"must" list on the agenda. Defeating the so-called bonus bill was on the
"must" list. I think Roosevelt honestly felt it would cause inflation. He was
budget-conscious, too. But he had to change. He realized the facts of life.

*Do you have the feeling that you've been pretty well kept out of the news these
past thirty years or so . . . ?*
Why, certainly. I should have been chairman of this committee twenty-five
years ago. But they kept me off on account of that fight for the veterans.
They knew I knew too much about the money business. They didn't want a
man like that.

Oh, I made news when I authored the Full Employment bill. They
called me a Communist, a Socialist and everything else. But we got the bill
through. They all now recognize it as a good bill.

When I get kind of low, I'd think about a verse I learned at one time,
when everybody was fighting me. It went something like this:

> He has no enemies, you say,
> My friend, the boast is poor.
> He who hath mingled in the fray
> Of duty that the brave endure
> Must have foes.
>
> If he has none,
> Small is the work he has done.
> He has hit no traitor on the hip,
> Has cast no cup from perjured lip,
> Has never turned the wrong to right,
> He's been a coward in the fight.

I'd often repeat that, you know. (Laughs.)

POSTSCRIPT: *"I live near the Water Gate Inn, but I'm not in that fat cat area. (Laughs.) They pay a half million dollars for condominiums down there. Of course, they have to pay ten or fifteen thousand dollars a year just to keep the corridors clean. From my apartment, I can see where the cabinet lives."* (Laughs.)

Peroration

Colonel Hamilton Fish

His office is on the far side of the lobby: a downtown Manhattan hotel. Once upon a time, it may have been deluxe, many, many years ago. Elderly people, a few, are seated in this bleak anteroom.

Inside the office, it is cramped with mementos of better days: a bust of Alexander Hamilton; the face of Lincoln; autographed photographs of Warren Gamaliel Harding, Calvin Coolidge, General Douglas MacArthur and Senator Everett McKinley Dirksen; and the adjacent bookshelf on which are sprawled numerous works dealing with military matters, a photograph of himself: a bareheaded young football player, Harvard, '08, Walter Camp's choice as All-Time, All-American tackle.

The Colonel, tall, lean, remarkably vigorous for his years, crosses his legs. His eyes half-closed, he appears to be addressing multitudes.

THE FIRST BILL I introduced in Congress was in December 1920. It was a bill to bring back the body of the Unknown Soldier. It was signed by Woodrow Wilson, the last piece of legislation he signed. That's almost fifty years ago. There were at least fifty thousand people there. . . .

As a World War I vet, did you have any thoughts concerning the Bonus March of '32?
I was always for the veteran. Veterans elected me. Those young fellows in those days knew how to fight—I wasn't connected at all with the Bonus March. It was ill-advised and caused a political issue, which it never should have. I was for a bonus certificate. I wasn't for these handouts. There were extremists on this Bonus March. They love to be in a march. They got a whole lot of extremists down there and they caused trouble. I kept away from it.

I was chairman of the first committee to investigate Communist activity in the United States. It was known as the Fish Committee. It only lasted one year, from '30 to '31. We didn't go after personalities. We didn't send people to jail or anything like that. Congress can't send people to jail, anyhow. We did go after their organizations, to warn the American people. It was educational.

We had only $25,000 to make the investigation. Now they give 'em three or four hundred thousand. We didn't even need the twenty-five thousand, because the four other members were also lawyers. Our $25,000 included traveling expenses and so on. I think I'm the first member of Congress, and perhaps the only member of Congress, that ever returned any fund allotted to committees. I returned $5,000.

I'm sorry I did it now. Because I would have liked to use the whole amount to have our report printed by the hundreds of thousands. HR 2290 is still the best report—it's only about sixty pages—is still the best report on Communism in America.

I wrote and got through a bill creating the Un-American Activities Committee, which came a few years later, chairmaned by Mr. Dies of Texas. I have a letter from him. It's interesting, because congressmen are prima donnas. They like to claim credit for everything for themselves: that he was responsible for the investigation of Communists, and so on and so on. But in fairness to Dies, he was certainly not, in this case, a prima donna. Because he sent me this letter, unsolicited, in 1962, from Texas.

In a ringing voice, he reads the letter. Tribute is paid him for his pioneering efforts and the information he provided Dies ". . . all records which our government had seized had mysteriously disappeared. I was able to get invaluable help from the work you did. . . ."

What did Congressman Dies mean . . . about the files disappearing?
What he said was the files were destroyed under orders from Roosevelt. I don't claim Roosevelt was a Communist. I don't even say he was pro-Communist. He was a Socialist. He said: Some of my best friends are Communists. Imagine the president of the United States saying that! And then going over and selling out to Stalin. What I wanted to do was to encourage Hitler to fight Stalin. Let them fight it out. And let the free nations sit down on the sidelines, just egging them on and saying: A plague on both your houses.

Dies did a very good job. Why do you think we have so little Communism in America today? Actually it's less than one percent, Communism in America. With fellow travelers, it's a little more, with extremists and others. Now why is this a fact? Because the Un-American Activities

Committee—American labor took it up, the American Legion took it up—all the patriotic groups. If it hadn't been for that, you'd have had ten percent Communists. We'd all have hell to pay in this country here today. We've got enough troubles already.

After Dies, came McCarthy, maligned, practically crucified and almost killed. He was hated because he was so fearless. He's still hated because they tortured the truth about him. Whether he'll ever get credit, I don't know. Although McCarthy is probably our most hated man in recent history, he always had the majority of the people with him—from Cardinal Spellman down. They spent millions to destroy this man. They destroyed him by putting through that censure resolution in the Senate. I'd like to have been at the Senate at that time, because I've always been able to talk, I'd a' given them hell. They killed him, you know, they killed him. They began to gang up on me first. Then they ganged up on Dies. And they ganged up on McCarthy a hundredfold. What they didn't do to him was a shame.

Franklin Delano Roosevelt . . . I represented, of course, the district which he came from, Hyde Park, Dutchess County. I represented it in Congress for twenty-five years, ten years before he was elected president, until the next fifteen years, until he practically died. I was never beaten in that district.

Roosevelt did his best every time to defeat me in Congress. He spent a great deal of money with the columnists and the radio commentators. He would rather defeat me, I think, almost than be elected himself.

It developed on his part, a good deal of bitterness. 'Cause I criticized him openly. Never personally himself. I always denied he was a Communist or a pro-Communist and so on. I'd say perhaps he was a Socialist, but if he wants to be one, he has a right to be one. He became bitterer and bitterer.

He really began to hate me. I had nothing against him. I don't belong to that school of Republicans that go around calling names, a lot of bad names. I fought him aboveboard, and I'm not sorry. I'm sorry I didn't fight him harder than I did, because he did a great deal of harm to this country. It will take us maybe a hundred years to live it down.

It was very amusing. He'd send in "must" legislation—some radical measure. I'd get up—I got along pretty well with the Democrats—I'd offer an amendment to the bill, which would really destroy it. And it carried. He'd have his leaders up there the next day: "What's the matter with you people here? What's the trouble?" And they'd say: "Mr. President, that's your own congressman that offered that amendment." They say he almost had apo-

A scene at the Fulton fish market, New York City

GORDON PARKS, 1943

plexy, almost died. And they'd come back to me, all these Democratic leaders—I knew them well—and laughing, saying, "You almost killed the president. He was trying to put the blame on us, and we put it on you." They'd say, he nearly dropped on the spot. This happened a half a dozen times, not once.

I was on the radio at least ten or fifteen times a year, on the big radios. That's what hurt him, 'Cause I'd accuse him: I accuse the president of this, of that, down the line. It infuriated him.

Roosevelt never went out of his way to attack me personally. He did talk about "Martin, Barton & Fish"* and inferred we were reactionaries. That isn't correct. I had voted for Social Security and the most progressive legislation. I always had the support of the American Federation of Labor. On social justice, I was left of center. He hired a columnist to attack me. Some of them absolutely slammed me, maliciously lied about me. Members of his cabinet, like Ickes,† were taking cracks at me. I naturally answered them. I spoke about Messrs. Jackson,‡ Ickes and Roosevelt. I called them Three Blind Leaders. (Reads.)

> *Three blind leaders, see how they run,*
> *They ran into a Depression*
> *Which they claim is a mere recession.*
> *Did you ever hear such deception*
> *By three blind leaders, see how they run,*
> *See how they squirm, see how they alibi,*
> *Those three blind leaders.*

When he first ran for president, I was very friendly with him. He ran on a very fine, middle-of-the-road or rather conservative platform. Perhaps the most conservative platform in history. My wife voted for him.

I supported Hoover. They asked me if I would take my keynote speech down to Washington and show it to President Hoover. He read it and approved it, all except the provision about the liquor amendment. I had put in a paragraph in favor of light wine and beer. I'm afraid that his wife, who was a white ribboner and a complete Prohibitionist, opposed that. He brought it back the next morning and he said, "You'll have to delete that light wine

---

* Congressmen Joseph Martin and Bruce Barton, Republicans.
† Harold Ickes, Roosevelt's tart-tongued secretary of interior.
‡ Robert Jackson, Roosevelt's attorney general; later associate justice of the Supreme Court; eventually, the United States' judge at the Nuremberg Trials.

and beer suggestion because I can't approve it." That changed the whole election, just that one thing. And, of course, the Depression.

People were unemployed and they were blaming Hoover. But certainly it would have brought him millions of votes. He lost by probably ten million and he would have halfed it. That would have made a great deal of difference, but it would not have elected Hoover, because they absolutely sabotaged his constructive programs. It would have softened the Depression and would have solved the Depression. They sabotaged that deliberately, the Democrats in Congress. Roosevelt was in on it. He wouldn't even confer with Hoover at the time. They wanted to continue this Depression so they could sweep the country. They wanted people unemployed, so they could reap the whirlwind of votes. It was shameful.

As soon as Roosevelt got in, he changed. He trampled his platform, brought into Washington a whole lot of young, socialistic, radical brain trusters, who sought to change the whole ideology of the United States. He had become finally an extremist.

During the first hundred days, I voted for practically every recommendation made by Roosevelt. The real break between me and my constituent was on the recognition of Soviet Russia. He recognized Soviet Russia without any support whatsoever in Congress. All former presidents, everybody was against recognizing Soviet Russia at that time. But he went ahead and did it by himself.

Up to then, we had been on very friendly relations. He okayed a stamp for me, and Jim Farley, who was a friend of mine and has been ever since, put the stamp through. I had letters from Roosevelt thanking me.

I broke with him, and began to be one of the leaders of opposition to the socialism of the New Deal and this big spending. There were ten million people unemployed all the time during the New Deal. That history has not been brought out clearly. Most of your historians of that period were New Dealers on the payroll. He had a hundred million dollars to spend without making an account. He gave large sums of money to his friends, who were authors and writers. Everything pro–New Deal was written and almost nothing against it. It's changed a little bit since then. . . .

Warming to his favorite subject, he speaks of "Roosevelt determined on a pro-war policy. In the 1940 campaign, he made a pledge to mothers and fathers that their sons would not be sent to fight in any foreign wars. It was absolutely a dishonest, dishonorable, contemptible statement, because he had been planning to get us in all the time. The Germans didn't want us fighting them, so they disregarded twenty or thirty attempts that we made to fight, attacking their submarines, bombing their submarines, giving away destroyers to England. . . . When he found he couldn't get Germany to fight us, he turned and tried to get Japan into the war."

There were three reasons Roosevelt wanted war. One: you had ten million Americans unemployed after six years of the New Deal. The other one: to be a war president, you became a great man overnight. And then, he hoped to put through a United Nations, of which he would be the author—and the uncrowned ruler of the world. With his dreams, I could speak at length. But that's another matter.

Roosevelt would have gone down in history as a great president after the first two terms. But he made a mistake, going for the third term. Jim Farley and all the rest fought it. His tragic mistake was when he was a sick and dying man, caved in, mentally and physically, and he insisted on a fourth term. "I'm the indispensable man." All that bunk.

He had all this fanatical, radical legislation introduced. They were not based on American customs. They were all Socialistic, and Socialism always fails. I know as much about this as anybody, 'cause I debated Norman Thomas, whom I have a very high idea of, at least ten different times.

Of course, Socialism has tremendous ideals. If everybody was an angel, Socialism would be wonderful. If everybody worked for everybody else and for themselves and for the country, it might work. But it's never worked in any big country. Maybe a small country of five million. . . .

I'm for the right of everybody to speak: Democrats, Republicans, left, right, freedom people, extremists, so on. The only thing Communism fears is the word "freedom," and they fear that like the devil is feared by Christians. HR 2290 was the best report ever written on Communism. I'm only sorry I didn't keep that $5,000 and spend it to print a million copies.

POSTSCRIPT: *"Al Smith was a very dear friend of mine. He loved this country, and he hated Communism. I was asked by Republican leaders if I would go down and see Al Smith at the Empire State Building . . . and ask if he would run on the Republican ticket for the United States senator against his old friend Robert Wagner. It was shortly before Al's death. Much to my surprise, he said, 'You know, Ham, I'd like to run and beat Wagner. I would like to go to Washington and as a senator, get up and oppose all the New Deal Socialistic legislation. And ridicule it. And I can do it.'" It was a matter of Smith's failing health, apparently, that kept him from making the race. "And he said, 'My* *heart is not as strong as it should be. And I have a very good job here, $50,000.'* *'Well,' I said, 'Al, as far as the job is concerned, we've been in touch with Mr.* *Du Pont, who pays the salary, and he will continue the salary, regardless.'"* The Colonel withdrew the request: "Because I, too, believed he could be elected. But not at the expense of his life."

Scarlet Banners
and Novenas

William L. Patterson

He is seventy-seven.

"My mother was born a slave in 1850. As the War Between the States *seemed inevitable, her grandfather sent his white family to Massachusetts and his black family to California. My father was a West Indian.*"

After graduating from law school in California, he signed up as a third cook on a steamship: ultimate destination—Liberia. While pausing in London, he met George Lansbury, the old Labour Party M.P., who urged him to return to America because "it was there the great struggle would develop."

In New York, he passed the bar, with an assist by Henry L. Stimson. Within a short time, his was the leading Negro law firm in the city. He became interested in the Sacco-Vanzetti case. "Most of the young Negro lawyers did not see any connection whatsoever . . . but I asked myself what was the purpose of practicing law when social issues arose and I played no part. . . ."

As a member of a delegation to Boston to protest the execution,* he met Ella (Mother) Bloor and other Communists. "They were very solicitous of my welfare. It was for me an experience with a new type of white American. However, it was when Mother Bloor linked up the Sacco-Vanzetti case with the oppression of the Negroes, I was struck by the clarity of her cause. I gave up the practice of law and joined the Communist Party."

For three years, he studied in the Soviet Union at the University for Toiling People of the Far East. Most of the students were young Asians, though there were "one or two Africans." He returned to America in 1930.

---

* He was in a demonstration on Boston Common. Upton Sinclair, in *Boston*, describes how "the mounted police tried to ride me down and chased me on horseback."

FOR A SHORT TIME, I was an organizer in Harlem. It was an interesting period that gave rise to the Negro literati. James Weldon Johnson was around.
And, of course, one of the great men of the century, Dr. W.E.B. DuBois.
Professor Alain Locke of Howard . . . and young Negro writers following
the path blazed by money-mad white writers. Two exceptions were the
poets Claude McKay and Langston Hughes.

I was asked by the party to go to Pittsburgh to take charge of a new
school there—of miners and metal workers. It was in the heart of the Depression. Unemployed Councils and hunger marches were organized.

I'd been arrested in a demonstration in which a thousand Negroes and
whites had carried the furniture of an evicted white family back into their
home. In the trial, I defended the other arrested men, as well as myself.
The jury brought out a verdict of not guilty.

I was arrested while speaking to black and white miners in western
Pennsylvania and eastern Ohio. On one occasion, there was talk of lynching me. White and Negro workers placed their picket line around the prison
and marched all night.

On another occasion, I was thrown into jail without any charges being
made. At twelve o'clock at night, gun thugs came to my cell, saying they
were going to transfer me to another jail. I knew the town had only one jail.
I thought this was it.

I was put into a Ford, and we started out of town. The three men began
to talk among themselves in a language I did not understand, but which I
recognized as Slavic. I asked them in Russian what they were going to do to
me. They were very much surprised in hearing a black man talk Russian.
We began to discuss my stay in Russia.

We soon came to a wooded section in the road. The car was stopped, and
I was told to get out. I thought I'd be shot trying to escape, as the charge was
usually made. But one of them kicked me, and they drove off.

The Unemployed Councils were a creation of the Communists, though
in the main their composition was made up of non-Communists. I recall
men and women being shot, engaging in these activities. There were
hundreds charged with sedition, conspiracy, on one pretext or another. But
it was a period of great schooling.

Many times, the councils started at a meeting in which it was proposed
that delegations be sent to City Hall or to the state assembly—demanding
food and work. These committees would come back and report to their
community. Out of these events came the Unemployed Councils. There
followed the idea of hunger marches. To city halls, to city councils. I led
one of a few thousand into Uniontown. When we arrived, the cossacks

Beale Street, Memphis, Tennessee

MARION POST WOLCOTT, 1939

were there in great number. I mounted the steps and began to speak. In a short time, the city council and the mayor came down and called a meeting. A delegation went into the City Council. I spoke for them. They immediately voted $6,000 for relief. It was a small amount, but it was a small town.

"Roosevelt emerged to talk about the necessity of giving people relief. One thing that many do not recall was his statement that he was out to save capitalism from itself. He did. With his WPAs and his PWAs, he brought back a measure of stability to American society.

"However, many illusions arose. Roosevelt carried out, in a very adroit manner, a program in which he doled out hundreds of dollars to workers, while millions were given to banks, the railroads and other industries. As contrasted to Hoover, he did, in fact, offer a New Deal to working people."

What do you feel was the Communists' role in the emergence of the CIO?

"John L. Lewis has stated it more clearly than anyone else. Without the organization ability of the Communist Party, the CIO might never have come to life. Youth today has no comprehension of the tremendous role played by the Communist Party in that period. It forced the Roosevelt administration to carry through some of the Social Security measures."

Wasn't the idea of black nationhood suggested, for a time, by the Communist Party . . . ?

"During the late twenties, the concept of self-determination arose, as a means of sharpening the struggle. The rights of Negroes to have a part of the United States in which they constituted a majority. There were separatist movements at the time. They were sharply challenged by DuBois. Black Americans are not Africans. To consider themselves so would be to surrender their heritage to the very forces which have been their greatest oppressors.

"Black power today is self-determination in a new form: autonomy of the black ghetto. It must be a positive force. Where it creates the idea of separatism, it must be combated."

I had been in Pittsburgh only a short time when the Scottsboro case broke. In April 1931, nine Negro lads were arrested, and the trial took place in Scottsboro, Alabama. They were riding a freight, seeking work. Some were seeking hospital care, which they could not get in their hometown. It was a freight train going from Tennessee to Alabama, in which a large number of white lads, who were also jobless and penniless, were moving restlessly from one place to another. When the lads were arrested, both white and black were charged with vagrancy. Until the sheriff found out there were two white girls, in overalls, on the same train.

Under pressure, the girls were forced by the police to say they had been raped by the nine Negro lads. Both these girls had been forced, by economic conditions, into prostitution at an early age.

He received a call from New York that the International Labor Defense (ILD) was undertaking the defense. The secretary of the organization was going to Europe with Mrs. Wright, the mother of one of the boys—to mobilize international sentiment in their behalf. He agreed to become acting secretary of the ILD.

I immediately sought the services of Samuel Liebovitz. He was one of New York's leading criminal lawyers and he had never lost a death case. He told me, "I'll bring these boys back and throw them in your lap." I told him, "No, you won't. These are political prisoners. They are arrested and being tried for a purpose . . . to terrorize the Negro people."

Liebovitz handled the case in a masterly fashion. The freight train on which these lads were riding had forty-nine cars. Liebovitz had a replica made of this train, every car placed in the position it originally occupied. In the trial, he forced the complainants, these two girls, to show what car the rape had taken place in. He showed the judge that this car had been full of gravel, that the gravel had come up to the level of the car's sides. Had these girls been raped, their backs would have been lacerated. . . .

Judge Horton reversed the conviction. He fairly analyzed the evidence and showed that much of it was inadmissible. And yet the case of the Scottsboro Boys lasted for seventeen years, from 1931 to 1947. That's when the last of them, Heywood Patterson, the most outstanding and courageous of these lads, was released.

It was a *cause célèbre*, which brought into action millions of people all over the world. And led me, inexorably, I think, to see the role of the American government in the persecution of the Negro people. The case went twice to the United States Supreme Court. There was evidence, both in law and in fact, sufficient to enable the court to dismiss the case. Instead, on each occasion, these boys were sent back to go through the torture and agony of their prison life, and the racist persecution to which they had been subjected. I began to see clearly this conspiracy to perpetuate racism as an institution in our life.

Didn't one of the girls eventually become a witness for the defense?
One of the most interesting features of the case. It showed the tremendous power of struggle to awaken both the consciousness and understanding of people. Ruby Bates, one of the young white girls, was a remarkable person. She told me she had been driven into prostitution when she was thirteen. She had been working in a textile mill for a pittance. When she asked for a raise, the boss told her to make it up by going with the workers. She told me there was nothing else she could do.

After she had been going with the white workers, the police called her in. They didn't want to arrest her for prostitution, but she had to have what they called Nigger Day. On a certain day, she had to go with black workers, so if they wanted to charge a black man with rape, to organize a lynching bee, they would have a man who could not deny he had gone with her.

Ruby and I had an opportunity of speaking together. We brought her to New York, when she expressed a desire to tell her story, the true story. She met Reverend Harry Emerson Fosdick. And I took her to see Elmer Rice, the playwright. When Wexley's play* appeared, she made a speech, and so did I.

She told how she had been threatened with imprisonment unless she charged these boys with rape. She told how Victoria Price, the other girl, had been implicated in a murder charge, and how this threat of prosecution was held over her head. She told how the authorities promised to give Victoria a house in Scottsboro, if she testified as they wanted. Ruby found it impossible to be a party to a crime of this magnitude.

Ruby Bates was a remarkable woman. Underneath it all—the poverty, the degradation—she was decent, pure. Here was an illiterate white girl, all of whose training had been clouded by the myths of white supremacy, who, in the struggle for the lives of these nine innocent boys, had come to see the role she was being forced to play. As a murderer. She turned against her oppressors. . . . I shall never forget her.

■　■　■　■

Max Shachtman

Formerly a Trotskyite leader, now a leading theoretician of the American Socialist Party.

---

* John Wexley's *They Shall Not Die*, a play based upon the case. Ruth Gordon enacted the role of Ruby Bates.

Fascism and Uncle Sam signs on boxcar, Crystal City, Texas

RUSSELL LEE, 1939

UNTIL THE CRASH OCCURRED, it was thought there was something unique about American capitalism. Even the radicals felt it. They were in bad shape. The Communists were wracked by internal strife. The Socialists were stagnating. Ford was paying his workers $5 a day—unprecedentedly high wages. It seemed the class struggle was coming to an end, and radicalism might disappear. But the 1929 crisis created a revolution in thought: it affected liberals and, in many cases, conservatives, as well as radicals.

What was called the collapse of American capitalism had an enormously stimulating effect on the American Communist Party. It underwent two phases in the thirties: the first five years of the decade, and the second. This phenomenon had something of a third phase, too.

At the beginning, it purged itself. It has nothing to do with events in the United States. As always, in the case of the Communists, it reflected happenings in Russia. On the eve of "the collapse of American capitalism," the CP expelled a group of us for espousing "the counterrevolutionary policies of Trotsky." Other expulsions followed. The conflict resulted in at least a dozen different factions. This bewilderment kept the party in a state of paralysis.

However, the oncoming of mass unemployment, on a scale hitherto unknown in this country, enabled the Communists to organize the unemployed and stage vigorous protests. They were initially the leaders of this movement. In New York, at Union Square, they were able to gather as many as 100,000 people at a rally.

Hoover was still president. Since he didn't offer even the mildest form of amelioration for the unemployed, the Communist Party seemed to be riding high. But its success was illusory. At bottom, the unemployed worker was uninterested in communism. He was interested in one thing only: a job. The CP could involve him in demonstrations, but it couldn't get him a job. It was the New Deal that subsequently did this—at least, for a few million.

With the election of Roosevelt, the party entered a new phase. It envisioned the complete decay of capitalism and the impending triumph of international proletarian revolution. It engaged in the most militant policies imaginable. Everybody to the right—and some to the left—of the party was considered the enemy. Socialists became social fascists. They were more vigorously attacked than the real fascists. During the first New Deal period, Congress was referred to as the fascist Grand Council.

Although it was of transitory nature, Communists were making progress among the unemployed. Unfortunately, they deepened the gulf between themselves and every other radical group in the country. "Red trade unions" were created. Their programs were revolutionary as all get out; their leadership was hot as a pistol. They had only one defect—few members. Consequently, their reputation among trade unions became really bad. There are few crimes as great in labor circles as dual unionism: dividing the ranks of workers in their confrontations with employers.

Nevertheless, capitalism looked pretty sick. Wide segments of the population were radicalized. In liberal and academic communities, Marxism, which had been considered passé, became popular again. There was more writing about Marxism—favorable, though not very perceptive, in many cases—during these years than at any other time in American history.

In the late twenties and early thirties, thousands of young people had joined the Socialist Party. They kept pushing the Socialists further and further to the left, in many instances borrowing the jargon of the Communists. This led to a split. The right wing, many older Socialists, pulled out. Especially after the Detroit Convention of 1934, when a platform was adopted in favor of the dictatorship of the proletariat.

These parallel developments among the Communists and the Socialists were influenced, aside from our domestic crisis, by two events in Europe.

The first: the triumph of fascism in Germany. Hitler had overthrown the Weimar Republic, without any real resistance by the world's two largest radical parties, outside Russia: the German Communist Party and the Social Democrats. They capitulated without firing a shot. There was conjured up a return to barbarism, in modern form, and the danger of a second world war. This was about 1933.

The second event was the Russian Five Year Plan, inaugurated by Stalin. The world outside knew little of its details. Later, it learned of the horrors associated with it. But what stood out in the minds of ninety-nine out of every hundred of American radicals was this contrast: there was no smoke in American factory chimneys; there, production was going on like mad everybody was working. And of all the great powers, it was Russia that was intransigently antifascist.

Yet in spite of all this, radicalism did not take deep root in the United States. The Communist Party had added a few thousand members, but it was still insignificant in the political life of this country. Especially, when contrasted to the American Socialist Party at its peak in 1918. It had over a hundred thousand members.

It was in the second half of the thirties that a big change occurred in the American left. There was the New Deal and especially the birth of the CIO. Labor entered politics, as the unorganized were organized. Radicals of all persuasion were deeply affected. The Communists and the Socialists, because of their experience, were virtually sucked into the movement. In many cases, they were the moving forces.

With the rise of Hitler and the Spanish resistance to fascism in the civil war, a most decisive event followed. A radical turnabout in Communist policy. The People's Front—the United Front—came into being. The party abandoned the theory of "social fascism." The United Front welcomed all radicals, all liberals and, for that matter, all "right-thinking" capitalists. (Laughs.) Everybody. The New Deal and Roosevelt were embraced. Speeches called for understanding of the National Association of Manufacturers. Had any radical suggested these ideas in preceding decades, he'd have been politically lynched. There were only two prerequisites: friendliness to Russia and hostility to Hitler.

As far as the Communist Party was concerned, it was quite effective. Certainly, unity among radicals is better than internal strife. It was the party of friendliness. How could anybody oppose it? You'd have to be against motherhood. . . .

Soon, the policy of working in the Democratic Party became accepted. This was natural. The labor movement was overwhelmingly behind Roosevelt and the New Deal. It wasn't a matter of taking it over. I don't believe all this right-wing nonsense about their capturing the Democratic Party. It was merely a matter of influence. In comparison with its utter isolation in the first half of the thirties, this was an enormous advance for the Communists. But it was all an illusion. Its Achilles' heel was its subordination to Moscow policy.

The party had been doing fine. It was against fascism, for the Loyalist government in Spain, for the CIO, for all the nice things in the New Deal. What the hell more do you want from a radical party? There's never been anything as nice as this in American history. (Laughs.) Then, virtually overnight, it destroyed itself. It backed the Hitler-Stalin pact.

The shock was volcanic. The labor movement drove them out of its ranks. It lost liberal support. It was reduced to insignificance. At the end of the decade, the CP appeared far more discredited, far more isolated than at the beginning of the thirties. And from that, it has never recovered.

There was a burst of respectability with the invasion of Russia by Hitler. Once again, radical and liberal intellectuals flocked to its banner. But it was a brief moment. Then came the Cold War. . . . Today, even the New Left looks upon it as obsolete, puritanical, conservative, establishment. . . .

It's funny, if it weren't so tragic. It's sad because of its effect on a genuine American radical movement. It looked for a moment, at the beginning, that it might become that. It never did.

The decline of the Socialist Party is even more regrettable. Especially to me. For the past ten years, I've been a member. This party did not understand—and now is only beginning to understand—the profound political revolution wrought by Roosevelt and the New Deal.

A new political coalition was created: labor, with its many ethnic minorities, and Negroes. At first it was sentiment on the part of the blacks; now it is organized. I'm convinced this coalition is going to remain a decisive element in American politics for a long time to come.

This coalition worked. It did not produce socialism, but then that wasn't Roosevelt's intention. (Laughs.) He saved our society in a new bourgeois reform way. I hate to use this jargon, but there you have it. Capitalism remains.

So the Socialist vote continues to decline. The enormous sympathy it once enjoyed in the labor movement has thinned down to nothing. The Communists, because of Moscow, are ruined. The American left is nothing as compared to its role in European countries. Nothing breaks my heart more than to say this: our stupidity in not recognizing the significance of the coalition, our failure to identify with this group, our isolation from the mainstream of American political thought, our special language, which no one understands. It's a pity.

I don't expect our power structure to build a radical movement. I expect the radicals to do that. Up to now, they have failed. As I watch the New Left, I simply weep. If somebody set out to take the errors and stupidities of the Old Left and multiplied them to the nth degree, you would have the New Left of today. . . .

The radicals of the thirties have gone their separate way. Only a handful retain their old commitments. I feel more strongly about the ideals of socialism than I ever did. Still, many thousands of old radicals, like myself, vote for the goddamn Democrats. And yet, as I look back on that decade, the thirties, it was for radicals the most exciting period in American history.

■ ■ ■ ■

Dorothy Day

The headquarters of the Catholic Worker: it is on the Lower East Side in New York. On a wall of the kitchen—an all-purpose room of "any peasant's lodging," as a young man says—is a framed quotation of Father Daniel Berrigan: "Men are called to declare peace as once they were called to declare war."

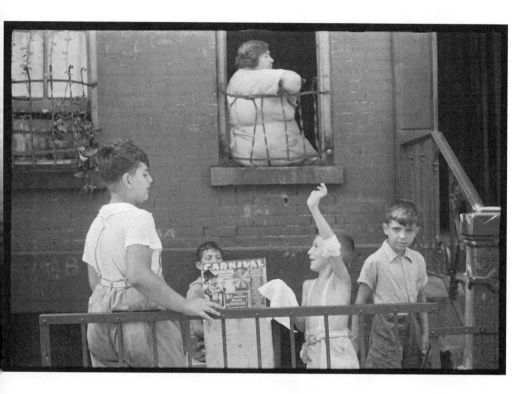

Children playing on 61st Street between
1st and 3rd Avenues, New York City

WALKER EVANS, 1938

Her room, two flights up, is bare of any luxury. A cot, a couple of chairs, a shelf of well-thumbed books, including a great many paperbacks. There are occasional interruptions by young associates—questions of the moment: the putting up of a stray couple; an unexpected visitor; will I share their meal? Nothing fancy, but filling. . . .

She is a large-boned, handsome woman. Though a white-haired grand-mother, touching seventy, her demeanor is that of a young, exhilarated girl. An intimation of weariness is now and then reflected. It passes quickly.

"My approach even as a child was religious. Some of my old friends from the Communist Party felt I was too religious to be really a good revolutionist. Pacifism was very much my whole point of view. I never could see a set of people killing off another set of people to bring a better society. People had to work nonviolently. I don't think I was especially influenced by Gandhi. I think it's the whole Christian message.

"My whole background before, as a Socialist and a Communist, was that things should be changed. There's always going to be human suffering, plain human orneriness. But it seemed impossible to me that we should be living with these extremes of wealth and poverty, where people lived like dogs and got nowhere."

IN DECEMBER 1932, I was covering the hunger march, down in Washington, of the Unemployed Councils. And a farmers' convention which was more or less Communist-inspired. I went down there to cover it for *Commonweal* and *America*.* I just sat in that shrine and prayed that a way would open up for me to work more directly with these issues. My prayer was obviously a fervent one. That was the year I met Peter Maurin. That was the year the *Catholic Worker* started.

She tells of Peter Maurin, the French peasant, who chose poverty as a way of life; a former teacher, he came to Chicago's Skid Row; worked the railroads, the wheat fields, the steel mills; was a janitor; engaged in all sorts of manual labor: "the man who digs the ditches, the man who cleans the sewers deserves just as much pay as the man who sits behind the desk. . . ." All reform, he believed, must come from the bottom up, not from the top down. His belief was in a "personalist communitarian revolution." It begins with the individual and his personal response to poverty. . . .

---

* Two Catholic journals: the first, a lay monthly; the other, a Jesuit weekly.

Ours is more the anarchist's point of view: the state is a tremendous danger. We were the first ones in the Church to oppose Mussolini and Hitler. We picketed the *Bremen*,* I remember, down there on the waterfront. The Communists were picketing at the same time. The Communists and the Catholics. . . .

It must have been in 1935. A group of Communists boarded the ship and tore down the swastika. Some of them were arrested, and one was shot. We were, both sides, issuing leaflets. Although atheism is an integral part of Marxism, according to Lenin, we still had these concordances. . . .

We joined them in a protest in front of the police station. We were dispersed by the police. When the Communists who were arrested were brought to trial, they proclaimed themselves Catholic workers. Most of them were longshoremen and they were Catholics, by birth. Cradle Catholics. It was amazing to hear them all get up and say they were Catholic workers. (Laughs.) Right away, they were identified with us. I found it very amusing.

We participated in the strikes that were going on. I remember a brewery strike. Why we picketed a brewery I don't know. (Laughs.) I'm practically a Carrie Nation about liquor. You see so much misery on the Bowery, you just have to carry on. . . . There was a department store strike. I guess we were the first Catholics policemen had ever seen on a picket line. They thought we were all Communists boring from within.

There was the Chinese-Japanese War going on that we started in 1932 or 1933. Then there was the Ethiopian War and the Spanish Civil War. Nonviolence had to be the role of the Church. How else could any one speak of the teachings of Christ, the Sermon on the Mount, the whole question of the Beatitudes . . . ?

Plenty of students came down and joined us, 'cause there were no jobs to be gotten. They came directly from college, with no experience. Mostly young men. That's what really began building up the *Worker*. We had thirty-two hospitality houses in the country before we were many years old.

There's a wide difference in point of view of the students then and young people today. State universities were cheap in those days. You could go to a state university and get yourself a degree easily enough. But there were no jobs. Now there are plenty of jobs and most young people are wondering what's worth doing. They don't want to be part of the system. The war hangs over their heads, the Bomb. They have a sense of constant crisis.

---

* A German ocean liner, bearing the swastika.

In the thirties, bread and butter issues . . .
Yes. They didn't consider the whole social order as students are doing today.
Or the whole peace issue . . .

In 1933, 1934, there were so many evictions on the East Side, you couldn't
walk down the streets without seeing furniture on the sidewalk. We used to
go ahead and try to find other empty apartments and force the relief stations to pay those first months' rent. We used to help people move into the
apartments and get settled. And give them a hand.

*Did you, like the Unemployed Councils, try to put people back in the apart-
ments from which they were evicted?*
No. We felt we couldn't use people in this way, to make a point. We tried to
forestall the marshal, and get them moved out, so they wouldn't be ashamed
and humiliated and debased. They had enough suffering without having
this suffering piled on them, being made part of a demonstration.

What was the attitude of the Communist Party toward the Catholic Worker?
There were a few articles in the *Daily Worker* trying to combat our ideas.
They considered it false mysticism. There was no contact between us, except
that some were friends of mine. . . . When it came to a certain kind of
strike or to a demonstration, such as the one in front of the German em-
bassy, there was a common cause.

We were never militantly anti-Communist. But we saw so many liberals
going over in the thirties, we had to put out the very strong differences in
point of view. In a way, they were not to be depended upon. They could
change their party line, it was the style, sort of. At the same time I can see
what Cuba's accomplishing. I think every single Latin American country
will have another brand of Communism. The Church could be a Communist organization.

The Communists contributed plenty in the thirties. Absolutely. They
were the ones that led the heroic struggles and risked beatings and imprisonment and death itself to organize in the South, for instance, in textiles.
They tried to organize the unorganized, wherever they were.

That hunger march down in Washington emphasized the need for all the
things we have now. They were marching on Washington, three thousand
of them, for unemployment insurance, old age pensions, aid to dependent
children. Every type of social security that we have now was on the Communist program at that time. But this was the philosophy of the state taking
over.

Did you campaign for Social Security at the time?
No, we were on the other side. The whole program of unemployment insurance, Social Security, was a confession of the failure of our whole social order. And confession of failure of Christian principles: that man, in fact, did not look after his brother. That he had to go to the state . . .

There's a terrific conflict here. The federal government again and again has to protect people against injustices—in the South, for instance. And yet, ideally, it should not be the business of the state. Popes and anarchists have emphasized the principle: subsidiarity. The state should never take over the functions that could be performed by a smaller body. The state should only enter when there are grave abuses. The Tennessee Valley Authority is a good case in point. It concerns the welfare of a great many people in a great many states. And begins a new social order right there—a communal order, to a great extent, autonomous.

The relation of the Catholic Worker *to the New Deal . . . ?*
We were against it. On the one hand, we had to go ahead. It was a time of crisis, as a flood would be. So we did try to get the people on welfare. Did try to get their rent taken care of. But what you had to do first of all is to do everything *you* could.

You were not opposed to the reform measures of the New Deal, per se?
No. But if it could be done by a smaller group, it would be better. We see the evils of gigantic associations. Their abuse of power. There must be decentralization. It's a tremendous problem. Autonomy as against immediate need. We emphasize our anarchism.

What do *I* do? That's how our houses of hospitality started during the Depression. A girl came in. She had read a letter we sent to the bishops about the Church's tradition. She had been evicted from her furnished room. She had a couple of shopping bags and was sleeping in the subway. We didn't have any room, we were all filled up. We didn't know of any place that could take her. The girl looks at us and says: "Why do you write about things like that when you can't do anything about it?" It shamed us, you know? We went and rented another apartment. Then we got a whole house. We were pushed into it. Everything we've done, we've been pushed into.

We never started a bread line. We didn't intend to have a bread line or a soup line come to the door. During the Seamen's Strike of 1937, six of them showed up. They said: "We're on strike, we have no place to stay, we have no food. We're sleeping in a loft on the waterfront." We took in about ten seamen.

At the change of the shift at the Penomah Mills Inc.,
Taftville, Connecticut

JACK DELANO, 1940

We rented a storefront, while the strike lasted for three months. We had big tubs of cottage cheese and peanut butter, and bread by the ton brought in. They could make sandwiches all day and there was coffee on the stove.

While we were doing that for the seamen, one of the fellows on the Bowery said, "What the hell are you doing down there feeding the seamen? What about the men on the Bowery? Nobody's feeding them." So when the men would come in for clothes or a pair of shoes or socks or a coat and we didn't have any left, we'd say, "Sit down anyway and have a cup of coffee. And a sandwich." We kept making more and more coffee. We brought out everything we had in the house to eat. That's how the first bread line started. Pretty soon we had a thousand men coming in a day, during the Depression. It started simply because that Bowery guy got mad.

Our good Italian neighbors recognized poverty. They'd bring all their leftovers to add to the soup. Storekeepers and neighbors. They'd bring over pots of spaghetti and their leftover furniture and clothing and things like that. The very ones who were poor themselves. We lived in their neighborhood and they accepted us.

They were also the ones who had little statues of Mussolini in their windows and gave him their wedding rings.* So you can't go ahead and say these are the bad guys and these are the good guys. You can't ever say it. They talk about the left and the right, yet all men are brothers. The Communists have a better understanding of this, but they want to bring it about through the use of force. Isn't it a shame? They do have the vision. Would they wipe out these people with Mussolini in the window?

When we moved into a more respectable type neighborhood, they used to throw things at us when we passed by, saying we were degrading the neighborhood. As soon as people get a little more comfortable, this is what happens. . . .

The attitude is much worse today. In the thirties, everybody was in the same boat. It was a general disaster. Ignazio Silone once said, "Everybody's disaster is nobody's disaster." The individual did not suffer as he does suffer now. Those on welfare today are despised as they were never despised before.

Another Depression might be a relief to many people. They know our prosperity is built on war. It might be so much better than war. People won't have to keep up a front any longer. They wouldn't have to keep up the payments any more. There would have to be a moratorium. The threat of De-

---

* In 1935, during the Ethiopian War, Fascist Italy was collecting gold, silver and copper. In exchange for their wedding rings, women received steel rings, inscribed: "Gold to the Fatherland."

pression is nothing to worry about. I wish to goodness the stock market would collapse for good and for all. I'd like to see a nonviolent revolution take place and an end to this Holy War. . . .

■   ■   ■   ■

Fred Thompson

"I'm just as old as the century." He is a member of the IWW (Industrial Workers of the World, popularly known as the Wobblies). He joined in 1922.

In his younger days, he had been a construction worker: tunnels, irrigation ditches, dams, quarries, laying track. "We always boxcared from one job to another, never paid any fare. I had heard of the Wobblies . . . weird stories, that they were a bunch of nuts trying to change the world by burning haystacks and stuff like that.

"I found a tremendous difference between this myth and the reality. They were a very serious bunch of men with understanding: even if we do win our immediate demands, the boss and I will still have a fight. Let's run the works for our own good, so we won't have to fight any more. They had this notion: someday . . . But, right now, let's clean up these camps, let's raise the wages.

"There's a belief that the IWW was killed by the repression following World War I, when a lot of us, including myself, were arrested for criminal syndicalism. The facts don't correspond. Our membership was at its peak in the summer of 1923.

"In 1924, we had a catastrophe, when an internal factional fight split us in two. But we built up again, following the Colorado Coal Strike of '27."

IN THE THIRTIES, OUR biggest growth was in Cleveland. As soon as this Depression got going, we hammered away at one theme: people who didn't have a job would do far more for themselves by going to every worker who still had a job, and saying, "If you strike, we won't take your job away from you. We'll come there and beef up your picket line." We put out a leaflet, I remember writing it myself: Bread lines, Picket lines. The theme was that bread lines lead to despair and picket lines lead to hope.

I was on a soapbox circuit. I used to go from Duluth down to Minneapolis, over to Milwaukee, down to Chicago. We'd usually hit places like the iron country in Michigan and Minnesota. In Chicago, we'd hit Swedetown, around the North Side. They'd be mostly men. The home guard. The fellows who weren't migratory workers, who didn't ramble around, who had a stationary job.

Henry Ford changed things for the IWW. We used to be rather strong with people who worked the wheat harvest. They went there in boxcars. But the combines* shut out the demand for extra harvest labor. Plus the fact that people became "rubber tramps," in broken-down tin flivvers. This meant our organizing technique was no longer workable. We had to go to the flivver jungles.

In '22, at the construction camps, you didn't see any females around unless they were visiting with their business agent (laughs), for short durations. You didn't see men and wives.

In '27, I had a little holiday that the State of California gave me for criminal syndicalism. When I came back, two years later, I found the whole industry had changed. Every camp had provision for married couples, but their children had to be working.

Quite a few people were living in nearby towns, if there were decent roads between town and job. The automobile made it possible for a man to live a fairly settled life and fill these out-of-town jobs. The migratory worker had practically disappeared in '26. You didn't hear much about him again until the Dust Bowl days. And a new kind of mobility arose.

Did the Communists or Socialists try to win away your members to their causes during these years . . . ?
The radical movement waxes and wanes. They jostle each other. We like to grab each other's members and things like that, sure. But the overall anti-capitalist movement grows and declines together. They all get bigger at the same time, they all get smaller at the same time. (Laughs.)

In general, there was cooperation—not entirely so. The IWW has always tried to avoid being dogmatic, doctrinaire. We don't ask a guy: what are your political beliefs? We ask 'em: what kind of work do you do? What industry are you in? We have never prevented any person joining because of his beliefs.

The Communists wanted us to join them in 1920. They had a misapprehension over in Moscow, where they got their orders, that we were a secret underground. Heywood† went over and tried to explain to Lenin that we had a great big printing plant in Chicago, where we put out twelve different weeklies and a bunch of magazines and so forth. We had trouble with the

* Machines for harvesting and threshing wheat.
† Big Bill Heywood, a top leader of the IWW.

government, but we were certainly not hiding. They knew we were doing these things. (Laughs.)

The IWW did not engage in internecine warfare, say, the way the other groups did . . . ?
We were forced into a certain amount of it. By 1923, the Communist Party had decided that we should be allowed to exist in agriculture and in the woods, but should not be allowed into any other industry. And if their members did join us, they should do what they could to disrupt us. Naturally, that gave us some concern. But even at that, we tried to get them to see the common sense, is all.

What did happen to the IWW membership in the thirties?
We had lean years. But we did get to far more people. People had time, all kinds of time. In the early thirties, up to '35, everybody might be flat broke, but they'd find a way of gettin' to a meeting.

In the depths of the Depression, did you hear much talk of revolution?
Oh, there was a lot of talk. But there was no anticipation that we were about to take over the works and run it. The IWW felt only an organized working class could do it. A working class that wasn't allowed to eat the food it produced . . . that had to go with patches on its ass after it had made too many clothes . . . was a working class that could be browbeat. A working class that had to beg for a soup bone wasn't a class that could take this world and run it. They had to organize first.

I ran into some ill-informed people who used the word *revolution* very carelessly—that things were so tough, we were going to have a revolution and so forth. I didn't run into any person who had given serious thought as to how you make one. I'd want a revolution. Sure, I'd like one now. But the circumstances are not propitious for havin' one, and they weren't in 1931, '32. It isn't just a bunch of starving people that are going to make a revolution. It's gonna be a people that have been asserting themselves. . . .

How did the IWW feel about F.D.R.?
When he died, I remember an obituary in our paper: "He was hated by those he had helped and loved by those he had harmed." A good many Wobblies felt that was hitting it right on the head. He made a big hullabaloo about what he was gonna do for labor. After he had labor by the tail, he seemed to figure he could disregard it and favor our enemy instead.

What were your feelings toward the New Deal?
Here was an economic system that had quit work. The logical remedy would have been for a working class to assert itself: we want at least enough of what we produce so we can keep on working. But you didn't have that kind of labor action. Consequently, the pigs who had been stopping the things from working by their own greed didn't disgorge anything. But certain adjustments were made that allowed people to eat. At the time of Hoover, you could use federal funds to feed animals, but not to feed people. It was up to your neighbors, he said.

You think, then, Roosevelt hurt the radical movement . . . ?
I don't know as he hurt it. He changed the situation. He did cause most people to feel if you could only find a good man and put him in office, he'll fix everything for you, and you can go back to sleep now. He certainly didn't help radicalism.

The kind of labor movement that grew up, that we have today, still has this birthmark. Unionism by permit—the NLRB, things of that sort.

In the early thirties, there was a resurgence of an almost dead labor movement. There were various radical activities: the Trotskyites up in Minneapolis, the Communists over there in Toledo, the Socialists there, Wobblies in Cleveland, Detroit and so on. The union literature was like the labor literature of a century ago—looking toward a successor to capitalism. Industrial democracy. In which you have a cooperative commune, you have a brotherhood of man. Even though the issue of the moment was five cents more an hour or better files for metal finishers to work with. . . . The literature carried a vision.

But then you saw, in the coal towns of Pennsylvania—Lewis and the CIO—great big banners: "The President Wants You to Join the Union." It worked. So radicalism was replaced by something else. The government had set up a way. Just sign your name, your authorization card. You can do it quite secretly, you don't have to be a hero any more. We can all vote in a union election, and nobody will know how you voted. Of course, the boss will have to recognize the union, and nobody will really have had to stick his neck out.

When I was a kid, if somebody asked me to define a grievance, I'd say it's something we don't like. Today, a grievance is something not in accordance with standards of arbitration. We're even *told what* the hell to be dissatisfied with these days. (Laughs.)

When I was a kid, the union was *us* guys, what *we* collectively did. Nowadays, people don't speak of the union as *us*. Almost everywhere, the union is *it* or *they*.

There is a growing perception that we should have something other than capitalism. But people aren't excited about it. It's a strange thing. I hardly find anybody today who doesn't agree that the ledger should not determine how we live. Most people think it's terrible that the pollution of Lake Michigan is being decided by how much it'll cost companies to cure it. People are realizing that an environment is being created that will be as dangerous for capitalists to live in as well as for working people . . . that it's insane to let major things be decided on the basis of black figures and red figures.

I find temperate people saying today that the business-motivated system isn't a safe thing to have around. (Laughs.) But I think there is less intensity of feeling.

I think a sense of powerlessness, of fatalism, has been growing from the thirties. Then, we just felt we didn't have the power, the organization. We never felt we were *inherently* incapable of achieving it.

The thing that gives me the most cheer are the young people today. You find them all over the world, having a sense of common fate. They're the least bookish radicals I've ever known, but the most literate. In the thirties, a guy read some kind of book and he wanted everything to go according to that text. Today, these college kids use books simply for insights. They don't have a dogma. They're far more flexible, far more open-minded, far more feeling. *They* have the feeling. . . .

■   ■   ■   ■

Saul Alinsky

Director of the Industrial Areas Foundation.

His work involves the creation of power bases in the community, autonomy in the neighborhood. Although his efforts have been primarily with poor whites and poor blacks, it is now extending to middle-class areas.

"There was a radical continuum that went on in the Depression. Today, there's a chronological cutoff for the kids. They don't believe anything happened in the past. It's a wonder these kids don't reinvent the wheel. Don't they realize that John L. Lewis was fifty-seven when he started the CIO? I think the McCarthy period broke the continuity—the handing over of the torch. There is a radical gap.

"I don't believe anybody has all the answers. I didn't believe it in the thirties, and I don't believe it now. Whenever anyone comes up with a pat prescription for paradise, I worry. Paradise, nothing! I don't want to be in paradise. I can't imagine a world without problems. It'd be hell."

Factory workers' homes, Camden, New Jersey

ARTHUR ROTHSTEIN, 1938

I HAD A FELLOWSHIP in criminology at the University of Chicago. My job was to get insight into crime. So I got in with the Capone mob and was with them for two years. I had enough of those classes in social pathology, social disorientation and all that crap.

How'd you get the boys to accept you?
I hung around the Lexington Hotel. It was their headquarters. I laughed at all the terrible jokes of Big Ed, one of the boys. He liked me and took me around. Different guys taught me the various operations. Jesus, did I learn! I learned what a fucked-up world this really is.

If you wanted to do something about crime, you had to start with the nice people, the respectable ones. I'd go around with a guy who headed the committee against vice. He owned a tenement, with call girls on every floor.

I found organized crime to be a huge, quasi-public utility. This was during the last years of Prohibition. People wanted beer, they wanted whiskey, they wanted broads, they wanted gambling and all the other stuff. It was a corporation. Everybody owned stock in it: City Hall, Democrats, Republicans, the world. . . .

Somewhere along the line, my interest in criminology waned. I remember my student days when I was starving and pulling funny rackets on restaurants, just to survive. Once, I came close to kicking in the goddamn window of Henrici's.* People were in there eating steaks about this thick and my stomach was empty. As a kid was telling me of an A & P store he robbed and another of a gas station he heisted, Hitler and Mussolini were robbing whole countries and killing whole peoples. I found it difficult to listen to small-time confessions. Most of my time was spent in antifascist and CIO activities.

That's how I found myself Back of the Yards. It was the nadir of all the slums of America, worse than Harlem is today. You had this dingy, gray mile-by-two-miles of track, south of the big slaughterhouses. Clapboard frame houses, one behind the other. Many of them with outhouses. The neighborhood was practically all Catholic. You never saw so many churches. It made Rome look like a Protestant Gothic town.

At this point, I decided to get the hell out of academic work and go in for mass organization. I had certain concepts I couldn't follow through on as a professional. If you're an academic and you're controversial, you're in trouble. You had to organize around issues, and all issues were controversial.

* It was, once upon a time, one of Chicago's finest restaurants.

I wanted to test out my ideas. Ideas on organization for change. If they would work in Back of the Yards, they would work anywhere. If you wanted to do something about crime and despair, you had to do something about its causes.

There were a lot of fascist groups in the area. It wasn't accidental. If you cut away a lot of your so-called political science analysis of why a totalitarian society develops, it comes down to this: If you're out of it, the demagogue comes along and says, "Follow me." If you haven't got a goddamn thing to lose, you follow him. Isn't that what happened in Germany?

There was a Benedictine priest, who was leading the Coughlinite movement around there. He was making speeches denouncing international Jewry. He had psyched out, because nobody had paid him any attention. He had about fifty followers. This was his only place in the world. So I made him chairman of the neighborhood's antifascist committee. He now had a thousand followers instead of fifty. He became one of the best antifascist apostles of the democratic process. He was given a sense of personal identification.

I'm going around organizing, agitating, making trouble. At the end of three months, I had the Catholic Church, the CIO and the Communist Party working together. It involved the Packinghouse Workers Union. I even got the American Legion involved, because they didn't have a goddamn thing to do. They all had one thing in common: misery. Powerlessness.

I'd go in to see this Catholic priest. I'd say, "I heard your sermon denouncing the union, calling it Communist. You know something, Father? Your people nodded and then walked out and joined the union. Know why? They're unemployed, their families are shot to hell and you're not doing a goddamn thing about it. You sit on your ass in the sacristy, and you're no longer a shepherd of your flock. Everybody is disregarding you. You want to be a leader? Get back with your people, get out in the streets and fight for the union. The enemy is the meatpacker; the enemy is low wages." So he'd do it. Purely on the basis of self-interest.

You don't talk Judaic-Christian moral principles to a priest, a rabbi or a minister. They wouldn't know what the hell you're talking about.

I had difficulty with only one priest. He was Irish. The Poles of the area had church wedding ceremonies involving bells. It broke down to a buck and a half a pull. The Irish priest passed the word around that he'd perform with bells at a buck a pull. The Polish shepherd went off his rocker. He said to me, "You're the guy who talks about people getting together, that we'll have power and so on. If you can get that Irishman to come back to the regular price, we'll join your organization. Otherwise, forget it."

So I went down to see the Irish priest. I made the mistake of posing the question on purely spiritual grounds. He told me to mind my own business. So I said, "O.K., I looked over the receipts of your last summer's carnival. Your big fund-raising affair. You made $18,000. I'll see to it, when the time comes for your carnival, the CIO, the American Legion, the Chamber of Commerce and every other church in this community will have some kind of affair on the same date. We'll rip your carnival apart. The most you can make at a buck a pull, assume you get all the wedding business, is ten grand. You'll drop eighteen." He ordered me out.

About ten minutes later, the phone rings. He reconsidered. On moral principles, of course. He was up to a buck thirty-five a pull. So I got three Polish churches to join the Back-of-the-Yards Council. So it went: different tactics for different circumstances.

John L. Lewis heard of it. He wasn't happy. The CIO was merely one component, and he wanted it to be the dog with the community as its tail. But he was converted. He offered me a job at $25,000 a year. All I had to do was go around the country organizing CIO unions into industrial communities. I turned him down, though I admired him, and my heart was with the CIO.

Three weeks later, Roosevelt called me to the White House. What a personality! What presence! He offered me a job as assistant director of the NYA. My job was simply to organize young Democrats across the country. Again, though my heart was with the New Deal, I said no.

These were the two most remarkable men of the decade. Why did I reject these offers? Easy. The secret of the Back-of-the-Yards Council—and all the other organizations I worked at since—was: The people weren't fronting for anyone. It was *their own* program.

In the thirties, I learned what is to me the big idea: providing people with a sense of power. Not just the poor. There is nothing especially noble about the poor. Everybody. That time may have been our most creative period. It was a decade of involvement. It's a cold world now. It was a hot world then.

The Doctor, Huey and Mr. Smith

George Murray

A journalist, Chicago's American.

From 1938 to 1945, he had been associated with the Townsend Movement as editor of its newspaper and, subsequently, as its general manager.

AT THE TIME I came over, there were twelve thousand Townsend Clubs all over the country. The little old lady secretaries of these clubs would write up minutes of the meetings in pencil or pen: we heard such and such a speaker . . . a lady baked a cake and we raffled it off. Club notes. My chore was to take all this indecipherable handwritten material and make little stories out of them. One-paragraph stories to give recognition to each club. It kept me busy all week long. I became editor.

He recounts his experiences with Dr. Townsend, the country doctor out of Nebraska. "He was so slender, so thin, never weighed more than 120 pounds, had a good thatch of white hair.

"In 1933, at sixty-seven, he was health commissioner in Long Beach, California, and selling a little real estate on the side. He was dealing with old people. He was aware of their lack of money and of anybody's interest in them. He wrote a three-hundred-word letter to the editor of the Long Beach Telegram. His idea: a gross income tax of two percent on everybody in the country, no exceptions. Proceeds to be divided among all people over sixty, the blind and disabled, and mothers of dependent children. They had to spend it within thirty days. He wasn't a great economist, but he had something figured out in his mind.

"It caught on so quickly, he didn't know what to do. It wasn't a movement at first. But then ten thousand letters came in a month. People from Long Beach

sent this clipping all over the country. Other papers picked it up. He turned his real estate office into headquarters. From then on, it was part of the American scene."

I remember the national convention in Indianapolis. 1939. H. L. Mencken was covering it for the *Baltimore Sun.* He liked Doc. At the press conference, Mencken was cheering Dr. Townsend on. A reporter turned to Mencken and said that all the established newspapers were against this crackpot plan, and "The way you talk, Mr. Mencken, it sounds as though you're for it." I remember Mencken saying, rolling his big cigar in his mouth, "I'd love to see the Townsend Plan enacted tomorrow morning. I'd also like to see New York City bombed from the air. I love a spectacle."

My work was unlike ordinary newspaper reportage. You also had to be a promoter. The plan was carried on by contributions. We would set up a Doctor's Birthday Party on January thirteenth every year. Then we'd have a Founder's Day on September thirtieth. Then we'd have a Homecoming Day. On these three occasions, the ladies would bake cakes and all. There'd be cake sales. We had organizers in each of the forty-eight states. Yet it wasn't organized as it might be by a computer. This was something that had grown unexpectedly, and nobody thought it would last. It was just thrown together. . . .

It was strictly a grassroots movement, nothing else. But it served its purpose. It brought the Social Security plan into being. When he signed the bill, late in 1935, Franklin D. Roosevelt was apologetic. He said: the Social Security plan has not been fully worked out yet by the actuaries. But he had to enact it to forestall the Townsend Plan. People were just screaming. They wanted pensions.

Dr. Townsend was called everything. He was called a charlatan, a man draining money from people, the hard-won pennies of the old. He never took a nickel out of it. He founded the newspaper and took a salary, $90 a week. Many years later, it was $150 a week.

He wasn't an economic genius but his common sense and instinct caused him to hit upon this plan. He was never strong in the cities. His strength was always in the rural areas and small towns. That's where the twelve thousand clubs were. Men like Father Coughlin and Gerald L. K. Smith sensed if they could get these people, they could put over any program they wanted. Dr. Townsend was a genius in politics, if nothing else. When these men came around him—and I'm sure they wanted to use him for their own purposes—he never said no. He never said yes, either. He always said, "That's very interesting." He would try to use *them.* He had a lot of native shrewdness. Nobody was going to take his clubs away from him.

The movement was at its height just before the war and went downhill after that. It lost its momentum. The Townsend Plan was a Depression movement. Now it became a pie-baking movement, just old people. But in the thirties, it had direction: it was going to influence the government, and it did.

■   ■   ■   ■

Senator Russell Long

United States senator from Louisiana.

IT WAS MY GOOD fortune to be the son of a man like Huey Long. He always provided wealth for his family, even in the Depression. I was born and raised in a laboring man's neighborhood, and I knew what wretchedness was. Even though our people were poor, you might say we did pretty well for the kind of folk we came from.

Huey Long had a great sympathy for the Negro, even though, unfortunately, very few were permitted to vote in Louisiana. He did not carry the racial fight for the black man in Louisiana. He thought he was carrying as many crosses as he could, the way it was. He didn't want to be crucified on that one.

I was about seventeen when he died.* I heard some of his speeches and I could see its effect on his audience. He'd go to places where he'd never been before, where they had never heard him. When he finished, he had 'em.

He had been a traveling salesman when he was a youngster and his approach as a political speaker was pretty much the same. Selling. He'd warm the crowd up with some jokes. After a while, he'd start explaining one point, then another, carrying his audience with him—to where he'd really score. He'd return to humor, an anecdote, and then bear down again. He had the audience so tense, you'd think something was gonna snap. Suddenly, he'd relieve the tension by reaching the climax, followed by quick jokes . . . and everybody just relaxed. He'd make them laugh and cheer, from the serious to the ridiculous. He wouldn't move the crowd to tears.

* In 1935, he was assassinated by Carl Austin Weiss in the capitol building at Baton Rouge.

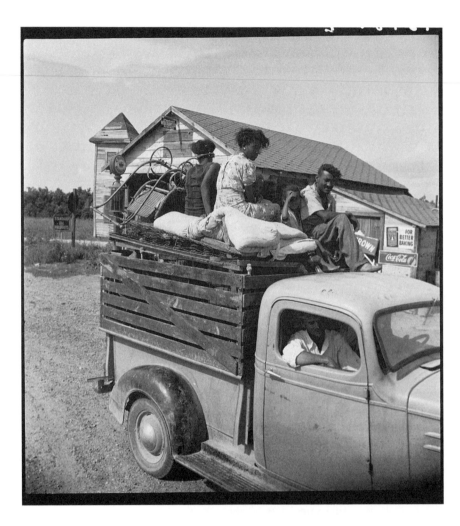

Mississippi Delta, on Mississippi Highway No. 1 between
Greenville and Clarksdale. Negro laborer's family being moved
from Arkansas to Mississippi by white tenant.

DOROTHEA LANGE, 1938

That wasn't his approach. But he certainly sold them points they'd never been sold before.

I enjoyed being in the crowd and hearing those speeches. One time, he was due to make a speech in the large football stadium in New Orleans. He was listening over the radio to the other speeches. Then he fell asleep and snored. He was tired. I could heard the crowd three blocks away. When he showed up, you might as well quit talking. The crowd shouted, "Let's hear Huey!" And that was it.

He never worried about how long he talked. He'd tell everybody to call their friends and neighbors and turn on the radio. He'd say, "I'm not gonna say anything important for the next few minutes, so make those calls." Because he wanted them to hear about all the stealing and corruption he'd found in Washington . . . that somebody else was engaged in.

You'd walk down the street, you couldn't escape the sound of his voice. Every home in New Orleans would have him turned on. His voice could be heard all over town till maybe one o'clock in the morning. New Orleans stayed open all night. It was that kind of town.

He was really catching on around the country. His plan was pretty well patterned after the old Populist philosophy. Money had gotten down to where a few people had practically all of it. He thought it was time you spread it among everybody. His share-the-wealth program was for one-third of the nation's money to be divided among all the people, even though you did permit the other two-thirds to be captured by the upper one percent. It had a lot of popular appeal.

His critics would say: In three or four years, the wealthy would have the money back in their coffers anyway. The Long people would answer: Maybe so. But think what a good time we'd have in the meanwhile. (Laughs.)

Huey Long had great impact on the Roosevelt administration. Dr. Altmeyer told me about it.* He was one of the people who put together the Social Security program. He said, when they'd meet at the White House to discuss the program, Roosevelt was talking more about Huey Long than he was about Social Security. It was designed in a large measure as a backfire against Huey Long.

It was to cut the progress Huey Long was making that Roosevelt moved to the left with liberal New Deal measures. He began as a reactionary. When Roosevelt sent down the economy bill, cutting government salaries and veterans' benefits, Huey made a speech, "The Victory over the Helpless." In one talk, he read from a veteran's letter: ". . . with the new Roose-

* Dr. Arthur J. Altmeyer. He was commissioner of Social Security for a number of years.

velt program, I won't be needing these. So you can wear 'em." The fella enclosed his false teeth. (Laughs.) The crowd just roared.

Roosevelt didn't buy all of Huey Long's program, but he certainly moved in that direction. His welfare programs paralleled in many respects what Huey Long was advocating. When the NYA was put into effect, Roosevelt gave my father credit as being a forerunner. We had a program very similar to it in Louisiana.

Westbrook Pegler wrote in his column that Huey Long had the support of the LSU student body because he had one-third of 'em on the payroll. About a third of the students did have scholarships to help work their way through college. He wanted to go far beyond that. He wanted to provide *every* young man and young lady who could make passin' grades the chance to work their way through college.

This was in the early thirties. A lot of people who today are bank presidents came to LSU with nothing more than a shirt on their back, and not so much as a change of underwear. Today they are prominent people.

Huey Long started out in favor of Roosevelt, and then they went their separate ways. Roosevelt, I think, made a mistake in underrating Huey. My guess is if my father had lived, he'd have run for president on the third party ticket in 1936. He might have kept Roosevelt from winning. I guess he was thinking in those terms. He probably would have caused Landon to win. If that had been the case, he'd have been a real prospect to win four years later.

Some people have suggested that this was a selfish approach, putting his own ambition above the good of the nation. His reply would be: If the public would suffer with Roosevelt or Landon, the sooner both are out, the better. Certainly, if Roosevelt hadn't moved left, Huey Long would have captured the public's imagination. He wasn't doing so bad as it was.

He knew Doctor Townsend and he knew Father Coughlin. I'm not sure they spent much time together, but they were all aware of what the others were doing. They were speaking from the same point of view. While each had a different approach, there was no fundamental difference.

I imagine he had many more good innings left, if the good Lord had let him live. He was thirty years ahead of his time.

■   ■   ■   ■

Evelyn Finn

I LIVED IN BATON ROUGE when Huey Long was shot. I coulda been up there at the capitol when it happened. My brother and I used to go there a lot. They had night sessions, because it was cooler at night. This time I said, "Oh, I'm tired of seein' 'im." So he went by himself. We was home listening to the radio and we heard the news. My brother came home. He'd been up in the spectators' gallery. He said, "There was a terrible commotion. They wouldn't let us out for a long time. I wonder what happened." I thought, "Well, no wonder. Huey Long was shot." He came home and didn't know it.

In 1933, she left St. Louis for a few years. Temporarily, she abandoned her work as a seamstress to run the family grocery store in her hometown, Baton Rouge.

The grafters, Huey's boys, till they got caught up with, they went to town. There was a fella came into the store. He was foreman of a WPA gang—it was called somethin' else before that.* Anyway, they was buildin' these beautiful homes on WPA money. The servants that worked in these homes, I'd cash their checks. They'd say: "We're So-and-So's maid, we're So-and-So's yard man." All these politicians paid their servants with WPA money, get it?

Negroes'd go in town and get their rations. But they couldn't eat it. Full of worms and weevils. They would tell me when they come into the store. They couldn't use half of what they got. But they went and got it. Otherwise, they wouldn't get anything. Because who dished it out would say: "If you don't take it, there's no use to give it to you." That's what they'd give the Negro.

One day, a couple of fellas came around. They said they were Huey Long's boys. Election was comin' up. We had a lot of votes in the family. They explained all the wonderful things Huey Long was doing. Our road was mud. I said, "You only come around when you want votes."

The next morning, there was a big truck-load of gravel, comin', with five or six men on it. They had plenty of manpower, the WPA did. The foreman said, "We give everybody what they want." Oh, that Huey! He was somethin'.

* CWA (Civil Works Administration).

■   ■   ■   ■

Gerald L. K. Smith

"Rev. Gerald L. K. Smith, D.D. . . . the gustiest and
goriest, the loudest and lustiest, the deadliest and
damnedest orator ever heard on this or any other earth."

—H. L. MENCKEN, *BALTIMORE SUN*, 1936

A rugged, though slightly subdued, seventy-one, he and his wife, Elna (after
whom the foundation is named . . . "she came into a handsome inheritance"),
are impresarios of a religious enterprise in Eureka Springs, Arkansas. Once
a celebrated spa, it had become ghostly until the energetic appearance of
Mr. Smith. It is something of a shrine now, offering The Passion Play, with
the latest in stereophonic equipment (". . . if this noble spectacle is anti-
Semitic, the New Testament is anti-Semitic." A General Motors executive
pronounced it better than Oberammergau's.), a gallery of sacred art, and the
Christ of the Ozarks.

This last is a remarkable phenomenon: the Christ of the Ozarks, a seventy-
foot statue on the peak of Magnetic Mountain. The sculpture is astonishingly
white, ". . . we ordered a special kind of mortar." It is visible from four states.
The Savior's outstretched arms appear to be blessing them with equally Won-
drous Love: Arkansas, Oklahoma, Missouri and Kansas.

At twilight, Mr. Smith is at the foot of the hill, his head bowed, his Stetson
at heart, his Lincoln Continental nearby. From within the circle of the Christ,
hymns pour forth. The voices of Kate Smith and Tennessee Ernie Ford are
stereophonically loud and clear.

"Let it never be said that Gerald Smith is using the name of his Savior to
make a fast buck. But if I were a young man, I'd take options on land out
here. . . ."

Mr. and Mrs. Smith ("We have been married forty-seven years, and I love
her as much now as the day she became my bride.") are gracious hosts: a coun-
try dinner and effusive conversation. He is grievously wounded at having been
"quarantined," these past years, by the mass media, though he is an admirer of
Ronald Reagan. . . .

He still keeps a hand in secular as well as sacred affairs: "Three girls are
busy every day, as I dictate articles for more than two hundred right-wing publi-
cations." His own journal, The Cross and the Flag, founded in 1942, is going

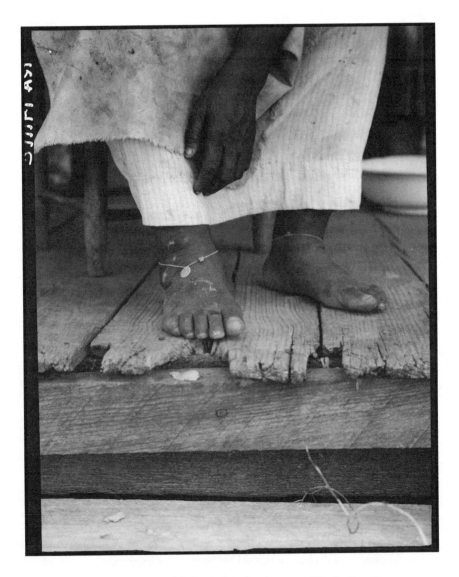

Fifty-seven-year-old sharecropper woman. Hinds County,
Mississippi. Thin dimes around the ankles to prevent headaches.

DOROTHEA LANGE, 1937

fairly strong . . . celebrated for its pungent philippics against the "Jewish Establishment" and recalcitrant blacks.

We are in a stately Victorian house: stained-glass windows, profuse with religious artifacts, portraits, statuary, Tiffany lamps and chandeliers, Persian rugs. . . . "Every stone in this house has been personally cut by hand." What was once the prayer room of the original occupant, a Confederate officer, has been transformed into a bathroom: "I don't think God makes himself available only at certain hours like eleven o'clock Sunday morning." In addition to paintings of the Savior, there is, facing the entrance, a portrait in oil of Henry Ford, the elder.

I WAS INTRODUCED TO the Depression while I was in Shreveport, Louisiana. I was pastor of the most sophisticated church. The leadership included the top men in the community. Then the curtain fell. I had the experience of standing at the door of the church on Sunday mornings, meeting weeping men and women who had lost everything.

In the meantime, Huey Long had risen to power. He referred to Louisiana as the last stand of the feudal lords. Human slavery was still being practiced. When a Negro or a poor white was arrested, he would be assigned by the judge, district attorney or sheriff to the deputy, who happened to own a plantation or sawmill. It was a matter of common practice.

Then came the Depression, and sophisticated people became penniless. Fifteen thousand homes were coming up for mortgage foreclosures in the city. The building and loan company decided to foreclose, before the HOLC could advance loans.

I couldn't stand the tears of these people, and I offered aggressive resistance to this. I urged the company to postpone these foreclosures. They said it was none of my business. Lo and behold, I was waited on by the leaders in my church. They brought pressure on me to resign. They were silent partners in this thieving enterprise.

I called my friend Huey Long: "The hypocrites in my church are planning to steal $50 million." In about thirty minutes, the phone rang. It was the head of the building and loan association. Weeping and wailing, he said, "Dr. Smith, what can I do?* You have no idea what Huey Long said to me. He's going to ruin me. He has told me to do anything you want me to do." I said, "All you need to do is cross the street to the courthouse and cancel the foreclosures." They were canceled. It confirmed my great affection for

---

* "Below the Mason-Dixon Line, all preachers are called 'Doctor,' whether they've been to school or not."

Huey Long, and it lost me my job as pastor of the King's Highway Christian Church.

"I've been asked, 'Why did you leave the formal ministry?' I said, 'Because I want to go to Heaven.' I insist on being called Mr. Smith. I don't like a man that hits me and says, 'Don't hit back, I'm a clergyman.' Take all these preachers causing all this trouble, stirring up the anarchists and all. They go out and tell these people what to do. Take off your collar and just be a private citizen in this controversy. So when someone hits back, they're not slapping a priest or beating a clergyman."

Huey Long and I developed a mutual respect for each other. When his power was at an apex, he said to me, "If God was governor of Louisiana, he couldn't find enough honest men to make a chairman for each county. If anything happens to me, Gerald, you're the only one of this gang that shouldn't go to the federal penitentiary. These boys who were barefooted when I found them just can't keep their hands out of the public till."

Huey Long developed a philosophy in which I helped him along. He was the only man of this century who knew how to think like a statesman and campaign like a demagogue. His share-the-wealth program sounded like demagoguery to reactionaries, but it was sound. The barons of monopoly came into the state. They bought up all the natural resources: the oil, gas and timber concessions—everything from oil to trees, from sulfur to fish. Huey Long said the wealth on top of our ground and underneath must be shared with the people. He said: No man should be allowed to accumulate a fortune of more than $5 million without a progressive levy against him. Imagine. We appealed to intelligent conservatives.

My strategy was to project Huey Long as candidate for president in '36, as Wallace was in '68. It was the understanding we'd split the Roosevelt vote. But we would have a say about who the Republican candidate was. If Huey Long had lived, we would never have nominated this protoplasmic substance, Landon.

The conservatives lost because they didn't know how to support a statesman. They only knew how to buy senators and congressmen. When the real crisis came, we had no one to defend the cause, because the man that can be bought isn't intelligent enough to think for himself. His footwork is too slow.

I remember saying to the Republican leaders personally—in the days of the Mellons—we're willing to split the Roosevelt vote, but we can't promise to lose. Our man is becoming so popular so fast, he might win. Jim Farley said if Huey hadn't been killed, he would have been president of the United States.

When Georgia was upstaging Louisiana and wouldn't let us into the football conference, Huey threatened to impose an extra penny tax on Coca-Cola. The Cannons, who own Coca-Cola, run Georgia. Naturally, Louisiana was brought into the conference.

Everybody came to us. The most subtle, the most cunning Communist leaders on the face of the earth, from Moscow and New York, visited us. They knew we were sincere friends of the people. They wanted to sell us on the Marxist philosophy. The moment we repulsed them, they called us Fascists. The moment we repulsed the reactionaries, we were called Communists. We were dealing with men who felt other men should go to work for a dollar a day and go to church in overalls.

We think our congressmen pass laws and levy taxes. That is done by the money changers. We raise interest from four percent to six, six to eight, eight to ten. A conservative insurance company tried to persuade people out here to finance enterprises at twelve percent. When I was a boy, they'd shoot the three balls off a man's store and put him in jail for that. (Laughs.)

"You say money changer, and they think you mean Jew. The word anti-Semite is a dirty word given to people who take issue with aggressive Jews. My theory is the aggressive Jew is not an honest representative of his community. If I were to attack Rap Brown, would you accuse me of being anti-Negro?* I don't think the Jews should control Palestine any more than they should control New York. I don't mean they should be driven out. Not one ounce of their liberty should be affected. Their citizenship should not in any way be jeopardized, but they shouldn't control everything, either. . . .

"Here we have these liberal regimes. Yet it's the greatest tyranny man has ever known. Cannibals are swallowing cannibals and dinosaurs are swallowing dinosaurs. The conglomerates. Under the leadership of the great impoverished statesmen like Harriman, the Kennedys, the Rockefellers, the Roosevelts (laughs),† we have developed the most super-monopolistic octopus of the human race today. . . ."

---

* "Nigger, as used down South, wasn't a dirty word. Today we can't even say 'chiggers,' we say 'chigg-roes.'" (Laughs.) "Now we have to say 'black,' don't we?"
† "The only way they could fill the football stadium was for Huey to attend the game. In one case, he agreed on condition that the newspaper, begging him, cancel Westbrook Pegler's column. Pegler started out as a Gerald Smith hater and Huey Long hater. Later, he turned on the Roosevelts. A few years ago, in Tucson, he said, 'The greatest mistake in my life was not joining Gerald Smith 25 years ago.'"

Huey Long died in my arms. We were walking through the hall, and this man shot Huey. The boys killed the killer, before he turned loose on the others. He missed me.

It was the largest public funeral in history. It took three acres of ground just to lay the bouquets. They came from everywhere on the face of the earth. There were people backed up eight miles on the other side of the Mississippi, couldn't get across the river.

I sat down beside the bed and wrote the eulogy by hand. Later on, I had it photostated.

It concludes: "His unlimited talents invariably aroused the jealousies of those inferiors who posed as his equals. More than once, yea, many times, he has been the wounded victim of the Green Goddess; to use the figure, he was the Stradivarius, whose notes rose in competition with jealous drums, envious tom-toms. His was the unfinished symphony."*

He recounts his one-man efforts, after Huey's death, in battling the Long machine—"the aggressive pigs in the trough." It was their compact with New Dealers that most incurred his wrath: the promise of several millions to be spent in the state, withheld during Huey's life—on the condition of their backing Roosevelt in the 1936 convention. . . . "Out of the nine men in the machine, I was the only one who refused. I arose in the meeting and said I had catapulted to prominence on the wet grave of Huey Long. There was nothing they had I wanted. So those others, who hadn't reported their income taxes, who had stolen money, were coerced by the Internal Revenue Department and lined up. I coined the term: The Second Louisiana Purchase.

"I went to the people. It was one of the most dramatic nights in Louisiana history. I took the last dollar I had and bought time on every radio station in the state. I announced I was going to speak in the plaza and seventy thousand people came out. I spoke past midnight. I talked about the blood of Huey Long sold on the auction block. It was months before the crooks dared leave their homes or drive through the country, because of what people heard me say that night."

"I used to have a lot of fun with Eleanor myself. I said she was a very generous woman. She left her teeth at the Elks Lodge. (Laughs.) I used to talk about the children. We were raised up to believe that if you married cousins, the children would be silly. It was never more graphically demonstrated than with the Roosevelt family. (Laughs.) When Eleanor came back from the South Seas and said the boys in the hospitals looked sad, I said, 'If I looked up into a puss like that, I'd have a relapse.'" (Laughs.)

* "It was a political speech to himself," said Senator Russell Long. "He anointed himself as Huey Long's successor. He made a great impression."

Many believe that Huey Long was largely responsible for the quick passage of the Social Security Act. . . .
Modern politicians would like to romanticize things. Social Security is the substitute for the real thing. Henry Ford, for instance, never believed in charity. He believed in a job rather than a pension.

Yet . . . why was a man like Henry Ford so fond of you?
Henry Ford wasn't entrenched wealth. He turned a bolt into a nut, a nut into a fender, a fender into a car, and a car into a genius-like formula. That is American wealth. He wasn't part of a combine designed to destroy everyone else. He wasn't part of the money market.

I gravitated to Detroit and started the Christian Nationalist Crusade. Frank Murphy was coming up fast. He played possum while the CIO destroyed Mr. Ford's factory.

You came to Detroit just about the time the CIO was being organized . . . ?
Oh, I was for organized labor. For years, I was an honorary member of the American Federation of Labor. But I believed that labor was moving in the same direction as capital—toward giant monopoly.

"I came so completely into the confidence of Mr. Ford that he specified: Everyone who sold merchandise to the Ford Motor Company contribute to the Christian Nationalist Crusade. We were seeking to enlighten all schoolteachers, all clergymen, all public officials.

"Then one day I was waited on by Mr. Ford's personal secretary, my personal friend. He said he'd been waited on by a personal representative of the White House and that unless Mr. Ford withdrew his support of me, they'd seize the factory and operate it in the name of the wartime emergency. . . ."

In 1942, he ran for the United States Senate in Michigan. He came within twenty thousand votes of winning the Republican nomination. "Both parties united against me." But not Henry Ford.

The time came for a coalition of the people—1936. There were three big mass groups: Huey Long's following, Doctor Townsend's and Father Coughlin's. I was instrumental in effecting this coalition.

Townsend was a sincere, good, unselfish man. I was in Washington when they were crucifying Townsend—the wolf pack. They called in a bunch of neurotic women to testify against him. Hired perjurers, they tried to say it was a racket. They had a Roman holiday with the old man.

I said, "Doc, they're going to destroy you. You treat them with courtesy. You should hold them in contempt." He had two or three hangers-on, who were turning pale. They're the ones who watch over the dues. (Laughs.) I said, "I would stand up, pronounce my contempt, walk out and *defy* them to come and get me." He said, "If I had a young man like you beside me, I'd do it." I said, "You've got him."

So the stage was set. We didn't tell any of those shortstops there, it would scare 'em.

The old man stood up. He pronounced judgment and contempt on the whole congressional committee. He defied the gavel. I just took him by the arm, and we ran out. In the meantime, I was in touch with Henry Mencken. I told him I'd kidnapped the old man and would bring him to Baltimore: "Find a place to hide him."

Mencken was delighted. We hid him for three days in defiance of the committee. The sympathy for old people was such that if any congressman had offered a motion to cite him for contempt, he would have committed political suicide. If I may say so, that was the budge that made the Townsend movement a political factor.

He asked me to speak at his convention in Cleveland. You can hardly realize how the multitudes moved.* It was a Populist movement.

The little machine makers who organized the program said the meeting must be unbiased. We must have a Republican, a New Dealer and so forth. I was scheduled to speak at ten thirty. The Roosevelt friend was set for eleven thirty, and the Republican for twelve thirty. So I spoke for three hours. (Laughs.) Every time the chairman made a move toward me, the crowd wanted to lynch him.

Recalls Mencken: "Twice at Cleveland [author's note: the other event, the Coughlin convention], I saw the rev. gentleman torpedo even the press stand. In that stand were journalists who had not shown any human emotion above the level of cupidity and lubricity for twenty years, yet he had them all howling in ten minutes. . . ."

Everybody was hungry when I was through. The meeting was over before they got to anyone else. Of course, Dr. Townsend loved and revered me in those days. Later on, we had a little quarrel. I felt as he grew old and vegetated, he was exploited. But I respected him to the very hour of his death.

* "In those days, I spoke at the Rose Bowl to 110,000 people. Think of that."

In the meantime, Father Coughlin had developed a great following. He asked if I would deliver the principal address at his convention, aside from his own. The gathering was as big as Townsend's. At the baseball stadium in Cleveland.

One day I was out at Royal Oak. We were discussing a tour. Out of the clear sky, Coughlin's door opened, without a knock. There stood Bishop Gallagher, his superior. Beside him stood the proverbial prelate—tall, wide-brimmed black hat—serious, pallid, no color. As though he were about to announce the governor had denied clemency.

Gallagher tapped Coughlin on the shoulder and said, "Come with me, Charlie." They were gone about twenty minutes. Coughlin came back as white as my shirt. He said, "The arm of Jim Farley is long. I'm finished. Our Church has always wanted an ambassador, but Protestant America won't give one to the pope. The Vatican is willing to settle for a Fraternal Delegate. Mr. Roosevelt has served notice there will be none, unless I am silenced." He never spoke out again.

Imagine a man, who had been speaking to twenty million people every Sunday, imagine such a man being silenced. What frustration!

So I was left alone. Huey Long was dead. Doc Townsend was dead. Coughlin was silenced. General Wood lost himself in his business. Lindbergh told me, "I don't know how to fight Walter Winchell and those others. . . ." But that didn't stop *me*. My background wasn't that of a pantywaist. I've been mobbed and rotten-egged. Once in lower Louisiana, I grabbed a heckler by the collar, drew him up and held him through the entire speech. Every time I'd make a point, I'd shake him. (Laughs.)

Did I ever tell you about that time in Georgia? A state with a lynching tradition. I was going to speak in a nearby town. We set up the sound equipment in front of the courthouse. Here came the mob. All the little farmers were there, all the little rich. The backbone of America are these little rich.

They grabbed the cable of our sound truck, threw it over the limb of a tree and screamed, "Hang the son of a bitch!" I stepped into the shadows of a store building. The sound men all ran and hid. The mob released the brake and the truck wound up somewhere in a ditch. They began to yell: "Where is he? Where is he?"

I jumped up on a big square of cement and I yelled at the top of my voice: "Here I am. The man that touches me touches a man of God. Who dares be the first?" (His voice breaks; with difficulty he stifles a deep sob. Across the room, his wife weeps softly. A long pause.) They went away.

A few nights later, I got a phone call about three o'clock in the morning. The voice said, "I am the man that led the mob. I'm a member of the state

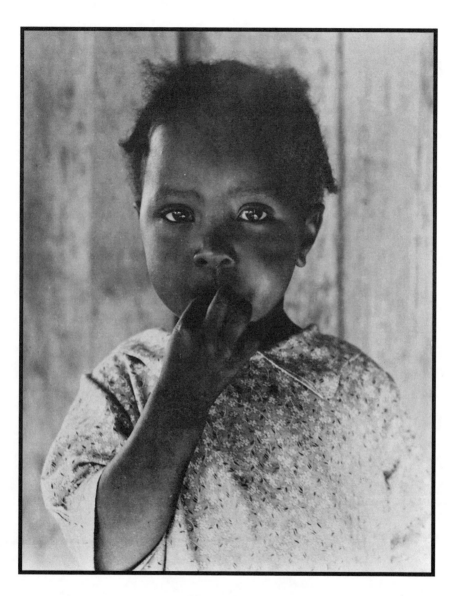

Child of former tenant farmer,
now a day laborer, Ellis County, Texas

Dorothea Lange, 1937

legislature. Mr. Smith, I am convinced you're a good man. If I can't have your forgiveness, I won't sleep another night." Isn't that something?

POSTSCRIPT: *From the airport at Fayetteville to Arkansas Springs is a stretch of some fifty miles. On the car radio was a continuous flow of hymns—the singers all white—interspersed with commercials. At no time was a black face visible, during the drive. Of young people, there were remarkably few, aside from little children in the company of their pilgrim parents.*

The Gentleman
from Kansas

Alf M. Landon

Two-term governor of Kansas; elected in 1932; reelected in 1934. Republican candidate for president in 1936.

We are in Topeka. As we are approaching Landon's office, there's casual conversation with the cabdriver. He is thirty years old. He was born and raised in this city.

"There's Alf Landon." *(He was sauntering up the pathway.)*

"Never heard, of him."

"Don't you know who he was?"

"Can't recall the name."

"Folks never told you . . . ?"

"No."

"They ever tell you about Roosevelt?"

"Roosevelt was in service. He was Rough Riders."

"Teddy Roosevelt . . . ?"

"Right."

"Did they tell you about Franklin Roosevelt?"

"No. Not so much about that. Most people called him Teddy."

"Did your folks ever tell you about the Depression?"

"Things were hard to get, things were bad, fight for what you got."

Alf Landon is a sprightly and genial eighty-two. Booted, he appears as though he'd just come in from the wheat fields. The walls of his office are decorated with mementos and photographs; friends and colleagues of another day: Colonel Frank Knox (his 1936 running mate), Congressman Joe Martin, H. L. Mencken, World War I buddies, college football teammates, his father and a young Alf. . . .

THOSE WERE HARD TIMES for governors, especially in '33. For sixty days, there was not standing room in my reception hall. Men with tears in their eyes begged for an appointment that would help save their homes and farms. I couldn't see them all in my office. But I never let one of them leave without my coming out and shakin' hands with 'em. I listened to all their stories, each one of 'em. But it was obvious I couldn't take care of all their terrible needs. If I could make some suggestion, I did that. It was a harrowing experience. I've never forgotten it.

On top of the Depression was the drought. It set in around '30 and lasted till about '37, '38. Black blizzards. Even here in Topeka, visibility was three blocks at most. In the spring of '35, I saw President Roosevelt. He sent M. L. Wilson out here—assistant secretary of agriculture. We spent two days driving across Kansas. At times, we couldn't see past the radiator. I told him all about our flood problems and drought. As a result, President Roosevelt established a farm pond program. Federal aid. Prior to that, farmers did the best they could. The state today is dotted with these farm ponds.

And the farm mortgages were coming due. That's why my reception room was so jammed. As part of Mr. Roosevelt's program, I appointed a conciliation committee of three men in each county. To extend time wherever possible. In many cases, I personally called the local bank or insurance company and succeeded in working out a moratorium. Since the bankers got their holiday, why shouldn't the farmers? We were among the first states to declare mortgage moratoriums. The courts declared it unconstitutional, so we worked out the committees. We practically stopped all the sales. And there were no riots in Kansas.

My relations with Mr. Roosevelt were always very pleasant. I never went to Washington that I never failed to call on him to pay my respects. But I always respected the pressure on his time. The president never failed to clear his appointment list for me. Once I kept Mrs. Roosevelt and General Marshall waiting. Some enthusiastic Republicans would criticize me. Didn't bother me.

The New Deal accomplished practices in land management that farm colleges had been teaching. These programs were necessary at the time. In '36, I advocated a long-range land-use study, which we'd never had. There were two uses that were hardly considered: reclamation and recreation.

How come the Republicans chose you as the 1936 candidate?
The campaign started in the grass roots. I didn't pay too much attention to it. Some friends of mine formed a committee. My campaign strategy was this: I would not fight against any favorite sons. But it was like a brush fire,

Farmer of Franklin County, Kansas

ARTHUR ROTHSTEIN, 1936

I guess. The Ohio delegation wanted to name me. They said the campaign would be underwritten by the head of a big banking chain. I said, "That's the very reason I won't enter Ohio. I'm not gonna be under anyone's obligation." I've never been owned by anybody.

We put a $2,500 limit on contributions to our campaign. Roy Roberts* said he never saw so much money being waved under the noses of candidates in his life. Hoover addressed the convention. It was in Cleveland. Frank Knox told me afterwards there was a plan to get together on Hoover. He was eager to run again. But he didn't have much delegate support.

Why would they seek you out—an old progressive Republican, an old Bull Moose man . . . ?
(He had started out as Bull Moose county chairman in 1914. In 1922, he bolted the Republican Party to support the Emporia editor William Allen White as independent candidate in a campaign against the Ku Klux Klan.)
I don't know.

Did you express much disagreement with the New Deal program?
Not too much. In my telegram to the convention, I wanted a declaration in favor of the gold standard. The platform committee—Eastern establishment, if you want to use a current phrase (laughs)—was all for a little snack of inflation. I challenged them. "The wild jackasses" of the prairie states were with me. I interpreted the plank on social security very liberally. This was before the roll call started. I made it known that the platform didn't suit me. But they nominated me unanimously. (Laughs.) I assume my feeling fitted the feeling of the delegates more than it did the platform committee.

I was accused of being too much of a me-too New Dealer by some of the staunch Republicans. They couldn't see the necessity of staying in tune with the times. They were out of touch.

This so-called welfare state is a unique combination of socialism and capitalism, and we'd better make it work. I've said this many times. I had not used the word "socialism" in any speech I made during the campaign. I was not afraid of "creeping socialism" as much as I was of creeping inflation.

I always felt if we kept our money sound and recognized the rights of labor to protect themselves as well as their women and children, and of farmers to

* For fifty-six years, he served, in sequence, as reporter, editor and president of the *Kansas City Star.*

organize, we'd work out of this. I've always been in favor of collective bargaining. And co-ops for farmers.

If you take Mr. Roosevelt's program today in light of what both Republicans and Democrats are standing for, he'd be pretty conservative. I've never
condemned Roosevelt's objectives, just his administration.

Do you feel the New Deal saved our society?
By and large? (Pause.) Yes.

In a nutshell, the basic problem of any government today is to keep alive
circulation from the bottom to the top. Through collective bargaining and
cooperatives.

You sound to me like a Populist nominated by the wrong party.
*(He laughs. He discusses the early Populists and their contributions to many of
the reforms, accepted today. He expresses particular admiration for Bob La
Follette.)*

Weren't the eastern bankers worried about you?
I don't know. A lot of 'em were for me. They knew how I felt. Maybe they
were just desperate. (Laughs.)

If I'd been Mr. Hoover in '30, when Senator La Follette—Bob, Jr.—
introduced a bill for a $10 billion appropriation in public works, I would
have passed it. We needed those dams that were subsequently built for
flood control and the pollution of rivers. Hoover vetoed it.

I didn't feel too bad when I lost in '36. I probably could have gone to the
Senate, but I felt the Republican Party needed one leader, who was not a
candidate for public office. Politics with me was an avocation, not a vocation.

Did you ever feel you were going to win?
Once. When I was in New York for the Madison Square Garden meeting,
Henry Allen, the former Kansas governor, received a call from the editor of
the *Literary Digest:* Come over and see our polls. Landon's going to win.
That night, I got as far as picking my secretary of state—and then I woke
up. (Laughs.)

Could you explain the Digest *poll?*
No. (Chuckles.) I think they deliberately weighted it.

On my way to New York for the big parade down Fifth Avenue, I stopped
off at Newark. I asked Governor Edge what chance I had in New Jersey. He
said, "No chance." He asked, "What's the chance in the country?" I said,

"No chance." A young fellow was sitting in the corner. I thought he was in Edge's party. He was a reporter. Edge jumped up excitedly. "I'll call his publisher. I know him, he's a Republican. I'll stop it." I said, "Sit down. I'll handle this." The young fellow was scared. I called the editor and I said, "Your reporter is perfectly entitled to that story. And if you print it, I won't deny one word of it. But you might as well call off the election. I'm not going to call your publisher or anyone else. Your reporter is standing here, and it's up to you." They didn't print it.

The campaign did have its good moments. I was invited to speak at the Union League Club. Their annual Lincoln Day Dinner in 1936. I said, no, I'm not coming. I was told no one had ever been nominated at a Republican convention who hadn't spoken to the Union League Club. I said, "So what?" (Chuckles.)

I did speak there the following year, after I'd lost. I met Ray Moley there. He said, "Do you know what Roosevelt was most afraid of in the campaign?" I said, "I didn't think he had anything to be afraid of." Moley said, "He was afraid his radio delivery had become so perfect that people would think it's artificial." I said, "Good. There might be some benefit in the antithesis of our radio deliveries." I was pretty rough. I guess I got too much antithesis. (Laughs.)

I was endorsed by every Democratic ex-presidential nominee, except Cox. When I got to New York for the big meeting, my room was jammed. Al Smith was there. I'd never met him before. As he was about to leave, I said, "Governor, I just want you to know that I understand you walked the floor many hours before you decided to support me, a Republican—thinking of the men and women that have worked for your nomination for governor, have driven through rain and snow to get out and vote for you, tacked up your cards on trees and fence poles all over the state. I realize only your belief that America is in great danger ever induced you to support me." Al's eyes filled with tears. He said, "I thought you'd understand." And he turned and walked out.

You felt he really felt that . . . our country was in great danger?
Yes.

Did you feel that?
No.

On the way back to the airport, a forty-eight-year-old cabbie responds. He's a World War II veteran.

"Does Alf Landon's name ring a bell?"

"Oh yeah. He ran for governor. I was a kid. He even run for president."

"Who did he run against?"

"I don't remember that. I remember he ran just because he was a Kansas governor."

"Franklin D. Roosevelt."

"Oh yeah. That's right."

"What about Roosevelt?"

"He brought this country out of it. You bet. I remember it. I'm afraid we're gonna have another one. . . ."

Book Four

Merely Passing Through

Edward Burgess

Like most guests in this once-elegant hotel, he's a pensioner. His room is overwhelmed by old-time appliances. There are light-housekeeping facilities. A table radio . . . "I used to build 'em, battery set. I still got things to do. I got a set of tools there that would knock your eyes out, worth about $200. All kinds of tools. . . ."

He is eighty-two. During the thirties, he had a steady job as a printer at Donnelly's.

I SPOTTED THIS STUDEBAKER in the window at Twenty-sixth and Michigan. So I says to May, let's buy that car. So we just stopped in, give 'em $600, all we had with us, and bought the car. The sales manager—his name was Compton—I told him that's the one we want. So we just had a couple of fellas push it out and put air in the tires and a couple of gallons of gas and away we went, down South Parkway. So we went all around, down Field Museum. . . . It was a six-wheel job.

The foreman down at Donnelly, he said, "You sure did your bit for the Depression." He bought one, he bought a new Ford. I said, "If everybody would spend ten cents more a day than they ordinarily spent, we'd sneak out of this in a hurry." (Laughs.) I said that. My theory, I felt that way. Because we were makin' money. We never got laid off or nothin'. There was no cause to feel otherwise.

When did you become aware of the Depression?
I really didn't pay no attention to it. The way I looked at it, without advertising there'll be no business, of any kind. And you can't have no advertising without printing it. See what I mean?

Did your standard of living change during the Depression?
It didn't change mine. I never did spend money foolishly. Never drank very
much, just a little bit here and there. But I was kind of liberal, too, in a way.
Always tried to help the other fella. Never hurt me any.

I co-signed a couple of times for loan companies and things like that.
Fact I did that for a fella in Fort Wayne, and he skipped out. And I had to
pay it, $55. When my dad died in 1919, he was on a train going to Ohio. I
wanted him buried with my mother. I always tried to help out the other
guy.

You don't remember bread lines?
No, we didn't have that here in Chicago, that I know of.

■   ■   ■   ■

Billy Green

Among his enterprises in the thirties: bookmaker.

I DIDN'T GET HURT too bad. I didn't own any stocks. I didn't believe in the
market then, I'm not too crazy about it now, if you know what I mean.
(Laughs.) The stock market is like shooting craps or playing horses. You
hear about the ones that win, but you never hear about the ones that lose.
There's more losers than winners, I promise you.

Any time you're guessing, you got to lose. The only way to win is to have
the other fella guess. That's my theory: never be a guesser. Never take a position in life. You give the other guy the first guess, and you always come out
best. You can't make a mistake that way. You always wind up the winner.
I've proved that on many, many occasions. Many occasions.

All the people around me in them days—successful businessmen—the
stock market just knocked 'em right out of the box. Oh, do I remember the
panic. Bedlam.

I never worked, always went in business for myself. I was lucky. You got
to have that Guy Upstairs with you. You got to have his arms around you. I
made a buck.

From an orange juice stand to a hotel, I branched out into a bowling alley. Made some investment in real estate. And here I am, with nothing to
do. Call it semiretired. But I'm always interested in a new proposition.
Action.

I got no reason to be discontented. It's just lookin' fer somethin' that I don't think I'm gonna find. You just can't call your shots any more. Everything is regimented today. Understand? Maybe it's from the Depression days, who knows? So what I'm lookin' fer don't exist, strange as it may seem. You follow me? But I have no complaints. I'd be the last guy in the world to complain. Because, like I say, life's been good to me. God has been good to me. You gotta have Him.

* * * *

Scoop Lankford

He is seventy-five years old. He spent thirty-one years of a life term in a state penitentiary: 1919 to 1950.

THE DEPRESSION HIT THAT prison pretty bad. We were practically not eating. We really scratched. One time they wanted us to eat some kind of fish. They called it halibut. This had black skin all around—didn't have that little white side, you know. This was baby shark they tried to feed us. It smelled so the entire building was stunk up. (Laughs.) So they all threw it on the floor and refused to eat it.

If you know what it was like for you, just multiply. The quality of food was low to begin with. We would get some kind of meat once a day. It was kind of scraps you wouldn't even keep in a butcher shop. Just tiny pieces all boiled up in a pot. It was rich enough so one man would get about a fourth of what his system needed. More people died during that Depression there than they ever did at any other time.

It wasn't starvation. They called it malnutrition. It woulda been starvation if they died quick from malnutrition. They just barely gave you enough to keep you alive. You lost weight. They made you lose weight until the doctor got after them and said they have to get at least one meal a day. A thousand men woulda died if it hadn't been for that doctor.

Did the guards ever talk to you about the Depression?
They were as bad for it as we were. A lot of them was eating in there on the sly. I've even actually given to them a piece of corn bread to take out. Nearly all of 'em were family men.

You wouldn't know there was a Depression as far as the talk was concerned. There was nothing to say. We at least had a place to eat and sleep.

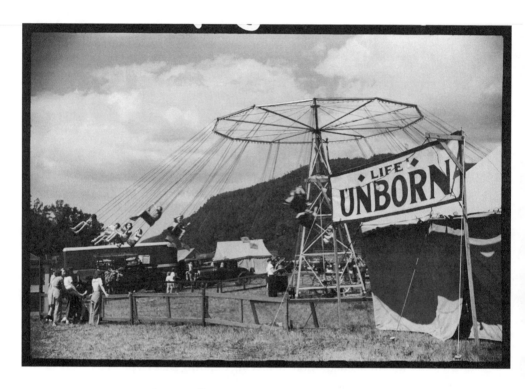

At a small American Legion carnival near
Bellows Falls, Vermont

JACK DELANO, 1941

The prison itself was a protection from the outside. The people outside, they had to hustle. We were just down almost as low as we could get. We had to dig a hole in low to get any lower than we was. (Laughs.)

We fared lots better when the war was on. Food and more food, during the war. Yeah, the fellas talked about it. They said, "Long live the war!" That was our attitude: Long live the war. 'Cause we were eating pretty good.

A Cable

Myrna Loy

Film and stage actress.

MUNICH, THAT WAS '38, wasn't it? I was at Malibu, down at the beach. I heard Jan Masaryk on the radio, speaking from London. It was about four o'clock in the morning there. I was so moved by this man. I was upset by the sell-out of Czechoslovakia. On an impulse, I sent him a cable. It was the first one he had received from anyone in the world.

Later on, he came to this country and he looked me up. It had meant so much to him. He said it cheered him in the darkest hour of his life. That was Munich. He said one of the reasons he broadcast to his country was that if he could reach me out on the Malibu coast six thousand miles away . . .

My wire was published in the London *Times*. Then it got to Prague. And then to Berlin. As a result, my pictures were banned in Germany. I didn't know that until 1939. In Amsterdam, I met a man who had fled Germany. He said I was on Mr. Hitler's blacklist. (Laughs.) "You're on the second page," he said. (Laughs.) I said, "My God, I didn't know that."

Some months later, one of the men at MGM* came to me very, very upset. "I have something here that I am ashamed to give you." It was a call-down about having mixed my politics with my work: How about watching out for this? He said, "What do you want me to do with this?" I said, "Tear it up."

When the Depression came, I had a very good job in Hollywood. It was just at the beginning of my career. It was really distant to me. Everybody around me was working. You get up at five-thirty. You're in the studio at seven. You're made up and ready at nine and work until six. They now call those the Golden Years of the Movies. Perhaps they were. People needed

---

* Metro-Goldwyn-Mayer.

films, needed some diversion. I wasn't deeply involved in politics myself. I kind of dialed out. I didn't come to life until Roosevelt. . . .

I was told I was F.D.R.'s favorite actress. I had never met him. Later on, when I was in Washington, at a cocktail party, Henry Morgenthau* said, "The old man thinks we're keeping you away from him. You've never come to see him. Tomorrow morning, put your hat on the dresser, and I'll call for you." The next morning he called to tell me the president had gone to Canada.

Later on, they sent for me to attend his birthday celebration. I bought myself a John Frederick hat. I came tootling into the White House with a big bunch of violets and this black hat. I looked down the hall and I saw Mrs. Roosevelt. I walked up to her. She said, "Oh, my dear, my husband is going to be so distressed." He had gone to Tehran. (Laughs.) Here was this glamour girl all done up. I fell in love with her then and there. I was very lucky to have spent quite a lot of time with her. I miss her very much. There aren't too many people you miss that way. . . .

* Secretary of treasury.

Book Five

The Fine and Lively Arts

Hiram (Chub) Sherman

At sixty, he is an established Broadway actor. Much of his time, whether "at liberty" or while engaged in a play, has been spent on the Council of Actors Equity.

I LEARNED IN THE twenties that you could exist on very little. To paraphrase Tennessee Williams, you can depend on the kindness of strangers. When the Depression actually began in '29, I was just on my way to New York. It wasn't any demarcation point in my life. There were no stocks to be lost, 'cause we didn't have them.

There were no jobs in New York. I worked in summer stock and touring companies. In 1931, I played a season in Newport, Rhode Island. It was as if the Depression had never existed at all. All the functions were duly reported as going on at the Viking Hotel and the Casino Theater. Sitting in the middle of the Casino, covered with flowers, were Mrs. Vanderbilt and Mrs. Moses Taylor, arriving in their limousines. I hadn't seen men in panama hats, blue blazers and white shoes since. There was discreet drinking in china cups during Prohibition in all the best hotels in Newport. One could sit there nursing a teacup filled with bootleg gin or whiskey. But it was all elegant. In teacups, china cups.

It was rock-bottom living in New York then, it really was. Cars were left on the streets. There were no signs about restricted parking. (Laughs.) If somebody had a jalopy—a few friends you know would have some old car—it would sit there for months on end neither molested nor disturbed. It would just fall apart from old age.*

---

* Ben, a nineteen-year-old college student: "My grandfather owned a car, but it never left the garage. He had it jacked up for two years. Gasoline was just too expensive. He told how

You didn't count your possessions in terms of money in the bank. You counted on the fact that you had a row of empty milk bottles. Because those were cash, they could be turned in for a nickel deposit, and that would get you on the subway. If you took any stock in yourself, you looked to see how many milk bottles you had, because that counted. Two bottles: one could get you uptown; one could get you back.

I remember being employed once to stand in front of St. Patrick's Cathedral on Fifth Avenue, Easter morning. With a clicker in each hand. A fashion woman had engaged me to note the acceptance of patent leather purses and white hats. Each white hat I saw, I clicked my right hand. And each patent leather purse I saw, I clicked my left hand. Then I had to go home and tote up what the clickers said. White hats were in that spring, patent leather purses were out.

I remember also what you'd pick up odd dollars doing. There were sightseeing buses—see Chinatown, see the Bowery, see New York. They were lined up right on Times Square. If you've ever noted a sightseeing bus, there'll be a couple of people sitting on the bus. And they'd say: It's leaving right away, guided tour, just leaving for the Bowery and Chinatown. Well, the people inside were usually shills. They're engaged for a quarter or fifty cents to sit there and look eager. I shilled in Times Square sightseeing buses. (Laughs.) As people came on, you got off: "Excuse me for a moment." And then you got into another bus. It's a sitting job.

The summer always provided work for actors. I don't know why this happened, I can't explain it. But there was a great proliferation of turning barns into summer theaters. During the Depression, that's when it came.

In 1936, I joined the Federal Theater.* I was assigned to Project 891. The directors and producers were Orson Welles and John Houseman. The theater we had taken over was the Maxine Elliott. A lot of theaters went dark during the Depression, and the theater owners were happy to lease them to the government.

One of the marvelous things about the Federal Theater, it wasn't bound by commercial standards. It could take on poetic drama and do it.† And

he polished the car once a week. How he took good care of it, but he never drove it. Couldn't afford it."
* One of the Federal Arts Projects (WPA) under the auspices of the New Deal. "It was an idealistic concept to encompass the whole country—to make the unemployed actor an entertainment worker. To do his share." It employed not only legitimate theater actors and dancers, but vaudeville and circus performers as well.
† T. S. Eliot's *Murder in the Cathedral* was the most celebrated case in point.

experimental theater. The Living Newspaper made for terribly exciting pro-
ductions.* Yet it was theater by bureaucracy. Everything had to go to a higher
authority. There were endless chits to be approved. There were comic and
wasteful moments all over the country. But it was forward-thinking in so
many ways. It anticipated some of today's problems. The unit I was in was
integrated. We did Marlowe's *Doctor Faustus*. Mephistopheles was played
by a Negro, Jack Carter. Orson Welles played Faustus.

Our next production was *Cradle Will Rock*, words and music by Marc
Blitzstein. And we rehearsed those eight hours a day. We worked every moment, and sometimes we worked overtime because we loved it.

Cradle Will Rock was for its day a revolutionary piece. It was an attack on
big business and the corruption involved. It was done à la Brecht. We had it
fully rehearsed.

On opening night, when the audience was assembling in the street, we
found the doors of the Maxine Elliott closed. They wouldn't admit the audience because of an edict from Washington that this was revolutionary
fare. And we would have no performance. Somebody had sent down the
word.

Well, when you have an alert company, who are all keyed up at this moment, and a master of publicity such as Orson Welles, this is just grist for
their mills. (Laughs.)

It's a nice evening in May—late May or April. Balmy evening. An audience not able to get into a theater, but not leaving because the directors of
891, Orson Welles and John Houseman, were haranguing them in the
street: "Don't leave!" They expected to get a reversal of the edict. We're told
not to make up. We're told not to go home. We don't know what's going to
happen.

No reversal came from Washington. So Orson and John Houseman got
their friends on the phone: What theater could we do this in? Somebody
suggested the Jolson Theater. An announcement was made to all these
people, without benefit of microphone: if you go to the Jolson Theater you
will see the show. And we marched. Walking with our audience around
into Broadway and then up Seventh Avenue to Fifty-ninth Street, we acquired an even larger audience.

---

* Documentary theater, based upon circumstances and controversial issues of the time:
Triple-A Plowed Under concerned the New Deal's farm program; *Power* dealt with rural
electrification; *Third of a Nation* (a phrase taken from the F.D.R. Inaugural Address of
1937) commented on the housing crisis.

Walking down the middle of the street?
Oh yes. Walking with no police permit. (Laughs.) Just overflowing the sidewalks. Obviously something was afoot. The Jolson Theater hadn't had a booking for months and was very dusty. But it was open.

Word came from Actors Equity that proper bonding arrangements had not been made. The actors would not be allowed to appear on the stage. Because now you're not under the aegis of the Federal Theater. You're under some obscure private management. You don't know what, because you haven't found out yet.

This didn't daunt us. We had a colloquy right in the alley. We decided, well, if we can't go on the stage, we could wheel out the piano and Marc Blitzstein could do what he had done in so many auditions: describe the setting and such, and we'll all sit in the audience. Equity didn't say we couldn't sit in the audience. When our cues come, we will rise and give them. So, that we did.

The theater filled. I don't know how the extra people, who didn't hold tickets for the opening, how they got in. I've often wondered. Did the box office open or did they just say: come in for the laughs? But it was packed with people.* The stage was bare, the curtain was up, and you suddenly missed all your fellow actors. You couldn't find them. We were in different parts of the house.

Eventually the house lights lowered a little. Marc Blitzstein came out and laid the setting and played a few bars and then said: "Enter the whore." I didn't know where Olive Stanton, who played the whore, was. Suddenly you could hear Olive's very clear high voice, from over left. A spotlight suddenly found her and she stood up. She was in the lower left-hand box. One by one, as we were called up, we joined in. We turned around if we were down front, and faced the audience. People were scattered all over. It was a most exciting evening. The audience reaction was tremendous.

One of those summers, '38, '39, I don't know which—Marc Blitzstein corraled most of us who'd been in the original company and asked us if we'd give up Sunday to go give a performance of *Cradle Will Rock* in Bethlehem, Pennsylvania. I thought this was marvelous. Because we're now going to take *Cradle Will Rock* to the workers, to the people for whom he wrote this piece. We were all corraled into a bus and off we went on a nice, hot summer's day. I thought, well, pretty soon the mills will close down and the steel workers will pour into this amusement park, as twilight comes, and they'll hear this marvelous saga. No one showed up.

* The Jolson Theater was larger than the Maxine Elliott.

A few men drifted in, and the first thing you find out is that many of them do not understand or speak English. And this was written in, supposedly, common American speech. Here we were preparing an opera for the proletariat, and the proletariat neither wants nor understands it. It's a rather shocking occurrence. But you don't give up.

You're in a hot, sort of open auditorium. And Will Geer,* never to be discouraged, scrounging around for an audience. He found a picnic of church ladies over an adjoining hill. They were spreading out their picnic baskets and he asked: "Would you like to be entertained with an opera?" They allowed as how they would, and they packed their gingham tablecloths, all the sandwiches and brought them over to this little amusement place. And sat down.

Marc Blitzstein came out and announced the name of this piece was *Cradle Will Rock*, the setting was Steeltown, U.S.A., and it begins on a street corner at night, and enter the whore. When he said those words, our audience got up and packed up their picnic baskets and left us. We never did do *Cradle Will Rock* in Bethlehem, Pennsylvania.

We were to report back to the Federal Theater, to Project 891. We had no assignment at the moment. But all of us in the stock company had to spend eight hours a day in the Maxine Elliott Theater. We could bring no food in the theater. We had a lunch hour. We could read, but we could not write. We couldn't deface anything, we couldn't rehearse. We sat. Forced sitting, with nothing to keep you interested, is one of the most grueling punishments I've ever been through. I've never been in jail as yet, I expect to. But prisoners are paid for work.

I don't know if I'm partisan to the underdog or whether I'm the underdog. My political convictions were my own. But this is not the case in life. You're stigmatized, anything you do. I was active in my union, I was playing benefits—there was Spanish relief, you know, the Spanish Civil War. My life was very full. I didn't sleep very much. I got excited about everything. They were tearing down the Sixth Avenue Elevated and selling the scrap iron to Japan. I was going to protest. . . . (Laughs.) There was a cause every second.

I was horrified one morning to find that a congressman from Kansas had stated in the *Congressional Record* that I was one of the seven Communists that dominated the Council of the Actors Equity Association. I thought that was unusual. So I sent the congressman a wire and I said: I read this news story, and if you'll repeat your accusations outside the halls

* Veteran character actor.

Seating now in all parts of the house, Chicago, Illinois

JOHN VACHON, 1941

of Congress, I would sue you for loss of employment. I never heard from him again.

I found the Equity Council in an uproar and I was asked to resign. I said I have no intention of resigning because a man has made such a statement, and he's never answered my telegram. "If you don't like me, don't elect me next time to the council. But I'm certainly not walking out." Several councillors walked out in protest to me being there. I was so politically naïve, I wouldn't know then how to go about joining the Communist Party. I wouldn't know just how to do it. (Laughs.)

There comes a time when you cannot think seriously about left and right. And people would come up to you, your dearest friends, and say: "Listen, tell me, really, are you?" I'd say: "Am I what?" They'd say: (whispering) "Are you a Communist?" Now if you say no, you're immediately accused of lying. I don't know why this is. But as soon as you say no, they look at you as if—oh boy! If you say yes, you're also lying, because no Communist says yes when asked. I found myself in this terrible bind, being assailed at every corner by people asking me.

One old Equity member—I was really at the breaking point—during a recess in the Equity Council meeting said: "Look, I really want to know." And I just couldn't care less at this time. He said: "I want to talk to you." And I said: "Yes?" And he said: "Tell me, are you a Communist?" I thought: I can't say yes and I can't say no. I said quickly, I said: "We're not allowed to tell." And there wasn't a laugh on his part at all. It was just as if I'd sealed my death warrant, being facetious. It haunted me for years, that remark. (Laughs.)

I remember going into a theatrical office looking for work. You'd go up and say: who's casting today? And the sign hanging over the railing: NO COMMUNIST NEED APPLY. It was hanging there. Indignantly, I ripped off the sign and went to the girl at the desk and said: "Why don't you reduce this to the basic fact that no actors need apply? You're not doing anything anyway." Making the little gesture. It probably got hung back on the door again.

So then the war broke out and the Depression, as we know it, ended. . . .
It didn't for me.

I enlisted in the navy—I was a bit too old for the immediate draft call. After being vilified in the halls of Equity I was told I was a marvelous human being and that my seat on the council would always be waiting for me. Five years later, I got out and went back and said: "Where's my seat?" And they said: "You'll just have to run like everybody else."

I had incurred a few debts before the war with high Depression living, and they were still waiting for me after the war. Not the seat, the debts.

The average actor clings to whatever job's providing money, the longest time possible. I've now come to an age where I can't do that any more. I find I want very little in the way of possessions out of life. Here we are in a hotel room, and there're unanswered letters piled up on my desk. And that's my life. I don't care. I've got a suit on, and that's about all I want. I'd like to answer the letters before I die. (Laughs.) But I don't know that I will.

■   ■   ■   ■

Neil Schaffner

It is a comfortable trailer home in Wapello, Iowa. He and his wife, Caroline, both retired, spend their winters in Florida.

Though both had "trouped" from childhood, the Schaffner Players were organized in 1925, and "we never missed a year—come war, catastrophe, the Depression—till a heart attack laid me low" in the late forties. It was a tent dramatic company, touring the towns of Iowa. After its first ten years, other Midwestern states were "trouped."

The Schaffner Players were among the more celebrated of such companies that performed in the rural areas of the country, since before the turn of the century.

The fare was primarily comedy, though a serious theme was occasionally part of the "repertore." "All these plays always had a good moral, a thought to carry away." In most of them, he appeared as Toby. With red wig and freckles, he was the rural comic hero, who always outwitted the city slicker. Whether he appeared as a GI, an FBI man or a country editor, he always was Toby. His wife was, invariably, Susie, recognized by her pigtails, freckles and equally pungent wisecracks.

The company would usually work a week in one town, a different play each night. Their regular appearance was always a major event in the entertainment life of the community. "Crowds would line up sometimes two, three hours before the performance was scheduled to start." The box office was always busy. . . .

WHO TOLD EVERYBODY THE Depression was on on the sixth day of July, nineteen hundred and thirty? In the middle of May we opened our season in Wapello. We had heard talk of hard times being back East. We couldn't see it. We had normal crowds at the show. A normal amount of candy and popcorn was being sold. We ended up our usual big week on the Fourth of

Fiddlin' Bill Hensley, Asheville, North Carolina

BEN SHAHN, 1937

July at Ollie, Iowa. We moved down to Fairfield, where we had always had big crowds.

On the night of July sixth, we played to about $30 gross business. That week, we took in $200 with a show costing us $1,500. We couldn't understand it. Somebody must have told everybody to quit going to shows. Well do I remember that day.

I jumped into a car and drove to Belle Plaine, where J. Doug Morgan had a show. He said, "I did the smallest business in the history of the Morgan Show." How everybody found out the Depression was on that day I'll never understand. All of a sudden, the plug was pulled out of the bathtub.

I have a wife, a baby and a mother-in-law. All I've got to sell is my ability as an entertainer. But it appeared nobody had any money to buy. The audience had become benumbed. They just accepted it as a horrible thing. You'd accept anything you couldn't do a thing about. The show was an escape from the trials and tribulations of everyday scratch for existence. The company had to survive. It was a groundhog case—root hog or die. We had to keep going, and that's all there was to it.

Mediapolis had always been one of our very good towns. We heard a rumble that people on relief were going to our show. They were threatened to be taken off the rolls. That night I made a little speech: "Many of our dear friends, who have always come to our shows, don't have the money. If anyone comes to me and tells me he can't afford it, I'll be happy to have him come as my guest." It took all the thunder away from these birds. I couldn't see whose business it is if people would sacrifice a hamburger to see a show.

We had to work all kinds of gimmicks to survive. At Burlington, I made a deal with the merchants. 110 paid me a dollar apiece. I gave them all the tickets they wanted to give away to their customers. That's how circle stock was born. Out of the Depression. A company would have a base and book six or seven towns nearby. A different town each night. They'd explain to the merchants, "We'll be in your town every Tuesday night." Another town, another night. We give them all the tickets they'd want for a dollar, which they'd give away. That plus ten cents would admit you.

Since time immemorial, "repertore" shows opened: ladies free. As a result, we'd have a big crowd on Monday and on Tuesday hardly anyone. We reversed the nights. So we had good Tuesdays and bad Mondays. I'd send postcards out to all the rural mailboxes: an absolutely free season ticket. But it had to be used every night. So the farmer would give it to someone, if he couldn't go. And we'd get a dime for the chair.

During the early Depression, Chatauqua was murder. They were our biggest competition. They started out as educational programs—lectures,

Swiss bell ringers. They were subsidized by the local citizens. But then they changed to entertainment. They tried to tie up all the choice lots in town for their tents. Sometimes they'd get in with the mayors and try to raise our license fees. But we survived.

Talk about desperate ideas. We decided our titles weren't catching. So we changed *Rebecca of Sunnybrook Farm*—that is, my version of it—to *Her Unwelcome Relative*. A play I wrote called *Chain Stores*, we changed to *What Mothers Don't Know*. We sat up till broad daylight thinking up these titles. Business doubled.

In about '32, I paid $150 royalties for *The Family Upstairs*. The audience enjoyed it, all right. They'd say, "I tell you, Toby, it was the best show I ever saw. Enough to last me for a month." So they never came back.

I made a serial out of the whodunit *Jittering Spooks*. After opening night, we'd invite the audience to remain and give them the opening act as a free gift. On the second night, the second act, and so on. Anything to get them back. . . .

Talk about bad luck. They had a terrible dry spell. On this hot night, I announced, "Toby predicts that tomorrow you'll have rain." They hooted and howled. It did rain. They marveled so at it, they never came back to see the show.

We worked all kinds of dodges. This guy comes up one day with the idea of a balloon ascension in front of our tent. For $10. So I made the deal. I advertised the free balloon ascension. He gets up there, and it floats five miles out into the country. The crowd follows him, and the sonuvaguns never came back.

Sure, I made gags about the Depression. The traveling salesman called on the farmer. He sees him out in the field with a fishing rod, casting. So he turns tail. He visits another farmer tying a rope around a pullet. The farmer says, "That other guy's gone daffy. It must be the Depression's done it." So the salesman asks, "Why are you wrappin' the rope around the pullet?" The farmer says, "When I get this outboard motor started, I'm gonna join 'im." (Laughs.)

The Depression ended for us in 1936. We did a Toby-Susie act on the radio, five times a week, fifteen minutes. Then, went on the *National Barn Dance* for Alka-Seltzer over NBC. 550 stations. We got thousands of letters. Stores wouldn't wait on customers when the show was on. They had loud-speakers where the men were pitching horseshoes. Farmers would come in out of the fields to listen. . . .

POSTSCRIPT: "*The Federal Theater had no connection with us. It was an idea of Mrs. Roosevelt. She thought it would alleviate unemployment among actors.*

Instead of putting William A. Brady in charge or some other recognized theat-rical man, they chose Hallie Flanagan, who had gone to Vassar. It became a haven for all the short-haired gals and long-haired boys and weirdies of all kinds. And legitimate actors were walking the streets.

"A friend of mine ran the project in Peoria. He made a profit. This horrified Miss Flanagan, She said: 'This is art, not commercial theater. You're not sup-posed to show a profit.'

"They could have solved actors' unemployment at very little cost. All they had to do was make a survey. If they said to each manager of each show: Add one more actor to your company. Uncle Sam will pay his salary. That would have been the easiest way. But, no, they couldn't do that. That's the practical way. . . ."

■   ■   ■   ■

Paul Draper

Solo dancer.

I HAD NO MONEY before the Depression. I had no money then. So I wasn't aware of anything affecting my life. I was a dancer. I worked up in the re-hearsal hall every day, looked for jobs, and auditioned.

In '33, we were performing on what was known as half-salary—breaking in. Whenever we got through with the break-in period, this manager would replace somebody in the act—make up another name for the act, and it would become another break-in. So we always worked on half-salary. I wasn't aware of it for a long time. I worked on half-salary for years.

Vaudeville was still alive. We used to do five shows a day at movie houses. You did thirty-five shows a week. I was always being hired for 19/35 of one week's work. Some act would get sick, and they'd say: Who can come in with-out rehearsal? I was at the time a flash act soloist. I used to work on a mar-ble tabletop and had one number, "Bye Bye Blues." I was not hard to place in a show.

A flash act goes on and off. It is without personality in any way. It is only the *act.* A juggler or acrobats. A dancer was, at that time, a flash act. It was only the exhibition of one's physical skills. You could always be fitted into a show without interfering with anything else.

In the late thirties, he perfected the tap dance technique to the accompaniment of classical compositions. He became a nightclub headliner and, subsequently, a concert performer. "I was no longer on the marble pedestal. I had achieved a sort of status."

My political awareness had nothing to do with the Depression. It was the Spanish Civil War. It was around 1937, '38. I danced to raise money for the Spanish Loyalists. Of course, I had a little more stability as a performer and could afford the luxury of outside interests.

If I have any nostalgia of the thirties, it does not concern the social-economic changes which took place. It's the memory of the Persian Room.* It was a very smart room. Everyone was in evening clothes. You weren't able to get in without a black tie. If the host didn't like the way someone looked, he would say there are no more tables.

I used to work there three months straight. You'd often get the same audiences, but it was all right. On last nights, every table had champagne. We all stood up, made a toast and sang "Auld Lang Syne." This was '37, '38, '39.

We thought of the poor, at that time, as quite divorced from us, who were not poor. By the exercise of one's charity, life could be made all right. You would always have the poor with you, they were the unfortunate, and you made donations. You could handle them. It was mildly unpleasant, but not fundamentally upsetting.

Now, for the first time, we face the dreadful reality that we are not separated. They are us. They are something we have made. There is no conceivable way today to say: Fish, and you'll be all right. In hurt, in anguish, in shock, we are becoming aware that it is ourselves, who have to be found wanting, not the poor.

■   ■   ■   ■

Knud Andersen

The studio of a portrait painter and sculptor. Piercing eyes are fixed upon us: a self-portrait of the artist as a young man. The eyes of others illuminate the twilight of the room. They are in oils: Senator Henrik Shipstead, among others. Of this portrait, Harold Laswell said, "The blue eyes of the subject do not stare vacantly into the future, but intently into reality. . . ."

He had come to Chicago from Norway forty-five years ago: "It was a grand adventure, the arts in the new land." Powerful men in the worlds of politics and finance had commissioned him to do their portraits, in times past.

---

* An expensive dining room club in the Plaza Hotel.

His eyes wander from work to work, from face to face, as he remembers. . . .

YOU SEE, TO ME the Depression was a blessing. When the shock of losing what you had worked for comes, I found refuge in my art. To stew in a deplorable situation . . . where people were affected . . . some to suicide . . . I lost myself in my art. The pain that came with economic loss, I felt would pass. These things, like the eclipse of the sun . . . People first observed it and committed suicide . . . not realizing that this would pass.

I felt quite prayerful, and so I was at peace. Of course, the knock on the door of economics . . . disturbed. But you survived. I constantly counseled myself on the best way of survival.

Did you join the Federal Arts Project?
No, no, no. It was so disappointing, I couldn't participate. If it is done in the right way, the gifted artist benefits from the state and contributes: thus, body and soul are nourished. Then I would have participated. But the program went against my grain. I did not recognize true artistry in evidence.

Oh, the Depression years were hard. I managed with a commission now and then.

Days without food . . . ?
Those are days I don't recall. Self-respect never allowed anyone to know I was in that state. I had quite a duplex studio. I had Bach and Beethoven. Nothing else mattered. I worked in the cathedral of the spirit. My body may have needed food, but I was unaware.

Once in the studio, a rat ran across my arm and bit me. Luckily, a visitor had left a bottle of whiskey, without my knowing about it. The bottle came of good use, I told him afterwards. I poured the whiskey over the wound. These are accidents, like the Depression. I avoid bringing accidents to mind.

■   ■   ■   ■

Little Brother Montgomery and Red Saunders

The first is a jazz pianist and the other a band leader, who devotes much of his time to finding jobs for black musicians.

MONTGOMERY: I was making a dollar a night on Sunday nights. And a spaghetti dinner. Playing house rent parties. On a Saturday night, I was playing for $3. No supper there. Weekends is when the stockyards workers would go. Tuesday night, I was playing for $2. My weeks were filled up with two, three dollars a night.

Monday night, that was the biggest night I had. $4. They had Blue Monday parties, the sporting people. Everybody who'd been out all Saturday and Sunday night, gamblers and hustlers. If they'd been hustlin' anything, they'd be poppin', buying moonshine, having fun, on Monday. From five o'clock in the morning until the wee, wee hours, way through the night.

SAUNDERS: Those Blue Monday parties had a meaning. The night life, the gambling, the prostitution and the pimps—they weren't just something that happened. They were a necessity. Survival. Women had to sell their bodies for twenty-five cents, fifteen cents. You find fewer black pimps today, because the black woman is more independent.

In a flat, everything would go. In one room, they were playing a piano and drinking whiskey. In another room, they would have Georgia skin, poker or whatever game. In another room, they'd have whores, hustlers. Everything went. A person had to have some kind of life.

MONTGOMERY: They were houses where people lived. With a piano in the front room, where people danced. And moonshine, twenty-five cents a half pint. Pulverized alcohol. No admission. The money came from the sale of moonshine and supper. Spaghetti and chili . . . The house'd be packed, all kinds a ways. Six, five, sometimes four rooms, a hundred, eighty people would be in it. They were givin' a party to get their rent together.

Lots of times we were raided by the police. Catch moonshine or catch 'em gamblin'. They had some bad policemen around at that time. They had Jesse James, Big Six, Callahan's Squad. . . .

We had a lot of house party piano players in them days—a guy called Forty-Five, Cripple Clarence Lofton, Pine Top Smith, 'Sippi Wallace, a guy called Toothpick. Piano'd be ringin' all night. Guys would come in, weren't workin', they'd play. You'd find all kinds of piano players, great ones. Boogie-woogie began in house parties. But we didn't call it that then. Doodley Joe, we called it . . . 1928, '29, '30. I paid $4 a week for a room. We made $15 a week. We got along pretty good.

SAUNDERS: There was a pickup in business when beer came in in '33. They could go out publicly and drink. And the price was right. Beer was fifteen cents and you could get entertainment. With repeal, you began to see a new light. You had to have these rent parties during Prohibition because there were no night clubs, to speak of. They were black speakeasies.

MONTGOMERY: I left around the early thirties and organized a band around Jackson, Mississippi. Sometimes we'd play at a dance and make

A trio of musicians from Duke Ellington's orchestra during the
early morning broadcast, New York City

GORDON PARKS, 1943

fifteen cents apiece. (Laughs.) You'd travel maybe two, three hundred miles in a secondhand Cadillac, and a beat-up Lincoln. The whole band. We'd get to a place and couldn't make gas money. Places like Meridian, Hattiesburg, Vicksburg, all up in the Delta. 1935, '36 and up to around '38.

The main times is when they're pickin' cotton. They got a dollar a hundred for pickin'. (Laughs.) Some people could pick two, three hundred pounds a day. We played in tobacco barns down through the South. I remember one band was burned up in one of those warehouses. We played a white dance tonight and a colored dance tomorrow. But we didn't mix.

SAUNDERS: In those days, the black artist was at the mercy of the promoters. In later years, MCA* and others took them on, but at first they weren't booking black bands. The hotels and ballrooms were for white bands. This was a time when radio was great. White musicians were having a field day, making all kinds of money in studios, in concerts and legitimate theaters. Big money. The poor black musicians just had the beat-up Lincoln. They were what you called starvation bands. Did you know black musicians created the one-nighters?

They didn't have any homes. Out of five years, they'd maybe sit down ten weeks. They lived in the auto. The location jobs were for the Benny Goodmans and the Tommy Dorseys, hotels and ballrooms. The only time they would sit down would be like the Apollo in New York, the Regal in Chicago, the Howard in Washington. . . . †

MONTGOMERY: Even their music was taken from them. Clarence Williams wrote "Sugar Blues" and that was called Clyde McCoy's. "Dorsey Boogie" is Pine Top's, which he played at house rent parties. . . .

■　■　■　■

Jack Kirkland

Writer-producer. His play Tobacco Road, *based upon Erskine Caldwell's novel, ran "almost eight years."*

IN THE SPRING OF '32, I woke up with a violent hangover. An agent gave me this book to read for that afternoon: "You're a southerner, you'll dig this." I went home with my hangover and read it and said: this is a play. So I took

* Music Corporation of America.
† Black theaters, featuring live artists. The films were merely stage-waits.

the book under my arm and went to live in Majorca for three, four months.
I was quite broke at the time.

He completed the play in Hollywood, where he wrote films at "very big sala-
ries." One was a highly successful Shirley Temple movie. "Shirley Temple's re-
sponsible for Tobacco Road, really." (Laughs.)

It opened December 4, 1933. I couldn't get anyone else to produce it. They
all were afraid of it. They thought it wouldn't run. So I put up all the money
myself. No one else had a nickel in it. I gave away a great deal of it to
associates. . . .

The whole thing cost about $9,000 to produce. The reviews in the dai-
lies were not too good for the play, except the raves for Henry Hull's performance. I just had to get up another five or six hundred dollars a week to
carry the play. Until the *Daily News** had the editorial. Captain Patterson[†]
fell for it and wrote an editorial. And the next day we were in. Later on, the
monthlies came out—George Jean Nathan, Bob Benchley, Dorothy Parker,
all came out for it.

Did you have any doubts during the five weeks before the editorial and the
magazines appeared?
No. Or I wouldn't have spent that money. The play was dealing with poverty. The audience understood and they were concerned. Of course, it was
based on a period preceding the Depression. It had existed for some time in
the South. Cotton was five cents a pound, and all that sort of thing. There
was shock value, sure. But I think its success was determined by its reality
and honesty.

Mrs. Roosevelt helped. She loved the play, because it was about social
conditions. When it opened in Atlanta, she went down there in case any
trouble happened. But there was none whatsoever.

Did you encounter much censorship trouble?
No. Mayor La Guardia threw out burlesque, but he wouldn't throw out
good theater. Later, in Chicago, they called us intellectual New Yorkers.[‡]

* New York *Daily News.*
[†] Publisher of the paper.
[‡] A couple of years after its Broadway opening, the play came to Chicago. "We opened to
rave notices. They carried me down the aisle on their backs, the audience did. Opening
night in Chicago was just the greatest opening night I'd ever known. A couple of months
afterwards, I was in California. I heard, over the air, we were closed by Mayor Kelly. He

From then on, the Depression was a swinging time for me. Everything was so reasonable, and my income was so big. (Laughs.) I never had it so good. When you're involved in making a living, gambling all your money, it was just something that passed in front of you without any feeling about it. And I was getting married quite often in those days, too. (Laughs.) Besides my artistic occupations, I had some marital preoccupations. (Laughs.)

Heaven knows I saw Hoovervilles—out of train windows. It was appalling to look at, even through train windows. But it didn't touch me.

A great many people felt it, especially the young. That's why so many at that time joined the party. It wasn't a lack of love for the United States so much as thinking some other system would correct this blasting horror of hunger. They were soon disillusioned. . . .

But it was a more generous time then. There wasn't this miasmic fear of unnamed things out there. Then it was specific: hunger. We had a more specific enemy to overcome. We were all in such a mess. When you're in trouble, you never go to rich friends to help you, you go to poor friends. I was more fortunate, so I was able to help out friends.

Don't forget, we were all younger. There was a spirit of adventure then, too. When you're thirty years old, you don't have much fear. You don't have the same kind of fear I would have now after thirty, forty years. As I'm talking to you now, I'm seeing it with the eyes of a young man. Oh, it was a magnificent time for me. There was certainly no lack of girls. (Laughs.) I'm awful glad I was young at that time.

---

exercised his power capriciously in revoking the theater's license. As I understand it, Mrs. Kelly walked in with her priest, and she was offended by it." The case was in the federal courts; a district court decision in favor of Kirkland; a reversal by the circuit court of appeals. . . . "so we moved down to St. Louis. We kept our full company on full salary in Chicago for five or six weeks, waiting for a decision. . . ."

Public Servant—
The City

Elizabeth Wood

She is chief of social services, Housing Assistance Administration. In the late Thirties, through the late forties, she was head of the Chicago Housing Authority.

IN '33, I'D JUST been hired as a social worker by the United Charities. Social work at that time was beginning to get psychiatric. I found this absolutely obnoxious. I got taken by some of my clients in a way that made me keenly aware of how stupid were some of our approaches. The irrelevance of the kind of goodies we were handing out. It was the psychiatric approach. Sit, be passive, and let your client tell you what's wrong. It was my first contact with poverty. I found out the hard way.

I saw the impact on one family. There were nine children and two parents living in three rooms. I found them a great big, sunny apartment, with enough bedrooms for a decent sleeping arrangement. And a dining room table for the first time. And enough chairs for the first time. I saw the magic that house performed. The family bloomed. I learned my first lesson about the meaning of a house. But that wasn't the whole story. This is my point.

There was a drunken father and a tough little German wife, toothless. I'll always remember that. The children had every ailment in the book. The twelve-year-old boy was a truant because he had to wear his sister's shoes. He was very proud, the only possessor of a toothbrush in the whole family.

I remember the girl I thought was feebleminded. She changed completely when they moved into the new house. I couldn't quite understand it. Her mother confessed to me that she used some of the food budget to get this little girl a permanent. She was scared to death I was gonna scold her.

But that was one of the things that helped this girl out of her condition. She found a job.

In that three-room apartment, when the father came home drunk, he beat up his wife. The girl was right there, next to it. It obviously had an effect on her. In the new place, when the father wanted to beat up his wife, the boys would put him in the back bedroom and lock the door. So there was no more of this savageness near the girl. These things happened just by the virtue of *room*. But there was the quality of the mother, too. She was one of the best social workers I ever knew.

She made the house work its full magic. When the other girl, the sixteen-year-old, started to date, there was a front parlor for her to sit in. There was a plant, there was a sofa. I had kept this room bare. She filled it. The mother had the girl buy a pink electric lightbulb, so it looked pretty when she had a date. That's what I call social work. (Laughs.)

In a way, this shows a falsity of the New Deal concept: All you need is a good, sanitary house. The person herself had ideas.

In 1937, the United States Housing Act was passed. The concept was a good one, different from those sterile words. We built quite beautiful projects throughout the country. The standards of the federal administration were high. But it never occurred to anybody that the people might make their own decisions about playgrounds, housing design or management policies. So the institutions became more and more institutionalized, while we took in more and more deprived people. In many cases, we tried to pick the nicer of the deprived and avoid the less nice. We had absolutely no insight . . .

Our legislation is still not phrased in concepts which work today: that sometimes these people have awfully good ideas, better than ours. We're just beginning to learn. Tenants have a right to make their own decisions.

In the early forties, we ran out of '37 money. By that time, austerity had set in. The new policy seemed to be: Because public housing was for poor people, it ought to look poor. There was a great resentment if it looked nice. That was the beginning of the sterile, barracks-like housing projects.

It had a multiple effect. We housed fewer and fewer people who benefited by the house alone. We found that housing itself was not enough for people who were really defeated. So the rules of the New Deal era aren't good enough today. 'Cause at best we were awfully kind, benevolent Lady Bountifuls. And, boy, that doesn't work these days.

"Project people" was a term of pride back in '37 and '38. Incredible pride. Our problem was preventing the tenants from becoming snobbish about

Sick migrant child, Toppenish, Washington

DOROTHEA LANGE, 1939

their belongings. I had to get it clear to them that the children across the street had a right to use their playground. There wasn't any other around.

I can remember a young woman who moved into Jane Addams.* She got married about the time we planned to build the project. From the day she saw the houses go up, she wanted to move in. She got pregnant and bought new furniture to store in the barn where she was living at the time. When she moved in with her new baby and new furniture, she was the proudest woman in the world.

I remember Mrs. Pacelli. She said, "I never used to talk to my neighbors when I lived in the slums. But here we've all been selected." There was a sense of aristocracy which was very funny. It's quite the opposite today.

There were lots of unsystematized, uninstitutionalized, good native works. After two babies died of whooping cough, a group of women in the project volunteered to find out about preventives. They knocked on all the doors, so that all youngsters under six got whooping cough inoculations. They had so many creative ideas.

This was in spite of us. And we had a perfectly good staff. Nothing wrong with them. We simply had no idea of the independence, the role of citizens. . . .

It remained that way until '49. Then we had to purge. The eviction of high income families, God bless us. The average income for the Addams families was $1,027. When their incomes reached over $1,250, they were evicted. It was a vicious, dirty thing to do. All over the country, I meet people who say: I was evicted from the project and moved into very inferior housing.

Fights over the selection of sites didn't exist in those days. It was a honeymoon, ten years of pure honeymoon. The only limitation on our capacity to produce was our brains. We didn't know how to foster the idea that these people could think for themselves.

By and large, they were two-parent families. Most of them were middle-class oriented, caught in the Depression. A large percentage were WPA families. They were people who were naturally mobile. They sought out a house because it was a good house.

We had a pitiful percentage of Negroes. The sites for the early projects were vacant lands in white areas. It was the official Ickes policy that you did not change the complexion of a neighborhood. Race relations advisers, good people, didn't go any further.

---

* One of the first public housing projects in Chicago. It was open for occupancy in the spring of 1938.

We put twenty-four Negroes on single, segregated stairwells. Then came the turnover in white families, but none among the Negro occupants. We promptly broke up the segregated stairwells and had a steady increase of Negro intake. It was not until the veterans' program in the late forties that we really adopted an integrated policy.*

There followed a descending pattern. The poorest people were heading that way by virtue of relocation—urban renewal. If they didn't know what to do with a family, they'd send them to a project. So there was a crash input of people on welfare and broken families. The feeling of the "project people" changed. It wasn't a question of their right any more. I can still hear the voice of one woman. In a bored tone, she was saying, "I got me a project. If I can't get anything else, I'll move in." At that moment, I knew most clearly our families no longer felt as they used to.

It was no longer a step up. It was a place where you were investigated. Private habits were never investigated in the old days. Because investigators felt they were being rooked by welfare families, the counting began of toothbrushes, birth certificates and sleeping arrangements. The institution of public housing fossilized, stiffened.

If you're the female head of a household and you don't have an identifiable father of all the children, you're really up against it. Welfare has broken up families because of the man-in-the-house rule. It's venal. The damage we've done to human beings is incredible. Today, we don't build homes, we build institutions.

The New Deal was an enormous step. It was a leap forward. The government assumed a responsibility toward subsidized housing. But we didn't realize that the house is not enough. There's the person. In ignoring his possibilities, we have a welfare generation. We begot it.

■   ■   ■   ■

Mick Shufro

He is public relations director of Roosevelt University; he works in a similar capacity for the American Association of Social Workers. In the late thirties and early forties, he was assistant director of the Chicago Housing Authority.

---

* Miss Wood was subjected to violent attack for insistently pursuing this policy, particularly by local and state politicians.

A MOTHER OF NINE children was receiving two quarts of milk. Because of a budgetary crisis, she was cut down to one quart. She raised hell at the relief station. She became vituperative. The case worker wrote her up as a psychotic. And sent her to a psychiatrist. Fortunately, he responded as few did at the time. He said: When this woman stops reacting the way she does, let me know. Then she would be abnormal.

At the time of the budgetary cuts, I found out that large dogs at the animal shelter received more per meal than a man on relief. I said so. One of the papers streamered it on the front page. The skeletal budget remained until, suddenly, more money was found.

I couldn't understand this sudden change of heart. Later I learned that shoplifting on State Street had become so great that the merchants petitioned the welfare people to give more monies, so that shoplifting costs would go down. It may have been that if a kid didn't have clothing, his parents shoplifted a pair of pants or a sweater or something of that sort.

I was once director of the Seamen's Division of the Transient Bureau. These men had traveled and were well organized. They never came in to see me alone. It was always a committee. They objected to the rules. I suggested they make up their own rules about people staying there. There were about three hundred people living there at the time. They themselves made up a set of rules that was much stiffer than the administration's. I wouldn't have made them for Alcatraz. But they made them up, followed them and came through.

The answers they gave to the questionnaires were about eighty percent false. They would tell case workers personal problems that didn't exist. It was deliberate. They were objecting to going through their personal history. They formed a committee. I agreed with them. I said: I don't give a damn about your personal lives. If you're eligible for relief, you're going to get relief.

Many laboring men were able to take relief without losing their self-respect or breaking down. The office worker or the professional very often broke down.

There were all kinds of rumors going on then as now: the Negroes who lived in public housing projects couldn't take care of their property. One day I saw a man in his Sunday clothes, digging in the garden out there. He said, "We have so many visitors watching over us, and telling others how the Negro lives, so I dress up in my best clothes when I'm gardening." You'd see a mother snatch her little children when visitors came around, and they'd come down a few minutes later in absolutely pure white dresses. It was show business and also made its points.

Is there a difference between "relief" then and "welfare" now?
At that time, when we said relief, we meant relief. Everyone then you assumed was an able and willing worker, simply out of work. Today there are people society does not accept as workmen. Never having been given the opportunities, they are *almost* unemployable—"welfare people."

■ ■ ■ ■

Elsa Ponselle

She is the principal of one of the largest elementary schools in Chicago.

I WAS THE YOUNGEST one in the family, so I got the college education. My brothers and sisters wanted me to go. They couldn't. It was a step up for us to have one daughter go to college.

I began to teach in December 1930, and I was paid until June 1931. When we came back, the city had gone broke. We kept on teaching, of course. I didn't go hungry and had a place to live. My father provided me with enough money to get by. But it was another thing for the men who were married and had children.

They began to pay us with warrants, which carried six percent interest. A marvelous investment. But not for the teachers who had to take them for pay. They had to peddle those warrants for what they could get. It was a promise to pay when the city got some money. We didn't think we'd ever get paid, but the businessmen knew better.

There were some stores downtown we will always remember with gratitude. They took those warrants at a hundred percent. Remember the Hub, Lytton's? They were wonderful. Old-timers like us still go there. There are some stores that will not be remembered with any love. They took it with a sixty, seventy-five percent discount. Many teachers were credited with only fifty percent. As time went along, they got it up to ninety. One of my friends bought a grand piano because she got a hundred percent on the warrant. (Laughs.) That was—if I may be forgiven for saying so—a hell of a note.

Finally, with F.D.R. in the White House, somebody went to Washington and we got a federal loan. And that didn't happen without a shove. At the time, the chairman of the Board of Education said we should be happy with what we were getting. We asked him if his wife could live on what we were making. A group got together and organized us. Everybody was heart and soul in the unions those days. Somebody said, "Why not a teachers' union?" And why not?

There were objections, of course: We're not tradespeople, we're not laboring class. We're professionals. As professionals, we're entitled to starve to death quietly and with refinement. Some of us weren't that much interested in being refined and professional. We were much more interested in improving our conditions.

We didn't have sit-ins, of course. That would hurt the children. We determined on one thing: We were not going to hurt the children. We went on teaching, whether we were being paid or not. We kept them apart from it.

We marched down LaSalle Street, we marched down Dearborn, we marched down Michigan Avenue. We marched everywhere. People were appalled. Teachers were supposed to be meek and mild. We were supposed to be the bulwark of the status quo and here we were, joining the revolution. (Laughs.) We were on the side of the great unwashed. How could we do that? I'm really surprised at how many teachers joined the movement, especially the older ones. They marched. It gave the establishment a turn. One of them went to Washington and got the money for us.

The Depression hit other members of my family. My brother, a tailor, like my father, was working one day every three months. He had a wife and two children. We were able to help him out. My sister-in-law came to me one day and said: "You want to hear something really funny? Johnny came home and said he had to bring some canned goods to school for the poor children. Where the hell is he gonna find kids poorer than we are?" We protected the kids from any idea that they were deprived.

Today the kids blithely make $50 and off they go and spend it. As they very properly should. One time, somebody said to me, "What these kids need is to experience a Depression." Two of us, remembering the hard times, screamed at him, "Never! Not in a thousand years!" I don't care how blithe they are in spending money. Nobody should experience a Depression. No young person should.

Do you realize how many people in my generation are not married? Young teachers today, they just naturally get married. All the young men are around. There were young men around when we were young. But they were supporting mothers.

It wasn't that we didn't have a chance. I was going with someone when the Depression hit. We probably would have gotten married. He was a commercial artist and had been doing very well. I remember the night he said, "They just laid off quite a few of the boys." It never occurred to him that he would be next. He was older than most of the others and very sure of himself. This was not the sort of thing that was going to happen to *him*.

Suddenly he was laid off. It hit him like a ton of bricks. And he just disappeared.

At our school, we had many Mexican children. When I get violent against big business, I think of those poor little kids. The Mexicans were imported to come up and work on the railroads, and when the work gave out, well, brother, can you spare a dime? They were thrust out, just like that. And they acccepted it. I mean, this was the way the world was.

At a time, when it was raining and snowing and the middle-class children were all bundled up, or else kept at home. Our kids came to school every single day, whether they had anything to wear or not. 'Cause it was warm, the classroom was warm.

The Mexican and Negro children were more used to being poor and hungry. The Italian and Greek children and their parents were stunned by it. You hear the saying today: if you really want work, you can get it. My nephew, not so long ago, said to me, referring to the Negroes: Ah, if they want a job, they can get it. I said, "If you ever say that again—I don't care if you're damn near forty years old—I'll slap you! Your father couldn't get a job in the Depression, and he wanted one." Of course, he's forgotten. But, ohhh, I felt all that old rage coming back.

The parents of the children I have today are working, but some of them are very, very poor. During the Depression, when you were poor, you weren't looking around and seeing . . . here's a society in which everybody has something except me. What's wrong with me? What's wrong with my parents, that we don't have these things? By God, I'm gonna get some. I can't blame them. They watch television, and everybody has everything. Why not me?

In the Depression, it wasn't only "not me," it was "not you," too. The rich, then, had an instinct for self-preservation. They didn't flaunt their money, if you remember. They didn't have fancy debutante parties, because it was not the thing to do. They were so Goddamned scared they'd have a revolution. They damn near did, too, didn't they? Oooohhh, were they scared! What's more scared than a million dollars?

The Depression was a way of life for me, from the time I was twenty to the time I was thirty. I thought it was going to be forever and ever and ever. That people would always live in fear of losing their jobs. You know, *fear*. And, yet, we had, in a way, a wonderful time. We were young.

Remember? The one great thing was the end of Prohibition. The liquor we drank before was awful. Whoever thought about enjoying a drink? I'm talking about the bootleg. To this day, I can't drink gin, because every time

I get a very fine Beefeater martini, all I can remember is that white stuff I drank during Prohibition.

How can you talk about the Depression without talking about F.D.R.? I remember when he was at the Chicago Stadium and all of us ran from school to get there. He came in on his son's arm. We didn't realize that he was really and truly crippled until we saw the braces. He got up there and the place just absolutely went up in smoke. What was tremendous about him was—with all the adoration—his sense of humor. He acted as though he didn't take himself seriously.

And Eleanor. Eleanor. I think she's the greatest thing that ever happened to anybody. I think of the way they talked about her, about her looks, about her voice. I used to get so rabid. Why I didn't have high blood pressure, I don't know.

Not so long ago, one of the parents said to me, "You know, you kind of talk like Eleanor Roosevelt." I said, "You mean her voice?" She said, "Oh, no, your voice isn't like hers." I said, "What do you mean?" She said, "I don't know. You just talk like Eleanor Roosevelt." Wasn't that something?

■ ■ ■ ■

Sergeant Vincent Murray

A police headquarters on Chicago's South Side.
"I worked for the American Express Company for ten years. In 1933, I was laid off. I was out of work for a year. I went to different aldermen, but there were no jobs to be had. I was recalled by the express company when business picked up a little. . . ."

I JOINED THE FORCE in 1935. Five hundred young fellows were sworn in on that particular day. We were saddened when a reporter announced that Will Rogers and Wiley Post were killed in a plane crash in Alaska.

Our starting salary was $2,300 a year. We purchased our own uniforms, guns and shirts, et cetera. At that time, there were very few policemen drove automobiles. We'd come to work in a streetcar in uniform. When we'd get to the police station, there'd be fifteen or twenty policemen in uniform on that streetcar. Ninety-five percent of us went to work on streetcars.

I look outside the window there, and to my right, looking west, I see 150 automobiles owned by detectives and owned by uniformed men. What I'm trying to bring out is the difference between 1935, '36, '37, '38 and 1968.

Now when I go and ride a bus downtown, I never, never see a uniformed man on a bus. They come here to work in all kinds of cars, Fords, Chevies, Chryslers, you even seen 'em come up in Cadillacs, Mustangs. At that time, we lived within our means. We didn't live over our heads.

These young fellows in the police department today, ninety percent of them are living over their heads. They have cars they can't afford. They have colored televisions they can't afford. And some of 'em are talking about summer houses. And every one of 'em I will say are in debt over their heads. It's impossible on what they're gettin'. If they want to keep up, their wives will have to go out and work. Or else, they moonlight, get extra jobs. At that time, they couldn't get two jobs. They were lucky to have one. Just here in the last month, they have allowed policemen to moonlight by driving taxicabs.

Today there are twenty squad cars where there used to be two. They probably had fifty foot men around the Loop. Now they might have ten foot men, the rest of them are in squad cars. It was interesting working in the Loop, back then. Every twenty minutes, we were stopped by visitors from out of town. They'd see a policeman in uniform and they inquire about different buildings, different restaurants.

It was at the tail end of the Depression. Around the Loop, you had quite a few employment agencies. And we had an epidemic of con games. When these fellows would come out of this employment agency, this confidence man would walk over and pat him on the shoulder and say, "Pardon me, are you looking for a job?" He'd say, "Yes, I am." "Well," said this fellow, his name was Parsons, "I've got a job for you right now over in the Garland Building. Running an elevator. The job pays $30 a week." Now $30 a week is a lot of money at that time.

So the two of them go over to the Garland Building. This confidence man would take this young fellow on the elevator to the office of the building, and he would tell him to sit in the corner. And he would converse with somebody in the building. He'd walk back and say, "You got the job. You start to work tomorrow. But you need a uniform. The uniform'll cost you $50."

So they'd get in a cab and they would go out to his house, and if this fellow didn't have the $50, he borrowed it from his in-laws or his neighbors. He was so desperate to get that job. So he'd give 'em the $50 and Parsons'd say, "O.K., report tomorrow morning, and I'll have your uniform for you."

The following day, the fellow would go down to the Garland Building and he would go up to the office and he would set there, and he's looking for this fellow, Parsons. Mr. Parsons failed to appear. Then he'd go over and talk to the girl. She'd say, "I don't know any Mr. Parsons."

Negro going in colored entrance of movie house on
Saturday afternoon, Belzoni, Mississippi

MARION POST WOLCOTT, 1939

We had about fifty complaints about this Parsons, who was taking these young fellows. Things got out of hand. The sergeant of the district took about ten young fellows and put them in plain clothes and told them to go around these employment agencies. We had a good description of him.

We found him. About thirty people came in, and all thirty identified him at the show-up. We put that fellow in the penitentiary for five years. That gives you an idea how desperate fellows were to secure work. They'd go for almost anything.

Did you have any encounters with strikers at that time or labor organizers . . . ? There was nothing wrong with those fellows organizing the CIO. *Left wing* is a term that was used, where you don't go around with the rank-and-file. They organized the fellows that worked hard for a living up at the stockyards. The American Federation of Labor did nothing for the laborer, nothing.

I can remember when my father worked at the stockyards when I was a little boy. That's fifty years ago. His salary was ten cents an hour. My brother worked up there for the same. He worked ten hours for a dollar a day. If they mentioned unions up there, they'd get fired. American Federation of Labor did nothing for these men. It was during the Depression, the CIO came along.

That's when they started calling 'em left wings and bolsheviks and so forth and so on. Personally I don't think they were any more bolshevik or Communist than I was. They just wanted an honest living, that's all.

If all this happened today, I think the people would take it in their own hands, the way things are going. They're a different breed now. More educated today, more educated.

There was no basic race trouble at that time. The colored stayed by themselves, they never marched into any neighborhoods. People were more or less indifferent to them.

■   ■   ■   ■

Earl B. Dickerson

President of the Supreme Life Insurance Company. "It is written largely on the lives of Negro people. Now we are seeking to move into the mainstream, due to the fact that competition is coming in from white companies. All this has happened since the 1954 Supreme Court decision."

He has been president of the Chicago Urban League, as well as of the National Bar Association, the Cook County Bar Association* and the National Lawyers Guild.

From 1939 to 1941, he was a member of the Chicago City Council as alderman from the Second Ward.

"The Depression was like a hurricane. Fortunately these 'Acts of God' are not prejudiced. They kill whites as well as Negroes."

THE SOUTH SIDE WAS very much as it is now in the ghettos. People standing around on corners. The streets were crowded whether it was Saturday or Monday. People who didn't have carfare to even seek jobs. Hopelessness on their faces, as they sat on stoops. . . . Almost all the Negro companies went out of business. The banks in the community were closed. Though they catered to black depositors, they were operated by whites.

At almost every meeting of the City Council, delegations came down from the South Side, asking for better relief treatment. Many times on the floor of the council, I argued for more consideration of their needs. The council was grudging and niggardly in its response. An alderman from a West Side ward† accused them of being lazy: "That's why so many of them are on relief," he said.

I replied, "It's like tying a man's hands behind his back, beating him on the head and accusing him of being a coward because he doesn't fight back." During my investigations, I found very few Negroes employed by the city and none by most of the large State Street stores.

The council was run by Mayor Kelly just as it's now run by Daley. He was a ruthless, domineering figure. It was a one-man show. There were only three aldermen who really challenged him. Paul Douglas was one. John Boyle was another. I was the third.

At first, Kelly was friendly. But when I introduced resolutions challenging the way things were, he changed. I challenged the winking at restrictive covenants that had so much to do with the development of today's ghettos. The School Committee hadn't had a meeting in six years, I discovered. I asked why it was that white students could transfer to other areas at will, but Negro children couldn't. None of my resolutions passed. Kelly didn't approve.

Oh yes, once I succeeded. I urged that the traction ordinance include a nondiscriminatory provision. At the time, there were no Negro motormen

* An association of black lawyers.
† Popularly known as the "West Side Bloc," celebrated for its close syndicate connections.

or conductors working the Surface Lines. The pressure was so strong—
manpower shortage because of the war—Kelly acceded. Not that he was
personally in favor of it. He was never a friend of the Negro people. He rode
on Roosevelt's coat tails.

*He recounts Mayor Kelly's choosing a relative newcomer to the ranks of the
Democratic Party, William A. Dawson, who had been a Republican, as congressional candidate, over himself in 1942, "because I couldn't take orders."*

I have never been to the council chambers since the day I left. Sometimes
I regret those four years. I was denied my full development as a political
person. Every door I sought to open for the Negro people was closed. In
matters of housing, no success. In employment, no success. In education,
no success. All I was able to do was raise the questions and bring them out
in the open. . . .

POSTSCRIPT: *"I was appointed by Roosevelt to the first Fair Employment Practices Commission. I served from 1941 to 1943. I remember the hearings in Los
Angeles. A big aircraft company, employing twenty thousand, had hired no
Negroes. Not until the morning of the hearings did they employ fifteen. I asked
the personnel manager in what departments they worked. He replied, 'Custo-
dial.' That means they were sweeping floors.*

*"At another company, there were no black bricklayers. The reason given:
one or two couldn't work alongside whites. They'd have to get enough to work
one side of the building. Since they couldn't find that many, they'd employ
none."*

Evictions, Arrests and Other Running Sores

Mrs. Willye Jeffries

A wisp of a woman: the black of her skin is highlighted by the startling white of her hair. She is seated in her kitchen. From the portable radio, the announcer, in machine-gun tempo, offers the news of the day.

In the adjoining room, on a neatly made bed, a very small boy is curled in sound sleep. He is a neighbor's child.

NOW WE HAD WHAT was known as the Workers Alliance. Local 45, for which I was secretary and treasurer. And we were going into relief stations, sometimes gettin' arrested two, three times a day.

We were fighting for an old lady that had died. And the relief wouldn't give 'em that hundred dollars towards the burial. They didn't want to give you nothing anyway. We got a crowd of about fifty people and went to the station. We gonna stay until we get this hundred dollars for this old lady. We finally succeeded in getting it. But we were two, three days before we could catch up with this man. This man was the head of everything. You see, the police would arrest us then. But when they learned we were fighting for a good cause, then they would let us alone.

There were policemen who felt this way, who would let you alone?
Oh, that guy they used to call Two-Gun Pete.

*(Startled) Two-Gun Pete Washington?**

That's right. He was one of them. But here at this relief station that day, they had those big patrol vans. You turned that thing bottoms up. Didn't nobody go in. We turned it over. There were a lot of Polish women in this organization, too. They had cayenne pepper, and they threw it in those policemen's eyes, and nobody knew who done it, but they went blind. That cayenne pepper, that red pepper. A lot of the time, the men were knocked down, but they get right up and fight again. The women, they played the biggest roles.

We had, oh a gentleman to die. We went over to the headquarters, and the workers were all working on the first floor then. We had a white lady, weighed about two, three hundred. We called her Ma Kuntz. She looked out. We were marching up and down, you know, picketing the place, because they wouldn't bury this old man. So we just took the corpse over there—not the man, but something resembling the corpse—and just set it in there. Where the workers was. And they all went upstairs. We run them out, just marching around there. We shall not, we shall not be moved. Singing—meaning we shall not be disturbed. When it was lunchtime, those workers made up $5 and sent it downstairs and told us to get something to eat.

The police patrol came. Ma Kuntz, she spied them out there well nigh before they got there. She had that old stick, and she's just marching, keeping time with that stick, see? Well, she say, if the patrol should come, now don't nobody get panicky. Just keep on doing what they're doing. So they just come in and they just stood in the door, crossed their legs, kinda stood in the door like that and looked at us. Got back in that patrol and went about their businesses.

But we did get that old man put away. We stayed over two weeks on that first floor. We had blankets, we moved a piano in and we had a big time. We had plenty to eat, 'cause those that weren't picketing saw that we had food every day.

An old time sit-in . . .

Sure, that's what it was. It was a fight, too. But I enjoyed it, I really enjoyed it. I didn't let them think I was powerless, either.

When my husband fell dead, my daughter wasn't two years old. He died on the third of September on the job out at the packing . . . and she was

* Sylvester Washington, a black policeman, celebrated and feared on the South Side. He had a reputation as trigger-happy.

two years old on the eighth of November. Well, I had this little girl and I just thought everybody was pushing me around because my husband was gone. And I was very mean. Very mean.

So I moved in a place—the old building is torn down now. The bathrooms and toilets were all on the halls. You could meet the water coming downstairs. It wasn't fit for anybody to live in. I heard about it, and I moved in there to get into a fight. And I got a good fight.

I started organizing those people in there and every time I'd get one leaflet, they'd take 'em down stairs and pile 'em on the landlord's desk. He lived out in Beverly's Hill.* He'd come the next morning, with all those leaflets piled up there. Naturally he looked at me. "Miz Jeffries . . ." He was offering me $500 to stop organizing the building. I'd say, "Look, these people I'm organizing are my people and I do not sell them out. Your money is counterfeit."

And, honey, Wilkins† had him a paid-off bunch of police officers. They were detectives, plainclothesmen, from Forty-eighth Street.‡ He had a list of every widow woman living in the building, and was on relief. He gave those names to the police officers, and around eleven thirty or twelve o'clock, they'd come in and knock on your door to see if you had a man in there. See? Everywhere they found a man, they had those people on relief cut off.

So on this particular night, when the law knocked on my door, I say, "Who is that?" Me and a fella named Edward Gray was playing a game of cards. We had a drink. We had a pint of liquor settin' on the table, but it wasn't open. He knocked again. He say, "Police officer, open the door." Well, I had a broom handle. I said, "Come on in. You got your goddamn key." And that time, he kicked on the door. I threw it open. He run it ag'in. I hit him. I said to my daughter, she was nine years old, "Jean, get out of bed and get down to the next block." The president of the Workers Alliance was on the next block. She went down there and got Tony, and Tony couldn't get here fast enough.

I was having a fight with Malone. Tony said, "O.K., hit him again, Sis." And he stood and held his watch, forty-five seconds, he say, "Hit him again, Sis." I got an old pen knife that I still got in my place that I pick my corns with sometimes. It was lying on the table. When he got tired of taking those hits over the head, he run under the stick and caught this arm and twisted

---

* Beverly Hills. A middle-class suburb on the Far South Side.
† Landlord of the building.
‡ A precinct police station. The busiest in the world, then.

it. That made me fall against the table. It knocked the knife off. My daughter saw it and run off the bed and run and picked it up. About that time, he just shoved his gun right into her side like that.

So he finally called the patrol. He said, "There's a fighting woman here and can't do nothing with her." I was a big lady. I wasn't skinny like I am now. So here come the police, the patrol, the old black maria. They say, "Gray, you better get out of here. We don't want you." He said to them, "Look, I would be less than gentlemanly to walk out on this woman now. I visited with she and her husband when her husband was livin' and I would be less than a man." He said, "If she gets ninety-nine, I can certainly stand a hundred." O.K., they took us both.

During the time we were waiting to go for trial, we got out a leaflet. Everybody from the South Side that belonged to the Workers Alliance was over at the courtroom that morning. So they messed around that trial all day, talk a little and call us up there.

In the meantime, Malone saw that everything was against him, 'cause he was the intruder. He had no business at my door. He called Gray to come in the hall. So Gray come back and he told me what Malone wanted. He wanted Gray and myself to pay a dollar fine and plead guilty. I said, "Look, I was a free woman when I come in here. And when I walk out I'm gonna be free." I'm not gonna have no record when I got out of here.

Well, the case was called. Wilkins had about fifty people there to appear against us. They were sitting in the back of the courtroom. We went up and the judge say, "Case dismissed." Wilkins and his wife got halfway up there and we were already halfway back. They didn't know what happened. So they all went home.

Wilkins say, "Miz Jeffries, could I take you back to the South Side." I say, "No, thank you. The streetcar runs out there. That's how I got here, that's how I'm going back."

I was doing tenants' work then and, you know, I didn't mind going to court with all those other people. They thought I was a lawyer. (Laughs.)

You see, I had a big, brown briefcase. And after, they commence to holler in court every time I go in court, two and three times a day: "This old lawyer woman!" I got a whole lot of newspapers and tore 'em up and put 'em in that briefcase. (Laughs.) Them were my law books. I had people laughin' about that all the time: "Here comes that old lawyer woman!" Goin' up front, case called . . . and I got my rosary laying there on that thing. The judge had on some, too. And I had a little pocket, here, stick the crucifix down. He thought I was a Catholic like him. (Laughs.) I didn't lose a case.

Well, I went to Washington and came back.* It was rainin'. When I got home that morning around eight o'clock, that whole wall was wet. There was no gutter to throw that water off. I had a two-room apartment. I sent for him. So Wilkins comes up. I said, "You see this? You think I can sleep here tonight? You put some gutters up." He said, "Come here." He showed 'em to me layin' out in the yard. I said, "Those gutters have been laying out there for over three weeks. They're no good out there." I said, "Look, I'm not paying any rent until you get those gutters up there." He put the gutters up the next morning.

And I had asked him about enamel paint. He promised me. So he had a cousin that did his painting. He sent him up with cold-water paint. I sent him back: "You can't put that on my walls." He finally come up with the right paint. Painted my two rooms beautiful.

That evening, everybody in the building wanted to see my apartment, it was so pretty. I say, "Look, I'm gonna tie up this whole floor." I tied up the whole second floor. Nobody on this floor paying no rent, 'cause everybody wanted what I wanted, and he didn't give it to 'em. All right. I got everybody's rent. And I wouldn't give it to him. I said, "You're gonna pay your rent when you got the decorations that I got." Some of 'em wanted a bed and some of 'em wanted linoleum and some of 'em wanted chairs and tables.

They got Mrs. Griffin right across from me, they did hers next. I asked her, "Now, you need anything in the apartment?" She said, "I don't need nothing like that." I said, "Then go downstairs and pay your rent." Mrs. Saddler, the next little lady next to me, she had a lot of children. And her husband was dead. I said, "Now what you want in here?" She say, "I need a mattress for my children's bed and I need some chairs and a table." He got it downstairs in the store room, but he won't give it unless you protest for it, see. I say, "Go downstairs and ask for it. But I'm not gonna give you this money unless you get what you want." She went downstairs and got what she wanted. Major† up and brought it. As they did the decorating, whatever those people said they wanted, they got it, before he got any rent.

So then he proceeded to evict me. I let him evict me. I let the bailiffs come and set me out.

They put your furniture out on the sidewalk . . . ?
Mm-hmm. Yeah, I let 'em come and did that. But we had a committee, see. We had everything arranged. We stayed out there a whole week. That was

* She attended numerous poor people's conventions in the thirties.
† The landlord's building custodian.

to excite the neighborhood. To what was happening. I had a very dear friend that lived around that same building. Every morning when I got tired from picketing, I'd go up there and sleep. My little daughter, she slept upstairs every night. So finally he came. "Miz Jeffries," he say, "there's no need for all this." I said, "Sure, there wasn't, but you put me out. So I'm gonna stay here as long as I want. You can't put me off. I'm not on your property, I'm on city property. The block don't belong to you."

It rained, but the men had tarpaulins. Nothing got ruined. We cooked, we had more to eat out there than we had in the house.

A lot of 'em was put out. They'd call and have the bailiffs come and sit them out, and as soon as they'd leave, we would put 'em back where they came out. All we had to do was call Brother Hilton, he's about ninety some years now. Look, such and such a place, there's a family sittin' out there. Everybody passed through the neighborhood, was a member of the Workers Alliance, had one person they would call. When that one person came, he'd have about fifty people with him.

Well, now the landlord'd disconnect that stove and put that piece of pipe away. If it wasn't up the ceiling, they'd take it, and just put the lights off. We had in the organization some men who could do electrical work, see. We'd sneak around through the crowd, and all this nice furniture sittin' on the street, and sometime it snowin'. Find out who own it, see. "If we put it back, would you stay there?" "Yes." "All right, let's go." Take that stuff right on back up there. The men would connect those lights and go to the hardware and get gas pipe, and connect that stove back. Put the furniture back just like you had it, so it don't look like you been out the door.

She moved in and out of several buildings in the area, getting in and out of trouble. She remembered precisely all her old addresses. During the 1936 campaign, she was assistant to the Democratic precinct captain. She carried every vote in her building for Roosevelt. The landlord was a Republican. "He was gonna put me out because I carried his building Democrat. I said to 'im, 'You shoulda been in that boat.'" As for the other Roosevelt campaigns, "I have swang him every time he got elected."

Nobody had any money. And we formed this organization. We would allow people to pay ten cents a month dues. Then we would give parties and raise money so we could carry on the work. But the majority of people when the war come along, they got ahold to a little money. Then you couldn't tell 'em nothin'. They didn't need you, see. Back in the thirties, when it was really tough, and nobody was working, we divided whatever we had with each other. Being on relief, I'd get that little piece of check, pay off my rent. They were givin' you then a little surplus food, remember? You'd have to go to the station and pick up some meat and some beans and bread and stuff like that. We'd divide it with our friends.

Now, if they see you ain't got nothing, they ain't thinking about you. They'll throw it in the garbage first. Some of them think they're better than you are. Some of 'em say, "I wouldn't give 'em the time to die."

The same is when we had the picket lines and struggled to get these colored fellas on these streetcars and els. That was a tough struggle, too. But we got 'em on the jobs. Now some of 'em don't know how to treat us. Some of 'em are so nasty when you get on these buses over here. They don't know how they got it. And sometimes I call out and say, "You don't know *how* you got on here. You *got* on here, but you don't know *how* you got on here." There are some of 'em who are sympathetic and will talk about it. I say, well, it was a struggle.

Most of the people from the thirties are gone in. I'm just around here, me and Drummer Yokum. That's about the only two from the thirties that I know of.

■　■　■　■

Harry Hartman

It is somewhere in the County Building. He overflows the swivel chair. Heavy, slightly asthmatic, he's a year or two away from retirement. He's been with the bailiff's office for "thirty-three and a half years"—elsewhere, a few years. He had begun in 1931.

During the Depression, "I was the only guy working in the house at the time. So the windup is they become big shots and I'm still working." But he has had compensations: "It boils down to having a front seat in the theater of life." As court bailiff, he had had in his custody a sixteen-year-old who had killed four people on a weekend. During the trial, "he bet me a package of cigarettes, understand, he'd get the chair. And I bet him a package of cigarettes he wouldn't. When the jury come up and found him guilty, he reached back in a nonchalant way back to me and said, 'O.K., give me the cigarettes.' I gave it to him in open court and pictures were taken: KILLER BETS PACKAGE OF CIGA-RETTES. *You know what I mean, and made a big thing about it." The boy got the chair—"it was quite a shock to him."*

During the thirties, "I was a personal custodian to the levy bailiff." Writs of replevin and levies were his world, though he occasionally took part in evictions.

"Replevins is when somebody buys on a conditional sales contract and doesn't fulfill their contract. Then we come out and take the things back. 'Cause it ain't theirs till the last dollar is paid for. Levy, understand, is to go against the thing—the store, the business—collect your judgment."

WE HAD 'EM EVERY single day. We used to come there with trucks and take the food off the table. The husband would come runnin' out of the house. We'd have to put the food on the floor, take the tables and chairs out. If they were real bad, we'd make arrangements, you understand, to leave a few things there or something. So they could get by. But it was pretty rough there for a lot of people.

Once we went to a house and there were three children. The table seemed to be part of the furniture company's inventory. That and the beds and some other things. The thing that struck us funny was that these people had almost the whole thing paid for, when they went to the furniture company and bought something else. So instead of paying this and making a separate bill, the salesman said, "You take whatever you want and we'll put it on the original bill." They paid for that stuff, and then when they weren't able—when the Depression struck—to pay for the new articles they bought, everything was repossessed.

You know, like radios. You remember at that time, they used to take the radio and put it in a cabinet that would cost $200 or so. The cabinet was the big thing. These people paid off the bedroom set and the dining room set. Next thing they'd want is a nice radio. The radio was put on the bill and boom! everything, the whole inventory, went.

It was a pretty rough deal. But we arranged that we left a lot of things there. On the inventory, we overlooked the beds and some of the other stuff. When we got enough, we said that the mattresses were unsanitary and we weren't gonna take it. If we had our way, we'd see that these people—if the original bill was $500 and they paid $350—we'd figure, well, you could leave a bed for $350 and you could leave a table. Or we'd say the mattress was full of cockroaches. We'd never touch the stuff. I'd just put down: bed missing. I'd ask the guy, "Can you identify that bed as the one sold?" And I'd say to the guy, "Hey, that ain't your bed. Say your brother-in-law's got it, and he gave you this one instead." Or something like that.

I mean, we always had an out. It was a real human aspect. If you really wanted to help somebody, you could. By making it easier for them, you made it easier for yourself. In most cases, people had plenty of warning that if they couldn't pay it, something would have to be done. They were broke and they were holding out as long as they could. But when it came around, a lot of cases they just gave up.

Some of the most pitiful things were when you went into a fine home, where if they were able to sell an oil painting on the wall, it could more than pay their judgment. When you went into factories, where the guy pleaded with you, so he could have his tools, understand, and do his work at home. When you took inventory, if you let him take his stuff, you know, if there was a beef, it'd be bad. But if you let him take what he needed, he didn't care about the rest. 'Cause he'd have bread and butter to go. So you'd use your head in a lot of cases.

It was a question of going in like a *mensch*. There was a rewarding part of it. If you treated that guy good, he appreciated it. And in the long run, we did better than any of the guys that went out on the muscle stuff. When we took inventory, it was our inventory that stood up. I could open a brand-new box, say in haberdashery, for shirts. What's to stop me from marking one box "partly full"? All I had to do is take out a shirt and throw it out and I can call it "partly full."

We'd even go out at night to repossess cars in a different way. The attorney would want this or that car, and he'd give you an order to take it. But if we thought the guy was a nice guy and he could get some money up, understand, and he needed the car for his business, we'd tell him to park it half a block away and be sure to get hold of a lawyer, or otherwise we'd tow it in the next time. You see? We did some good.

At that time, they tried all their pullers, the companies, they tried to recover on their own. So they wouldn't have to file in the municipal court. They tried to save that. They had their own pullers. We put a check on them and we took all kinds of phony stars away from them. Chicken Inspector 23, you know. They tried everything. It got so, people were so mad at me—or, you know, anybody to come out. These guys would come out with their fake stars and say they were deputies. Then when we come out, they were ready to shoot us.

One of your greatest guys in town, a fella that's a big banker today, when we went to his home, he met us at the head of the stairs with a rifle. And my boss at the time said, "Yeah, you'll get one of us, but we'll get you, too. Why don't you cool off, and maybe we can discuss this. We don't want this place. We knew you had the money, we knew that. Why don't you get together with the lawyer and work something out? What good would it do if you shot us? We didn't ask to come here." People would get emotionally disturbed.

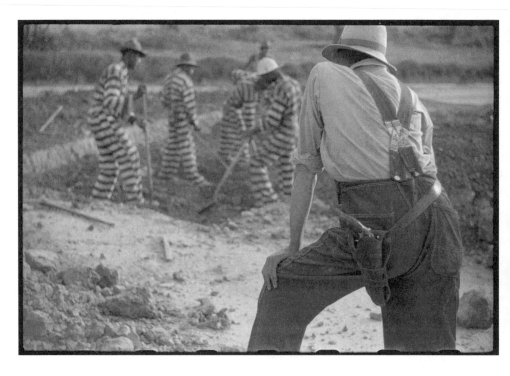

Convicts and guard, Oglethorpe County, Georgia

Jack Delano, 1941

One time I went to take out a radio and a young girl undressed herself. And she says, "You'll have to leave. I'm in the nude." I said, "You can stay," and we took it out anyhow. All we did was throw her in the bedroom and take the thing out. But we had to have a police squad before the old lady'd let it out. Screamed and hollered and everything else. It was on the second floor and she wanted to throw it downstairs. There were many times we had sofas and divans cut up by a person in a rage.

The only way to gain entrance is if people would open the door for us. Whoever wouldn't let us in, we'd try to get it another way. There are ways, if you want to get it bad enough, you can do it.

I used to work quite a bit at night. We'd go around for the cars and we'd go around for places we couldn't get in in the daytime. We did whatever the job called for.

Remember your feelings when you had to go out on those jobs?
In the beginning, we were worried about it. But after you found out that you could do more good and maybe ease somebody's burden—and at the same time, it was very lucrative as far as you were concerned—why then you just took it in your stride. It was just another job. It wasn't bad.

But we had places where we had to take a guy's truck and take his business away, and he's gone to the drawer and reached for a gun. We'd grab him by the throat, you know what I mean, and muscle and something like that. I don't know if he reached for the gun to kill himself or to scare us or what. Anyway, he went for the drawer and boom! I slammed the door on his hand and my partner got him around the neck. I opened the drawer, and there's a gun there. I said, "Whataya goin' for the gun for?" He said, "I'm going for my keys." (Laughs.) The keys were in his pocket.

We've had guys break down. We've had others that we thought would, and they were the finest of the lot. No problem at all. No matter how much they were burning on the inside.

There were some miserable companies that wanted to salvage *everything*. When we got a writ from them, we didn't want it. But we had to take it. Some of 'em really turned your guts. And there were others, it was a pleasure to know. All in all, we used to look at it and laugh. Take it for whatever it was. If you got so, you knew how to allay hard feelings there, and you knew how to soft soap 'em, you did all right.

Aside from the bed, the table—I suppose the humiliation . . .
We tried to keep if down. That they were sending the stuff back or that they were gonna get new stuff. Frankly, their neighbors were in the same

classification as they were. It was things that people knew. It was part of the hardship.

When you saw guys around the house, they'd just stand by . . . ?
Depressed . . . if you came in there and they thought they were failures to their wife and children. But like everything else, they always got over it. Look, people were trying to get by as best they could, and this was our way of getting by. We might as well make it as pleasant as we possibly can. And that's what our boss wanted: less trouble. Because after all, he held a political office and he wanted goodwill.

The poor people took it easier and were able to much better understand than the people who were in the middle or better classes.

If I walked in a house, say, where they had furniture from Smyth* and you come into them . . . first of all on account of being ashamed of never having had things of this type . . . they were the ones who hit hardest of all. They never knew anything like this in their whole career. They'd have maybe a Spanish cabinet, with all the wormwood and that. And realize that if they could have sold that, they could have paid their bill what they owed, what the guys were closin' in on 'em for. We had men walk out of the house with tears in their eyes. And it was the woman who took over. The guys couldn't take it. Especially with cars, you know what I mean?

The poor mostly would make the best of it. They knew it was gonna be taken. They knew what they were up against and they knew it was only a matter of time, you know, until somebody took it away. We had less trouble with the poor. Not, I mean, that we enjoyed going against them, 'cause if they were poor, you had to help 'em more than anybody else.

It was a real rough time, but we tried to make it along with a smile. Instead of being a vulture, we tried to be helpful. But they were interesting times.

Did you encounter much resistance in your work?
No. I'd say one in a hundred.

If you'd walk in another room and somebody all of a sudden gets hot and grabs a knife and goes for one . . . I mean this can happen. But you usually get 'em when they start crying, understand. When they start crying, they're already spent. Most of all, it was surprising how they accepted their fate.

What we did then, I don't think we could do today. With the way the people look at the law. And with their action and their feeling, you know

* John M. Smyth Co., one of the better furniture stores in Chicago.

what I mean. They wouldn't accept today as they did then. What we did then was different. People still respected the courts and respected the law. They didn't want to revise our laws to satisfy them. (Weary, resigned.) What am I gonna tell you?

Today you get a guy in court, you don't like what the judge says, he calls him a *m f*, you know what I mean? So how can you go in a house, understand, where we had law-abiding citizens like we had in the thirties? Today we'd possibly run into a lot of trouble. If we started these evictions, we'd move 'em out on the street, they'd move 'em right back in. Whataya gonna do then? Today I think it's different, a different type people.

Before if you wore a badge, it meant something. Today you wear a badge, you better watch out, 'cause somebody'll try to take you to see if they're as good a man as you are. And we're getting older, not younger. (Laughs.)

Today it's tougher for evictions than it was in our day. Today if you evict anybody, you not only have to evict the people, you have to evict about seven or eight organizations that want the people in there. And each can come up with some legal point, why they should remain without giving the landlord any rent. Now I'm not for the landlord. They bled 'em in some of these buildings, I understand. They may be perfectly right. But as far as following the law is concerned, that's something else.

■　■　■　■

Max R. Naiman

A lawyer. He is sixty-five, though his appearance is that of a short, forty-year-old wrestler.

"*I was a restless youth. In 1918, at the tender age of fourteen, I shocked and thrashed grain. I made three treks to the western states. I worked the harvest fields of the Dakotas, Montana and so on. I used to ride the rods and the blinds. I was a hostler* in the freight yards of Idaho. I met the Wobblies. I lived in jungles. They were great educational centers.*

"*As a farm worker I was victimized. One farmer beat me out of my pay. Where was I gonna find a lawyer to defend me . . . ? I graduated law school in 1932. Out of a class of eighty-five, there was just six that threatened to shove off. The mailman stayed on his job, the bank clerk stayed on his job, the policeman on his job, follow me? But I joined the International Labor Defense.†*

---

* He services engines at the end of a run.
† Hereafter referred to as the ILD.

Defending workers. My clients educated me. We spent many hours, waiting to be called. This was the practice of the court, to keep us waiting. . . ."

THERE WERE QUITE A bit of evictions taking place. As good fortune would have it, the Unemployed Councils developed. They were a bunch of Robin Hoods. They would wait until the bailiff put the furniture out in the street and put it right back where it came from. If there was a padlock in the way, well, then, it was removed, you see? The people were placed back in to the despair of the landlord.

Sometimes these Robin Hoods were so forthright and brazen, they put up a label, stick it on the door: This furniture was moved back by Local 23 of the Unemployed Council.

There was a case where the bailiff and his deputies came to move out a Negro family. The family was a little bit on the alert. They were expecting some legal action, not having obeyed the court's order to get out. The head bailiff shoved his foot in the door and yanked out his pistol to command attention. And also to compel the people to open the door. A struggle developed between the bailiff and the lady of the house. In the course of the struggle, the plank that constitutes the outer edge of the door came off. So the woman picks up the plank and—in the language of the streets—socked him across the wrist and forced him to drop his gun. With the leader of the deputies being thus disabled, they abandoned their attempts to remove the people.

Naturally, warrants were issued for the arrest of this lady and a male companion. It might have been her husband. My clients. It was my practice in those days, trusting very few judges, to always demand a jury trial. It was a long process as against bench trials, where you stand up and give your ditty and it's all over in a matter of minutes. Both my clients were deeply depressed. It's common knowledge when an officer is a victim of bodily harm, of course, a job is done on 'em. There was confusion, the lying that went on. The prosecution's witnesses were thoroughly discredited. The jury found my clients not guilty.

I was hurrying down the corridor to get over to another court. My client had her arm wrapped into mine. She was trying to hold me still for a minute. Finally she stuttered and she says, "Counsel, I loves you so much. I wish I had you in the bushes." (Laughs.) Cases such as those ran into the hundreds. This was my greatest reward. (Laughs.)

Another type of arrest was where clients used to sit at relief stations and wait all day in distress. The distress could be a baby left at home. It could simply be the red tape in getting processed. I had a woman who asked for an increase in the supply of milk for her children. She became very impatient and began to remonstrate. The relief staff could become irritable if the clients attempted to be persuasive. Naturally she was arrested.

She was taken over to the psychopathic hospital. It was a new development in administration tactics at that time. Before it was just straight out-and-out prosecution, subjecting you to fine or imprisonment. This was a new technique: the judge and two psychiatrists, no jury.

The director of relief, Raymond Hilliard, was well known to me, and I, to him. He apparently took a very hostile attitude toward me. As I went to telephone why the psychiatrist, who was gonna testify on behalf of my client, hadn't yet appeared, I passed by Hilliard and a police officer. He made a very disparaging remark. Provocative. I paid no attention.

Suddenly I was wheeled around on my heels. I find myself face to face with Hilliard. He says to me. "I promised you something. Here it is." And delivered a blow to my face. I was flabbergasted. I backed off. He kept on advancing. I got tangled with my briefcase and my arm in getting my coat off. Somehow I managed to untangle myself before he got much closer. I went over on the counteroffensive. I know a little about the art of fighting. I learned from Jack London that you have to get the first blow and make it decisive. This is from his *Call of the Wild*.

So I advanced with all the energy I could and delivered about two or three blows to this big hulk of a man. He buckled at the knees and down he went. Of course, when you saw him again, he was bleeding profusely. The policeman rushed up and grabs ahold of me. A little, diminutive woman, who was sitting in a car rushed up she said, "Arrest that man. I saw how that big fellow came behind that little one and hit him." (Laughs.)

He talks to Hilliard, who is now mopping the blood off his face: "Do you want me to arrest him?" Hilliard says no. Then he turns to me as though he wanted to effect reciprocity: "You want to arrest him?" I says no. The little woman persisted: "I'm from Milwaukee and I saw what happened. Arrest that man." Meaning Hilliard.

As I got to the office, lo and behold, I face a gentleman and he says, "I know what happened to Hilliard. He was taken in for emergency aid. I heard you were all beat up." I said, "You got the facts wrong." "Aw," he says, "the city editor sent me to get a picture. Point at your face with your index finger." I says, "I'll give you about ten minutes to get out of here." "Oh," he says, "don't take offense. Give me a fighting pose, then." I says, "This I'll do." The next day, the *Tribune* knighted me "Battling Naiman." (Laughs.)

The ILD would defend anyone engaged in struggle. As far as I know, it did not discriminate concerning one's politics. The police would often refer to them as Communists. I never stopped to ask.

Few people are aware that brutality did not start yesterday. It's a well-established way of the past, especially in the thirties. Some people were holding an open-air meeting in Peoria in the park. The police came around to break it up. They pulled the speakers off the stands and hauled 'em all off to jail. They also grabbed hold of a preacher who protested.

The victims were taken into a large room, say twelve by fifteen. The police made each one run a gauntlet, where they could each take a sock at 'em as they went through. They were put in jail without an opportunity to communicate with anybody. Before the local justice of peace, the whole five of 'em were convicted and sent down to the prison in Vandalia, Illinois. The ILD found out and asked if I would go down and see what it was all about.

In those days, not only were the clients impecunious. Some lawyers were impecunious. I once led a relief organization of three hundred lawyers. I was in a delegation of six that went to Washington. Ultimately, they did set up a project for lawyers. You think it's only workers who were affected by the Depression? (Laughs.) I had very little dough. I was not paid for this activity. The first three or four years of my practice, I had to borrow to live. Occasionally, one would pick up a little case and make a few dollars.

Be that as it may. On this occasion, I ran a writ of habeas corpus—that's a high and holy writ—and got all five of 'em released from custody. Outside the courthouse on this hot July day, we examined our finances, collectively. I must have had about $1.57 in my pocket. The others, of course, had nothing and they were far from home. What could be done with $1.57? We deliberated on the subject.

If one man availed himself of $1.57, there'd be nothing left for the others. We were going to divide and eat to satiety or starve to the extent $1.57 would permit us. We bought a quantity of bread and milk, basic food. (Laughs.) We had our supper in the park, and then we laid to sleep for the night. We formed a ring around a huge tree and each one's head had for a pillow the butt of the fellow in front of him. (Laughs.) The canopy of heaven and the stars above were our blankets. (Laughs.) And our guard was a most beautiful moon.

The police invariably arrested these labor leaders. A little skirmish took place in South Chicago. Three or four people were beaten and sent to the Bridewell Hospital.* The police lieutenant pulled out a leaflet that announced a picket line and protest. He lifted his eyes very dramatically and lifted his hands with his palms to the ceiling and said, "Man, is there gonna

---

* An adjunct of a Chicago jail at the time.

be trouble!" I didn't press him for what he meant. The next day was the Memorial Day Massacre of 1937.

I handled other matters in the thirties. Some young men were going to Spain to fight on the Loyalist side. They joined the Lincoln Brigade. A lot of them streamed into my office, to look over their insurance policies, their wills. What lingers in my mind is the caliber of these men. There was this young lawyer. He was an editor for the publishers of legal books, but he wrote briefs on the side for the ILD. In the summer of '36, along that time, I got a card from this fella. Postmarked around the Pyrenees Mountains. He was crossing from France into Spain. The next I hear is that he volunteered to go over the top with hand grenades in his belt to silence a fascist machine-gun nest. The snipers got him.

Virden. A little town in southern Illinois. I stayed in the home of a miner's family. Just because the mine was shut down and he had nothing to pay his rent with, he's thrown out on the street. The furniture of the five defendants. . . .

They had a local council of unemployed. These fellows took the furniture out to the heart of the square and piled it right up against the monument . . . the mattresses and the chairs and the stove. To call attention of how courts, real estate operators and the Main Street boys treated an old pioneer family. This so infuriated the pillars of society that they brought charges of unlawful assembly.

Well, for miles and miles around, long caravans of broken-down Model T Fords, with flat tires and whatnot, packed the courthouse in support of these arrested miners. Neighbors would come around and visit the house. And share their food with each other. And share their little old rackety cars, going places. The warmth that existed in, let's say, a little joint misery.

Today people are so busy with their cars and with their TVs and so on that humanism has a little blow to it.

I'm looking forward to Social Security that I may be entitled to. This is one of the programs that always appeared on leaflets raised by people in the struggle for better conditions. There was a slogan among the people: Pass Social Security Legislation. Today thousands of people, when they walk to the mailboxes and pick up their Social Security checks, owe it to these pioneers, who were called every bad name you could think of. . . .

NOTE: *He was the original after whom Richard Wright created the lawyer Max in his novel of the thirties Native Son.*

Honor and Humiliation

Eileen Barth

In 1933, she graduated from a university, where she majored in social service administration. Immediately, she was engaged as a case worker for the county.

I WAS TWENTY-ONE WHEN I started and very inexperienced. My studies at school didn't prepare me for this. How could I cope with this problem? We were still studying about immigrant families. Not about mass unemployment. The school just hadn't kept up with the times. We made terrible blunders. I'm sure I did.

There was a terrible dependence on the case worker. What did they feel about a young girl as their boss? Whom they had to depend on for food, a pitiful bare minimum? There was always the fear of possibly saying the wrong thing to her. The case worker represented the agency. We seemed powerful because we were their only source of income. Actually, there was little we could do.

I had a terrible guilt feeling. I was living rather well sharing a nice apartment with two other girls. My top pay was $135 a month, which made me well off. Yet there were constant layoffs. I always felt that if I lost my job, I might go on relief, too. So I never really had a sense of security myself.

I think most case workers felt as I did. Though there were quite a few who were self-righteous. They felt some of the people weren't looking hard enough for work. Or they were loafers. They believed some of the stuff that came out in the newspapers. Even then. They sometimes made it very difficult for the clients. There was a lot of hypocrisy and sham.

I worked with both whites and blacks. One could say the blacks were more accustomed to poverty. But they still said, "I wouldn't come here if I had work." There was a lot of waiting around the relief offices. Where they came to pick up their food orders. These places were mostly old warehouses, very dismal. That was another thing, dispiriting. Sitting around and waiting, waiting, waiting. . . .

The case worker was often the object of their anger. Where else could they give vent to their feelings? So they took it out on us. They didn't know the cause of their problems. Of course, there were tensions. At one time, my job was to cover the entire city. I often worked at night. I found myself in very strange neighborhoods at all hours. I took it as a matter of course. Yet I knew when these people felt put upon. . . .

In 1934, a case worker was killed by her client, while sitting in the chair at his home. A youngish white man living with his mother. The story is: she had promised him a job. CWA was coming in. He was so overwhelmed by his joblessness he became maddened to the point where he shot her. He dragged his mother to the district office. He killed the supervisor, a clerical worker and then killed his mother and himself.

We were all frightened. Bulletins were issued to all the offices: case workers could take a moratorium on visits. We weren't told we *must not* visit. So I decided I'd go anyway. I was young and felt the clients needed me. (Laughs softly.) If this were to happen now, would I go? I don't know.

I remember, for a time after that, peering into the window, before I rang the bell. I guess I was pretty scared. One family said to me it was terrible, but some case workers deserve to be killed. He looked at me and smiled, "But not you, Miss Barth." (Laughs.)

I'll never forget one of the first families I visited. The father was a railroad man who had lost his job. I was told by my supervisor that I really had to *see* the poverty. If the family needed clothing, I was to investigate how much clothing they had at hand. So I looked into this man's closet—(pauses, it becomes difficult)—he was a tall, gray-haired man, though not terribly old. He let me look in the closet—he was so insulted. (She weeps angrily.) He said, "Why are you doing this?" I remember his feeling of humiliation . . . this terrible humiliation. (She can't continue. After a pause, she resumes.) He said, "I really haven't anything to hide, but if you really must look into it. . . ." I could see he was very proud. He was so deeply humiliated. And I was, too. . . .

■   ■   ■   ■

Ward James

He is seventy-three. He teaches at a fashionable private school for boys, out East. He was born in Wisconsin; attended school there.

BEFORE THE CRASH, I was with a small publishing house in New York. I was in charge of all the production and did most of the copy. It was a good job. The company was growing. It looked like a permanent situation. I was feeling rather secure.

I realized that people weren't secure in the publishing business. There was no tenure. We didn't have any union. That was the first move I made, organizing the Book and Magazine Union in New York.* A lot of white collar people at the time felt unions were not for them. They were above it.

Until 1935, I had my job with this publishing house. They insisted I take a month vacation without pay and a few other things, but it wasn't really too distressing. It became tougher and tougher.

I was fired. No reasons given. I think my work with the union had a good deal to do with it, although I couldn't prove it. What hurt was that I'd gotten pretty good in writing technical books for boys. I had three published. By now, with things getting tight, no publisher wanted any book that wouldn't be a best seller.

I was out of work for six months. I was losing my contacts as well as my energy. I kept going from one publishing house to another. I never got past the telephone operator. It was just wasted time. One of the worst things was occupying your time, sensibly. You'd go to the library. You took a magazine to the room and sat and read. I didn't have a radio. I tried to do some writing and found I couldn't concentrate. The day was long. There was nothing to do evenings. I was going around in circles, it was terrifying. So I just vegetated.

With some people I knew, there was a coldness, shunning: I'd rather not see you just now. Maybe *I'll* lose my job next week. On the other hand, I made some very close friends, who were merely acquaintances before. If I needed $5 for room rent or something, it was available.

---

* "I was also engaged at that time in organizing the Consumers Union. Our idea was to help people of what we now call the inner city to buy more intelligently. Advertising was even less regulated than it is today. Merchants were on the make. Now, Consumers Union, still a worthwhile organization, serves the middle class well. But I'd like to think some day it will get into the ghettos and do some real work."

I had a very good friend who cashed in his bonus bonds to pay his rent. I had no bed, so he let me sleep there. (Laughs.) I remember getting down to my last pair of pants, which looked awful. One of my other friends had just got a job and had an extra pair of pants that fit me, so I inherited them. (Laughs.)

I went to apply for unemployment insurance, which had just been put into effect. I went three weeks in succession. It still hadn't come through. Then I discovered the catch. At that time, anybody who earned more than $3,000 a year was not paid unemployment insurance unless his employer had O.K.'d it. It could be withheld. My employer exercised his option of not O.K.'ing it. He exercised his vindictive privilege. I don't think that's the law any more.

I finally went on relief. It's an experience I don't want anybody to go through. It comes as close to crucifixion as . . . You sit in an auditorium and are given a number. The interview was utterly ridiculous and mortifying. In the middle of mine, a more dramatic guy than I dived from the second floor stairway, headfirst, to demonstrate he was gonna get on relief even if he had to go to the hospital to do it.

There were questions like: Who are your friends? Where have you been living? Where's your family? I had sent my wife and child to her folks in Ohio, where they could live more simply. Why should anybody give you money? Why should anybody give you a place to sleep? What sort of friends? This went on for half an hour. I got angry and said, "Do you happen to know what a friend is?" He changed his attitude very shortly. I did get certified some time later. I think they paid $9 a month.

I came away feeling I didn't have any business living any more. I was imposing on somebody, a great society or something like that.

That ended with a telegram from Chicago, from the Illinois Writers Project. I had edited a book for the director, who knew my work. He needed a top editor to do final editorial work on the books being published, particularly the Illinois Guide. I felt we really produced something.

This was the regional office, so I worked on guide books for four or five other states. The *Tribune* said it cost two million and wasn't worth it. No matter, they were really quite good.

The first day I went on the project, I was frightened as much as I'd ever been in my life. My confidence had been almost destroyed in New York. I didn't know a single person here. But I found there was a great spirit of co-operation, friendliness. I discovered quickly my talents were of use.

Had been in Chicago about a month or two. I remember I wanted to buy a suit on credit. I was told nobody on the WPA could get credit in any store

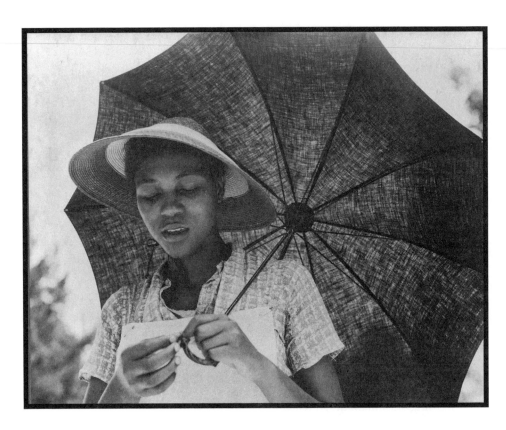

Louisiana Negress

DOROTHEA LANGE, 1937

in Chicago. It was some years later before I could establish credit of any kind.

I bought an inexpensive radio, an Emerson. My son, David, who was four or five, dictated letters to his mother to be sent to his grandmother: "We have a radio. We bought it all ourselves. Nobody gave us it all." Apparently, he had resented that he and his mother had been living rent-free in Ohio. And she may have been getting clothes from her sister. Yeah, there was an impact even on the very young.

Do you recall the sentiments of people during the depths of the Depression?

There was a feeling that we were on the verge of a bloody revolution, up until the time of the New Deal. Many people, among them intellectuals, without knowing what else to do, worked with the Communist Party. The Communists naturally exploited this. It began to change with the New Deal and pretty much came to an end with the Russian-German pact.

I remember a very sinking feeling during the time of the Bank Holiday. I walked down to the corner to buy a paper, giving the man a fifty-cents coin. He flipped it up in the air and said, "This is no good." And he threw it in the middle of the street. (Laughs.) Some took the holiday as a huge joke. Others had hysteria, like this newsboy: there isn't any money, there isn't anything. Most people took it calmly. It couldn't get much worse—and something was being *done.*

Everyone was emotionally affected. We developed a fear of the future which was very difficult to overcome. Even though I eventually went into some fairly good jobs, there was still this constant dread: everything would be cut out from under you and you wouldn't know what to do. It would be even harder, because you were older. . . .

Before the Depression, one felt he could get a job even if something happened to this one. There were always jobs available. And, of course, there were always those, even during the Depression: If you wanted to work, you could really get it. Nonsense.

I suspect, even now, I'm a little bit nervous about every job I take and wonder how long it's going to last—and what I'm going to do to cause it to disappear.

I feel anything can happen. There's a little fear in me that it might happen again. It does distort your outlook and your feeling. Lost time and lost faith. . . .

■ ■ ■ ■

Howard Worthington

I DON'T KNOW HOW I survived. I was working with a bond house on LaSalle Street. We were specializing in foreign securities. I was so grateful we were not mixed up in the stock market. Thank goodness, it wasn't going to affect me. The next thing I know, we failed. The head of the company disappeared with $7 million worth of assets.

Oh gosh, a friend of mine was making $25,000 a year. They cut him to $5,000. He walked right over the Board of Trade Building, the top, and jumped. I wasn't even makin' five at the time. (Laughs.)

I don't think I should have been in the investment business. It was pressure from my wife. A man in that business has to know lots of people with money. I was never an opportunist. I like people because they're people. They could be broke.

I got a job with the Cook County Board of Public Welfare. I had to eat. I earned $95 a month—I was going to say a week. (Laughs.) My boss was as nice a colored woman as you ever met in your life. I had a title—I keep saying it. I don't know whether it was true or not. I was director of occupational assistance and self-help. There was no status working for Illinois Emergency Relief. My wife felt it a great deal more than I did. She dolled it up. She used that title among her friends. I really enjoyed some of the experiences, I really did.

I have to pay tribute to my wife. She managed an apartment building in Evanston. We got a six-room apartment free. I also picked up gadgets that I bought for fifty cents and sold for a dollar. It bought my lunch, paid my carfare. I drove some of my friends nuts. Every time I got a new gadget, I was in to sell it to 'em. They had jobs.

There was a fellow invented something called Bergenize. It was beautiful to demonstrate. You'd dip your hands in a can of it. It was colorless. Then you'd dip your hands in the dirtiest grease, wash it off with cold water, and they'd be as clean as could be.

I had six cans of Bergenize. Before I went out to sell, I'd dip my hands in this stuff. I walked into a garage and went to the grease pit. I dipped my hands into it, walked over to the faucet and turned the water on. My hands got dirtier and dirtier and dirtier. (Laughs.) You see, I had washed my hands back home and forgot to put the stuff back on. I can still remember the garageman looking at me and shaking his head. I panicked and walked out. (Laughs.)

"My dad was sales manager for a leading coffee house. He was over sixty-five and still earning an excellent salary. This was in the early thirties. Jesus, I remember this as though it were yesterday. My mother was playing the piano, I was playing the mandolin, my brother and sister were singing. The doorbell rang. A special delivery for my dad. He was fired. After thirty-eight years with the company. Just like that. A cloud over the whole festive. . . .

"Dad opened an employment agency for salesmen. He had been president of the Sales Managers' Association. He had a lot of friends. But he never made it. A salesman would come in, suit not pressed, needed a haircut. My dad would give the guy two bucks. The guy'd get the job and my dad never collected his fee. (Laughs.) He died in 1936."

I think I drank more than I should have. It was a release. I didn't lose my job because of it. But . . . my wife's mother lived with us. She wasn't a member of the WCTU* but she was close. She considered it a weakness on my part that I wasn't able to withstand all the tensions without some release. In the afternoon, I had a few drinks. I had to time it so I didn't get home until after she was in bed. (Laughs.)

My wife did such a good job of managing that Evanston building, the bank moved us to a four-room flat on the South Side. A hell of a neighborhood. She had rented all but our own apartment, so the bank said: out. They got $150 for it. This was the reward for doing a good job.

We had four generations living in that four room. My son, my wife, her mother and her mother's mother. Grandma was delightful, but trouble! Margaret and I slept under the table.

Oh, I tell you. . . . If I only had the guts and knowledge I could have done so much better. I would have gone into something that I felt . . .

When I got out of school in 1921, we had kind of a depression in '21. (Laughs.) While at the university, I managed the *Illinois Agriculturalist*. I think my place was with *Prairie Farmer* or something of that nature. But I happened to get into the investment business. If I had gone into agriculture . . .

POSTSCRIPT: *"I'll never forget that Depression Easter Sunday. Our son was four years old. I bought ten or fifteen cents' worth of eggs. You didn't get too many eggs for that. But we were down. Margaret said, 'Why he'll find those in five minutes.' I had a couple in the piano and all around. Tommy got his little Easter basket, and as he would find the eggs, I'd steal 'em out of the basket and*

* Women's Christian Temperance Union; headquarters, Evanston.

re-hide them. The kid had more fun that Easter than he ever had. He hunted Easter eggs for three hours and he never knew the difference. (Laughs.)

"My son is now thirty-nine years old. And I bore him to death every Easter with the story. He never even noticed his bag full of Easter eggs never got any fuller. . . ."

■　　■　　■　　■

Horace Cayton

Sociologist; co-author (with St. Clair Drake) of Black Metropolis.

He had come to Chicago from Seattle, where his father was editor of a Negro newspaper, and he himself had served as a deputy sheriff. His grandfather Hiram Revels was the first black senator from Mississippi, following Reconstruction.

I'LL TELL YOU HOW naïve I was. This was along 1930, 1931. When I first got to Chicago, I came into the Union Station, got into a taxicab and told the driver, "Take me to the best Negro hotel." He turned around and looked at me like I was a fool. He took me to the only hotel he knew. It was a whorehouse. I was never so hurt in my life. I don't know what I imagined. Something, oh, fancy, like the Ritz. Only it wasn't the Ritz.

I had a romantic notion about the black belt, the cabarets, the jazz—that was there, too. When we rolled out Michigan Boulevard and cut over to South Parkway, it was exciting. I walked around the streets, day and night, just like I did in Paris. It was a fantastic world. I met wealthy Negroes, but I knew nothing of the masses.

I was eating lunch on the South Side. I saw a group of Negroes marching by, marching by twos together, and silent. Not loud and boisterous. These people had a destination, had a purpose. These people were on a mission. They were going someplace. You felt the tension.

I still had my dessert to eat, but I was curious. I got in the back and marched along. I was dressed better than they were, but they showed no animosity toward me. I said to the chap next to me, "Where we going?" He said, "We just gonna put some people back in the building. They were evicted."

It was a ramshackle building. A shanty, really. A solid crowd of black had formed and they were talking great . . . what Robert E. Park* called an

---

* Professor of sociology at the University of Chicago; mentor of Horace Cayton.

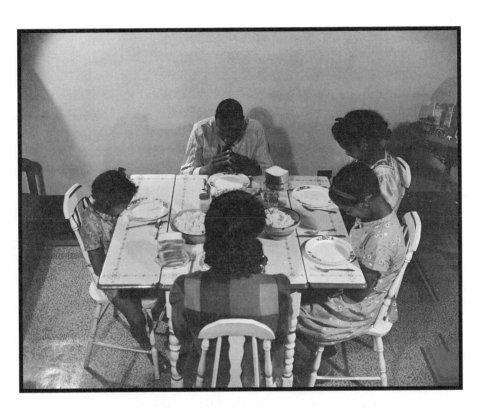

Mr. Branch, resident of the James Creek dwellings,
saying grace, Washington, D.C.

GORDON PARKS, 1942

"indignation meeting." They used to have these indignation meetings down South, where Negroes just let off steam because they couldn't contain themselves, from some injustice that had been done. They'd lock the doors and have an indignation meeting and curse out white people. Here was action.

They moved out from the church just rags of covers, broken down bedsteads and a chiffonier back into the house. Then they had a spiritual meeting. The weather was below zero at the time. We stood there and heard the sirens. Police cars. Everyone grew tense. A frail, old black woman waved her hand and said, "Stand tight. Don't move." They started to sing: ". . . Like a tree that's standing in the water, we shall not be moved. . . ." Then they sang another wonderful song, "Give Me That Old Time Religion." (He sings a phrase, ending with ". . . It's good enough for me.") They added Communist words: "It's good enough for Brother Stalin, and it's good enough for me." And they had other verses, like: "It's good enough for Father Lenin, and it's good enough for me."

While they were singing, the tension was felt in the crowd. The sirens were there like a Greek chorus, coming from all directions. Somebody said, "It's the Red Squad." The old woman said, "Stand fast." But they came through like gangbusters, with clubs swinging. They pulled the old woman off, but in the general confusion, she disappeared in the crowd.

I didn't run because I was so taken up with this great drama. I had never really felt the Depression and what it had done to human beings till then. I don't know why I wasn't clubbed. I was on the outside and I was better dressed.*

Truth is, the Communists made very little inroads with the Negro people. The Communists embraced many of the causes, but the black people didn't take them seriously. For example, the party would have a float in the Bud Billiken parade down South Parkway.† But they really didn't penetrate. They raised issues that Negroes were interested in and they learned a lot from the Communists. They accepted help from anybody. Why shouldn't they? They'd be damn fools if they didn't.

One of the reasons the Communists flopped is they didn't know how to deal with the Negro church. The church was the first Negro institution, preceding even the family in stability. Even in slavery where there was really no family tie, the first organization was the church. The Communists

---

* His impressions of this incident appeared as an article that year in *The Nation*.
† An annual parade on the South Side, sponsored by the *Chicago Defender*. It was a feature for children. Merchants and social clubs of the area would have floats.

came in flat-footed with this vulgar Marxist thing. I was lucky I didn't join. Now I say that, 'cause at my age, I don't give a damn what I join. Hell, I mean, let them drop dead, the bunch of them.

The church played a role in the black community during the Depression . . . ?
Adam Clayton Powell's Abyssinian Baptist Church, his dad had, had led that church and got a great deal of strength from it. Father Divine epitomized that whole period. He was the essence of it. Father Divine was God in a brass bed.

One time in New York, I was in the Village. There was a little fish and clam juice restaurant. A pretty little white girl worked there. She said, "I was born in Father Divine's Heaven." She was ten or twelve before she found out Father Divine wasn't God. She was white as snow. She was from Crumb Elbow, that was his community. All his churches were called Heavens. He would buy hotels, and they'd be Heavens. He fed more people during the Depression than anybody.

That indignation meeting in Chicago shocked me to my depths. The grimness of hunger and no place to sleep, of cold, of people actually freezing to death.*

I remember the original lie-in. Negroes were out of work, after promise after promise after promise. One day a group of them lay down in front of the streetcar tracks. They all had white conductors and white motormen. They couldn't come through. Mayor Kelly tried to make a deal with them. They were going to lay down and stop the goddamn traffic from running through. They would erect a wall of human beings, a black wall. They hoped for jobs. They didn't really hope for and didn't get platform jobs. But there were people digging ditches for the utilities, just common labor. And Negroes weren't on there. So they said, "We'll just shut off the damn thing." It can't work and we're starving and these gangs of workers doing most of the menial work were white. Right in the black community.†

---

* "Mrs. Mary Eggleston's apartment at 1449 E. 65th Street is without heat in Saturday's near-zero temperatures because the building's owner hadn't connected a furnace. . . . For warmth, Mrs. Eggleston and her four children wear sweaters and overcoats and huddle around a kitchen range. . . . There used to be five children, but 14 year old Nadine died Monday. She had sickle anemia and her mother thinks her death was hastened by the cold . . . 'the doctor told me to keep her warm. . . .'" (*Chicago Daily News,* January 25, 1969)
† †"They were laying that track from Fifty-first and South Park to Cottage Grove and none of the colored boys was workin'. And some of 'em said, 'What the hell are we gonna do?' So one of the fellas, said, 'Follow me.' So they fell in line right there on Fifty-first Street, and that gang of men walked up to them fellas that were working and take the shovels away from them. And told 'em to get the hell outa there. They'd taken them jobs, they been wor-

Do you remember the attitude of the black community then in contrast to today's . . . ?

In spite of the Depression, there was hope. Great hope, even though the people suffered. To be without money is a disgrace in America today. The middle class looks upon welfare Negroes as morally corrupt because they haven't worked. But in the Depression, there were so many whites who were on relief. So the Negro would look, and he wouldn't see any great difference. Oh, there was a difference: a disproportion of Negroes on labor than on skilled jobs in WPA. But if Negroes were on relief, so were whites: we're gonna have a better day. That was the feeling. That hope is gone. It's crystal hard now. It's hatred and disillusion.

What was the black people's atitude toward Roosevelt?

Oh yeah, that was something. He broke the tradition. My father told me: "The Republicans are the ship. All else is the sea." Frederick Douglass said that. They didn't go for Roosevelt much in '32. But the WPA came along and Roosevelt came to be a god. It was really great. You worked, you got a paycheck and you had some dignity. Even when a man raked leaves, he got paid, he had some dignity. All the songs they used to have about WPA:

> *I went to the poll line and voted*
> *And I know I voted the right way*
> *So I'm askin' you, Mr. President*
> *Don't take away this W P and A.*

They had a lot of verses. We used to sing them:

> *Oh, I'm for you, Mr. President*
> *I'm for you all the way*
> *You can take away the alphabet*
> *But don't take away this WPA.*

When they got on WPA, you know what they'd mostly do. First, they'd buy some clothes. And tried to get a little better place to live. The third thing was to get your teeth fixed. When you're poor, you let your teeth go. Especially, the child. If she's got a rotten or snaggle tooth and that tooth

kin' on the surface lines ever since . . ." (Clyde Fulton, an eighty-five-year-old black man, recalling the early thirties.)

may ache, dulled by aspirin or something or whiskey. Then they'd pull them out. They'd get their teeth fixed. WPA. . . .

There was some humanity then. We don't have humanity today. No, goddamn it, these bastards, they're not going to do right, as sure as I'm sitting here, they're not gonna do right. I've withdrawn. I feel like I felt when I was in France and Germany in 1935. We're heading, driven like figures, toward a tragedy. I see nothing to do. It's futile.

NOTE: *At the time of this conversation, he was working on a biography of Richard Wright.*

■ ■ ■ ■

W. L. Gleason

He is eighty years old; lives by himself in Minneapolis. He types out a diary— "daily happenings just for the hell of it, to keep boredom from my door."

WELL, I WENT THROUGH that Depression, which took place during the good years of my life. The good physical years, the best mental years. But they were years which made a lot of bums out of good people.

In 1922, I bought a lot and, with my lily-white hands, I built a summer cottage on it. In the same year, I bought a Ford touring car. In the same year, I bought a modern six-room house for six thousand bucks. And in the same year, my wife bought a four-hundred-buck piano.

Damned if I didn't pay it all off, every penny. And then give the whole damn thing away as a divorce penalty, along with barrels and barrels of interest at six and a half percent.

However, when my thoughts run back over the years, as they often do in my dreams, both day and night, one incident, event, happening, never fails to come in for a review. . . .

My oldest boy, Bob, managed to hook on to a job, cutting lawn down on the lake shore. There was no power for the lawn mower, other than legs, arms and lungs. Bob used all of them. In order to spend the two bits, which he was to get for the job (twenty-five cents to you, $00.25 to the bank).

The old gal who owned the place was in the money. Bob completed the job in record time, and knocked on the door to collect his two bits. The old gal opened the door and exclaimed, "Oh, but you didn't trim the trees." She closed the door. Bob took off down the road, and never, never did come back for his two bits.

And the hell of it is that all these many, many years, it sticks out in my mind like a damn sore thumb. I suppose it will be growing like a cancer through all the days I have left. There were so many things happened during the Great Depression. There were some nice things happened, there were worse ones. Like three major strikes, which touched closely on my friends. So why in the billy hell has this happening taken the limelight for me over all the others?

Strive and Succeed

This was Luke Larkin, the son of a carpenter's
widow. . . . He had a pleasant expression, and a bright,
resolute look, a warm heart, and a clear intellect, and
was probably in spite of his poverty, the most popular boy
in Groveton.
He has struggled upward from a boyhood of privation and
self-denial into a youth and manhood of prosperity and
honor. There has been some luck about it, I admit, but
after all he is indebted for most of his good fortune to his
own good qualities.

—*Struggling Upward* BY HORATIO ALGER, JR.

Harry Norgard

A freelance commercial artist.

IN 1933, I LOST my job. It was the year of the Century of Progress. It came
as a shock. 'Cause one day the man tells me I'm set for life, and the next day
he tells me I'm all through. "We have to tighten our belts."

I went out to freelance, find my own accounts. Within two months, I
was making half again what I left. This was in the heart of the Depression.
I always felt deeply in my heart, you could always sell something if you offer
the buyer something better than he's getting.

It didn't matter to me whether there was a Depression or not. Bemoaning
your fate gets you nowhere. I knew wherever you make an effort, you make
headway.

It's true a great many people lost their shirts. In many ways, it was their
own fault. There were millions of people buying stock, being hot shots. It

stands to reason when people engage in a business they know nothing about, they're gonna get hurt.

One man I know made a killing in the market—on paper. "I'm gonna have a house on Sheridan Road, I'm gonna have a Packard, I'm gonna have a chauffeur, I'm gonna have everything." Hoggish. He used to take his children to see four or five apartment buildings: ". . . this one is for you, that one is for you, this other is for you." He was gonna leave his children a big legacy. He had no business calling it his property. His equity in each of them was so small, they were topped by first, second and third mortgages. The man was up to his eyebrows in debt on each one. His dominoes fell, one on top of the other.

People with real money didn't get hurt during the Depression. Because they were able to take advantage of the distressed property. Buying them up. The people who got hurt were people who had no business doing what they were doing in the first place. They were lambs in a den of wolves.

I was prudent. I always liked to feel liquid. I knew where I could lay my hand on a dollar whenever I needed it. The Bank Holiday didn't even touch me.

Some people were victims of circumstance. It was no fault of their own. Many people did their best to find something to do. I heard of a former banker who became a caddy at the golf club he had at one time been a member of. There were people with a great deal of spunk, who wouldn't frighten easily.

Someone once said to me: The worst thing that can happen to a man is to have a good job. Because when you have a good job, you're in a safe, secure, snug harbor. People will stay where it's nice and warm and cozy. A man really does better for himself if he's thrown to the wolves, so to speak.

Our greatest successes in business were made by illiterate men. They couldn't speak the language. They couldn't write. They made no appearance you could be proud of. From sheer necessity, they had to go into business for themselves. They had to roll up their sleeves and go out. If they became junk men, they opened a junk shop. Then they were dealing in scrap metal. Before you know it, they were steel tycoons.

The Depression *made* a lot of people. I know one man who found himself out of work. He began thinking and thinking. He wrote sixteen letters to manufacturers and explained he could offer them a service at no cost. Three or four of them wrote back. In a few short years, he became an extremely wealthy man. He gave them something they needed, even though at the time they didn't know they needed it.

Al Capone operated a soup kitchen. People would line up a half a block long. He was becoming kind of a Robin Hood in that era. He would go to ball games, people would get up and cheer him. They didn't regard him as an underworld character. They thought of him as a sport. He was spreading good cheer among the poor. Things like that were happening everywhere.

They don't give you medals for money. But they don't give you medals for being poor, either.

Roosevelt was to the people like the Holy Father was to the Catholics. At first, I felt pretty much the way everyone else did. Later on, it became apparent to me he was selling the country down the river to the big unions.

The consequence: when the first sit-down strike happened in Detroit—I happen to know some people who lived through it—these strikers tore the place apart inside. They tore up the pipes, they broke the windows, they ripped the machinery out, they did hundreds of thousands of dollars damages.

You heard this from . . . ?
People who saw it, people who sat it. And they weren't even punished for a thing like that. I'm sure if General Motors had sent in a squad of goons to wreck the headquarters of the United Automobile Workers, something would have been done about it. Unionists got special treatment all along the line.

I think a great deal of this was encouraged by Socialist agitators. I never marched up and down the street to help myself. It never occurred to me to blame anybody but myself for what was happening to me. It would be the last thought to enter my mind.

As for the WPA, a picture comes to my mind of men leaning on shovels, as I'm driving through Outer Drive. I've seen photographs of these people, sitting on curbs and smoking cigarettes.

So today a man will do the least he can for the most he can get. In the Depression, those who acted that way never lasted very long. In those days, you could pick up an employee any hour on the hour, just open up the window and yell and somebody would come in for a job. Those who retained their job had the fear of God put in 'em. One thought was uppermost in their minds: I got to do as good a job as I can or else I'm gonna get canned. I firmly believe the only way you can get most people to do a job is to put the fear of God into 'em.

Do you think another Depression might be good for us?

No, I wouldn't say that. What I do say is we are not all deserving the sympathy some of these bleeding hearts have for the people. A great deal of their misery is self-inflicted. These people are constantly looking for assistance. What would happen if we all had this attitude?

■   ■   ■   ■

General Robert E. Wood

In the library of his Lake Forest home, he is watching a television baseball game. At eighty-nine, "I have three bosses—my wife, my secretary and my nurse. It's terrible." (Laughs.)

"MacArthur and I were great friends. We were cadets at the Point together. We were in the same class. When he formed the Rainbow Division, he offered me a colonelcy in it. I was transferred to Pershing's general staff and became quartermaster general of the army."

He had left Montgomery Ward, a mail-order house, in 1924 and came to Sears, Roebuck as a vice president.

I ALWAYS ASSOCIATED THE Depression with one of the best things I ever did for Sears, Roebuck. I founded All-State Insurance in '31, which was the depth of the Depression. It proved an enormous success. Now its earnings are in the neighborhood of ninety million a year. All-State started out pretty slow. But it never lost money, even in '31.

It was a mail-order business. I transferred it into a chain store as well as mail order. Pass goods over the counter instead of through the mail. I gradually converted it from mail order serving the rural people exclusively to a chain store in the cities. That's what made me president. In 1928. The same year as Hoover, who was a friend of mine.

With the Crash, you became aware of trouble because your sales absolutely disappeared. Business didn't drop off gradually. It took a plunge, just like that. Of course, it hit me as well as everybody else. But I felt sure things would come back.

I voted for Roosevelt in '32. Yeah. That surprise you? I thought it was time for a change. While I was a Republican, I voted for Roosevelt. I've forgotten just when I became disenchanted with Franklin D. It was sometime during his administration. I liked him, couldn't help liking him. I was one of the few men in so-called Big Biz that voted for him and supported

Stalled on the desert, facing a future in California. No money, ten children. From Chickasaw, Oklahoma. Southern California.

DOROTHEA LANGE, 1937

him. He was very kind to me. He offered me several appointments. Had me down to Washington several times. But he did oversell the truth, you know. He'd shift from one thing to another. I lost confidence in him.

Did the Wagner Act affect you in any way, the emergence of the CIO?
Not with Sears. We've never had a strike. We had no organization. Sears was one of the first firms in the United States that shared the profits with employees. We've always had peaceful labor relations. For over fifty years, we never had a strike. We're not unionized. But we never lifted a finger. We told employees they could join a union if they wanted to: if you want to join, go ahead and join it. But they never figured it brought them anything.

Things began to pick up around '34 and '35. It was '36 before they began to pick up strong. '32 was bad, '33 was bad, '31 was the worst of all. We cut, including myself. I started with a salary cut. We had to cut or we'd have perished.

We had to lay off thousands of people. It was terrible. I used to go through the halls of the building and these little girls, they were all terrified. I remember one Italian girl I called in. She had a family of ten, father, mother and eight children. She was the only one working. It was terrible. But we had to lay 'em off. I could see how frightened to death they were.

The Depression ended in '33. But it didn't begin to recover on a big scale until '36.

Some people say it didn't end until the war.
Oh, that's ridiculous. You began to pick up in '36. It wasn't big but it was all right.

Were there friends of yours who suffered?
Neighbors and friends. Not my college friends because I went to West Point and all my classmates were in the army. They were immune at that time. It was a good place to be. (Laughs.)

I was very fortunate. While I had no capital of my own, I had a very good salary. I didn't have to shut down, so to speak. (Laughs.) No, I didn't have to cut down on servants or anything like that.

I always felt the Depression was temporary. You couldn't stop this country. I founded All-State in the darkest period, didn't I?

POSTSCRIPT: *"I was an isolationist, you know. I still think it was a mistake for us to have gone into the war. We've got an empire here, and we've got two great undeveloped continents, North and South America. Why should we get mixed up in the affairs of Europe which is an old-time continent? We've got unlimited room to expand, and why we should get mixed up in an old, tired Europe, I couldn't see."*

■ ■ ■ ■

A. A. Fraser

For thirty years, he looked over the books of a lumber company. At last, he became an officer and a member of its board.

WE HAD SAWMILLS IN Arkansas, Mississippi and South Carolina. The money was flowing in so fast, we didn't know what to do with it. But that year, '28, we liquidated these holdings. There wasn't any more timber to cut. We left in Arkansas 45,000 acres of stump.

We bought it at $1, $1.50 a thousand. But we figured by the time it ran out, it was worth $5 a thousand. So when a million feet went through the mill, you could deduct $5 million from your income tax return. Depletion allowance. You see, when the stump is left, that's the end of the capital. Like oil and coal.

Was an attempt made to replant?
No, not in those states. We had houses to liquidate and a railroad and a big store. These towns belonged to the company. You should have seen our offices, beautiful. Like old plantation mansions. Our money was made with cheap wages. A dollar a day. Mostly Negroes. We sold it en bloc to speculators.

People would fight for those jobs. A case of supply and demand. Why didn't we pay more? That was the going wage. You had to make money. You see, without money, we would never have been able to build those mills. We were capitalists. It was free enterprise. We employed a lot of men, so you certainly can't blame us.

What did these people do when the homes were sold?
What did who do?

The people who lived there.
Oh. Some of them got jobs with other companies. Some of them lost their jobs. That was a tragedy.

Then I realized my lifelong ambition to be on the board of directors of several companies. First thing I know, I'm sixty-eight and in good health. So

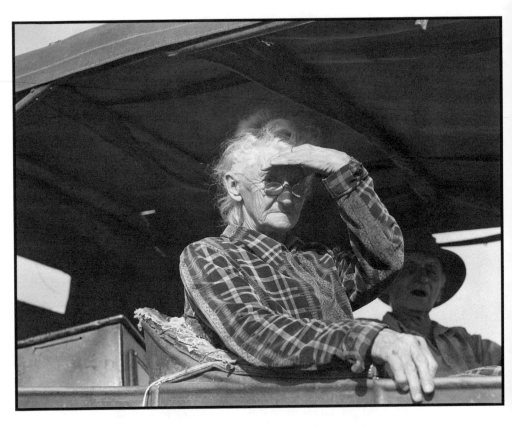

Eighty-year-old woman living in squatters' camp on the outskirts of
Bakersfield, California, says "if you lose your pluck you lose the
most there is in you—all you've got to live with"

DOROTHEA LANGE, 1936

I quit. I finally made it to the Gold Coast. So I just follow my own investments. Got rid of all the cats and dogs. I only buy blue chip stocks. All I do is study stocks and give advice to widows, who live in my building. They stop me in the lobby every day: "What's good today?" I give 'em free advice.

■ ■ ■ ■

Tom Sutton

A lawyer, with offices in a suburb, west of Chicago. His wife, a physician, shares the quarters.

He heads Operation Crescent, an organization of white property owners:

"The wealthy have a place to run. My people are caught in a trap. They're lower middle class, the forgotten ones. Every member on our board is a former liberal. Our best ideas come from the skilled laborers. They have the pulse of the people. They feel abandoned by their priests and their schools. They are hurting, hurting, hurting. . . . They have no place to go but themselves. They don't hate Negroes. They may prefer whites, but that doesn't mean they hate Negroes. And nobody really wants to admit hate. . . ."

THE REASON A MAN works is not because he enjoys work. The only reason any of us work is because if we don't work, we don't eat. To think that any man may sit in society and say: I don't wanna. O.K., if you want to starve, starve. He'll work. Believe me, he'll work.

Those who went through the Depression have a little more pride in their possessions, have a little more pride in the *amount* of possessions they have. They know that it was a fortunate person in the thirties who have as much as they have today. They're much more money conscious.

Money is important to people, especially children of the Depression. You can see when they come into the office here, they're trying to see: Am I a wealthy or am I a poor lawyer? If I'm poor, they don't have that much confidence. They're sort of happy that they're shaking hands with some of the wealthy.

I hate people to know how much money I have. I would never want to admit it if I was broke. I would never want to admit I was a millionaire. One thing the Depression did was to make us secretive. It was ours. During the Depression, nobody would admit that they were broke. My friends who went through the Depression with me, I'll never know how much money they have, because they won't talk about it. Whether they're broke or wealthy.

In the Depression, you didn't want to admit you had problems, that you were suffering. This is mine. If I don't have the money, that's my problem, not your problem. If I did have money, that's not your affair. I don't know if our family was particularly secretive. . . .

The last Depression was blamed on the lack of regulation. This Depression which is coming will be blamed on too much regulation. The way we'll try to get out of it is to truly go back to a free system of exchange. Whether that'll work, I don't know.

People blamed Hoover for the Depression. He had no control over it. If the Depression hits now, they'll blame the government. You always have one danger when you blame government: disturbances tend to create chaos. Chaos will create a demand for a strong man. A strong man will be most repressive. The greater the Depression, the greater the chaos.

I don't think we're basically a revolutionary country. We have too large a middle class. The middle class tends to be apathetic. An apathetic middle class gives stability to a system. They never get carried away strongly, one way or the other. Maybe we'll have riots, maybe we'll have shootings. Maybe we'll have uprisings as the farmers did in Iowa. But you won't have revolution.

I remember standing in my father's office in the Reaper Block,* watching a march on City Hall. I was seven or eight. I remember his comment about red flags and revolution. He said, "The poor devils are just looking for bread." They weren't out to harm anyone. All they were marching for was food. I thought: Why were they looking for food? There were plenty of stores.

There was always talk in the house about the financial crisis. I remember listening to Father Coughlin about money changers in the temple. I lived in a Protestant neighborhood. It seemed there were more Protestants listening to Father Coughlin than there were Catholics. My father listened to him. He was like everybody else: anybody that had a solution, they'd grab on to it.

But he was a liberal and a Democrat and a strong supporter of Roosevelt. One of my favorite pastimes, during the campaign, was sitting across the front room, watching him repeat after Roosevelt as Roosevelt talked. You know, telling off the other side. Since most of his brothers-in-law were conservative Republicans, he enjoyed that particularly.

I went along with him. I can remember writing a term paper in high school: "The Need for a Planned Economy." I take it out and read it once in

---

* An office building in the Loop, since torn down. Many lawyers had their quarters there.

a while, just to see how foolish youth can be. How could anyone take that seriously?

The income tax changed me. I was making some money. It burned me up thinking now I had to file it with the government. It was the fact that I had to sit down and report to somebody what I made. I had to keep records. And I'm so tired of keeping records.

I'm a happy-go-lucky Irish type. As long as I've got enough money to pay rent next month, I'm happy. I don't like to sit down: Did I make a big fortune or did I lose a deal? How much did I pay the secretary? How much did I pay for the cabs? Half the time when I had arguments with Internal Revenue, I don't keep track of those things. We have to be bookkeepers: ten cents for the cab tip, twenty-five cents for a meal, what have you. We're building the bookkeeper type. The New Deal and all those agencies contributed to this. . . .

Of course, we had social problems thrown in with the Depression. We had the beginning of the liberal movement in which Communists were in the forefront. They made use of labor with strikes, sit-ins, the many problems we had at that time. A free economy would have straightened out these problems.

Looking back, many individuals would have been hurt, etc. But as a result of the programs, many more are now hurt than would have been hurt at the time. In an attempt to alleviate a temporary situation, they've created a monstrosity.

Many of the people I knew in law school, children of the Depression, talked about how they had to quit school for help. The father who had been a doctor took a janitor's job. They would do anything rather than take public money. Then it was just the thought that you couldn't take someone else's money. It was a matter of pride. Now I have some of that leftover. . . .

POSTSCRIPT: *"And there's the added feature: I am somewhat of a snob. My children are going to know some of the best of society. Not the best, necessarily. Though money is an indication. They're going to know the best who are working a little harder, applying themselves with greater effort, and will be going further. We work a great deal for our children. It's nice to think there are wonderful ditchdiggers in the world, but that's for somebody else's daughter."*

■　■　■　■

Emma Tiller

In the mid-thirties, she found herself "on my own, and the world was sorta new to me. I wasn't no longer where I had to take orders. I'm grown, I can do as I please, go where I want to, come back when I want to. . . ."

I TRAINED MY OWN self to cook. I always been a listener and a long memory. I could listen to one of Betty Crocker's whole programs and memorize for years afterwards. Cook it. I never doubted myself in nobody's kitchen. Which always means I had a job. You felt this independent because you knew they needed you. That's why I studied to be a good cook.

If it was an ordinarily rich family, you had the whole house under your control. So I ordered the food and I cooked somethin' and it didn't turn out the way I want it, I dumped it out and cooked somethin' else. 'Cause I'm tryin' to learn how to be a good cook. Rich people could afford me. 'Cause when you make mistakes, if I got money, I ain't gonna cry about you wasted sugar, you wasted this, you wasted that. I quit those jobs.

In 1937, I was workin' for a very wealthy family in Wichita Falls. Her husband was a doctor. She told me she was going to have forty people for lawn dinner, ate outdoors. When you work for them rich people in the South, you don't go and buy no frozen peas and beans and rolls. Uh-uh, you cook them rolls, you shells them peas, you string them beans. . . .

She was supposed to get some caterers in to serve this food, because this food has got to be cooked in the kitchen and served outside. I kept askin' her: Has she seen the caterer mans? No, she said, she'd get 'em. So this week came and I asked her again. The dinner was to be Tuesday. No, but she'd get 'em.

So I said to myself: This woman intends to make me serve this meal from this stove, after cookin' for forty people. And you serve it in courses, yeah. So I said: Mm-hmmm, I better start plannin' what I'm gonna do with her now. Another thing I didn't like about her, she was a very stingy person. I was gettin' kinda bored with this house anyway. And gettin' more independent, too. Remember, I was a pretty good cook by now. She'd have this habit . . . when I get through work, I want my money, and I don't want to have to ask you for it or wait two hours, while you fool around. Give me my money. I tell 'em: give it to me while I'm livin'.

Every week when I get through workin' she would go and get in bed. She would lay there and pretend she was sleepin'. I come in. (Utters a mock sigh.) Oh, go in there, Emma. I think my purse is in there. And when I get

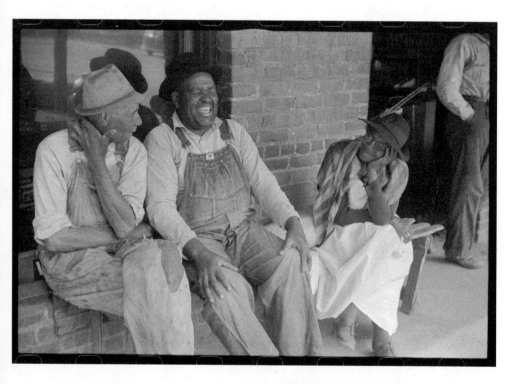

Saturday afternoon in Franklin, Heard County, Georgia

JACK DELANO, 1941

back with that purse, she'd be dozed off again. And you gotta stand there and call her gently: here is your purse.

So I knew she wasn't gonna get anybody to help me. So that Monday, week before, we had to start the gatherin' of vegetables. She says, "We'll start orderin' the stuff Monday." They always say "we" when they mean "you." So Monday we brought about a bushel and a half of green beans, washed 'em, packing 'em away. She ordered about three hundred pounds of ice, 'cause the refrigerator couldn't hold it all. Then she was gonna serve peaches with cream on 'em. I opened all the peach cans and poured 'em in crocks and then put that down in ice.

She recounts, in loving detail, the other foods to be prepared: the caviar and a variety of other hors d'oeuvres: the nature of exotic condiments; the scores of capons, . . . "all the fancy dishes, all the little extra things. . . . I fixed up special puddings and salads. . . ."

This you also has to serve. This is before dinner, along with the drinks. They is the whiskiest folks you ever saw. *Then* you serve this hot dinner. Imagine anybody putting all this work on one human being.

I know I'm gonna leave. But since she has been so nasty, I'm gonna put her into a real doozy. She got forty people, doctors, teachers, oil mens, that all hadda be big shots. Some of 'em comin' from New York. Mm-hmm this here is real nice.

So I works up until Saturday. All the food is prepared for the Monday cookin' for the Tuesday servin'. That Saturday, I had to wake her up again, that sleep: give me my money. I said to myself: Sister, if you knew what I had on my mind, you wouldn't lay down.

That Sunday, I was supposed to go back at eleven and fix their lunch. I got my money and I didn't see no point to it, because I'm not goin' back there. With all this food stacked up, corn cut off the cob, big tub and half full of that . . .

She did call Sunday the lady next door: Was I sick? I didn't answer. She didn't worry much. She know *I had to be there* on Monday. That Monday, I went visitin'. I'm a week advance on my rent and I got about $6 in my pocket. I'm rich. I was supposed to be on the job at eight o'clock. I didn't get out of bed till nine. I decided I'd lounge around till the last of the week. A good cook is always in demand.

So on Monday she calls the lady where I rented from, where I had servant quarter in the back. You see, when I'm workin' for a family like that, I always rent some place else. Because when you lose your job, you don't lose your house.

So eleven o'clock, I come back from visitin'. This other white lady said, "That woman you work for says you had all the food fixed up out there and she's got forty rich people that is comin' there for dinner Tuesday, and you left and didn't say nothin' about it. Is you sick?"

"No, ma'am, I'm not sick."

"How come you didn't go to work?"

I said, "Didn't I pay you your rent Saturday?"

"Yes, you did."

"When the time comes you don't get your rent, that's the time you says somethin' to me. But when I work, whether I work or don't work is none of your business. That woman been knowin' for six weeks she was gonna have forty people there. She thinks she's gonna make me do all that work for that same $7. Not on your life."

She was to pay you $7 for that day?
Seven bucks a week, honey. So this landlady says, "My, my, my, you should be ashamed of yourself." I said, "I'm not ashamed. I done enough work for that woman. I have to wake her up every time it come time for her to pay me, she go to sleep. If that woman had died, her husband woulda said he didn't owe me. I don't like anybody sleepin' on my money." And I said, "And where would *you* be without Rosalie?" Rosalie used to do all *her* slave work. That shut 'er up.

How did the lawn party go?
I had it all figured out, don't think I haven't thought of every bit of it. I could see them big pot-gut doctors and their wives with all their fancy dresses and all, comin' into her house, and sittin' up there with her eyes full of tears. . . .

If you was stupid enough to let 'em get away with it, they'll give you an extra dollar or two. And she figure on some of these people givin' you a little tip—and that was gonna be your pay. You got your tongue hangin' out . . .

That was my awakenin'. I felt good. I think all Negroes have this feelin', when they feel secure enough they can hold up their heads like mens and womens. It's like that old sayin': as long as you got your hand in the lion's mouth, you have to be easy till you get it out. Well, I got my hand out. . . .

■   ■   ■   ■

W. Clement Stone

"The attainment of one goal should be the springboard to another higher and more noble effort." Signed—W. A. Ward. "Optimism is the faith that leads to achievement." Signed—Helen Keller. "Smile, be happy, keep smiling."

There are numerous such inspirational messages in the corridors and elevators of the Combined Insurance Company of America Building. Happy, fox-trotty string music is heard through the halls, a soft background.

Behind a huge desk, sits the ebullient president. He has a pencil-thin mustache ("in those days, movie stars, Ronald Colman, John Gilbert and others, did it"); he wears a wide bow tie ("it's an indication of an extrovert, someone with a high energy level, someone who has drive, who gets things done"); he smokes long, thick Cuban cigars ("when we had our Castro troubles, I bought up the equivalent of three warehouses"). He offers me a couple. "When you take the label off, you'll see it's '59." His laugh is unique; it has a five-note rise. He happily concedes these phenomena are carefully planned. It's a matter of image.

He is a celebrated philanthropist and was listed in Fortune as one of America's new centi-millionaires. His companies employ at least four thousand, with sales representatives in many other countries. Some are welfare states, where he sells "supplementary coverage."

"I started selling newspapers at the age of six on the South Side of Chicago. I found if I tried to sell at a busy corner, the larger kids would beat me up. So I found out that if I'd go in a restaurant, and even if the owner would push me out a few times, sooner or later I'd sell my pile of papers. Actually, that's what started me on cold canvassing—calling on people unannounced."

MANY OF US LEARNED in the Depression how to turn a disadvantage into an advantage. First of all, we have what is known as PMA, positive mental attitude. It's based on the premise that God is always a good God, that with every adversity there's a seed of greater benefit.

During the Depression, there were tremendous advantages to a sales manager. A man was willing to accept any kind of job. All I needed to do was to take a man out and show him how to make twenty, thirty, forty dollars a day, and I had a salesman. We—I use the editorial we—know how to make supermen out of ordinary men.

Would you mind expanding on this?
Rrrrrright!

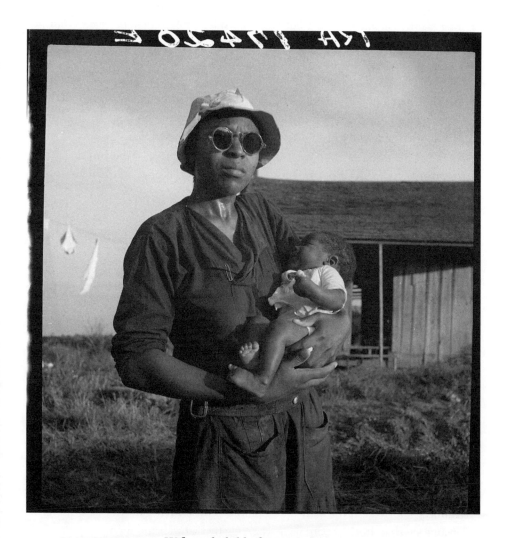

Wife and child of tractor driver,
Aldridge Plantation, Mississippi

DOROTHEA LANGE, 1937

(He presents me with several books: Success Through a Positive Mental At-
titude, The Success System That Never Fails and Think and Grow Rich.
He refers to the last: "That's the greatest book that came out of the Depression.
In 1937. By Napoleon Hill. That book motivated more people to success than
any book you can buy by a living author.")

Actually, in the Depression years, many men who were successful in the
twenties became has-beens. They had a negative mental attitude. They
were men making $30,000 a year and didn't have the courage to start at
the bottom and work up. Others realized opportunities were unlimited, if
they were willing to think and willing to pay the price. A person doesn't
have to be poor. Anyone in the United States could acquire great wealth
today.

I said to myself: Why shouldn't I earn in a day what others earn in a
week? Why shouldn't I earn in a week, what others earn in a month? Why
shouldn't I earn in a month, what others earn in a year? How can I do it?
The answer was simple. Work scientifically.

First of all, I'd always thank God for my blessings. Then I'd use a very
simple prayer: Please, God, help me sell. Please, God, help me sell. Please,
God, help me sell. Please, God, help me sell. Please, God, help me sell. This
did many things, the mystic power of prayer. It got me keyed up. I threw all
the energy I had into it. Immediately afterward, I'd unwind and relax.

Do you recall any sad moments during those hard days . . . ?
I don't believe in sadness. I believe if you have a problem, that's good. When
I'd have a poor day, I would try to figure out what's wrong with me. Maybe I
needed more rest or go see a movie. The next day would be a rrrecoooord day!

When the Depression hit, I had over a thousand licensed salesmen in
the United States. I soon found out they weren't selling. So I traveled the
country and wound up with 235. I trained these men. And we sold more
insurance than in the boom days when we had a thousand men.

Here, he discusses the self-motivator: self commands, affirmation. "You say fifty
or a hundred times in the morning, fifty or a hundred times at night, for, say,
ten days, until it affects the self-conscious mind: 'Success is achieved by those
who try.' Or, 'Where there's nothing to lose by trying and a great deal to gain,
by all means try.' Or, 'Do it now.' Or, 'Do the right thing because it is right.'"

My man'd go into a place, he might be nervous. So we'd have him talk loudly,
talk rapidly, emphasize certain words, hesitate where there's a period or a

comma, a smile in his voice, and when he talked for a long time, he'd use modulation. It worked a hundred times out of a hundred.

In the thirties, I sold accident insurance. Cold canvass. Unannounced, I'd call on banks, stores, offices, during business hours. And sell the manager and get permission to sell in the establishment.

First of all, you'd need a good introduction, so they'll listen. I've used one continuously since, because it works: "I believe this will interest you also." *You* is a very important word. At that point, if I'd hesitate, he might say, "What have you got?" "Well, since you asked me, I'll tell ya." Ordinarily, I wouldn't wait I just go in about the time the prospect gets a little nervous and wants to get away. I'd release tension by using humor.

If you don't see anything funny about your standard joke, you'd laugh at yourself for telling it. (Laughs in a five-note ascending scale.) Right! I'd say, "If you're hurt—we even pay if your feelings are hurt, how's that?" (Laughs.)

Of course, I used the directional force of the eyes and my fountain pen, so the individual looked at what I'm pointing to. Thus, he concentrates through the sense of sight and the sense of hearing. If you had an objection, it wouldn't occur to you in that short span of time. You have a nervous system, I know how to tap it.

You'd have to have an effective close. If you wanted the person to say yes, you'd ask an affirmative question: "You see what I mean?" Now you just shook your head yes, whether you understood me or not. Why? Because I made it easy for you. If I want a no, it's very easy. Make a negative statement. Now you don't have accident insurance, do you? Be frank. . . .

No, no, I haven't. No.
You see? I made it easy for you to say no. That eliminated a lot of argument. So it was a matter of a one-two-three sale. I made 122 sales in one day in the Depression. Since then, we've had men who've done much better. If I wanted to sell you an accident insurance policy, it would never occur to me that you wouldn't buy. There's no reason why you shouldn't.

(Quickly) So, during the Depression, you'd call on the top man. . . .
The reason I'd call on the head of a company, you find a man who has worked his way up from the bottom is much more generous than one who hasn't. What I really wanted was his permission, and I made it easy for him to give it to me. If he didn't take the policy, I'd say: (enthusiastically) "Well, thanks just the same. I'll see you again next year!" Then, as I would leave, I'd say. "Oh, by the way, would it be all right to see the others? If they're not

too busy, I'll show it to them. If they want it, all right. If not, all right." I'd
be on my way out and the answer would always be yes. Because it's a reflex
action.

I would certainly not be in the sight of the president too frequently. I'd
go from department to department. If it were an office, I'd go from desk to
desk.

Unannounced?
I wouldn't even tell 'em my name. Every man, every woman, every child
needs protection. In a Depression, they need it more than any other time. If
a person had enough money for a ton of coal, it was more advantageous for
him to have a half a ton of coal and my policy than just a ton of coal without
the policy. The system worked.

I was a student of the human mind and would get keyed up. If I wanted
to sell you an accident insurance policy, you're sold. Give me one of your
liabilities, and I'll turn it into an asset.

*It's the Depression, I have three children, my wife is ill, the company is failing,
I'm afraid they'll lay me off. . . .*
The first thing to do is pray for guidance. Then engage in thinking time.
You condition your mind to determine what you want. Figure out the logical
way to achieve it. Don't worry about the thousand reasons you shouldn't
achieve it. All you need is one good reason why you should. If you had
PMA, a positive mental attitude, you'd do more than that for which you are
paid, so the firm couldn't afford to let you go. Instead they'd push you up.
This is in the Depression, right?

*Right. Now you come up to me. You're gonna sell me. I'm really worried, I say
to you: "I'd love to buy your insurance, but I'm so frantic, I just can't—"*
The response is so simple: "That's exactly why you need it." I'd close in on
you. If you didn't have money, that wouldn't bother me. I'd say, "You can go
next door and borrow it." And if you wanted it badly enough, you would.
Why not?

As a student of the human mind, what you'd do is push the right buttons.
If someone would say, "I don't believe in insurance," you'd go along with
them: "I'll be truthful with you, I don't think you'll have an accident. If I
did, in fairness to my company, I wouldn't sell you a policy." You'd hesitate.
Then he'd say, "You can't tell." I'd say, "You're right." And I'd show him the
policy and sell 'im.

All this time, with bread lines, apple sellers, people on relief, crisis, you just went along. . . .

Rrrright! Because of mental attitude, the power every human being possesses—the human mind.

In those days, it was very easy to do what others were afraid to do. There might be ten salesmen ahead of me and ten salesmen behind me and it was very interesting. They might be trying to sell insurance. But with my PMA, I sold. Whether they sold or not, I never took the time to find out.

■ ■ ■ ■

Ray Wax

He is a stockbroker, living in a middle-class suburb, just outside New York City. It is a recent endeavor. Previously, he had been a builder and a real estate broker.

Though his words come easily, he feels he has little of worth to recount. He is restless, a fever possesses him. . . .

MY OLD MAN IN 1928 had a million dollars in cash. Between the market, the races and the numbers racket, he lost everything. Going to the horses, sitting in a box for almost four years, with the touts who were supposed to pick the winners for him . . . he went through a million. In '31, my old man gave me $5: "Here, take care of the house."

It took me twenty years to figure out what happened. I always figured there was some kind of logic I didn't understand. Maybe it was some kind of lack in me. 'Cause I was brought up in a middle-class family: all the privileges, the house with the servant—all of a sudden, one day it's all gone. Now I had to find out who the hell I was.

Here I am being thrown into some kind of goddamn pot and I had to learn how to live. Really, without Horatio Alger I wouldn't have made it. I really believed there was room for you in this society, that there was work, that you could overcome adversity.

One day I started out looking for a job. Within three hours, I found one as a shipping clerk. $10 a week, of which I gave six home. I became a good shipping clerk. I worked alone. My world was the four walls of the shipping room.

I had no illusion about getting an education. I didn't have the drive, didn't know what I wanted to be. I began to feel I was peripheral. I didn't fit

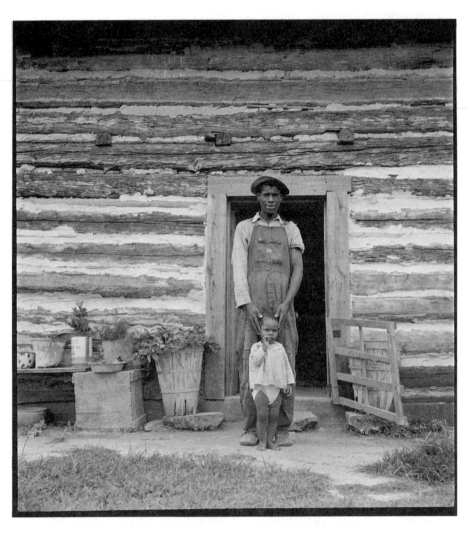

Young sharecropper and his first child at Hillside Farm,
Person County, North Carolina

DOROTHEA LANGE, 1939

into a world where people spent four years in a institution and came out with a guaranteed job or point of view. Or became a doctor or dentist.

I used to ride the New York subways and look at the chalk board at employment agencies. In the street, there'd be hundreds of men looking at these boards. I did chance jobs.

One day on the subway, I picked up a paper and it said: "Experienced Florist Wanted." The date on the paper was the day before, but I figured the hell with it, I'll try.

I showed up at Everybody's Florist, that's what it was called. I saw a gang of men in front of Everybody's Florist and I said, "Are they hiring anybody?" And a guy said, "No, they hired everybody yesterday." Another guy said, "Look kid, they don't know who the hell they hired. Just get in the crowd." So I got in the crowd. As we moved through the door, he said, "What's your name?" I said, "Ray." He said, "We didn't hire you." And I said, "Yes, you did hire me." He said, "You're full of shit." I said, "So help me God, you really did hire me." He said, "All right," and he gave me a batch of flowers.

Roses and carnations, three cents for this and five cents for that. These guys were buying the glut of the New York flower market. They had the concession to put men out on any station of the IRT system, for which they gave a cut to the IRT. This is the way I became a flower vendor.

In the early thirties, guys made a living by buying a batch of flowers and working for themselves. The IRT bull would come along and chase them. But if they worked for Everybody's Florist, they had a set spot. These guys would say: Look, you poor bastards, don't go hustling for yourself. Come in with us and you'll be able to make a living.

Here I am selling flowers, and they don't look bad. You can put up a little sign: Thirty-five cents for a dozen roses, fifty cents for a dozen carnations. The only place you can set up is where the turnstiles are. You try to find yourself a little living room and you're up against the wall, up against the tile. All these people, hundreds and thousands pouring out of the subway, and there I am looking like some sort of sick dog making a chance sale.

I think the first day maybe I sold $8. My pay working for Everybody's Florist was $2 a day. Later when I became top drawer, my top pay was like $3.

How'd you get to be top drawer?
I grew up on Horatio Alger. I remember reading every Horatio Alger. I was really bit in the ass. I really believed that if you ran out and stopped the horses, you married the boss's daughter. So help me God. And if you get a fucking job and worked harder than anybody else and they saw the gleam

in your eye, they somehow recognized that you had it. There were all these
other guys struggling behind you, but somehow you were sitting at the desk
and you were calling the orders. It was only right. It was the way the world
was made, it was the way it was supposed to happen.

The next day I brought 'em back the money I got, the $8. And the guy
said, "You fucking little bum, is this all the money you brought? Look, you
little bastard, you gotta do better."

At first, with the roar of the train, up against the wall, with your box on
the floor, they wouldn't see you. So I put up a stand: a board with the stuff at
eye level, at a height where every one could see it. And I found out that if I
began to open my mouth and hollered a little, I did better. "Here y'are, getcha
roses here!" I'll always remember the peonies: "Get your peeeooonies here!"

It used to get so cold down there. I used to wear two pairs of pants. No
relief. If you had to pee . . . I used to time the trains so I could get into the
fuckin' pissoir and unbutton two flies so I could pee before the next train
came in. It was a joke trying to get through two pair of pants to get to your
pecker and pee and get back out in time for the next train.

In the worst hour of the Depression, if you were aggressive, if you
wanted to scrounge, if you believed in Horatio Alger, you could survive. If
you were on your own, you could stumble through, wearing a monkey suit
or finding an off-beat job. For me, people that worked all day and went
home to their families, they were fags. They were the ones who could come
up behind me when I was working and put their hand on my ass. Respectable men going home to their wives and children: Drive you back? Won't
you let me come back later and drive you back? I wanted to sell the son of a
bitch flowers, so I wouldn't put him down completely.

Every day I took back more money and took out more flowers. By the
time I came in after the third or fourth day, they were kinda glad to see me.
I worked for Everybody's Florist for twenty-three days without a break. In
the course of those twenty-three days, something happened to me.

Wherever I worked, I made more money than anybody else. In my igno-
rance, I thought I was a better hustler than anybody else. The reason I
made more money than any of the other guys was that they stole. I used to
work and bring them all the money, for a lousy $2 a day. But these other
guys, the hustlers, were making a lot of money and every day, depending on
what their gross take was, stole a proportionate amount of money. They
didn't steal it. Clipping, they called it. They clipped a few bucks.

After I worked there ten, twelve days, I said to the three thugs who ran
Everybody's Florist: I want to tell you how to run this business. I began to
tell them their checkout stinks, half their flowers come back, they don't

know what the hell they're buying. Right out of Horatio Alger. I'm twenty years old and they're listening. O.K., but there's one thing wrong. The transom's open.

I walk out the door, two guys grab me by the throat. They put me up against the wall and they say, "Listen, you little son of a bitch, when you work here, you work like everyone else. If you're gonna work here and sell flowers, you're gonna steal. And then you'll make a living." From then on, I never make less than $75, $100 a week and a hundred and a quarter. I became one of their top men.

I could clip ten, fourteen, twenty dollars on a good day. I'd have to hustle $100, $150 in flowers. And that was a lot of hustling 'cause they were selling roses at three cents apiece and 'mums at, big deal, five cents apiece. To live in that atmosphere, you had to play their game. Eventually, I became one of the boys.

When you'd come in at ten o'clock or whatever, Tommy or Harry would say, "You little bastard, how did you do today?" I'd say, "Gee, Harry, I had a good day. I did $40." "That stinks," he'd say. Then, "Have a drink." And toss a bottle of booze over to you. I hadn't eaten all day and that goddamn subway, between trains I'd run up and grab a sandwich and be right down. Now they push the bottle in your face and you take a slug because you got to prove you're one of the boys.

And they'd say, "You wanna get laid? We got a hooker downstairs. Three ways for a half a dollar." I'd walk down the goddamn stairs and sure enough there'd be a black broad on the table and some guy banging away at her and her hollering and moaning and slightly drunk. . . . What are you gonna do? This is the world I lived in. At least twice a week, there'd be a broad in the basement. There'd be booze on the table. Somehow you had to survive. I never went down in the basement.

Under the Brooklyn Bridge, you'd find the guy with a pink cat sittin' on top of a fire hydrant. He's the pimp. He'll say, "Wait a minute. There's another guy that wants to go up. I'll take you both up." You go through a locked door and you'd be trooping up and through another locked door and you'd come out into a kitchen. You'd come into an apartment which was made up of a hot stove—heating douche water—and a round wooden table, where there'd be an old Italian man, sitting there, looking down. . . . This was a Luciano house, a syndicate house. I guess the cops got paid off.

Myself, when I would come in I'd look down, sit down, not look at the other men. And you didn't know what would come out. There would be two girls, a little beat around the edges. If you went in a room, you made it quick with the girl. It was the best thing you could do for the girls. She'd say, "Honey, you were great, don't worry about it. You'll be around when these old bastards won't be able to get it up." The girl was good for forty, fifty men a day. I came back to the house often. This was a dollar house in the thirties.

I've been to a few houses later in life, in Europe, but I've never gone through a locked door or up some stairs without me being back in Sand Street . . . following Louie up the stairs with my heart beating, to break into a room with a couple of old men sitting around a wooden table, looking down.

The whorehouses on Sand Street were the only thing that saved my sanity. I had no relationship to the rest of the world.

I lived in a world completely alone. The only thing that sustained me during that period: I continued to read, I continued to hustle. I had a vague sense of myself. Every guy had a gun or a knife except me. I carried a book, so they called me the professor. But finally I began to forget English. Everything reduced to four-letter words.

Also the money I made was slowly being eaten up by my family. I used to keep the cash I stole in *The History of the Jews in Poland*. I used to come home and find a note from my old man: Dear boy, took twenty. Signed, Pop. At the end of that year, I had $150 for all my effort. I left them a note saying I was going to Baltimore for a week. I never came back. I felt I had paid my debt in the subways.

His Baltimore experiences involved "Textile U," a huge shipping room, where the employer urged long working hours on the promise of his "finding a place in the firm," where colleagues put him wise to the way of things; setting up lending libraries in drugstores. . . . "I liked handling books," meeting radicals, intellectuals, students at Johns Hopkins. . . . It was the time of the Oxford Pledge and the movement against Fascism; his temptation to go to Spain as a member of the Lincoln Brigade. . . . "I was an ideal recruit, alone, on the run, searching for something"; a serious affair with a schoolteacher, running away. . . . "This is part of the Depression. You lived in a fear of responsibility for another person. You backed off when someone got close."

New Orleans, Corpus Christi, Houston, Port Isabel, down the Gulf to Mexico. "The Richard Halliburton dream, I had that one, too. There was a great world of adventure. If you believe in Horatio Alger and Richard Halliburton, you believe something will work out."

The Depression ended for me about '37. There seemed to be more work available. You weren't feeling guilty if you drove through the streets with a car. I moved into the middle classes, a little unhappy. . . .

Where I lived in this suburb, there's so much hostility. They feel the welfare people are getting a ride on their back, playing a game. During the Depression, you felt they had a right. . . . Oh, they were crazy for Roosevelt, my neighbors. They'll even tell you why. He was a good man to them because he saved the economy.

The young people growing up in that hour, they were not afraid of the society, they weren't threatened by it. They had great hope. They felt some-how they would overcome it. Today the young people are in rebellion, but they're frustrated. They haven't the illusions we had. . . .

I was born out of the Depression. I gave up my illusions. No more Horatio Alger. I had a few bad hours, a few bad years. But I found excitement. It was an awakening.

Epilogue

Reed

THE RAFT

He is from an upper-middle-class suburb of Chicago, attends college and has worked during the summer months. He is nineteen.

CHESTER AND I PLANNED to go down the Mississippi on a raft. Prompted, of course, by Mark Twain. We'd build ourselves a raft, start at Joliet and go down to New Orleans. My father thought I was joking. He said I couldn't go. I called Chester and told him to come over.

As the conversation started, it was good-humored. When my father saw we were serious, tears began to well up in his eyes, and he got a lump in his throat.

He started saying he had dreams when he was young, wanted to do the same sort of things. He was young during the Depression. To put himself through school at Amherst—and all the time very emotional about it—he'd gone with no money and had little to eat. That he and my mother had to scrimp during the early years of their marriage. I had an opportunity which he never had.

What struck me as rather strange was his saying: if I saved some money this year, maybe next summer I could go to Europe. Which is something, he said, he'd always wanted to do. While he was talking about the Depression, he was almost on the verge of crying.

Why would he agree to a European trip and not to the other one?
I think the Mississippi trip was just not his idea of fun. He saw it as a hardship. It might just be that he'd like to tell his friends that his son is off to Europe. He wouldn't want to tell his friends that his son is on the Mississippi River on a raft.

How often has he brought up this subject—the Depression?
Oh, very rarely. It was a surprising thing. And never before in such terms,
never as emotionally. He said, "Why, now, Reed!" As if I'd done something
very wrong. Very seldom have I been addressed in that tone of voice, as if I
had committed some serious insult to him.

CHESTER: *What struck me was his talking about dreams. Dreams was his
word. We didn't talk about this as our dream. "You boys have dreams. I had
dreams, my wife and I have dreams we haven't accomplished." Our Mississippi
thing didn't strike him as the right kind of dream to have somehow.*

I've noticed recently they've been concerned with status more than I
thought they were before. He would like to send himself to Europe. I don't
know what to make of it all. It was a side of my father which I'd never seen
before. Something we touched off, innocently enough, which just got out of
control. I was amazed and a little embarrassed. He reacted as though I was
making some decision in my life which was contrary to everything he ever
wanted for me. It was just a trip down the Mississippi.
    He said: Too often you look at our generation and say we did nothing. We
did an awful lot of things.

CHESTER: *We didn't start talking about the Depression. We were talking
about a raft. He started talking about the Depression.*

He kept on saying: You people don't seem to realize what we did. You seem
to disregard the American tradition. We countered by saying that, of course,
this raft trip was exactly in the American tradition. More so than going to
Europe, I think. He said: Although America is messed up, it's better than
we found it, and I don't want you to forget this. Too often you look upon our
generation and say we did nothing. We did an awful lot of things.
    (Musing.) It wasn't as if it was a memory, but an open wound. He talked
about the Depression as if it had just happened yesterday. We touched a
nerve.
    You know, his ship's come in. He doesn't want to see our raft go out.

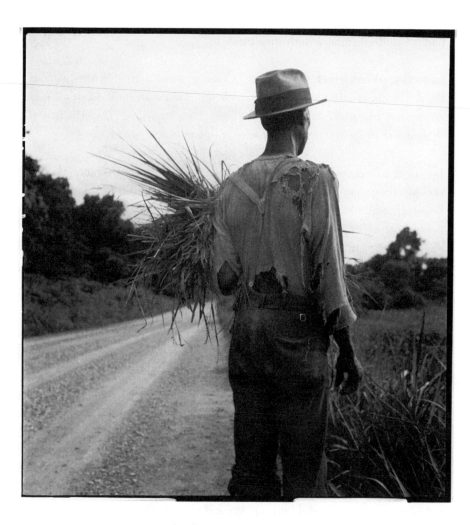

Worker living on cotton patch
near Vicksburg, Mississippi

DOROTHEA LANGE, 1936

Virginia Durr

A Touch of Rue

Wetumpka, Alabama. It is an old family house on the outskirts of Montgom-
ery. A creek runs by. . . . She and her husband, Clifford, are of an old Alabam-
ian lineage. During Franklin Roosevelt's administration, he was a member of
the Federal Communications Commission. She had been a pioneer in the
battle to abolish the poll tax.

OH, NO, THE DEPRESSION was not a romantic time. It was a time of terrible
suffering. The contradictions were so obvious that it didn't take a very
bright person to realize something was terribly wrong.

Have you ever seen a child with rickets? Shaking as with palsy. No proteins, no milk. And the companies pouring milk into gutters. People with
nothing to wear, and they were plowing up cotton. People with nothing to
eat, and they killed the pigs. If that wasn't the craziest system in the world,
could you imagine anything more idiotic? This was just insane.

And people blamed themselves, not the system. They felt they had been
at fault: . . . "if we hadn't bought that old radio" . . . "if we hadn't bought
that old secondhand car." Among the things that horrified me were the
preachers—the fundamentalists. They would tell the people they suffered
because of their sins. And the people believed it. God was punishing them.
Their children were starving because of their sins.

People who were independent, who thought they were masters and mis-
tresses of their lives, were all of a sudden dependent on others. Relatives or
relief. People of pride went into shock and sanitoriums. My mother was one.

Up to this time, I had been a conformist, a Southern snob. I actually
thought the only people who amounted to anything were the very small
group which I belonged to. The fact that my family wasn't as well off as
those of the girls I went with—I was vice president of the Junior League—
made me value even more the idea of being wellborn. . . .

What I learned during the Depression changed all that. I saw a blinding
light like Saul on the road to Damascus. (Laughs.) It was the first time I
had seen the other side of the tracks. The rickets, the pellagra—it shook
me up. I saw the world as it really was.

She shamed, cajoled and persuaded the dairy company into opening milk dis-
pensaries. When they sought to back down, she convinced them that "if these

people got a taste of milk, they might get in the habit of buying it—when they got jobs."

When the steel companies closed down in Birmingham, thousands were thrown out of work. She was acquainted with some of the executives; she argued with them: "You feed the mules who work in your mines. Why don't you feed the people? You're responsible."

The young today are just playacting in courting poverty. It's all right to wear jeans and eat hamburgers. But it's entirely different from not having any hamburgers to eat and no jeans to wear. A great many of these kids—white kids—seem to have somebody in the background they can always go to. I admire their spirit, because they have a strong sense of social justice. But they themselves have not been deprived. They haven't experienced the terror. They have never seen a baby in the cradle crying of hunger. . . .

I think the reason for the gap between the black militants and the young white radicals is that the black kids are much more conscious of the thin edge of poverty. And how soon you can be reduced to living on relief. What you *know* and what you *feel* are very different. Terror is something you *feel*. When there is no paycheck coming in—the absolute, stark terror.

What frightens me is that these kids are like sheep being led to slaughter. They are romantic and they are young. I have a great deal more faith in movements that start from necessity—people trying to change things because of their own deprivation. We felt that in the labor surge of the thirties. The people who worked hardest to organize were the ones in the shops and in the mills.

The Depression affected people in two different ways. The great majority reacted by thinking money is the most important thing in the world. Get yours. And get it for your children. Nothing else matters. Not having that stark terror come at you again. . . .

And there was a small number of people who felt the whole system was lousy. You have to change it. The kids come along and they want to change it, too. But they don't seem to know what to put in its place. I'm not so sure I know, either. I do think it has to be responsive to people's needs. And it has to be done by democratic means, if possible. Whether it's possible or not—the power of money is such today, I just don't know. Some of the kids call me a relic of the thirties. Well, I am.

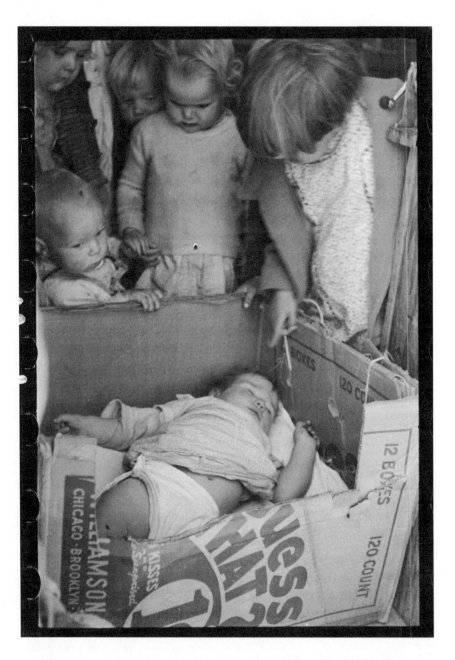

While the mothers are working in the fields, the preschool children
of migrant families are cared for in the nursery school under
trained teachers, Kern migrant camp, California

DOROTHEA LANGE, 1936

Photo Credits

All photographs are courtesy of the Library of Congress, Prints & Photographs Division, FSA/OWI Collection.

Pages iv–v
Negroes in the lineup for food at mealtime in the camp for flood refugees, Forrest City, Arkansas
Walker Evans, 1937
LC-USF3301-009217-M3

Pages 12–13
Employment agency, Sixth Avenue, New York, New York
Arthur Rothstein, 1937
LC-USF33-T01-002672-M3

Page 17
Toward Los Angeles, California
Dorothea Lange, 1937
LC-DIG-fsa-8b31801

Page 24
Negro field worker, Holtville, Imperial Valley, California. "He has just made himself shoes out of that old tire."
Dorothea Lange,1935
LC-DIG-cph-3a50903

Page 28
Mother and baby of family on the road, Tulelake, Siskiyou County, California
Dorothea Lange, 1939
LC-DIG-fsa-8b34842

Page 35
Carpenter, Westmoreland County, Pennsylvania
Walker Evans, 1935
LC-USF3301-009020-M1

Page 44
Daughter of migrant Tennessee coal miner. Living in the American River camp near Sacramento, California
Dorothea Lange, 1936
LC-DIG-fsa-8b29876

Page 52
Farm boy with sack full of boll weevils, which he has picked off of cotton plants, Macon County, Georgia
Dorothea Lange, 1937
LC-USZ62-130145

Page 58
Mexican mother in California: "Sometimes I tell my children that I would like to go to Mexico, but they tell me 'We don't want to go, we belong here.'"
Dorothea Lange, 1935
LC-USF346- 000825-B-B

Page 65
Under the elevated railway, Chicago, Illinois
John Vachon, 1940
LC-DIG-fsa-8a06711

Page 68
Bootblack, Fourteenth Street and Eighth Avenue, New York, New York
Arthur Rothstein, 1937
LC-USF33-T01-002678-M4

Page 76
Was Nebraska farmer, now migrant farmworker in the West, Merrill, Klamath County, Oregon
Dorothea Lange, 1939
LC-DIG-fsa-8b34833

Page 86
Child living in Oklahoma City shacktown
Dorothea Lange, 1936
LC-DIG-fsa-8b38490

Page 91
Destitute family. American River camp, Sacramento, California. Five children, aged two to seventeen years
Dorothea Lange, 1936
LC-DIG-fsa-8b29879

Page 94
Young mother of twenty five says "next year we'll be painted and have a lawn and flowers"; rural shacktown, near Klamath Falls, Oregon
Dorothea Lange, 1939
LC-DIG-fsa-8b34857

Page 100
Housing conditions in Ambridge, Pennsylvania, home of the American Bridge Company
Arthur Rothstein, 1938
LC-DIG-fsa-8b34857

Page 105
Employees of Coca-Cola plant on strike, Sikeston, Missouri
John Vachon, 1940
LC-USF33-T01-001899-M2

Page 112
Newsstand, Memphis, Tennessee
Russell Lee, 1938
LC-DIG-fsa-8a23587

Page 116
Pullman porter at the Union Station, Chicago, Illinois
Jack Delano, 1943
LC-DIG-ppmsca-01568

Page 122
In Memphis, Tennessee, hundreds of colored laborers congregated near the bridge every morning at daylight in hopes of work chopping cotton on a plantation. They are hauled to and from work on trucks. Reduced cotton acreage has made employment scarce for this class of seasonal labor in all towns. "You can't live the commonest way on six bits a day. Not alone nor no way. A man like me can't get no foothold. It's a mighty tough old go. The people here in the morning are hungry, raggedy, but they don't make no hungry march."
Dorothea Lange, 1938
LC-DIG-fsa-8b32356

Page 131
Strike pickets, New York, New York
Arthur Rothstein, 1937
LC-USF33-002677-M1

Page 134
Street corner, South Second Street, Camden, New Jersey
Arthur Rothstein, 1938
LC-DIG-fsa-8a10213

Page 141
Picket line at Mid-City Realty Company, South Chicago, Illinois
John Vachon, 1941
LC-USZ62-130701

Pages 146–147
Ladies who live in rooming house, St. Paul, Minnesota
John Vachon, 1939
LC-DIG-fsa-8a05214

Page 152
Tap dancing class in the gymnasium at Iowa State College, Ames, Iowa
Jack Delano, 1942
LC-DIG-ppmsc-00250

Page 157
Homemade swimming pool for steelworkers' children, Pittsburgh, Pennsylvania
Arthur Rothstein, 1938
LC-DIG-fsa-8a10004

Page 164
Crowds in downtown section of Providence, Rhode Island
Jack Delano, 1940
LC-USF33-020754-M2

Page 175
Bethlehem graveyard and steel mill, Pennsylvania
Walker Evans, 1935
LC-DIG-ppmsc-00231

Page 178
Coal miners, Birmingham, Alabama
Arthur Rothstein, 1937
LC-DIG-fsa-8a08362

Page 188
Cotton sharecroppers. Greene County, Georgia. They produce little, sell little, buy little.
Dorothea Lange, 1937
LC-DIG-fsa-8b32081

Page 191
Farmer on a load of hay, farmers' market, Weatherford, Texas
Russell Lee, 1939
LC-DIG-fsa-8a26549

Page 197
Melons on Frank Tengle's porch. Hale County, Alabama
Walker Evans, 1936
LC-USF3301-031296-M5

Page 201
Wife of a migratory laborer with three children, near Childress, Texas (Nettie Featherston)
Dorothea Lange, 1938
LC-DIG-fsa-8b32434

Page 203
Inhabitants of Nethers, Virginia, in front of post office
Arthur Rothstein, 1935
LC-DIG-fsa-8b26686

Page 208
Florida migrants studying road map before
leaving Elizabeth City, North Carolina, for the
state of Delaware
Jack Delano, 1940
LC-USZ62-130588

Pages 216–217
Negroes waiting at streetcar terminal for cars,
Oklahoma City, Oklahoma
Russell Lee, 1939
LC-USF33-012345-M1

Page 223
The windshield of a migratory agricultural
laborer's car, in a squatter camp near
Sacramento, California
Dorothea Lange, 1936
LC-USF33-015329-M1

Page 224
San Francisco, California. After forty-four
years of Republican administration, California
gets a Democratic administration. The
California "New Deal" faces same opposition
as the national "New Deal."
Dorothea Lange, 1939
LC-DIG-fsa-8b32862

Page 229
Railroad workers, Port Barre, Louisiana
Russell Lee, 1938
LC-DIG-fsa-8a24699

Page 237
Dorothea Lange, Resettlement Administration
photographer, in California
Dorothea Lange, 1936
LC-USZ62-128944

Page 242
Washington (southwest section), D.C., Negro
woman in her bedroom
Gordon Parks, 1942
LC-DIG-ppmsca-12887

Page 252
Flood refugee encampment at Forrest City,
Arkansas
Walker Evans & Edwin Locke, c. 1937
LC-USF33-031345-M1

Page 256
"We made good money in the cherries this
year. From then on we made just beans."
Merrill, Klamath County, Oregon. Woman in
mobile unit of FSA (Farm Security Adminis-
tration) camp.
Dorothea Lange, 1939
LC-DIG-fsa-8b35692

Page 261
Scene along Bathgate Avenue in the
Bronx, New York, a section from which many
of the New Jersey homesteaders have come
Arthur Rothstein, 1936
LC-DIG-fsa-8b28421

Page 269
A scene at the Fulton fish market, New York
City
Gordon Parks, 1943
LC-USW3-028722-E

Page 276
Beale Street, Memphis, Tennessee Marion
Post Wolcott, 1939
LC-USZ62-130116

Page 280
Fascism and Uncle Sam signs on boxcar,
Crystal City, Texas
Russell Lee, 1939
LC-USF33-012094-M4

Page 285
Children playing on 61st Street between 1st
and 3rd Avenues, New York City
Walker Evans, 1938
LC-USF3301-006717-M3

Page 290
At the change of the shift at the Penomah
Mills Inc., Taftville, Connecticut
Jack Delano, 1940
LC-USF33-020743-M2

Page 297
Factory workers' homes, Camden, New Jersey
Arthur Rothstein, 1938
LC-DIG-fsa-8a10291

Page 304
Mississippi Delta, on Mississippi Highway No.
1 between Greenville and Clarksdale. Negro
laborer's family being moved from Arkansas to
Mississippi by white tenant.
Dorothea Lange, 1938
LC-DIG-fsa-8b33011

Page 309
Fifty-seven-year-old sharecropper woman.
Hinds County, Mississippi. Thin dimes
around the ankles to prevent headaches.
Dorothea Lange, 1937
LC-DIG-fsa-8b32018

Page 317
Child of former tenant farmer, now a day
laborer, Ellis County, Texas
Dorothea Lange, 1937
LC-USZ62-130887

Page 321
Farmer of Franklin County, Kansas
Arthur Rothstein, 1936
LC-DIG-fsa-8b27586

Pages 326–327
Five members of Ola self-help sawmill co-op,
Gem County, Idaho
Dorothea Lange, 1939
LC-DIG-fsa-8b35367

Page 332
At a small American Legion carnival near
Bellows Falls, Vermont
Jack Delano, 1941
LC-USF33-021089-M1

Pages 336–337
School youngsters, Red House, West
Virginia
Ben Shahn, 1935
LC-DIG-fsa-8a16722

Page 344
Seating now in all parts of the house, Chicago,
Illinois
John Vachon, 1941
LC-USF33-016076-M5

Page 347
Fiddlin' Bill Hensley, Asheville,
North Carolina
Ben Shahn, 1937
LC-USF347-006257-M5-B

Page 354
A trio of musicians from Duke Ellington's
orchestra during the early morning broadcast,
New York City
Gordon Parks, 1943
LC-USW3-023926-C

Page 360
Sick migrant child, Toppenish, Washington
Dorothea Lange, 1939
LC-DIG-fsa-8b34329

Page 369
Negro going in colored entrance of movie
house on Saturday afternoon, Belzoni,
Mississippi
Marion Post Wolcott, 1939
LC-USF331-030577-M2

Page 382
Convicts and guard, Oglethorpe County,
Georgia
Jack Delano, 1941
LC-USZ62-125970

Page 394
Louisiana Negress
Dorothea Lange, 1937
LC-USZ62-130298

Page 399
Mr. Branch, resident of the James Creek
dwellings, saying grace, Washington, D.C.
Gordon Parks, 1942
LC-USW3-010684-C

Page 409
Stalled on the desert, facing a future in
California. No money, ten children. From
Chickasaw, Oklahoma. Southern California.
Dorothea Lange, 1937
LC-DIG-fsa-8b31796

Page 412
Eighty-year-old woman living in squatters'
camp on the outskirts of Bakersfield,
California, says "if you lose your pluck you
lose the most there is in you—all you've got to
live with"
Dorothea Lange, 1936
LC-DIG-fsa-8b29843

Page 417
Saturday afternoon in Franklin, Heard
County, Georgia
Jack Delano, 1941
LC-USF331-020841-M2

Page 421
Wife and child of tractor driver, Aldridge
Plantation, Mississippi
Dorothea Lange, 1937
LC-DIG-fsa-8b32107

Page 426
Young sharecropper and his first child at
Hillside Farm, Person County, North Carolina
Dorothea Lange, 1939
LC-DIG-fsa-8b34256

Page 434
Worker living on cotton patch near Vicksburg,
Mississippi
Dorothea Lange, 1936
LC-DIG-fsa-8b29633

Page 437
While the mothers are working in the fields,
the preschool children of migrant families are
cared for in the nursery school under trained
teachers. Kern migrant camp, California
Dorothea Lange, 1936
LC-USF33-015328-M1